THE FINANCIAL DECLINE OF A GREAT POWER

The Financial Decline of a Great Power

War, Influence, and Money in Louis XIV's France

GUY ROWLANDS

OXFORD
UNIVERSITY PRESS

This book has been printed digitally and produced in a standard specification in order to ensure its continuing availability

OXFORD
UNIVERSITY PRESS

Great Clarendon Street, Oxford OX2 6DP
United Kingdom

Oxford University Press is a department of the University of Oxford. It furthers the University's objective of excellence in research, scholarship, and education by publishing worldwide.

Oxford is a registered trade mark of Oxford University Press in the UK and in certain other countries

Reprinted 2013

British Library Cataloguing in Publication Data
Data available

Library of Congress Cataloging in Publication Data
Data available

ISBN 978-0-19-958507-6

For Bridget and for Thomas

Acknowledgements

This book, more than most on early modern France, bears the imprint of the time in which it was written. It was researched over a decade but was conceived and written as the western world entered a prolonged period of financial crisis and as British universities entered a period of existential angst not unrelated to fundamental funding issues. In such times one turns for solace and support to sponsors, friends, and family—Burke's little platoons. I am once again in debt (metaphorically) to the British Academy, which provided me with a Small Research Grant in the mid-2000s, and which, together with the Leverhulme Trust, awarded me a Senior Research Fellowship in the academic year 2010–11 to take me away from normal duties in the University of St Andrews. Without their support the book would have been far harder to write. I must also thank the St Andrews School of History and the university for agreeing to release me for this work, and more generally for continuing to provide a good level of basic financial support for speculative research. I would also like to thank the Centre Marc Bloch of the Humboldt Universität zu Berlin, and especially Daniel Schönpflug (as well as other Berlin-based colleagues), for providing intellectual sociability much as Voltaire, when in Prussia, might have appreciated. Thanks, too, are owed to the Carnegie Trust for the Universities of Scotland for a research grant in 2009, and to the staff of the Archives Nationales in Paris and the Service Historique de la Défense in Vincennes (especially Emmanuel Pénicaut, Bertrand Fonck, Son Bernard, and Olivier Delplace) for facilitating my research. Thanks also to Benjamin Darnell for his help and to Bettina Holstein for her generous hospitality in Paris. I would also like to express my gratitude for the exemplary professionalism of the OUP staff who have worked with me on this book—Seth Cayley, Stephanie Ireland, and Emma Barber—as well as my copy-editor Elizabeth Stone, and my proofreader Clifford Willis. My deepest gratitude for assistance goes to the anonymous readers for OUP, as well as Robin Briggs, Rafe Blaufarb, Joël Félix, and Geoff Heal for reading through drafts of the book and providing suggestions and further context for my thoughts. Above all, though, I would like to thank my wife, Bridget Heal, who once again supported me as I wrestled with a difficult subject. It is to her I dedicate this book, but also to our son Thomas, whose generation will not suffer too much, I hope, from the recent profligacy and fecklessness of western politicians, bankers, and borrowers.

Contents

Abbreviations

Archival sources	
AN	Archives Nationales de France
Ars. Ms.	Bibliothèque de l'Arsenal (Paris) manuscript
BNF	Bibliothèque Nationale de France
Maz. Ms.	Bibliothèque Mazarine (Paris) manuscript
SHD	Service Historique de la Défense (Vincennes)
Printed sources	
CCG	*Correspondance des contrôleurs généraux des finances*, ed. A. M. de Boislisle (3 vols, Paris, 1874–97)
Claeys	Thierry Claeys, *Dictionnaire biographique des financiers en France au XVIII*[e] *siècle* (2nd edn: 2 vols, Paris, 2009)
Chaussinand	Guy Chaussinand-Nogaret, *Les Financiers de Languedoc au XVIII*[e] *siècle* (Paris, 1970)
Clamageran	Jean-Jules Clamageran, *Histoire de l'impôt en France* (3 vols, Paris, 1867–76)
Dangeau	*Journal du marquis de Dangeau . . .*, ed. E. Soulié, L. Dussieux, and P. de Chennevières (19 vols, Paris, 1854–60)
DAPS	Daniel Dessert, *Argent, pouvoir et société au Grand Siècle* (Paris, 1984)
Depping	*Correspondance administrative sous le règne de Louis XIV*, ed. G. B. Depping (4 vols, Paris, 1850–55)
Dictionnaire des surintendants	Françoise Bayard, Joël Félix, and Philippe Hamon, eds, *Dictionnaire des surintendants et des contrôleurs généraux des finances* (Paris, 2000)
Esnault	Michel Chamillard [*sic*], *Correspondance et papiers inédits recueillis et publiés par l'abbé G. Esnault* (2 vols, Le Mans, 1884)
Forbonnais	François Véron de Forbonnais, *Recherches et considérations sur les finances de France, depuis l'année 1595 jusqu'à l'année 1721* (2 vols, Basel, 1758)
Iung	Jean-Éric Iung, 'Service des vivres et munitionnaires de l'Ancien Régime: la fourniture du pain de munition aux troupes de Flandre et d'Allemagne de 1701 à 1710' (dissertation for the *diplôme d'archiviste-paléographe*, École Nationale des Chartes, Paris, 1983)
La Chesnaye	François de La Chesnaye des Bois et Badier, *Dictionnaire de la noblesse* (19 vols, Paris, 1863–76)
Legohérel	Henri Legohérel, *Les Trésoriers généraux de la Marine (1517–1788)* (Paris, 1963)
Lüthy	Herbert Lüthy, *La Banque Protestante en France de la Révocation de l'Édit de Nantes à la Révolution* (2 vols, Paris, 1959–61)
Malet, *Comptes*	Jean-Roland Malet, *Comptes rendus de l'administration des finances du royaume de France* (Paris, 1789)
McCollim	Gary Bruce McCollim, 'The Formation of Fiscal Policy in the Reign of Louis XIV: The Example of Nicolas Desmaretz, Controller General of Finances (1708–1715)' (unpublished Ohio State University PhD dissertation, 1979)

Michaud	Claude Michaud, *L'Eglise et l'argent sous l'Ancien Régime: Les receveurs généraux du clergé de France aux XVIe–XVIIIe siècles* (Paris, 1991)
Pénicaut	Emmanuel Pénicaut, *Faveur et pouvoir au tournant du Grand Siècle: Michel Chamillart, Ministre et secrétaire d'État de la guerre de Louis XIV* (Paris, 2004)
Rowlands	Guy Rowlands, *The Dynastic State and the Army under Louis XIV: Royal Service and Private Interest, 1661–1701* (Cambridge, 2002)
Rupprecht	Benoît Rupprecht, 'Michel Chamillart, contrôleur général des finances' (*Mémoire de maîtrise*, Université Paris-Sorbonne (Paris IV), 1997)
Saint-Germain, *Bernard*	Jacques Saint-Germain, *Samuel Bernard, le banquier des rois* (Paris, 1960)
Saint-Germain, *Financiers*	Jacques Saint-Germain, *Les financiers sous Louis XIV: Paul Poisson de Bourvalais* (Paris, 1950)
Saint-Simon	*Mémoires de Saint-Simon*, ed. A. M. de Boislisle (43 vols, Paris, 1879–1928)
Seligmann	Armand Seligmann, *La première tentative d'émission fiduciaire en France: Etude sur les billets de monnaie du Trésor Royal à la fin du règne de Louis XIV (1701–1718)* (Paris, 1925)
Spooner	Frank C. Spooner, *The International Economy and Monetary Movements in France, 1493–1725* (Cambridge, MA, 1972)
Vuitry	Adolphe Vuitry, *Le désordre des finances et les excès de la spéculation à la fin du règne de Louis XIV et au commencement du règne de Louis XV* (Paris, 1885)

A Note on Monetary Circulation in Louis XIV's France

Although three chapters will be devoted to the manipulation and use of coins and paper monetary devices, a preliminary basic explanation of the system of monetary circulation in France during the age of Louis XIV is required. The French currency system was based upon bimetallism, the use of both gold and silver for setting the value of the monetary unit; and, like most European currency zones in the early modern period, it was characterized by a division between the coinage and the unit of account.[1] Monetary transactions were denominated in the unit of account.

The key French unit of account was the *livre*, which was not represented by a specific coin but against which larger denomination coins were valued. From 1667 the *livre tournois* was adopted as the unit of account for the whole ancient kingdom, while the *monnaie parisis* standard ceased to be used. Much like the British currency before decimalization in 1973, the *livre* was subdivided into 20 *sous*, and each *sou* (or *sol*) was further subdivided into 12 *deniers*. In this book coin values will occasionally be written, for example, as L10:8s:6d (representing 10 *livres*, 8 *sous*, and 6 *deniers*). There were a variety of coins representing multiples of *sous* and *deniers*. There was a copper 1 *sol* coin, and some other copper coins worth more than a *sol*, but more important were a number of silver and gold coins which were worth multiples of *sous* and *livres*. A variety of smaller silver coins were created at different times for daily circulation within France, particularly from the mid-1670s, such as the 4, 3, and 2 *sou* pieces. The most important gold coin was the *louis d'or*, created in 1640–1 in a serious effort to 'nationalize' gold coins and reduce dependence upon Spanish *pistoles*, whose rough equivalent they were deemed to be. Hitherto the main French gold coin had been the *écu d'or* and the *demi-écu*, which gradually fell out of major use. The worth, or *fiat* value, of the coins (which can be referred to as the 'rating', or even the 'tariff') was officially set by the crown, in the case of the *louis d'or* at somewhere between 11 and 20 *livres* under Louis XIV. The principal silver coin was the *écu d'argent* (sometimes known as the *louis d'argent* or *écu blanc*), which was commonly considered to be worth 60 *sous* after the government set the rate in 1577, though this rating would also be regularly altered. The ratings were adjusted by government decree and implemented by restamping or recoining in the royal mints as coins were called in. Upward reratings are referred to as augmentations or enhancements of a coin's value, downward reratings as diminutions or abatements. It should be noted that the *enhancement* in value of a physically unchanged coin (the *écu*) is the same as the *debasement* of its corresponding unit of account (the *livre*).

[1] Generally, see Luca Fantacci, 'The Dual Currency System of Renaissance Europe', *Financial History Review* 15 (2008), 55–72.

Not all of France was on the *livre tournoisis* standard. Newly incorporated provinces on the edges of the kingdom often retained separate monetary arrangements, thus making the process of resource transfer, even within the king's lands, more complicated. Noteworthy is Alsace, which from 1681 (when Strasbourg was acquired) until 1718 used the *livre d'Alsace*, worth 11/12 of a *livre tournois*, as its unit of account. The coins in which this *alsatien* value was expressed also enjoyed a higher official rating (in terms of *livres, sous*, and *deniers*) than their *tournois* equivalents, and these coins were different from those of old France. Louis XIV kept this system separate from the old kingdom as a recognition of the region's trade bias towards the Holy Roman Empire and in order to reduce potential coin outflows across the Rhine. A very similar system pertained in the province of the 'Trois Évêchés'—Metz, Toul, and Verdun—which was intertwined with the independent duchy of Lorraine in the Meuse and Moselle region. Also worth noting is the separate system in the so-called 'pays conquis' on the northern French frontier. In the Lille Mint were struck specific coins used in French Flanders and Hainaut, though they were also used freely on the other side of the border in the Spanish Netherlands. These coins differed in weight and in fineness/purity (and thus intrinsic value) from those struck in the old kingdom.

At this point a brief explanation of the quality and rough value of the larger coins needs to be provided. French coins were measured for their value in terms of *livres, sous*, and *deniers*, but also in terms of a 'weight' value known as the 'marc d'or' and the 'marc d'argent', and like all coins in terms of their purity. From the 1640s the French coinage was much in demand across Europe, and it acquired a degree of respectability as standard milling of the edges reduced opportunities for fraud. For all the manipulation of the coins vis-à-vis the *marcs* and the *livre*, the *louis d'or* and the *écu* remained very high quality coins which were not debased metallurgically under Louis XIV. The fineness/purity of the major coins—the ratio between the actual alloy and the main metal on which they were based—was not altered in this period. What did change, though, was the relationship of the *livre* to the *marc d'or* and the *marc d'argent*—the marc being both a unit of mass and the unit in which the price of gold and silver was calibrated—as coins were officially rerated (up and down) by the government, exercising one of its rights of sovereignty. The great recoinage of 1709 also saw changes to the weight of the silver *écu* and the *louis d'or* after decades of stability.

N.B. The alterations in the weight of the major coins in turn altered the gold and silver values of the *livre* as the unit of account. If one takes this together with the reratings of the coins, it can be estimated that in 1688 the *livre* was worth roughly 8 grams of fine silver, but in the Nine Years War (1688–97) it was devalued by around one-third before stabilizing during 1699–1713 in the region of 5.3–5.5 grams.

Alongside the coinage, the French financiers and bankers made extensive use of bills of exchange—*lettres de change*. These did not have legal tender status but their use was sufficiently widespread within restricted mercantile, banking, and state finance circles for them to count as an alternative monetary instrument alongside coinage. In order to avoid transporting huge amounts of coinage across vast distances, bills of exchange were used for moving large sums of money between towns and cities across France (inland exchange) and over different currency boundaries across Europe (foreign exchange). When 'foreign exchange' and its costs are being discussed, this usually means the price of moving money by bill of exchange. Generally it was expected that these bills would be honoured fairly quickly after transmission and upon presentation, though by the end of the seventeenth century these instruments were being prolonged and 'toured' around various major European exchange centres, for a price. They could become expensive, but that depended upon the person issuing them, the person on whom they were drawn, the state of the currencies involved, and the health of trade relations between the various locations concerned. Like other instruments, by 1700 a bill of exchange could be negotiated across almost all of Europe—with the notable exception of Venice—and it was reassigned with the inscription of the name of the third party who purchased it on the back. As negotiable and discountable instruments they reached full maturity in the final decades of the eighteenth century, but by the end of the seventeenth they had already achieved a level of sophistication that would make them the crucial method for financing international war over a wide geographical area. For France the most important 'place' in 1701–9 for exchange using such bills was Lyon, which operated a clearance system for Europe-wide transactions, based on quarterly money fairs, that had been settled in its essentials for well over a century. The French state 'piggy-backed' on Lyon's mercantile and banking settlement arrangements. The system had already been handling a markedly growing volume of finance since the late 1670s, but from 1701 Louis XIV's foreign exchange demands for his armies put extreme pressure on the quarterly 'Payements', producing credit crises in 1704 and 1707, and finally a credit meltdown in 1709, from which the system never really recovered.

Glossary

In this glossary readers will find technical French words, and some English expressions, that crop up in several places throughout this book. Many are explained in passing in the chapters, but this glossary is designed as a reference aid.

abonnement a lump-sum payment in order to secure exemption from an imposition; also known sometimes as a *rachat*.

affaire extraordinaire a specific contract (*traité* (*q.v.*)) between the royal council and one or more financiers, most notably for the contractor to collect ad hoc taxes, sell venal offices, or impose forced loans on venal officials, in return for lucrative commission.

aides wholesale excise duties and sales taxes on a variety of goods, especially alcohol, manufactures, and foodstuffs.

appropriations the process of earmarking revenue sources for specific expenditure tasks.

assignation an appropriations (*q.v.*) order, issued by the *Trésor royal* (*q.v.*), and drawn upon a particular revenue source.

augmentation des gages a forced loan upon existing venal office-holders, in return for which their office's *gages* (*q.v.*) were increased.

bail a lease based upon a contract for collecting some types of revenue.

billet a bearer bill or promissory note, drawn for the most part upon fisco-financiers (*q.v.*), and normally for short-term loans; in most cases highly tradable by the 1700s; also 'billets de Monnoie', bills issued by the royal mints.

bureau an office in which a team of officials, clerks, or agents work.

caisse a chest containing money and financial instruments; also refers to a general fund held by a financier.

capitation a direct tax introduced in 1695 as a graduated poll tax on all French subjects; modified in 1701 to become part of the *taille* (*q.v.*) for commoners.

Chambre de justice special royal tribunal set up to investigate the conduct of fisco-financiers; it had the right to impose large fines, imprisonment, and even the death penalty.

commis a clerk in ministry or agency bureaux; or an agent of a ministerial or para-royal body employed under commission in the provinces or working with troops.

comptable a senior financial official obligated to provide accounts to the royal council and the Paris Chambre des comptes for their handling of royal money; could be either primary or secondary receivers of revenue.

département an administrative jurisdiction: e.g. a ministry, or a range of territory under the oversight of a royal *intendant* (*q.v.*).

dixième a 10 per cent tax upon private revenues and upon wealth, levied mainly on property, investments, and paid work; based in part on self-assessment, it was introduced in 1710 and imposed on privileged as well as non-privileged subjects.

don gratuit literally a free gift, a grant of revenue to the king voted upon by a corporate body (e.g., provincial estates, urban municipalities, the Church); in effect an imposition, with the sum arrived at through some negotiation.

exercice a duty-year handling royal finances undertaken by a fisco-financier (*q.v.*); often carried out in alternation with one or more colleagues.

Extraordinaire des Guerres the principal military treasury, responsible for channelling the vast majority of funds to the military and its suppliers; operated as an agency under the jurisdiction of the War Ministry, headed by two or three alternating treasurers general.

fisco-financier a financier whose interests were based to a great extent on handling royal revenues either as a *receveur* (*q.v.*), a treasurer, a tax farmer, or a contractor.

gabelle salt tax, varying in intensity and collection methods depending upon the region.

gages income from the capital invested in a royal venal office, in effect a form of interest for a long-term loan.

généralité financial province, largely concerned with collection of the *taille* (*q.v.*) and its adjuncts, usually presided over by two alternating *receveurs généraux* (*q.v.*).

intendant royal commissioner despatched to oversee the government of a province on behalf of the royal council for several years; army *intendants* were also the principal logistics managers for field armies.

intendants des finances several senior venal officials who worked with the *contrôleur général des finances* at the centre, and whose bureaux together loosely constituted a Finance Ministry.

lettre de change a bill of exchange: a financial instrument for moving money from one urban location to another, either within one or across two currency zones; subject to varying costs imposed by the exchange rate, by losses arising from differential currency quality, and by commissions.

mémoire a memorandum, in common use in French government as policy documents, reports, and proposals.

ordonnance de paiement an order signed by both the king and a minister authorizing the release of funds for a purpose, on the basis of which *assignations* (*q.v.*) would be issued to the recipients of the funds.

Paulette annual payment by venal office-holders to the crown, worth 1/60 of the office's value; payers could pass on their offices unimpeded as inheritance upon their death.

Payement one of the four quarterly clearing periods for financial transactions at Lyon.

promesse see *billet* (*q.v.*).

receveur a collector and receiver of royal revenues on the king's behalf; always a venal office; two *receveurs généraux* were responsible for a *généralité* (*q.v.*) by alternation; within each *généralité* there were also lesser *receveurs*.

régie an administrative arrangement involving contractors—either for tax collection or military supplies—in which the agents were given commission for costs and loans by the royal council, but they made no large advances to the king and they received no profits from their operations.

remise a rake-off awarded to contractors by the government in one-off financial contracts, or given to royal *receveurs* (*q.v.*) as part of the regular system of direct tax collection.

rente a financial instrument providing the holder with an annuity, and offered by private individuals and corporate bodies; those drawn on the Paris Hôtel de ville were used as a form of long-term, lower-interest debt by the monarch.

rescription/récépissé a formal written pledge or promissory note, issued by a revenue collector, to pay upon presentation the sum designated; more flexible than an *assignation* (*q.v.*), and usually not tied to a specific revenue stream; *récépissé* was also the name of a receipt for coin handed in at royal mints.

taille the principal direct tax, mainly on land; varied in weight and form by region; nobles were exempt from the *taille* by virtue of their status, although in the south the privilege of exemption was attached to the status of the land itself, not that of the person.

taxation a rake-off to cover expenses and salaries, based mainly on so many *deniers* for every royal *livre* handled; given mainly to military/naval treasurers and tax farmers.

traitant a financier contracted by the royal council to manage an *affaire extraordinaire* (*q.v.*).

traité a financial contract to collect a tax, or sell a new batch of venal offices, or impose further forced loans on venal office-holders.

Trésor royal the central royal treasury which processed most of the crown's net income, either as cash or as paper, under the oversight of Finance Ministry officials.

ustencile a tax in cash and kind levied locally and paid to army units as additional living-expense allowances.

vivres the business of supplying bread to the troops, organized in large private companies by fisco-financiers (*q.v.*) known as 'munitionnaires'.

The Treasurers General of the Extraordinaire des Guerres: Years on Duty, 1688–1715

YEAR ON DUTY	TREASURER GENERAL	YEAR ON DUTY	TREASURER GENERAL
1688	Charles Renouard de La Touanne	1702	Montargis (shared with the king himself)
1689	Jean de Turmenyes, sieur de Nointel	1703	Pleneuf
1690	La Touanne	1704	Durey de Vieuxcourt (and Montargis as *adjoint*)
1691	Turmenyes	1705	Montargis
1692	La Touanne	1706	Mongelas
1693	Turmenyes	1707	Montargis
1694	La Touanne	1708: until 5 April	Louis Feste de Noisy (by commission)
		5 April onwards	Joseph Durey de Sauroy
1695	Turmenyes	1709	Mongelas
1696	La Touanne	1710	Michel François Le Bas Duplessis
1697	Jean-Louis Arnauld de La Perrière and Romain Dru de Mongelas	1711	Sauroy
1698	La Touanne and Jean de Sauvion	1712	Gérard-Michel de La Jonchère
1699	Arnauld and Mongelas	1713	Duplessis
1700	La Touanne and Sauvion	1714	Sauroy
1701	Arnauld and Mongelas THEN Claude Le Bas de Montargis, Jean-Etienne Berthelot de Pleneuf, and Jean-Baptiste Durey de Vieuxcourt	1715	La Jonchère

General Introduction

History does not repeat itself but it sometimes rhymes.
(attributed in various forms to Mark Twain)

In the course of the last twenty-five years of his seventy-two-year reign (1643–1715) Louis XIV dramatically reduced the power of France on the international stage and weakened the internal financial stamina of his realm. While his provocation of the Nine Years War (1688–97) caused France major logistical difficulties, forced up borrowing, and tempted the government into unwise manipulations of the currency, this demanding conflict did not set the country up for severe financial or military decline. With time France could have recovered and its relative decline, against the emerging and still-unstable British state, would have been gentler and more manageable. The War of the Spanish Succession (1701–14) shut off that hypothetical historical path. With the acceptance in November 1700 of the will of the last Habsburg king of Spain, Carlos II, Louis XIV not only put his grandson Philippe on the Spanish throne but took on the responsibility for defending an enormous agglomeration of territory against a Grand Alliance that coalesced in 1701–3.[1] This undertaking came at huge financial cost. The tragedy was that France locked itself into a commitment to the Spanish empire not just for dynastic reasons but for economic motives too: Versailles was by now acutely aware that the extra-European world was ripe for exploitation, but the king and his ministers overestimated what the Castilian elites would ever let the French get from the Spanish Americas. Dynastically the War of the Spanish Succession was worth the struggle, economically it was far from worth it.

In the decade after the Bourbon dynasty inherited the Spanish *monarquía* France experienced chronic military overstretch, and to mount the huge war effort the king had to increase state spending massively, especially in 1705–7. Unfortunately the tax base remained weak in relation to the country's surplus wealth, and politically difficult to widen. This forced the monarchy into dangerous expedients that drove up the price of credit, foreign exchange, and supply commodities, and into higher and higher debt commitments that proved unmanageable. The system of financial contractors and officials so central to French state operations was thrown

[1] Britain, the Dutch Republic, Savoy, Portugal, and most of the Holy Roman Empire plus the Habsburg Emperor, its head.

into chaos, there were a number of bankruptcies and near-collapses among state financial agents who had to be bailed out by the king, and the government was forced into the hands of international bankers for a good proportion of its financial operations, thanks to the pattern of warfare. The widespread employment of relatively unfamiliar financial instruments, and the expanded use of older ones enjoying increased velocity in the international market, allowed the war to be conducted on a length and scale that would otherwise have been impossible, but ironically all this only enhanced the financial disorder inside France. Ministers found themselves navigating the War of the Spanish Succession with apparently little idea of what was likely to happen to the state's finances or to the credit markets if they pushed various financial techniques too far. By contrast, a few men—with strong nerves and deeper insights into the financial and banking worlds—managed to exploit their privileged positions inside the financial machinery, or as the king's banking auxiliaries, to protect themselves if not advance their own interests considerably. In the eyes of some contemporaries these men were in league with the devil.[2]

The size of the debt provides the key index for appreciating the strains inflicted upon France. In 1683—at the time of the death of the Finance Minister Jean-Baptiste Colbert, the dominant financial figure of the previous twenty years—the state debt had stood at only 240 million *livres*. After the two subsequent great wars, the exact size at the end of the reign has been variously estimated by serious contemporaries and scholars at between 1.25 billion and 2.4 billion *livres*. The full debt on 1 September 1715, the day Louis XIV died, was most likely somewhere between at least 1.2 and 1.7 billion *livres*. To this should be added the amount of capital invested in venal offices and which was privileged with government interest payments (not all of it was): this was a further 600 million *livres* by September 1715, perhaps double the venal investment in the state in 1688.[3] The total capital value of state debt requiring service was therefore at least 1.8 billion and perhaps as much as 2.3 billion *livres*. In other words, the state debt was at least three times what it had been just thirty or so years earlier, and it represented somewhere between 66 per cent and 85 per cent of national output during a century of very low economic growth.[4] The proportion of expenditure spent on servicing the debt during the War of the Spanish Succession never rose to the earlier

[2] See e.g. the satirical *Pluton maltôtier, nouvelle galante* (Cologne[?], 1708).

[3] William Doyle, *Venality: The Sale of Offices in Eighteenth-Century France* (Oxford, 1996), 48, 55; Forbonnais, II, 395.

[4] My own estimates are non-committal because of the weakness of the sources. The level of overall debt one chooses depends largely on the amount of downgraded government bonds that may or may not have been circulating and what capital sums they really represented in 1715. The level of short-term debt not yet earmarked for discharge was far less than the 553 million Desmaretz claimed: the total paper unfunded debt accepted in the 1715–16 visa was worth 241 million. For estimates other than my own, and on the earlier situation, consult: Mark Potter, *Corps and Clienteles: Public Finance and Political Change in France, 1688–1715* (Aldershot, 2003), 13; McCollim, 359; Richard Bonney, *The King's Debts: Finance and Politics in France, 1589–1661* (Oxford, 1981), 306–7; Margaret Bonney and Richard Bonney, *Jean-Roland Malet, premier historien des finances de la monarchie française* (Paris, 1993), 57, 60, 73; Malet, *Comptes*, 417; Vuitry, 194–5; CCG, III, 681: 'Compte rendu de M. Desmaretz au Régent', 1716.

catastrophic heights of the era of Richelieu and Mazarin: whereas in many years between 1624 and 1660 debt *servicing* exceeded actual spending on the war effort, it only seems to have done this in 1709–13, and then only because so much expenditure was being deferred for later payment. Nevertheless, from 1695, and especially from 1701, the relationship between revenue, borrowing, and expenditure was becoming disordered, and the interest rates paid from 1708 were becoming exorbitant.

The size of the debt indicates the growth of the burden on France, but in per capita terms it was not so very far off the level in Great Britain at the same time. However, during the War of the Spanish Succession the French state fell markedly behind its British neighbour in its capacity to service its debts, certainly by 1705 if not by 1703: France had higher interest rates, poorly organized appropriations, an inadequate sustainable revenue base, and relatively illiquid credit instruments for covering the bulk of the debt. The spending on debt service was consequently perhaps half as much again as it was in Britain. If France was a 'fiscal-military state'—an expression used nowadays to describe seventeenth- and eighteenth-century states that taxed and borrowed in order to support expenditure devoted overwhelmingly to standing armed forces and war—then during the years after 1703 it was descending into the second or even third division, way below Britain and the Dutch Republic for efficiency and orderliness.[5] France still had its size, large population, and economic diversity going for it, but by the end of the War of the Spanish Succession this added up to very little raw military and naval power. And the financial situation was appalling and unmanageable given the French aversion to higher taxes for servicing loans. It would take well over fifteen years after Louis XIV's death to bring things back into a semblance of balance, using drastic measures to achieve this, while the monarchy would never liberate itself of enough of the debt amassed by Louis XIV to allow it to undertake future wars without periodic crises.

The bulk of this book is accordingly an attempt to reconstruct what happened in the final fifteen to twenty years of Louis XIV's reign, and to explain how and why things transpired in the way they did. This is important not only for understanding the enormous difficulties that the superpower of the age got itself into at the time, but also for appreciating the long-term legacy Louis XIV handed to his great-grandson Louis XV and his great-great-great-grandson Louis XVI. This is not an easy task, largely because so many of the sources for French financial history under Louis XIV have long since disappeared, especially through the ravages of fire; but also because the records were unreliable and imprecise, even at the time. Statistical exactitude is all but out of the question and would, in any case, be methodologically unsound.[6] All one can really hope to do is to weed out what appears unlikely from the surviving accounts, correspondence, and other records, and then

[5] On the fiscal-military state, see notably: John Brewer, *The Sinews of Power: War, Money and the English State, 1688–1783* (London, 1988); Christopher Storrs, ed., *The Fiscal-Military State in Eighteenth-Century Europe: Essays in Honour of P. G. M. Dickson* (Farnham, 2009).

[6] Where statistics have been used in this book, readers should bear in mind that they are of varying accuracy and not to be accepted as gospel.

try to establish a rough sense of developments, trends, pressures, and influences in royal finances.

Reconstructing and explaining France's financial troubles in the period 1700–15 has never been attempted before in as broad and comprehensive a fashion. Most historical writing on Louis XIV's finances and financiers has focused upon the Colbert era before 1683, while the problems of the following decades have been treated largely as a background run-up to the Regency and John Law's great experiment with royal finances. Daniel Dessert's *magnum opus* drew principally upon his deep knowledge of the period before 1683 as he sought to explain Colbert's system of financiers, and for the period after Colbert's death Dessert continued to focus upon discovering the revenue-gathering financiers' sources of power and funds.[7] There has been little on Michel Chamillart as the penultimate finance minister of the reign except a French masters dissertation, and the doctoral thesis of Gary McCollim on Nicolas Desmaretz, Louis XIV's last finance minister, is only now (after over thirty years) going into print.[8] Otherwise, there are a number of thematic works on Mint bills, on French economic relations with the Spanish monarchy and empire, on the bankers (most notably as part of a huge study by Herbert Lüthy on the period *c.*1685–1789), and on the financiers of Languedoc (again covering a century). Studies of venality and of corporate bodies, such as law courts and provincial estates, have also brought serious fresh insights into the problems of royal finances in the later seventeenth and eighteenth centuries.[9] But none of these works has focused on asking how and why France's finances declined so badly after 1700. Only a single article and Adolphe Vuitry's book on financial disorder and speculation—both well over a century old—have sought to provide a more focused look at the problem of the French state's finances in the War of the Spanish Succession, and neither work was sufficiently comprehensive.[10] If the literature generated by historians of France is strong but selective and specialized, the shallow and simplistic comments on French finances in works on British financial history only reinforce the need for an in-depth examination of the agonies of Louis XIV's financial system.

The approach of this book is therefore to integrate for the first time the history of taxation, borrowing, and spending in this period, and relate them where appropriate to the strategic imperatives of the War of the Spanish Succession. While it draws heavily and gratefully upon printed primary evidence and specialist secondary literature about various aspects of the financial system, it breaks new ground in its analysis of the spending side of the French state and how this related to borrowing. In particular, I have sought to use the royal papers on the military treasury and

[7] DAPS.

[8] Rupprecht's *mémoire* and McCollim's thesis. McCollim's revised study in book form appeared too late to be used for this study.

[9] See notably the works of Seligmann and Lüthy. Also, Chaussinand; Doyle, *Venality*; Potter, *Corps and Clienteles*; Julian Swann, *Provincial Power and Absolute Monarchy: The Estates-General of Burgundy, 1661–1790* (Cambridge, 2003).

[10] See Vuitry. Also, Philippe Sagnac, 'Le crédit de l'État et les banquiers à la fin du XVIIe et au commencement du XVIIIe siècle', *Revue d'histoire moderne et contemporaine* 10 (1908), 257–72.

the army paymasters to tackle the broad question of France's financial decline.[11] This has made it possible to relate royal finances more closely than before to the nature and conduct of the war effort. I have also used royal papers concerning bankers to try to shed further light on taxing, borrowing, monetary manipulation, and spending. There is no detailed treatment in this book of the bankers whom the government used for sending remittances to the armies abroad, although they appear where relevant throughout the chapters. They also enjoy a section of the Conclusion to themselves to explain the high costs of their operations and how these account for some of the elevated expenditure on the war effort after 1701. But it is the royal financiers' activities that provide a better way into explaining many of the dubious practices that were also used by the bankers, with similar costly effects for the monarchy.

THE FISCO-FINANCIER SYSTEM

Understanding the financial decline of the French monarchy involves attention to some of the more salient details of what happened in the years 1700–15, but it also requires an appreciation of the underlying financial structure on which the French monarchy depended. From the fifteenth century onwards, all those who collected or otherwise handled the king's monies, with the exception of private bankers who remitted them under specific contract, were known as 'financiers' or 'publicains'. 'Finance' three hundred years ago in France did not have the wide sense it has in the twenty-first century, instead designating anything connected with the king's money. In order to avoid confusion it is advisable to refer to those involved in this business—whether they were contractors or regular revenue and expenditure officials—as 'fisco-financiers'.[12] This label, however, covers a multitude of functions, and several different categories of financial operative. In some cases fisco-financiers ran what can be described as 'para-royal' administrations or agencies, with personnel running into the hundreds if not thousands and with their own credit at the heart of their operations. Those who owed detailed accounts of their handling of royal revenues were known in a literal fashion as 'comptables' (the French word meaning 'accountable men'), and there were a number of them, together with the great tax farmers, who were the core of the royal financial machinery below the ministerial bureaux. All fisco-financiers were subject to a greater or lesser amount of ministerial direction, but even for those among the highest ranks in daily contact with the ministers, supervision was largely a matter of maintaining a watch over their macro-activity. It was not a question of micro-management, which would have been impractical. For the most part the fisco-financiers were kept in

[11] Only cursory, superficial use has been made of these papers before, despite an earlier appeal for their exploitation: Henri Germain-Martin, 'Le financement des guerres de Louis XIV et les trésoriers de l'extraordinaire des guerres', *Revue des travaux de l'Académie des sciences morales et politiques* 126 (1973), 15–29.

[12] Daniel Dessert used this expression as an adjective, but it can equally well be used as a noun.

check in a rather flimsy way, by the knowledge that either they could lose their positions or the government could ultimately sue them through the courts for defaulting on their obligations.

At the top of the *comptable* tree were the *Gardes du Trésor royal* who ran the king's main treasury and clearing house for revenues in Paris, and the *receveur des revenus casuels* for income from venality. On a local level the most important revenue-raising *comptables* were the *receveurs généraux des finances*, two of whom usually managed collection of the direct taxes by their subordinates in each *généralité*. These roughly thirty *généralités* were the major financial districts into which France was divided for financial purposes and which were only in some cases the same as the provinces. Alongside them in the *pays d'états*—those outlying provinces that retained provincial assemblies—were the treasurers of the local estates, who acted as both disbursers of expenditure and revenue-gathering managers. As to tax farming, it is worth noting that the *fermiers généraux*—the farmers general—and other tax farmers were not strictly speaking *comptables*, as they were not royal office-holders and instead worked on the basis of lease contracts. Although they were expected to produce accounts, the scrutiny they were under does not seem to have been as detailed as for the *receveurs généraux*. The activity of these revenue-raisers, and the mounting problems they faced, will be considered in Chapters 3 and 4. Below the *Gardes du Trésor royal*, the most important *comptables* of all, however, were the big spenders: in particular the *trésorier général de la Marine* (sailing fleet), the *trésorier des Galères* (the galleys), and above all the army's paymasters, the *trésoriers généraux de l'Ordinaire des Guerres* (who handled a small percentage of sums) and the *trésoriers généraux de l'Extraordinaire des Guerres* who dealt with the bulk of military expenditure. These army treasurers were answerable to the Secretary of State for War as well as to the *contrôleur général* (the Finance Minister) and they will play a significant part in the later chapters of this book.

The split between revenue-raisers and spending officials is not a clear-cut one, and individual *publicains* could perform both roles. It therefore makes most sense to think of the fisco-financiers instead in terms of men acting mainly as either primary receivers or secondary receivers of the king's revenues. The *receveur des revenus casuels*, the *receveurs généraux*, the tax farmers, and the 'traitants' (dealing with specialized one-off revenue contracts) were the main primary receivers, gathering funds from the populace in the forms of taxation, sales of office, forced loans, and regalian rights. The bulk of their funds was put at the king's disposal through the Trésor royal. The treasurers general of the Extraordinaire des Guerres and the other military treasuries were fundamentally secondary receivers because they were overwhelmingly dependent for income upon money passed to them from the primary receivers.

Getting money from the *caisses* (chests) of one receiver of funds to another, especially to secondary receivers like the Extraordinaire des Guerres, required an organized system of appropriations. In theory the primary receivers passed their funds, either in cash or notionally, to the Trésor royal in Paris. The king and a secretary of state or the *contrôleur général* would then issue general payment orders, the *ordonnances de paiement* that specified an overall sum, either to the Trésor royal or directly to secondary receivers. These *ordonnances* were in themselves very unlikely to produce any concrete funds.[13] Specific funds would then be pledged by the Trésor royal working with the Finance Ministry to meet those payment orders, and the pledges would normally come in the form of *assignations* given to secondary receivers. These were more detailed orders drawn upon a particular revenue source, for example the customs duties of Alsace or the urban tolls of Anjou, and they would be presented by, say, a military paymaster to the primary receiver of that revenue source for payment. The same process was also used to transfer funds from primary receivers to the king's remittance bankers (who usually traded or pledged them). This system of publicly used *assignations* was essential for as long as diverse revenues belonging to the king were in the accounts of a large number of chests whose funds rolled in at varying paces.[14]

A release date for the earmarked funds would be stated in an *assignation*, but these were by no means always paid on time, nor the sums paid up in full. *Assignations* might be formally prolonged for a limited period, cashed early for a discount, or cashed for less than their face value at the time of their maturity. As revenue sources declined in yields in the final decades of Louis XIV's reign, speculation on these instruments became widespread. Men who were in the market for these instruments—especially the shadowy *agents de change* (exchange brokers)—would set a 'present value' upon a revenue stream they suspected would not deliver in its entirety, and made offers (or not!) to *assignation*-holders on this basis.[15] As the revenue situation got worse, the value of immature *assignations* might come to reflect not the state of a particular revenue stream, but the needs of individuals to trade such instruments for cash or other paper. In other words, supply and demand could affect the value of an *assignation* just as much as the strength of its revenue stream. This caused a degree of discredit not just to particular streams but to the whole appropriations system, as a multitude of people trying to trade *assignations* could produce a downward spiral in present value on all revenue sources![16] Ministers therefore sometimes turned to another form of paper issued for decades now by the most important fisco-financiers, so-called *rescriptions* or *récépissés*. These were documents emitted personally by *receveurs généraux*, which confirmed their liability to pay up funds from anywhere within their designated sphere of responsibility, whereas *assignations* on them—issued by the crown—were couched in more specific terms, hypothecating a particular revenue stream. Secondary receivers such as the army paymasters liked *rescriptions*, as they made it easier to squeeze payment out of a primary receiver, but *receveurs généraux* were understandably less comfortable with them as they made it harder to juggle their various revenue streams.[17]

13 For example AN G⁷1784, no. 132: Saint-Macary to Desmaretz, 5 November 1709.

14 Alain Guéry, 'Les finances de la monarchie française sous l'ancien régime', *Annales ESC* 33 (1978), 222.

15 SHD A¹1699, no. 271: Titon to Chamillart, 17 February 1703.

16 AN G⁷1786, no. 154: Voysin to Mongelas, 6 April 1710.

17 AN G⁷1097: Mongelas to Chamillart, 2 February 1706; G⁷1784, no. 174: Trudaine to Desmaretz, 7 December 1709.

This was the basic revenue and appropriations framework for handling royal funds, and it involved massive amounts of financial trading and manoeuvring. That a good number of financiers could manipulate the state, and do so with relative impunity, was largely attributable to the needs of the monarchy, but it can also be put down in part to the weakness of the auditing framework in a context of financial crisis. For those fisco-financiers who were *comptables*, they were under the obligation to provide accounts first to the royal ministries and then to the Paris Chambre des Comptes, a superior court which had the responsibility to verify and certify the processes (but not the government decisions) of royal revenue-raising and expenditure. Yet the official audit process was extremely weak. The War Ministry and the Finance Ministry received the accounts of financial officials and agents, but they were too short-staffed to follow up the receipts and discharges in detail, while the Chambre was a cumbersome and hobbled creature. In the last resort it possessed judicial oversight over *comptables* and could try them for misdemeanours. In practice, though, it was only permitted limited investigative and auditing authority to prevent it disturbing hidden patterns of power and infringing on royal sovereign rights, as exercised through the ministers. In any case, by Louis XIV's reign it was struggling under such a weight of business that it could take decades for the court to process a single financier's accounts for just one year. Audit failure also arose because war threw up considerable confusion in accounts, while the effects of major conflict dragged out financial years as the delivery of revenues lagged further and further behind schedule.[18]

One reason why it was so hard to keep a check on the revenue-raisers and the royal paymasters was the hybrid nature of the world in which they operated. In France the revenue edifice became the main structure of public credit, meaning the king did not see the fiscal machinery purely in terms of maximizing revenue-raising efficiency. The whole financial system was based upon advances and short-term loans to the king because of the difficulties in matching revenue flow to expenditure needs, and this was institutionalized in the establishment of regular but widely spaced due dates for making collected revenues available to the crown. The need to pay the monarchy deposits and upfront instalments, the delays in funds coming into their coffers thanks to seasonal and geographical factors, and sudden requirements for extra crown expenditure meant that royal financial officials and farmers needed to take out very many short-term loans themselves at the best of times, and when circumstances deteriorated so their borrowing increased. Urgent short-term credit was most easily available through the fisco-financiers, so the crown needed to be indulgent towards the most powerful and useful among their number, and this involved a degree of permissiveness towards deficient accounting and suspect activity that provided great opportunities for profiteering.

By the end of the seventeenth century fisco-financiers were tapping credit at lower levels of society and in a more widespread fashion than ever before, and this enhanced the utility of this system for the king. At least before the eighteenth

[18] BNF F-23621, *édit*, June 1717; AN G[7]1787, no. 236: memorandum on Treasurer-General Arnauld, [late 1711].

century, very few fisco-financiers enjoyed large personal fortunes that could provide a sufficient cushion for their activities. Instead they relied upon their contacts, the monies they held for the king, and their own reputations to raise credit. As businessmen, naturally the fisco-financiers preferred to deploy what funds they held in as wide a fashion as possible to maximize returns. At their disposal were often large sums of royal funds belonging to the king but which they did not yet need to pass on. What they did was use this, and whatever wealth they owned or borrowed, to invest in a multitude of schemes that could profit them or protect their situation if adverse circumstances struck. They speculated and directly invested in each other's activities, but they also acted selectively as guarantors for the activities of other fisco-financiers. Moreover, the historians Bayard and Dessert reckoned that around two-thirds of those who between 1661 and 1715 were major food suppliers for the armies and navies—so-called *munitionnaires* organized in large 'vivres' companies—were also among the great collectors and handlers of the king's revenues.[19]

For all but a small minority of the leading fisco-financiers, most funds they provided were raised through credit mobilized by issuing paper debt instruments on a growing scale. Around the start of the Nine Years War fisco-financiers (notably *traitants* taking on one-off revenue contracts) began to issue bearer bills (*billets au porteur*) upon themselves in order to make it easier to get cash for the advances the crown increasingly expected of them. These were typically to mature within about three months. The rise of bearer bills that did not carry the name of the creditor made them a particularly useful method of borrowing from the great noble families, who were still rather shy about being identified with some of the most rapacious men of the kingdom. For the first few years bearer bills were payable to a named individual and were centred around Paris, but after 1700 they were increasingly anonymized and were extended to Lyon and elsewhere to garner provincial and foreign money. The increasing use of bearer bills with no individual named as the creditor made it easier to trade them, and by September 1704 bearer bills issued by *receveurs généraux* were circulating in Holland, Genoa, and elsewhere. Bearer bills were, in addition, issued as a way of pushing back the delivery of funds in cash to the king's secondary receivers, and secondary receivers, in turn, might make their payments in their own bearer bills, as the military treasurers did on a grand scale. On top of this, primary receivers such as the farmers general would be forced by the government to emit bearer bills in order to try to withdraw other, collapsed paper instruments such as Mint bills. Nothing like it had ever been seen on such a scale as it was in France during the 1700s.[20]

This was, in outline, the structure and instrument system for raising revenue and short-term loans, and getting the proceeds to the great spenders, the army and navy. It was a system—as we shall see—that had the problems of principal-

[19] Françoise Bayard and Daniel Dessert, 'Les financiers dans l'état monarchique en guerre au XVIIe siècle', in Emmanuel Le Roy Ladurie, ed., *Les monarchies* (Paris, 1986), 251–2.

[20] DAPS, 74–6, 207, 365; CCG, III, 323: Anisson to Desmaretz, 2 July 1712; Saint-Germain, *Financiers*, 38, 117–20; Lüthy, I, 110; AN G[7]1776, no. 236: Montargis to Chamillart, 13 September 1704.

agent distortion, rent-seeking, assymetric information, and moral hazard at its heart, and these became more of a problem in the 1700s than previously as financiers battled to protect and enhance their own private interests. Some brief explanation of what these terms, derived from economic and public choice theory, mean is required here. A 'principal-agent' problem is when state agents can escape the bounds set by their political masters, in large part because of an imbalance of de facto power in the relationship. This can stem to a very large degree from 'information asymmetry', when the agents can deal with the sovereign power on the basis of advantageous knowledge and superior understanding of the situation they are managing, a problem that was endemic at a time of poor communication and a compartmentalized 'public sphere'. With less than scrupulous agents, or in a context where private interests are treated quite legitimately as part of the wider public interest, this generates 'rent-seeking', a situation in which contractors and agents manipulate and alter the very frameworks within which they are seeking to gain advantage, or at least to protect themselves against disaster. The strength of private interests, in relation to the needs of the state, can become so great that the state needs to intervene outside the normal rules to support them in their mistakes and their losses, or because the state has deliberately forced them into overstretching their resources. Bankers and military paymasters, for example, become so essential to the king's needs that they are too important to be allowed to fail, and when they founder they need to be propped up. This creates 'moral hazard' for it makes it possible for people to conceive of the state doing something similar in future, and increases the likelihood of people behaving in a way that might force the state to provide assistance again in their favour. It shifts the loss risk of often hazardous ventures—such as contracting to supply money or bread or foreign exchange to the king—from private bodies to the state. Of course, if the king were to persuade people to lend to his financial agents or act as his financial agents he might have no choice but to prop them up, whether losses were a result of the agent's irresponsibility or beyond their control. These notions will appear in several places in this book. Such social science concepts should be employed with great care in relation to the distant past, yet they have a real value in helping to crystallize the problems of the fisco-financier and contractor system that was the body and soul of the French logistical machine under the old monarchy.

THE INHERENT WEAKNESS OF THE FRENCH CREDIT SYSTEM

All told, and we shall never be able to determine exactly the pattern of investments, it is clear that the major fisco-financiers as a group could draw on a real diversity of sources to back their operations. In the War of the Spanish Succession they would need to. Despite the many unendearing qualities of the fisco-financiers, the system seems to have been one that the crown—with regular wars, and managing endemic localism and a culture of all-pervasive clientelism—could not afford to unpick. This was because the French credit framework was unreliable, uncertain, and not conducive to low interest rates or easy lending. There was a severe problem of secrecy and therefore assymetric information in the credit process, and the credit market was getting too big to rely upon personal trust between individuals. Honour and reputation, not transparency, was therefore the bedrock of credit, and it required paying one's debts and handling one's debtors in a patient and mutually agreeable manner. All this prevented regular total breakdowns of credit, although sometimes creditors had little choice but to bear defaults (some of them cavalierly undertaken) with fortitude. In Louis XIV's France there were also legal and religious constraints on lending that hampered financial flows, for usury laws remained on the statute book and could be used. French law did not openly protect financial dealings involving credit that responded to market conditions. From December 1665 the legal maximum for private lending in the financially most important areas of the kingdom was a mere 5 per cent. Furthermore, repayment of the principal of a debt could technically not be demanded, and this anti-usury approach was internalized by many, sometimes in a duplicitous fashion: while a good number of people in France, 'out of the scruples of conscience', were apparently averse to lending money unless the capital were alienated in perpetuity, at the other extreme there were some—including the monarchy itself—who saw themselves bearing little moral obligation to honour their credit instruments in full if they had been traded, especially for a discount greater than 5 per cent. Respect for original financial engagements was thus somewhat lacking on the part of private individuals, state financiers, or the state itself.[21]

All of this helped to create a financial world characterized by subterfuge and higher-risk premiums. The legal and legislative structure pushed people into private credit agreements which were hard to enforce except through social pressures, and only the perpetual need for credit prevented more defaulting than there actually was. It all added up to a volatile situation in which credit arrangements were not dependable under law. It certainly put up underlying interest rates, to levels higher than those in the Dutch Republic or—after 1704 brought greater protection to creditors and credit notes—England. Moreover, limits on the rate of interest offered, whether by private individuals or by the state through its main annuity bonds, the *rentes*, may have reduced the willingness of people to lend in circumstances that were fraught with risk. It is striking that implicit French interest rates for private credit hovered around the maximum permitted from the mid-seventeenth century. Even if the state found ways around this, offering higher rates of interest in a variety of ways through a number of instruments and bodies, there remained an inherent risk in participating in a system whose structures and interest rates could, in effect, be altered at royal (or even private individual) whim. As Philip Hoffman and others have pointed out, French credit markets were weak under Louis XIV because of uncertainties and repeated shocks that made

[21] Laurence Fontaine, 'Antonio and Shylock: Credit and Trust in France, *c.1680–c.*1780', *Economic History Review* 54 (2001), 39–43, 53–4; Esnault, I, 96: 'Mémoire', [January 1702, probably by Desmaretz] (quotation); Vuitry, 188–9.

borrowers and lenders uneasy.[22] Government defaults at times hit financiers hard, and this in turn could penalize individuals who had invested in them. Government support for key state financiers in the form of debt relief orders and injunctions could be equally damaging, disturbing the patterns of credit and magnifying the moral hazard already inherent in the system: every time it happened, a signal was sent that royal agents would be protected from the normal rules of the credit system in which they operated.[23]

One of the ways in which this problem of trust could be mitigated was by maintaining the financial world and credit markets as a highly Balkanized set of arrangements. This could work in France owing to the enormous size of the economy and country, and the complexity of its commercial dealings within a structure of privilege and corporate identity. During Louis XIV's reign the financial 'public'—especially those who really mattered—remained very limited in size and nature, and was perhaps more a disaggregated set of 'sub-publics' possessing little informational unity and marked by continued great secrecy.[24] Defaulting could therefore be selective and hidden, and credit crises could unfold in slow motion. But aside from the risk that this would allow burgeoning disasters to go undetected by ministers until it was too late, this secrecy and compartmentalization of finances came at a high cost, as increasing unpredictability and risk pushed up the price of money and military supplies (obtained largely on credit) in the final two, highly demanding wars of Louis XIV's reign.

There was, however, a deeper problem of governance which destabilized French credit. When government depended so much on a single man, and backstairs access to him, no markets could be sure of what was coming round the corner, and it made the funding of the French monarchy more expensive in comparison with some of its international rivals. The truth of this was laid fully bare in early 1712, when it became clear that the country was likely to have to endure a regency government for a minor king in the not-too-distant future, with all the extra uncertainty as well as rent-seeking and infighting by well-placed vested interests this would bring. Two weeks after the death of the twenty-nine-year-old Dauphin (the former duke of Burgundy), the banker Samuel Bernard lamented to Desmaretz that 'since the death of Monseigneur the Dauphin minds are completely disturbed. It is not possible to do any negotiating at any price, and everyone is holding back their money.'[25] It has, of course, long been argued that France was at an inherent disadvantage in the 'Second Hundred Years War' with Britain, lasting from 1688 to 1815, because she was burdened with a state that was 'absolute' in nature and arbitrary in its financial dealings, and there is much to be said for this view. This is not to argue that the British state could not also change direction and act capriciously, but to do so in a significant and deliberate manner after 1688 it had to get the agreement of Parliament, in which holders of liquid capital had considerable

[22] Philip T. Hoffman, Gilles Postel-Vinay, and Jean-Laurent Rosenthal, *Priceless Markets: The Political Economy of Credit in Paris, 1660–1870* (London, 2000), 3, 22, 51, 58.
[23] Saint-Germain, *Financiers*, 110–11, 130–2.
[24] AN G^{7}1778, no. 112: [second] note by Montargis, 1 April 1706.
[25] AN G^{7}1122: Bernard to Desmaretz, 5 March 1712.

influence. Moreover, in the 1690s and 1700s various parliamentary statutes and legal judgments, plus the development of the Bank of England's practices, gave greater liquidity to financial instruments and helped to develop secondary markets, while loans were directly linked to parliamentary grants.[26] As one financier wrote from London in 1709,

> The public funds here not being like those in France, exposed to the caprice of those who govern, and it is [government] good faith that makes there be more foreigners and even Frenchmen who supply their money here than [Englishmen].[27]

The credit gap between the two states, indeed, first seems to have opened up significantly during the War of the Spanish Succession. Publicly floated French official instruments in 1701–7 offered de facto if not nominal interest rates of 8–10 per cent, and the short-term debt in 1707 required interest of 7.5–10 per cent per annum or more; this at a time when the British government's liabilities were edging down to rates of 5–6 per cent.[28] It is not hard to see why there was growing disparity between the rival powers. On top of the deeper deficiencies of credit in early modern France, on a general level the biggest underlying problem for the state might well have been the absence in France of *secure* or generally reliable hypothecation of revenues for servicing the debts contracted either directly by the crown or indirectly by its agents.[29] There were also outright government breaches of faith with the markets that could be disastrous in the short term, provoking one insider to ask, at the time of a rapid, unexpected, and particularly egregious volte-face over Mint bills in January 1707,

> What confidence do you wish, Monseigneur, that one has in future in the edicts and declarations? This frightful alteration will close up the purses of even the best intentioned.[30]

The absolutist monarchical system of government, in which the king was counselled in the financial *arcana imperii* by a very small, select few, was a significant cause of the French state's credit problems. Especially when the advice was ill-informed and ill-founded, and led the king into counterproductive policies too.

A MILITARY-INDUSTRIAL COMPLEX IN THE FRENCH STATE?

Sometimes the advice was highly self-interested too. In the course of the War of the Spanish Succession there emerged in France an early manifestation of a 'military-industrial complex', thanks, not least, to the all-pervasive use of financial and

[26] P. G. M. Dickson, *The Financial Revolution in England: A Study in the Development of Public Credit 1688–1756* (London, 1967), 401, 459–61, 487, 514.

[27] AN G[7]1119: 'Extrait d'une lettre écrite de Londres le 4 novembre 1709'.

[28] Forbonnais, II, 172–3; Dickson, *Financial Revolution*, 79–83, 373–8, 470–1.

[29] See Chapter 8.

[30] AN G[7]1120: Bernard to Chamillart, 11 March 1707.

supply contractors to support the logistics of the state. What this particularly important group of men had in common was not the mass production of armaments—though some of them were involved in munitions manufacture—but the supply of logistical services and of money, or rather credit, to the state. Is it, however, out of place or anachronistic to think of these contractors as a military-industrial complex? Most political scientists, many political activists, and President Eisenhower in his 1961 farewell address to the American people have associated the term with the developments in American government and the arms industries in the period after the Second World War. The label has also been applied to the situations developing in the western European powers in the decades leading up to the First World War. It is widely argued that the existence of such a complex poses a real threat to modern democratic government, either intentionally or unintentionally, as defence special interests lobby and enter government (especially defence departments and the US Congress) for their own advantage. Perhaps, however, we should not restrict our use of the concept to episodes when a modern representative government and constitution find themselves in danger. There were a small number of episodes in early modern European history when either a state was in danger of falling captive to a military-industrial complex, or a military-industrial complex damaged the interests and structure of a state.

A military-industrial complex should not be seen as a single, coherent interest bloc. Rather, the label encompasses a number of separate, war-related private interests attempting in similar ways to enhance their situation through the penetration of the corridors of power. Such interests are sometimes competing, sometimes cooperating, and can be composed of a very few people, who nevertheless wield considerable power and influence to the detriment of those they exploit, both above and below them, in the political hierarchy. This activity can have potentially baleful effects on the host state, whatever its constitutional set-up. At the heart of this problem lies the issue of principal-agent distortion, in which states find it exceptionally difficult to control their ostensible servants. Such a phenomenon can be seen in France in the early eighteenth century in an intense form, as a set of individuals and loose groupings with political and economic interests related to war managed to exert considerable influence over ministers to their own advantage or for their own protection. It was not that the French financial and supply contractors pushed Louis XIV into accepting the will of Carlos II, or into launching any of his wars for that matter. Nor do they seem to have made any discernible effort to prolong the War of the Spanish Succession for their own profit. Nevertheless, Louis XIV's problems with his contractors were extreme for the time—compared with similar lobbies in the Dutch Republic and England—in that they augmented the state's financial distress.

The financial woes of France were brought about not by military defeats,[31] but for the most part by the king's acceptance of the Spanish inheritance, by the consequent increases in military spending this made necessary, by the inadequate tax base, by the fall in revenues, and by some of the probably unavoidable revenue

[31] *Pace* Dickson, *Financial Revolution*, 59.

expedients that were used. But they were greatly exacerbated by mistakes in policy (some of them influenced by self-interested advisers and agents) and by the excessive use of increasingly powerful financial instruments that should have been employed with far greater restraint. The financial decline this book describes is as much about the degeneration of financial management as it is about the weakening of revenues, the increase in spending, and the accumulation of debts.

PART I

THE STRATEGIC MANAGEMENT OF WAR AND THE FINANCIAL CHAIN OF COMMAND

Introduction

From time to time a country gets locked into a deteriorating situation because of an overwhelming political imperative that then—because of enormous economic and financial stresses—engenders open-ended commitments to maintain essential components of that political project. It also pushes governments into decisions that are dangerous and, in hindsight, appear disastrous. For Louis XIV's France the Spanish succession produced just such a trap. It is therefore essential that we understand, if with a critical eye, the impulses behind the French government's decisions and the consequences thereof, and also consider the options available to the government. Accordingly, the first part of this book will begin by looking at the enormous fiscal and logistical challenge posed by the political and geostrategic demands of the War of the Spanish Succession. Chapter 2 will then relate the pressures of war and credit to the superstructure of power and the decision-making processes in royal finances.

1

Geostrategy, International Politics, and the Burden of War, 1688–1714

Louis XIV has a reputation as one of history's great warmongers. During his 'personal rule' of over fifty-four years, France found herself at war for approximately thirty-three of them and was conducting minor military operations during a further five. The wars of aggression and conquest against the Spanish monarchy and the Dutch Republic in the later 1660s and 1670s gave way after 1678 to a policy of annexing territories, known as the 'réunions', through a combination of legal subterfuge, diplomatic bullying, and military occupations. In 1683–84 Louis launched a war to acquire further Low Countries territory from the pitifully weak Spanish on his northern frontiers and to try to force the Holy Roman Empire into recognizing his Rhineland acquisitions as permanent. This, however, the Empire would only do temporarily, as de facto conquests, so the best that could be agreed was a fragile twenty-year truce. After Louis revoked the Edict of Nantes in September 1685, sending a flood of Huguenot refugees across northern and central Europe, made further interventions in German affairs, and pursued an increasingly personal dispute with the pope, he found nearly all of Europe hostile towards France. Fearful that Emperor Leopold, having made huge conquests from the Turks in the previous four years, would shortly turn his forces against French acquisitions in the Rhine-Moselle region, in August 1688 Louis launched a pre-emptive strike to consolidate his position and force the Empire into a formal, permanent recognition of his annexations. It was a colossal miscalculation, since the normally fractured Empire united against France while Louis' bitter foe, William of Orange, profited from the situation to remove his father-in-law, James II, from the British thrones and begin the consolidation of his own power. France would now face international warfare on a logistical scale and geographical range unknown since the 1650s, requiring mobilization on an unprecedented scale.

THE GEOSTRATEGIC POSITION OF FRANCE, 1688–1714

Two decades of intense warfare after 1689, with only a brief respite halfway through, proved draining for France. In the final years of the War of the Spanish Succession the French state machine did not completely collapse, as it had done when it was organizationally far weaker during the 1640s, but it did reach the verge of breakdown. That things got so much worse in the 1700s was not simply a function of accumulating war exhaustion, but stemmed from the geographical expansion in commitments taken on by Louis XIV when he accepted the Castilian poisoned chalice, the Spanish throne, for his grandson Philippe, duc d'Anjou, in November 1700. It is now commonly held that Louis had little choice but to accept the entire inheritance when presented with the will of the last Habsburg king of Spain, Carlos II, a document through which the Castilian elites hoped to preserve their *monarquía* by committing the most powerful army in Europe—that of the French—to its defence and preservation. It was a shrewd move on the part of the Spanish inner governing circle, if a hopeless one given the number of international players with a range of interests in acquiring parts of the monarchy or rights within it. The French government appears to have agonized about whether to renege on three years of diplomatic negotiations with William III of Great Britain: the two kings had sought to avoid a major conflagration over the Spanish inheritance by establishing a partition plan that the French and the British would enforce upon the Spaniards and the rest of Europe. In the end, though we cannot be certain, the French council of state—the Conseil d'En haut—appears to have been swayed by fears that the British would be unreliable allies in enforcing partition upon Emperor Leopold and the Austrian government. Moreover, the Spanish explicitly threatened to turn to an Austrian heir who would accept the entire inheritance should Louis not do so.[1] The wisdom of the French decision cannot be argued out here, although one might easily suspect that the War of the Spanish Succession would have been less bloody, less extensive, far less costly for France, and shorter had Versailles abided by the spirit of the March 1700 Partition Treaty, called the Spanish (and Austrian) bluff, and refused to accept the entire inheritance. It is doubtful, though, that the Bourbons would have eventually emerged with the main prizes of the Iberian and transoceanic lands, and this may have been a deciding factor for Louis at a time when the European powers were interloping in the Spanish overseas empire on an escalating scale.

Whatever the reasons, the Bourbons took on the entire inheritance of Carlos II, and the French were saddled with the responsibility of holding Philip V's disparate lands together. Even for the most populous country in Europe this was a terrible imposition, given that France was already weakened politically and financially by the Nine Years War. Between 1688 and 1690 Louis XIV had brought upon himself a coalition of enemies comprising the Holy Roman Empire, the British Isles, the Dutch Republic, the Spanish monarchy, and Victor Amadeus II, Duke of Savoy. The strategic imperatives of fighting this range of enemies imposed such demands on France that the supply of pay, food, and *matériel* necessary for war superseded

[1] An appreciation of the dilemmas and problems surrounding the Spanish inheritance can be gleaned from a number of recent works: e.g., John C. Rule, 'The Partition Treaties, 1698–1700: A European View', in Esther Mijers and David Onnekink, eds, *Redefining William III: The Impact of the King-Stadholder in International Context* (Aldershot, 2007); William Roosen, 'The Origins of the War of the Spanish Succession', in Jeremy Black, ed., *The Origins of War in Early Modern Europe* (Edinburgh, 1987). Campaigning details can be found in the monumental chronicle of the marquis de Quincy: *Histoire militaire du règne de Louis le Grand* (8 vols, Paris, 1726).

all considerations of budgetary control that had previously been attempted. But at least in the Nine Years War French armies had been fighting close to or within the country's frontiers for the vast majority of the time, and logistical costs did not therefore become crippling. Moreover, by 1695 a seismic shift had taken place in French strategic thinking, which was now much more closely linked with diplomatic negotiations and awareness of the king's unfortunate international image. A far more defensive approach emerged, to calm international anxieties.[2] All this made it possible to keep the costs of transferring resources out of old France relatively low, and though defensive stances were not cheap and required careful management, French armies had been able to live off enemy land to a limited extent, mainly just beyond the frontiers.

Unfortunately for the new, more restrained French approach, the War of the Spanish Succession took on a very different pattern. French forces very quickly found themselves operating way beyond their frontiers and home resources. By assuming lead responsibility for the defence of the Spanish Netherlands, the duchy of Milan, the kingdoms of Naples, Sicily and Sardinia, and the Spanish Iberian territories after 1700, France would face a considerable increase in the cost of war. How and why this should be so much worse than in the 1690s demands explanation. After the experience of the Thirty Years War it was considered vital to manage carefully any attempt to live off the land, otherwise large forces would disintegrate and territory would be lost to the enemy. However, regardless of the level of contribution income extracted from enemy territories in the Nine Years War,[3] after 1700 Bourbon armies were unable to live off the land to nearly the same extent, because they found themselves working with allies whose land they could not simply despoil. The huge costs of an intensified war effort in northern Italy in 1702 led Chamillart to urge the Franco-Spanish commanders to live off the region as much as possible, 'to make war German-style', but the Spanish Governor General of Milan explained that for obvious political reasons—a desire to entrench Bourbon influence throughout the peninsula—it was very hard to seize foreign resources from the Lombardy duchies and Venice, even though the material benefits would be huge. Supplies would generally have to be negotiated and seizures would mostly have to be paid for.[4] Matters were no better from that year onwards in the Low Countries. Such was the power of Dutch fortresses and the difficulties of crossing the Rhine that the United Provinces and western Germany simply could not be penetrated by anything other than small forces operating out of the Spanish Netherlands. After 1706 the Bourbons found themselves controlling only the southern third of these provinces, and after 1708 they were almost pushed out altogether. But this gave no boost to contribution income, since Philip V's authorities understandably wanted to continue treating the people of this area as loyal subjects under enemy occupation. Further east, it was hard for France to live off much of

[2] SHD A[1]1453, no. 25: 'Memoire' by Chamlay, 21 September 1695.
[3] See Rowlands, appendix 2.
[4] SHD A[1]1594, no. 84: Chamillart to Bouchu, 13 February 1702 (quotation); Esnault, I, 206: Vaudémont to Chamillart, 12 March 1702; AN G[7]1775, no. 322: 'Estat' [late 1702].

south-western Germany, except sporadically in some of the western Palatinate and the southern Black Forest and Breisgau region. Even in the better years (and there were few good years), contribution income from enemy territory probably only met around 10 per cent of total military spending in the 1700s. It was certainly somewhat below the rate of the 1690s.

Owing to the very limited possibilities of living off the land after 1700, Versailles was faced with what soon proved to be a monumental problem of moving resources abroad. As the number of France's enemies increased this was required on such a scale that the country came to suffer what is known as a 'wealth transfer problem', caused by a major international deficit in military spending. The defence of the Spanish Netherlands siphoned a modest amount of money out of France, but a certain proportion of it returned through domestic procurement. Here, only a few acute problems—as in 1706 when the cavalry lost two-thirds of their horses[5]—made very large additional outlays by government and army officers necessary. However, the situation was far worse in the south. The army of Italy, in particular, not only required huge remittances to be sent from France through Lyon and the Italian financial centres, often at very high cost, but it could suck much of the available money and credit out of the whole south-eastern quarter of France. Campaigning in Italy also caused 'extreme exhaustion' for troops and officers.[6] The other great drain on resources was Iberia, where the war was not only carried on in north-western Andalusia and the far west of Extremadura against the British and Portuguese, but spread rapidly into Aragon, Catalonia, and even, at times, Valencia and Old Castile. The huge scale of this theatre, where the financial, commercial, and transport infrastructures were comparatively underdeveloped and remittance possibilities were heavily circumscribed, was remarked upon frequently by French financiers, commanders, diplomats, and administrators.[7] On top of all this, France was subsidizing allies, most notably the new king of Spain Philip V, Elector Maximilian Emanuel of Bavaria, and the latter's brother Archbishop-Elector Joseph Clemens of Cologne. It was not merely the stagnation of revenues, thereby increasing reliance upon ever less favourable credit, that greatly exaggerated the French budgetary problem after 1700,[8] but the additional costs of moving money and other material resources to French armies and allies now some distance abroad. There were heavy foreign exchange costs associated with these transfers, costs that had been relatively small during the more confined, static, and defensive Nine Years War.

A more detailed sense of the strategic burden needs to be provided in order that the financial pressure can be appreciated in its proper, military context. In 1701 Louis XIV and Philip V faced only the Austrian Habsburgs in just the northern Italian theatre, but the pressures of this single zone alone soon proved painful. Already by December 1701 France was carrying the overwhelming burden here

5 CCG, II, 474: *mémoire* by Chamillart, 16 October 1706.

6 SHD Ya2: Voysin to chevalier de Maulevrier, 14 September 1710.

7 AN G[7]1778, no. 77: note by Mongelas, 7 March 1706.

8 *Pace* Margaret Bonney and Richard Bonney, *Jean-Roland Malet, premier historien des finances de la monarchie française* (Paris, 1993), 23.

because the Spanish forces and the Milanese revenue base were very weak.[9] With the prospect of war against Britain and the Dutch, and the conflict expanding to the Netherlands and Rhineland in early 1702, France found herself facing a strategic Morton's Fork, as the king's adviser, the sieur de Chamlay, recognized very well. He argued powerfully that remaining on the defensive actually required more troops than going on the offensive, owing to the sheer number of fortresses that needed defending. Equally, alas, a clear offensive strategy would yield little because the Dutch and Imperial forces would be too strong for France to attack with any hope of victory, their fortresses were too far from convenient Franco-Spanish bases, and they were not on rivers easily navigable by the Bourbon armies. Moreover, two full armies would be required to undertake the siege of a major Dutch fortress, such was the strength and sophistication of the sunken, bastion-traced emplacements in this part of the world by the end of the seventeenth century. Chamlay therefore recommended 'a sort of mixed war' for just about all of Europe: the Franco-Spanish should act defensively in protecting and maintaining those fortresses they absolutely had to hold, while offensive operations should really consist of aggressive posturing and positioning, living off enemy territory where possible, blocking enemy thrusts, and trying to engage them in battle where possible.[10] These recommendations were the basis of French military strategy for most of the war, though in 1703–6 major offensive operations were undertaken to conquer the territories of the duke of Savoy—Savoie and Piedmont—after he became a turncoat in November 1703, joining the revived Grand Alliance of Britain, the Dutch Republic, Portugal, and the Holy Roman Empire.

Already in 1702, though, the combined burden of maintaining forces abroad in several places had been proving problematic.[11] By this time, the French government was spending in the region of 80 million *livres* on the war effort, and this was before the British, the Dutch, or the Portuguese had entered the conflict. The situation would only get worse, until the combined effects of massive setbacks shrank France's war efforts after the summer of 1708. While one might imagine the turn to offensive warfare in the Po valley region would ease some of the pressure there, in fact the enormous logistical cost of offensives for the war in Italy between 1703 and 1706 contributed more than anything to bringing France to its knees in the final decade of Louis XIV's reign. Elsewhere, too, the commitments were only getting heavier. In both the 1703 and 1704 campaigns French armies were operating deep in southern Germany in alliance with Bavaria and against the Imperial forces, and the decision to increase support there only intensified the resource transfer problem in 1704, not least because much of south-west Germany was under enemy control and the route to the Danube valley was all but blocked. From 1704 France was also heavily committed to military operations in Iberia after the outbreak of war between Philip V and Portugal. By the time the pro-Habsburg Catalan uprising began in mid-1705 the Spanish government was unable to meet its

[9] Esnault, I, 72, 75: Memorandum by Bouchu, 25 December 1701.
[10] Esnault, I, 125–30: 'Mémoire...' [by Chamlay], February 1702.
[11] SHD A[1]1594, no. 104: Chamillart to Bouchu, 23 February 1702.

commitments for food and artillery supply to the French troops in Iberia.[12] And the failed effort to recapture Barcelona further depleted French energies in the spring of 1706, the military *annus horribilis* for Louis XIV. In 1707 expenditure on French forces in Spain amounted to over 12 million *livres*, a vast increase since 1705, though it had become even harder and costlier to move funds there than earlier.[13]

THE BURDENS OF DEFEATS

The costs of strategic overextension were compounded by the price of failure. From the summer of 1704 Versailles had to contend with a series of major defeats that gradually pushed the Bourbon forces back into the French and Spanish heartlands. These were no longer the minor setbacks that (along with successes) had characterized the years 1688–1703. First, on 13 August 1704, the Franco-Bavarian army was shattered at Blenheim, making it very unlikely that the Holy Roman Empire would now be forced into abandoning the Habsburgs, as had been Louis' plan. Just over a year later, in October 1705, the Allied capture of Barcelona pushed much of the eastern third of Spain into the arms of the Habsburg claimant to the throne, Archduke Charles, opening a major new front in the war. At this point the situation was not yet disastrous, but in 1706 it became so. The duke of Marlborough's defeat of the maréchal de Villeroi at Ramillies in Brabant on 2 May was followed by Bourbon military withdrawal from most of the Spanish Netherlands, even though the Allies proved to be in no way secure in their conquest of these lands: though they failed in the end, the French nearly clawed back much of the territory in 1708. In Italy, however, the events of 1706 were truly catastrophic, not least because so much had been invested, financially and politically, in the campaigns there since 1703. With a *dénouement* in the contest between Louis XIV and Savoy in the offing as the Bourbons closed in on Duke Victor Amadeus' capital Turin, Versailles increased funds for the army of Italy during 1705 from an initial allocation of 21 million *livres* to 23.45 million, up from a 'mere' 12 million in 1702. With a further increase in funds in 1706 for the Turin siege, to support two armies totalling 80,000 men, this was an unsustainable magnitude of expenditure.[14] It was in fact a logistical roll of the dice by a government gambling that the employment of so many resources would deliver a final knockout blow to Victor Amadeus, close down northern Italy as a theatre of war, produce solid revenues from Piedmont, and henceforth reduce the strategic—and thus financial—pressure on France. Resources could then be reallocated elsewhere. The effort was to no avail: the French army was routed outside Turin on 7 September, huge amounts of supplies and equipment were lost, the commanders evacuated the army over the Alps, and

[12] Henry Kamen, *The War of Succession in Spain 1700–15* (London, 1969), 75–6.

[13] AN G[7]1093: Amelot to Desmaretz, 12 March 1708; G[7]1094–5: 'Memoire au sujet des lettres de change tirées sur Lyon par le S[r]. Tiffaine...', [December 1710?].

[14] SHD A[1]1594, no. 40: Chamillart to Bouchu, 17 January 1702; AN G[7]1778, no. 83: note by Mongelas, 6 March 1706; Esnault, II, 143: La Feuillade to Chamillart, 24 October 1706.

the remaining forces in Lombardy, though facing only weak enemy forces, could not be relieved or make any headway against the Allies. They too were withdrawn in 1707. The following year, the final Bourbon effort to regain lost ground in the Netherlands came to grief at Oudenarde on 11 July 1708. Not only were the Bourbons reduced to a strip of frontier territory in the Spanish Netherlands, which would shrink further over the coming years, but by the end of 1708 the Allies had captured Lille, capital of French Flanders, the hub of the northern French forces, one of Europe's most formidable fortresses, and a symbol of Louis XIV's expansionism since he had annexed it in 1667.

The logic of Bourbon overextension should suggest that these withdrawals, first from the Danube basin, then from much of the Low Countries and from northern Italy entirely, would cut the costs of warfare for France, and in some respects they did. But the effect was not necessarily immediate. The return home of the debris of the French army of Bavaria in October 1704 meant that expenditure on field forces and the need for foreign exchange in this theatre were reduced,[15] but the defeat at Blenheim had also led to the loss of a great deal of the money and paper devices travelling with the army, worth at least 200,000 *livres*, and a number of completely devastated regiments had to be rebuilt as if starting from scratch. Similarly, the defeat at Ramillies in 1706 led to huge expenditure on rebuilding yet more regiments, and replacing additional lost financial instruments, this time worth 2.3 million *livres*. The lost instruments did not amount to a great deal of 'real' money but they disrupted a lot of the supply process and increased its costs. Two years later the defeat at Oudenarde and the failure to retain Lille cost the government enormous sums in borrowing since the army of Flanders had to live hand to mouth.[16] Meanwhile, the defeat at Turin at the end of the summer of 1706 had not only led to enormous losses in men and *matériel* but also caused an urgent and massive demand for money, while the prospect of the shattered and starving French army of Piedmont moving back across the Alps into the Dauphiné forced local administrators into considerable borrowing using their own personal credit as part of the guarantee. As one *commissaire* put it when Milan was being evacuated the following spring, 'the burden is greater still for leaving [Italy] than for staying'.[17]

After defeats and withdrawals the French left behind many men as prisoners in Allied hands for years to come, and the conventions of the time seem to have insisted that they should be maintained by their own sovereign through remittances. The French also trailed debts that, owing to the multilateral and international nature of state credit by this time, had to be honoured, with repayments making claims on the military budget for subsequent years.[18] As if this were not bad enough, heavy defeats increased the costs of war by causing crises in the money

[15] AN $G^7$1777, nos 314–18.

[16] CCG, II, 474: *mémoire* by Chamillart, 16 October 1706; AN $G^7$1778, no. 295: 'Estat…' of gratifications, n.d. [1706]; $G^7$1782, no. 24: 'Estat', [March 1708].

[17] CCG, II, 355: Trudaine to Chamillart, 2 October 1706; AN $G^7$1779, no. 94: Picon d'Andrezel to Chamillart, 18 March 1707 (quotation).

[18] AN $G^7$1120: 'Compte des fournitures faites pendant les huit premiers mois de l'exercice de M. Demontargis 1707…', [September 1707].

markets, not least because of worries over what might happen next and a likely increase in demand for credit to rebuild the armies. France was already suffering from signs of credit overstretch before Blenheim, but news of the defeat there caused jitters that built up into a state of near panic, the direct effects of which lasted over nine months. Chamillart thought that the 1706 defeats at Ramillies and Turin had wrecked his ability to control and maintain confidence in Mint bills that the government (as we shall see) was using to supplement the coinage supply. The defeat at Malplaquet on 11 September 1709 (and it *was* seen as a defeat by the markets), the subsequent loss of Tournai, and then the loss the following year of Mons in Spanish Hainaut also made it increasingly hard to finance the war effort, in part because the Allies were now lodged in the northern French provinces, depriving Louis of some revenues and even imposing contributions beyond their own lines.[19]

Defeats, then, unsurprisingly cost more than victories or military stability, and the additional burdens this imposed further sapped the strength and vitality of the French logistical machine. An end to the war was essential, but it proved very hard to achieve on tolerable terms. Already by September 1707 a desperate Chamillart was advising the king to renounce claims to some parts of the Spanish monarchy in order to obtain peace with the Allies and avoid complete financial breakdown, with the knock-on threat of domestic disorder. In 1709 Louis did cease to support French troops in Spain, withdrawing some and placing the others under Spanish logistical support. But the war dragged on because Allied demands were too strong for Louis to swallow. The Allied invasion of northern France was only stopped after the British cessation of offensive operations: most immediately, this allowed the maréchal de Villars to defeat the Imperial commander Prince Eugène and the Austro-Dutch army at Denain very shortly afterwards in July 1712, before he went on to recapture several key frontier fortresses by the autumn. Then, after Britain persuaded the Portuguese and Savoy to join them in making peace with the Bourbon powers, the Dutch too came to an agreement with Louis XIV.[20] At the start of winter in late 1712 offensive operations in northern France therefore came to an end, much to Austrian disgust, just as Louis was on the verge of full military defeat. Even after the 'miracle' of Denain, further campaigning in this region in 1713 would have finally exhausted France's logistical capacity. By the end of 1713, even after peace with the Dutch, British, Savoy, and Portugal had reduced the scale of the war dramatically, France was utterly drained. The navy minister Pontchartrain regretfully informed Philip V's government that the French navy could not assist with support for the recapture of Barcelona from the rebels, explaining that 'The King would gladly have taken on this burden if the German war were not absorbing all the finances.'[21] This 'German war' was now confined to the upper Rhineland. France's capability had been reduced to that of a one-theatre power, like Portugal.

[19] CCG, II, 476: 'Mémoire' by Chamillart, 17 September 1707; Malet, *Comptes*, 119.
[20] Quincy, *Histoire militaire* , VII, 161–3.
[21] Chamillart to king, 17 September 1707, cited in Vuitry, 20; AN G[7]1094–5: Jérôme de Pontchartrain to Orry, 5 December 1713.

THE GENERAL CAUSES OF HIGH COSTS IN THE WAR OF THE SPANISH SUCCESSION

Between the peak spending year in the Nine Years War (1692) and those of the War of the Spanish Succession (1705–7) there was at least a 66 per cent increase in military expenditure, if one takes the figures provided by the eighteenth-century financial official Forbonnais and compares them with other scattered data. Army pay in itself cannot be said to have been responsible for increasing state expenditure: the army was, in fact, for most of the time smaller during the War of the Spanish Succession than it had been in the Nine Years War, and there was also a stagnation in pay and allowances for officers and men from the mid-1680s. In addition, there was relatively little expenditure on the fortification infrastructure after 1700; indeed, there was a considerable decline from previous levels.[22] So what was driving up costs? Though it is impossible to provide exact figures for the additional costs that were imposed on France after 1700 by the geostrategic circumstances and the defeats, in comparison with the less volatile and extensive Nine Years War, there is little room for doubt that these influences weighed very heavily on the French fisc. The geostrategic situation in particular seems to have been the single most important factor in draining the country's resources, compelling not only the purchase of foreign exchange, but also the use of suspect, costly expedients that were ill-managed and accordingly put up the price of credit. Much of the rest of this book will attempt to explain how this occurred and what damage was done, but some brief consideration of a few other possible factors driving up costs is needed at this stage.

Speaking generally, because revenue sources were failing and 'war was being made on credit'—weak, badly organized credit—Forbonnais estimated that the War of the Spanish Succession cost at least one-third more than it would have done if sufficient tax revenues had been available.[23] That they were not available owes something to the stagnant state of the economy at this time. But was 'stagflation' (stagnation and inflation) also at work? The picture is not a simple one. Despite some serious inflation in the price of a few commodities such as candles from the mid-1690s, the overall rise in expenditure cannot be blamed on any underlying inflation in the wider economy (especially for foodstuffs): this was small before the problems of 1709–10 and subsequent difficult harvests pushed up food and commodity prices. A big hike in grain prices did take place in 1709–10, which increased the cost of bread supply for the armies to a record 45 million *livres*, but there had already been considerable inflation in army supply over the previous decade, and this was because the macroeconomic decisions taken by the government were by no means always helpful for maintaining downward pressure on the logistical costs of the army. Despite a number of price downswings because of some of the coinage manipulations, coinage enhancements did provoke some brief, acute inflation. Yet between 1692 and 1705/1707—the peak expenditure years, remember—the

[22] See the various tables in Forbonnais, II.
[23] Forbonnais, II, 165.

coinage was inflated in value by only one-fifth, while military expenditure increased by a minimum of two-thirds. Indirectly, however, the manipulations of the currency—in the shape of coinage reratings and Mint bill emissions—had a greater knock-on effect on the costs of the war effort, as later chapters will argue. The introduction of Mint bills had something of an impact on wholesale prices, especially in Paris in 1705–8, and while the great inflation of financial securities in the final decade of the reign affected mainly the financial and wholesale commercial circles, it also influenced the prices paid by the government and its agents to fuel the war effort.[24]

It was not that the French government was pursuing uniformly damaging policies in a wholly blinkered and ignorant fashion. In an era when the huge and resource-rich France was now up against other states that were thinking much more consciously about their fiscal-military systems than they had in the past, 'The issue of the struggle depended in large part on the capacity of each of the adversaries to exploit as fully as possible their gold and silver potential and the volume of the stock each disposed of', in the words of Daniel Dessert.[25] War now also required considerable attention to the place of finance in grand strategy and the use of finance as a tool of psychological warfare. French ministers were aware of this and sometimes felt they had no choice but to act on a short-term basis. In September 1707 Chamillart began a further round of desperate expedients to raise funds in order to persuade the Grand Alliance that France would be capable of a major effort in the 1708 campaign, while advising the king to fully support the intended Scottish uprising in the hope that this would cause a drying-up of the London money markets to match that in Paris, and therefore make it impossible for Britain to continue the war. The financial health of France's enemies was clearly also of interest in France, and growing British financial strength in particular could have deflating effects on expectations in the money markets in France.[26] The introduction of the *dixième* tax in 1710 (see Chapter 3) has always been considered 'one of the principal motives that determined [France's enemies] to make peace', and indeed the Holland Grand Pensionary and *primum mobile* of Dutch commitment to the war, Anthonie Heinsius, linked its introduction to other French efforts to prepare bread supplies for the 1711 campaign.[27] It was certainly a positive move by the then Finance Minister Desmaretz, and the French government did introduce some expedients that were healthy. Even some of those which were not are explicable, if deeply regrettable, in the circumstances.

Nevertheless, instead of revenues shaping the war effort, the demands of war in France before 1709 were driving expenditure and monetary policy in an extreme

[24] Marcel Lachiver, *Les années de misère: La famine au temps du Grand Roi* (Paris, 1991), 424–5; Lüthy, I, 111; Saint-Germain, *Financiers*, 88; Forbonnais, II, 194, 214, 216, 273.

[25] DAPS, 158 (my translation).

[26] Esnault, II, 157–8, 160–1: 'Mémoire', 22 September 1707; AN G[7]1784, no. 282: de La Garde to Desmaretz, 27 March 1709.

[27] Malet, *Comptes*, 147. Malet exaggerated: it may have kept some French forces in the field and helped influence the British government, but it is not clear whether the *dixième* pushed any other governments towards the peace table.

fashion. This approach produced violent lurches from one policy to another and ever more arbitrary, dangerous decisions, especially with regard to credit instruments, appropriations methods, and the coinage. The cumulative effects of this appear to have produced a marked increase in the cost of military supplies in the War of the Spanish Succession, and a brief outline of this will be useful at this point. With every crisis and at every announcement of a dubious expedient, those with the wherewithal to organize supplies for the crown became nervous about eventual repayment. It became safer for people to hold on to their goods and produce, thereby ensuring prices rose in the short term. More importantly, at the level of logistical contracting, suppliers also appear to have set high prices so that their returns could be insulated from weak government repayment methods. Higher prices for military supplies—whether delivered on a small scale to regiments for basic equipment, or on a huge scale as food or even as foreign pay for whole armies—were effectively an insurance premium built into their contracts by those selling to the crown on tick. Especially from 1705, the contractors were protecting themselves against the failure or depreciation of the instruments with which the government and its agents were paying them for their deliveries. Suppliers, because they were dealing with a host of small traders and middlemen, needed to be reimbursed in cash. If they were paid by the state in paper they would trade it in the market, thus causing general depreciation of such instruments, with knock-on costs for the monarchy in other expenditure; they would then seek further reimbursement for their loss from the government. It is no accident that the peak years for military expenditure, 1705–7, coincided with the widest geographical overextension of the army and the flooding of the financial markets with severely depreciated credit instruments on an unprecedented scale. Looking back, with more evidence at his disposal than we now have, Forbonnais reckoned that in the War of the Spanish Succession 'the state [...] deprived of money had paid for supplies half as much again as they would have cost in a time of order'.[28] Explaining some of these costs in terms of insurance is not to say that the government's financial, *matériel*, and food suppliers were innocents merely trying to make an honest living and protect themselves from the feckless financial incontinence of an imprudent dynastic state. They were very much part of that state, and they were policed in a weak fashion. Some of them, as we shall see, were ruthlessly focused on their own enrichment and advancement. They needed very close management. How far the king had a ministerial team capable of formulating sound policy, and of managing the logistical side of the war effort and controlling the financiers involved in it, now needs to be considered.

[28] Forbonnais, II, 152–3, 173–4, 190, 222 (quotation), 273.

2

The King, His Ministers, and the Direction of Financial Policy

Louis XIV's government set the legal and accounting framework and the spending parameters for the state. Its use, misuse, or even abuse of its sovereign powers in matters of money and revenue had a disproportionate determining effect on the logistics of the war effort, even though the machinery of government at the apex of the system consisted of only a few dozen people. Certainly the king and his ministers were constrained by practical questions of politics and logistics to operate in certain ways, but they did have room for manoeuvre and they also had a degree of choice in whom they appointed to carry out many of the detailed functions of the ministries under them. How the king and his ministers saw and performed their roles, and dealt with their inferiors in the business of fuelling the war effort, was therefore of considerable importance. The structures of power and the quality of the second-rank staff who supported the king and ministers need careful consideration, but first Louis XIV himself and those he appointed to the key posts of *contrôleur général des finances* (Finance Minister) and Secretary of State for War need to come under the spotlight: given the circumstances and the constraints of the time, how efficacious were the decisions they took, how well did they understand the financial world with which they were dealing, and how alert were they to issues of conflict of interest, moral hazard, and rent-seeking?

THE HARDEST PART ABOUT BEING KING?

By the War of the Spanish Succession it had become clear, especially through the painful experience of the 1690s, that the orderly conduct of war required considerable attention to state finances on the part of the king himself. When Louis XIV referred to the 'dur métier du roi'—the hard profession of being king—he was probably referring to the iron self-control, the sense of permanent performance, and the huge range of duties required of him. But the kinds of skill in financial management that lay behind the emerging fiscal-military states of the later seventeenth and early eighteenth centuries were exceptionally hard for any ruler to master, let alone one who had been brought up in a more cavalier era and who felt more of an affinity with the role of the 'roi de guerre', the warrior king. Nevertheless, Louis was a highly conscientious ruler, and throughout his personal rule (1661–1715) he ensured that the monarchy at least possessed and maintained a reasonably effective and organized system of central administration under his watchful eye, stray though his gaze did for periods of time.

In matters of finance he was surprisingly industrious. The *règlement* of 15 September 1661, issued in the aftermath of the arrest of the last *Surintendant des finances*, Nicolas Fouquet, gave the king direct oversight of both accounted and secret expenses, and his signature would be placed on all financial ordinances. It created a Conseil Royal des finances under the nominal direction of the Chancellor of France, the head of the judiciary and most senior royal official; and, with some adjustments over the years for changes in personnel and positions, this council generally handed responsibility for advising the king on the distribution of all funds to the *contrôleur général* of finance, who would then take the king's orders for appropriations, and who oversaw the central revenue clearing-house and treasury, the Trésor royal. The carrying out of expenditure was in the hands of the spending ministers, most notably the Secretaries of State for War, the Navy, and Foreign Affairs (in descending order of budgetary weight), as well as the *contrôleur général* himself for a small proportion of the total.[1] From 1661 Louis gave Jean-Baptiste Colbert the power to order most financial affairs without the participation of other members of the council, and allowed the senior ministers and their immediate underlings to approve details of spending while he kept track of the general flow of funds. For Louis XIV finances and the economy were essentially matters of 'intendance', by which is meant, in essence, aristocratic estate management. There was far less emphasis upon economic planning and even less concern with the relationship between macro- and microeconomic issues, as the government dealt for the most part simply with what had happened to crown revenues and expenditure, and what was needed.[2]

This approach (which, though becoming rather old-fashioned by 1700, nevertheless persisted among European monarchs ruling actively well into the nineteenth century) was complemented by an equally conservative (and suspicious) approach to credit and to money markets. When combined with the intrinsically arbitrary nature of French absolute monarchy, this would cause chronic financial weakness right down to the end of the *ancien régime*. Louis XIV's high-handed view of his authority made him a slow learner with regard to the power of markets. It has been suggested, with good reason, that his frustration with Colbert, who does appear to have realized the power of the emerging international marketplace, contributed to his turning towards a succession of *contrôleurs généraux* after 1683 who would not act as serious brakes upon his expenditure-driven priorities. This sounds like the orthodox historical idea of monarchs' lofty indifference and insouciance towards their finances, but though Louis was more interested in war, diplomacy, and display, he by no means ignored finance, especially when the situation was deteriorating and he had to consider the resources for his war efforts. By the

[1] Michel Antoine, *Le coeur de l'État: Surintendance, contrôle général et intendances des finances 1552–1791* (Paris, 2003), 296–7, 303, 315, 339, 379–80.

[2] Pierre Clément, *Histoire de Colbert et de son administration* (2nd edn, 2 vols, Paris, 1874), I, 153; McCollim, 111; Thierry Sarmant and Mathieu Stoll, *Régner et gouverner: Louis XIV et ses ministres* (Paris, 2010), 219.

last decade of his reign Louis had come to appreciate the extent to which there was an international competition for resources and this was at heart the greatest issue at stake in the War of the Spanish Succession. As he remarked to his ambassador in Madrid, 'The principal object of the present war is that of the commerce of the Indies and the riches they produce.'[3] The War of the Spanish Succession was utterly different from the Dutch War and the Nine Years War in that these conflicts had been focused upon power on the European continent, and had been concerned only indirectly with trade or, even less so, with overseas colonies. Even in the minds of Louis XIV and Queen Anne, this new war was really much more about trade and overseas empire, and it was therefore like only one other previous great European conflict, the Hispano-Dutch war of 1621–48, even though the fighting beyond Europe was on a smaller scale (ironically) than in the 1690s. This made it all the more essential that whoever took the helm of the finances under the king should be well-informed, fully in command of the complexities, and extremely sensitive to opinion, given that the scale of the war demanded so much credit. Unfortunately the government's knowledge of the complex financial situation, and the competence of some of those at the highest echelons of government who were running the revenue-raising, borrowing, and spending mechanisms, left a good deal to be desired.

THE *CONTRÔLEUR GÉNÉRAL DES FINANCES* AND THE CONTROL OF REVENUE

It is not even certain that the position of *contrôleur général* was well suited to the needs of the early eighteenth century. As Nicolas Desmaretz, the final holder of the post under Louis XIV, told the Regent in 1716, the *contrôleur général* was neither a person authorized to make expenditure of his own free will nor someone who had to render personal accounts for the sums he processed, but was really an organizer and executor for the king. His Majesty was his own *Surintendant des finances* in succession to Nicolas Fouquet and others like Sully before him. The contrôle général was not an office but a commission, though technically endowed with a 'pouvoir', or authority, to oversee all the kingdom's financial affairs. This meant managing the Trésor royal; the Trésor des parties casuelles which handled revenue from venal offices; all the king's fiscal receivers and farmed revenues; the Church finances; the navy finances, the army treasuries, and the larger suppliers for the armed forces; the king's properties; public borrowing; the *pays d'états* (those outlying provinces that still enjoyed their own deliberative assemblies); the mints; the judiciary; the transport infrastructure; and commerce in general. The *contrôleur général* exercised a form of 'contrôle', or inspection, over accounts.[4] Although

[3] Seligmann, 9–12; *Correspondance de Louis XIV avec Michel Amelot, son ambassadeur à Madrid*, ed. baron de Girardot (Paris, 1864), II, 121: Louis to Amelot, 18 February 1709 (quotation).

[4] Sarmant and Stoll, *Régner et gouverner*, 216; Pénicaut, 86–7; McCollim, 71–2; CCG, III, 673: 'Compte rendu de M. Desmaretz au Régent', [1716]; Dangeau, VII, 155–6.

he did have licence to look into other ministries' affairs, in practice he tended to steer clear of the details. He did settle on the revenue sources to be employed with regard to the needs of the army and navy, but unless he also held the ministries for these bodies he did not order payments relating to either of them, and this was one of the great weaknesses of French government by this time. France had no single minister responsible for the overall direction of all revenues and expenditure. The *contrôleur général*'s authority did not even approximate to Godolphin's contemporary control as Lord Treasurer in England. Desmaretz explained that:

> All the expenses ordered by the King are settled without being agreed with the *contrôleur général*: those of war, the navy and pensions between the King and Messieurs the secretaries of state, each for their own department.

For Desmaretz's clerk and chronicler of the country's finances, Jean-Roland Malet, the absence of a coordinating minister with supremacy in government allowed for a large increase in spending under Louis XIV.[5]

Be that as it may, the set-up by 1670 was a real improvement on what had gone before. Jean-Baptiste Colbert, despite the views of his more recent denigrators, was certainly a reformer and administrator of deep insight and massive stamina, and like his counterpart in the War Ministry, the marquis de Louvois, he had a real eye for the sort of mind-numbing details that make a system work well or badly. In these respects he compares favourably with his successors, even the knowledgeable (but reckless) Louis de Pontchartrain (1689–99). One of the reasons the financial system worked better under Colbert's direction than previously was his careful management of a significant group of major financiers whom he carefully deployed and who were very much beholden to him, but his successes were not just those of personnel management (as Dessert would have us believe).[6] Colbert cut right back on the profits of financial contractors, and restructured the administration of the *généralités* (the financial provinces), the royal domain revenues, and the government annuity bonds in such a way as to make royal finances far more sustainable over the long term. The big question is whether Colbert's reforms were far-reaching enough to cope with the financial problems of the future, even over the next generation. All the subsequent evidence is that they were not, though it would be unreasonable to expect Colbert to have anticipated the huge costs of the Spanish Succession war.

His immediate successor, Claude Le Peletier, did little more to protect the monarchy from the effects of the demands it would make on its financial system. He cracked down on a few systemic abuses that were occurring, but this mainly took the form of a purge of Colbert's creatures. He increased the burden of direct taxation, but more dubiously began afresh the manipulation of venal offices for the purpose of extracting more revenues from their incumbents. He was more relaxed about the idea of long-term state debt than Colbert, who had been allergic to an extension of government bonds—the *rentes* backed by revenues channelled to the

[5] CCG, III, 682: 'Compte rendu de M. Desmaretz au Régent', [1716]; Malet, *Comptes*, 55–6.

[6] Jean Meyer, *Colbert* (Paris, 1981), esp. 191–2. For the hostile view, see Daniel Dessert and J.-L. Journet, 'Le lobby Colbert: Un royaume ou une affaire de famille?', *Annales ESC* 30 (1975), 1303–36 Daniel Dessert, *Le royaume de Monsieur Colbert 1661–1683* (Paris, 2007), 222.

Paris Hôtel de ville—and in this respect Le Peletier was working more in the spirit of the times, but his attempts to absorb short-term debt with reimbursements or conversions into *rentes* were botched.[7] It is perhaps not surprising he took an early opportunity in the Nine Years War to pass his post on to Louis de Pontchartrain. Pontchartrain had a serious, detailed knowledge of royal finances, and like Colbert was meticulous in checking accounts. Less reputably, he was also an investor of colossal proportions in state financial activity, largely through financiers he used as proxies, and as such he can be compared closely with Claude de Bullion, *Surintendant des finances* under Cardinal Richelieu. Pontchartrain's tenure coincided with an increase in royal expenditure on the army and navy as the Nine Years War moved into a higher gear, with the war effort reaching a peak for the entire *ancien régime* in terms of troops under arms and ships in commission during 1692–93. Under him there was no endemic financial disorder of the kind that would afflict France in the following decade, but there was a punctuated series of acute crises, and he had to deal with the catastrophic economic and social situation brought on by climatic disaster and harvest failure in 1692–94. As revenues stalled and then began to fall he took the innovative step in 1695 of imposing a graduated poll tax, the *capitation*, on all French subjects from the Dauphin downwards, an expedient that in fact opened the path to future direct taxation of the privileged elites. Chamillart sought to give the impression that Pontchartrain had left finances in a very bad state, which of course helped excuse his own unpopular policies after 1699, but there is no doubt that the elevated royal expenditure (for which the king must take much of the blame), the emission of millions of *rentes*, the creation of countless more privileged offices, and the anticipation of revenues all weakened the country's revenue base. At the end of the Nine Years War in 1697 France needed a decade or more in which to recover, to return to the tolerable situation of the mid-1680s. Unfortunately, in his remaining two years in office Pontchartrain did little to set France back on the road to financial health.[8]

The development of the position of *contrôleur général* under Louis XIV before 1700 was paralleled by the development of the spending ministries, and what is little appreciated—especially by financial historians—is the extent to which the Ministry of War and the Ministry of the Marine (navy) ordered a great deal of their own financial affairs. Leaving aside the navy, the War Ministry and its administrative procedures had undergone a remarkable transformation in the decades after 1661, as three generations of the Le Tellier family—Michel Le Tellier, the marquis de Louvois, and the marquis de Barbezieux—grew in political power and social status with the active support of the king. They adapted regulations to make the funding of regiments more viable, particularly in the period to 1688; they worked year in, year out with the *contrôleur général* on the adjudication of major supply contracts, and with the bread contractors—known as *munitionnaires*—on the

[7] Pierre Clément, *Le Gouvernement de Louis XIV ou la Cour, l'Administration, les Finances et le Commerce de 1683 à 1689* (Paris, 1848), 78–80.

[8] There is no focused study of Pontchartrain as *contrôleur général*, but see *Dictionnaire des surintendants*, 98–101.

infrastructure of their businesses; and they refined the War Ministry's own administration. Even if many problems remained, there was a marked improvement on the miserable military administration of the era of Richelieu and Mazarin.[9] What matters more here is that they exercised control over most of the activity of the Extraordinaire des Guerres, the greatest network of military paymasters in Europe who were part of a semi-autonomous treasury working as a government agency.[10] The Le Telliers brought the various civilian contractors for the army under far tighter control than previously and subjected them to really quite ruthless discipline and treatment. They ran a regime that allowed these men some profits but kept them on a tight rein and dangled the prospect of ruin before them through arbitrary, if well-informed, decisions.[11] After January 1701 it was to be a somewhat different story, when the positions of *contrôleur général* and Secretary of State for War would be combined in a single pair of hands. For the following seven years the financial interest—tied so closely to logistical contracting for the army—was lucky to have a minister in post who was more naïve than Pontchartrain and less hostile than the Le Telliers.

AN ATLAS WITH FEET OF CLAY: MICHEL CHAMILLART, 1699–1708

Pontchartrain was succeeded as *contrôleur général* on 5 September 1699 by Michel Chamillart. Chamillart had briefly been provincial *intendant* of the *généralité* of Rouen before he was recalled to Paris in 1690 by Pontchartrain to be one of the *intendants des finances*, the principal under-ministers below the *contrôleur général*. He was diligent but did not appear to show a penetrating wisdom or a grasp of financial affairs. His elevation as a replacement for Pontchartrain owed much to the favour of the king's morganatic wife, Madame de Maintenon, who had put him in charge of her own affairs and given him the superintendency of the college of Saint-Cyr she had established for the daughters of distressed noble folk. By 1699 the king had reportedly become alarmed by Pontchartrain's financial policies, and took the opportunity of a vacancy in the post of Chancellor of France to kick him upstairs. But Louis may have chosen Chamillart to succeed Pontchartrain because he thought he could thereby exercise more personal oversight once again. Chamillart's first year in office was fairly successful, bringing an improvement in revenues and seeing the tighter control of expenditure, even if confidence among the financiers was shaky. On 23 November 1700 he was elevated to the status of *ministre d'état* with a seat on the inner advisory council, the Conseil d'En haut.[12] It was a sweet moment, but things would very soon afterwards turn sour.

[9] For a full treatment, see Rowlands, 27–108. On the Richelieu era, see David Parrott, *Richelieu's Army: War, Government and Society in France, 1624–1642* (Cambridge, 2001), 251, 366–462.

[10] See Chapter 7.

[11] Ars. Ms. 4494, fos 3v–4v, 6v: 'Discours de Mr. Paris de la Montagne', n.d.

[12] Antoine, *Le coeur de l'État*, 355; *Dictionnaire des surintendants*, 102; Pénicaut, 69–70, 84–5, 95; Seligmann, 39–41.

The essence of Chamillart's own troubles over the following years was his acquisition of a second major post, indeed the other biggest job in government, that of Secretary of State for War, on 8 January 1701. For all but seven years of Louis XIV's 'personal rule' the two positions were kept separate, though this had not been the case with the navy: during 1661–83 (under Colbert) and 1690–99 (under Pontchartrain) responsibility for the navy was held simultaneously with the post of *contrôleur général*, and while this combination had earlier been manageable it was less so by the mid-1690s.[13] Why Louis took the fateful step to hand the two largest workloads to Chamillart is not altogether clear, but it can be accepted that he wanted a harmonious war effort, and by January 1701 some sort of war was more likely than not.[14] The accumulation of the two positions may have made superficial sense to the ageing king in the absence of a chief minister who could provide overall strategic and policy coordination. Nevertheless, if the intention was to keep matters under control by better coordination of income and spending, using Chamillart as a chief civil servant while the king acted as executive decision-maker, then the effect was quite the opposite.[15] Claude Le Peletier claimed to have warned the king that the results would prove unhappy.[16] With both posts united in one man tensions between the revenue and the needs of expenditure—between the interests of War and of Finance—were negotiated less by the king and rather more by Chamillart and his underlings. And Chamillart was not someone with any real experience of running military affairs, except on a minor provincial level. Indeed, he was quite humble about his lack of strategic vision,[17] which, in the light of the expansion of the war in 1701–3, makes Louis' decision to put him into the War Ministry even more flawed. The effects on both the financial and the military worlds were far from positive. As will be seen, the financial machinery of the War Ministry and the army as a whole became part of the revenue-raising, expedient-generating, fiscal machine that soon began to devour itself and impede the effectiveness of the army. As to the management of finances, Louis' decision to double up Chamillart's responsibilities suggests he did not fully appreciate how much the post of *contrôleur général* now needed filling by someone who had to concentrate upon fostering credit and managing financiers with tact, diplomacy, close scrutiny, and real behind-the-scenes effort. Even had he had the aptitude, Chamillart simply would not have had enough time to do this, and his normal deputies would not have had full credibility and therefore the authority to stand in his stead.

Very early on it became abundantly clear that Chamillart was monstrously overburdened, and he let it be known to those closest to him just how unhappy he was about his responsibilities. Even after two *directeurs généraux* of finance were created to assist him as *contrôleur général* in June 1701 he was still absurdly overcommitted,

13 Legohérel, 212. Colbert became secretary of state formally in 1669.

14 Pénicaut, 97.

15 Chamillart had no preponderance in government, and was not superior to either the Secretary of State for Foreign Affairs, Jean-Baptiste Colbert de Torcy, or the Navy and Royal Household secretary, Jérôme de Pontchartrain.

16 Louis André, ed., *Deux mémoires historiques* (Paris, 1906), 166.

17 Pénicaut, 100–7, 208–10.

and in the summer of 1704 asked the king in all seriousness to relieve him of this position altogether.[18] He was wise to do so, for it is possible to see how the overburdening of Chamillart led both ministries to deteriorate from the administrative standards set under previous incumbents. To give just a few instances, there was chaotic management (rather than managed flexibility) in matters of passports and trade with the enemy; Chamillart struggled to keep on top of even the most important matters, such as providing resources for his top bankers to remit abroad; and the Finance Ministry regularly made a mess of financial appropriations.[19] After he left the contrôle général in February 1708 he turned to sorting out the disorder inside the War Ministry, confessing he was doing so 'in order to avoid the difficulty and confusion into which the affairs of royal finance had led me to fall'.[20]

The details of Chamillart's financial policies will emerge over the coming chapters, but other than being characterized by increasing desperation for money, there was little coherence to them. His tenure was, in fact, little short of abysmal compared with the other *contrôleurs généraux* of the reign, or to Jean Orry, who was busy reordering the Spanish finances at the same time.[21] His successor Desmaretz may have 'weeded' the files to accentuate the negatives in his tenure, and one has to remember that Chamillart was trying to cope with a huge workload. But this notwithstanding, it is clear that he simply did not have the aptitude for the job and had been overpromoted. He really only understood the mechanisms of finance, and not the psychology of the collectivity of lenders, nor how the economy, especially commerce, related to royal revenue. As an *intendant des finances* he had dealt with minor areas of tax business with which he had already been familiar, and though he paid attention to other financial matters they were not in his jurisdiction and he never worked on them in great detail.[22] As *contrôleur général* he turned out to be very short-termist in his thinking, preferring instant revenue-raising to longer-term, slower revenue generation (for example in his approach to encouraging the rebuilding of trade with Spain). Nor did he understand international transactions very easily, admittedly a fiendishly complicated world. He was also prone to grasping the wrong end of the stick, on one occasion confusing the availability of cash in a region with the hypothecation of notional tax resources there.[23]

Just as problematic, he was an emotionally sensitive, sincere, and religiously devout man with little concern for building a wealthy, powerful dynasty during his years in office.[24] His instincts were not only to distrust but positively loathe most (but not all) of those involved in finance. He found it extremely hard to take a

[18] Pénicaut, 90–8, 133–8, 142–3, 231–3; CCG, II, 476: 'Mémoire' by Chamillart, 17 September 1707.

[19] See Chapter 8.

[20] Maz. Ms. 2626, fo. 26r–v: 'Reglement fait par M. Chamillart'.

[21] Anne Dubet, *Jean Orry et la réforme du gouvernement de l'Espagne (1701–1706)* (Clermont-Ferrand, 2009).

[22] Pénicaut, 71.

[23] AN G^{7}1092: Orry to Chamillart, 24 August 1702; Saint-Germain, *Bernard*, 146; SHD A^{1}1699, no. 148: Jérôme de Pontchartrain to Chamillart, 31 January 1703, and Chamillart's marginalia.

[24] Unlike Colbert and the Le Telliers. See Pénicaut, 293, 307, 311, 329, 391–409; Esnault, I, 393: La Feuillade to Chamillart, 15 October 1704.

detached view of them, even though he knew they were vital for the functioning of the state. They were people 'whom I condemn because they love money too much'. Claude Le Peletier felt he had too little empathy or sympathy for 'le public', that is, the financial public, to make working with them a smooth business. As for the money markets, especially in Lyon, he had a total tin-ear for their interests, regularly threatening them rather than steering them as the pressure on the state mounted. He felt strongly that people in the money markets should invest honourably in government and Church annuities and in the tax-gatherers' debt flotations, rather than speculating on the value of currency devices that his own policies were wrecking. His offended Catholic sensibilities were joined to a crudely authoritarian and naïve view that the king's subjects should be willing to sacrifice their own interests for the good of the state. He overestimated royal power and simply could not understand that people in the market would buy and sell precious metal, money, and paper instruments for whatever price they could get, regardless of his orders and strictures. By 1707, despite all the evidence around him, he remained baffled as to why most people had no confidence in Mint bills when he felt they ought to![25]

He was not alone in his frustration and bewilderment as ministers across Europe faced dealing with the markets, which increasingly were taking on a life of their own, on a far greater scale than previously.[26] But Chamillart was an extreme example, and the French government as a whole struggled far harder and with far less success to understand and work with the markets than the governments of countries where sovereignty was shared with consultative bodies. If the British government could be just as inept at maintaining confidence and reassuring the markets during the Nine Years War, by the 1700s they had improved their approach dramatically while the French government only got worse.[27] What is particularly striking about Chamillart is that he simply failed to appreciate the need to honour debts on time if further credit was to be easily obtained and forthcoming.[28] This disastrous approach would contribute not a little to deteriorating financial confidence in the monarchy. Yet Chamillart retained considerable faith in his own judgement, even when almost everyone else was telling him not to pursue a particular policy.

If Chamillart could be arrogant and hostile towards 'la finance' and the markets as a whole, when he did trust someone he was willing to accept almost anything they said. As a man of his word, he expected that those he graced with his favour

25 Depping, III, 319: Chamillart to Harlay, 8 April 1700 (quotation); André, *Deux mémoires*, 163; René Dumas, *La politique financière de Nicolas Desmaretz, Contrôleur Général des Finances (1708–1715)* (Paris, 1927), 46–7; CCG, II, 411: Chamillart to all *intendants*, 11 May 1707; SHD $A^1$1699, no. 322: Bernard to Chamillart, 13 October 1703; BNF Ms. Fr. 10247, fo. 139: Chamillart to Vendôme, 20 May 1707.

26 J. Sperling, 'The International Payments Mechanism in the Seventeenth and Eighteenth Centuries', *Economic History Review* 14 (1962), 449.

27 D. W. Jones, *War and Economy in the Age of William III and Marlborough* (Oxford, 1988), 23–5.

28 For example, CCG, II, 391: Chamillart to Trudaine, 26 March 1707; SHD Ya2: Chamillart to all *intendants*, 26 December 1707.

would automatically be trustworthy too. He was, dare it be said, even a dreamer who, at least in 1694, had believed there were enough 'honnêtes gens'—honourable people—with huge financial reserves behind them to supply the king's credit needs. But as we shall see, he was arguably duped by people. The secretary of the comte de Toulouse, one of the royal bastards, remarked that Chamillart had been far too credulous of bad advice about financial arrangements, with the result that financiers he had trusted had profited excessively.[29] Indeed, though it is believed Chamillart was not really a partisan player or builder of a clientele, he closely surrounded himself with a select group of financiers (see Chapter 10), permitting them an influence over the *contrôleur général* unrivalled by any other clique between 1661 and 1789. Even though Colbert had relied on a few key financiers and Pontchartrain had profited from his financial clients' activities, neither had allowed the fisco-financiers such influence over policy and contracts.

CHAMILLART'S MEN IN THE MINISTRY: THE BUREAUX DES FINANCES, 1701–1708

Chamillart's mishandling of financiers extended to his management of the Finance Ministry and the team of subordinates staffing its various divisions. Unlike the War and Marine ministries, the Finance Ministry was not known by this title at the time, and it was a far looser organization, but it seems easiest to use this label to describe the complex set of offices working for the *contrôleur général.* Essentially cast by Colbert in a mould that would broadly survive to the late *ancien régime*, it was structured in the following manner: under the *contrôleur général* served several *intendants des finances* with semi-autonomous authority and specific responsibilities for aspects of government policy, each supported by a number of *commis*, or administrative-class clerks. In addition, under Colbert had emerged the post of *premier commis des finances*, who was separate from and superior to the *contrôleur général*'s own *premier commis.* He did not work directly with provincial agencies but was in effect the intimate collaborator of the *contrôleur général*, busying himself mainly with the Trésor royal, the Trésor des parties casuelles, the greatest financiers, and the overall flow of revenue and expenditure. Also of key significance for smooth operations was the *commis-garde des registres*, who was vital for keeping an eye on the detailed operations of the Trésor royal. The *contrôleur général*, the *intendants des finances*, and the *premier commis des finances* were collectively known as 'Messieurs des Finances'. The Finance Ministry was subdivided into a number of bureaux generally under an *intendant des finances* aided by his *premier commis*—their organizational principles remain obscure. Pontchartrain had raised the number of *intendants des finances* from two to six and turned them into venal offices. This had provided the second-tier bureaux which they ran with greater formal structure and prestige, but it also threatened to entrench heredity of office in such critical

[29] Esnault, I, 101–2: 'Mémoire' by Chamillart, [1694]; CCG, III, 254: Valincour to Desmaretz, 17 December 1709.

positions. In the post-1689 period, as the contrôle général changed hands, these subordinates tended to survive the ministerial transition, which may have increased their autonomy. By 1690, according to the great expert on French administrative history, Michel Antoine, the Finance Ministry should be conceived as seven separate 'départements', whereas the various spending ministries were in each case a single department subdivided in a less formal manner on the whim of the respective secretary of state. Unlike for the War and Marine ministries, there was no official 'Hôtel des finances' in which the *contrôleur général*'s staff worked, for the clerks remained orientated far more towards each of the 'Messieurs'. To an extent, Pontchartrain's devolution of a lot of authority to several of the *intendants des finances* was a justifiable recognition of the demands now presented by the expanded scope of royal financial activity. But the burden was now so great that the *commis*, too, were becoming more important and powerful.[30]

Also vital for the management of royal revenue and expenditure were the central revenue treasurers, in particular the *Gardes du Trésor royal* who occupied two venal offices that alternated being on duty biennially, and less importantly the *receveur des revenus casuels*, who oversaw revenues deriving mainly from the sale and further manipulation of venal offices. The *gardes* delivered receipts (*quittances*) to those agents and officials who collected revenues, upon full delivery of sums owed; and they issued annually thousands of documents specifying appropriations on the basis of spending *ordonnances* that the *contrôleur général* and secretaries of state had signed. Though the Trésor royal was technically subject to the king rather than the *contrôleur général*, there should be no mistake that in this period it was firmly in the latter's domain, one *garde* going so far as to describe him as 'my patron and my protector'. Le Peletier in the 1680s had improved the oversight of the Trésor royal by tightening up the system of reporting transactions in the registers kept by the *premier commis des finances*, but in the end such a system was only as sound as the men installed in these offices, and at least one *garde* (in 1704–8) had an astonishing array of conflicts of interest, even by the standards of the time (see Chapter 10).[31]

All these men were essential to the task of setting and managing the central state budget. Budgeting was indeed limited by modern standards and was not routinized at this time, but documents anticipating and planning revenue and expenditure did exist in a recognizable form by the late seventeenth century. The growing reliance on longer-term borrowing encouraged more precise calculations, as governments living in an increasingly statistical age and at a time of mounting indebtedness came to see just how disastrous it could be to fail to estimate revenue and expenditure with some kind of accuracy (however rough). 'Prévisions' were worked on in the summer or autumn before the next fiscal year (beginning on 1 January) to create an 'état général des finances', a general estimate. The *contrôleur général* then organized the 'arrangement des finances', earmarking specific revenue sources

[30] Antoine, *Le coeur de l'État*, 321–6, 346–9, 355; Sarmant and Stoll, *Régner et gouverner*, 117–18; Margaret Bonney and Richard Bonney, *Jean-Roland Malet, premier historien des finances de la monarchie française* (Paris, 1993), 13, 89.

[31] Antoine, *Le coeur de l'État*, 312, 322, 337; AN G^{7}1098: Montargis to Desmaretz, 11 March 1710 (quotation).

('fonds') to each area of government; another set of documents would then be drawn up specifying the projected incomings and outgoings of the Trésor royal. Over the course of the year this body, and all others that handled the king's funds, would issue outline (and rather rough) running accounts of how matters were proceeding. At the end of a fiscal year came 'états au vrai' from *comptable* financiers, giving an interim statement of what had actually happened pending full accounting in the years to come. These were verified by staff in a specific office within the Finance Ministry. The question is whether the alterations that were made and the extraordinary budgets that were decided in the course of a year were so regular and large that they make a mockery of the modern idea of a budget. It was hard to keep financial flows for each year discrete because of anticipations of future revenues, late payments by revenue-gatherers, and even the unexpected need to use current revenues to repay earlier loans. There was also a lack of budgetary discipline by the spending ministries under the king's direction in the circumstances of an evolving war effort. Furthermore, thanks to communications difficulties and accountancy weaknesses in the absence of double-entry bookkeeping, it was all but impossible to keep track of state finances in real time.[32]

With such a difficult scenario to manage at the best of times, it was axiomatic that the 'Messieurs des finances' at the very top needed to be men of the highest calibre. Unsurprisingly, though, they were a mixed bunch. Chamillart preferred to surround himself with a small number of very trusted close friends and relatives, and then leave to them many of the dealings with revenue contractors, bankers, and fisco-financiers—except those financiers to whom he was personally very close. He could be somewhat careless about whom he appointed to manage whole areas of his brief. In February 1703 Alexandre Le Rebours, his very close relative, was installed in the prominent post of *premier commis des finances* giving him responsibility for overseeing the Trésor royal, before he was promoted in August 1704 to *intendant des finances*. He then held both jobs simultaneously and remained at the heart of the decision-making process to the end of the reign. This put him in a powerful position to dominate the Finance Ministry and the appropriation of revenue sources to expenditure. The great chronicler Saint-Simon saw him as arrogant and slippery, comparing him to an absurd buffoon in a Molière play, and if the duke's usual embroidery of reality is here once again on display, there is no doubt Le Rebours made repeated and serious errors of judgement in office. In short, he showed manifest signs of incompetence for the capital tasks with which he was charged, lacking political touch and at times even common sense in his dealings with bankers, and earmarking revenue sources in a chaotic manner.[33] He was, at least, loyal to Chamillart, whereas others in the Finance

[32] Antoine, *Le coeur de l'État*, 324; Alain Guéry, 'Les finances de la monarchie française sous l'ancien régime', *Annales ESC* 33 (1978), 217–20; Michel Morineau, 'Budgets de l'état et gestion des finances royales en France au dix-huitième siècle', *Revue historique* 536 (1980), 290–6, 300.

[33] Pénicaut, 34, 51, 60; Saint-Simon, XII, 160–1; XVII, 449; AN $G^7$1097: Tourton to Torcy, 27 June 1708. Le Rebours was definitely the main figure responsible for appropriations: see SHD $A^1$1894 and AN $G^7$1774–88.

Ministry were almost certainly leaking sensitive inside knowledge to, *inter alia*, Swiss bankers no less.[34]

Good, bad, or indifferent, these men were neither sufficiently respected nor prominent enough to give Chamillart the support he needed. To give him this assistance, in June 1701 Louis XIV reluctantly agreed to the creation of two *directeurs généraux des finances*, both such offices selling for 800,000 *livres*. Sitting above the *intendants des finances*, they would take over much of the running of royal finances while Chamillart retained an 'inspection supérieure', continued to supervise earmarks and the issuing of receipts to revenue providers, and conserved direct oversight of the Trésor royal. For as long as Chamillart occupied the office of *contrôleur général* these two positions existed. But the demarcation of responsibilities was far from clear. Though each director general took on half the responsibilities of the *contrôleur général*, there was a good deal of overlap. More importantly, Chamillart continued to involve himself in a lot of the detail, especially of monetary policy and handling the markets, areas that he did not understand but where he acted as a drag upon those of his underlings who did possess greater insight.[35]

The strongest crutch for Chamillart was Colbert's nephew Nicolas Desmaretz. He had begun working in his uncle's offices aged only fifteen in 1664, gaining massive experience of a whole range of financial affairs and devices over the following twenty years. In June 1678 he succeeded to an *intendance des finances*, and in the final six months of Colbert's life was the sole such official. But his uncle's death brought catastrophe. Caught up in a major scandal involving illicit profits made by the minters of new, small, silver coins, he was ejected from office and exiled to his estates. Some have argued it was very likely that Desmaretz did have his fingers in the till, and certainly his intensive improvements on his estate and acquisitions in the previous few years had cast a cloud of suspicion over him; others have suggested he was merely too complaisant.[36] Alternatively, in an atmosphere of factional purging in the aftermath of Colbert's death he may simply have been unlucky, since people used the perfectly standard backhanders he had received from contractors as a stick with which to beat him, and they could do so because this particular coinage scheme had been undertaken so corruptly. Whatever the truth, Desmaretz was absent from court for twenty years, the object of the king's considerable distrust if not anger. Nevertheless, this abated to the extent that around 1695 he seems to have been made *chef de conseil* to the king's illegitimate daughter, the princesse de Conti, at her request. Successive *contrôleurs généraux* also turned to him for advice, and he remained particularly close to Louis de Pontchartrain. Chamillart called on Desmaretz to mastermind the 1700 investigation into financiers' profits, and he gradually worked on the king to promote Desmaretz's rehabilitation. He was too good an operator for the kingdom to do without him. Louis was clearly unhappy about installing him in a major office, but it

[34] For example, Germain Martin and Marcel Bezançon, *L'histoire du crédit en France sous le règne de Louis XIV* (Paris, 1913), 175.

[35] Antoine, *Le coeur de l'État*, 359–61; Saint-Simon, IX, 17.

[36] McCollim, 133–41; Antoine, *Le coeur de l'État*, 310–11, 334; Saint-Simon, VII, 133–4; Clément, *Histoire de Colbert*, I, 389–90; idem., *Le Gouvernement*, 81–2.

became ever clearer that his entire inner circle felt he needed to do this. Desmaretz's work behind the scenes could not be sustained without some kind of royal recognition, not least because the monarchy needed to maintain the confidence of the monied interests. Finally, in October 1703 he was appointed to one of the posts of director general of finance, with responsibility for much of the tax farming, waterways and forests, the Paris Chambre des Comptes, the postal system, gunpowder contractors, colonial income, and coinage policy. By this point he had a reputation as something of a financial wizard. According to Saint-Simon,

> Nobody was better versed than he in the tricks of the financiers and in the gains they made during his [earlier] era [in office], and by this knowledge, in what they could have done since.[37]

Desmaretz was not as brilliant as he later tried to make out, and during the period he was director general he evidently behaved in a factional manner. The particular object of his malice was Jean-Baptiste Fleuriau d'Armenonville, the other director general of finance, whom he associated with his earlier disgrace, and whom he undermined in the financial community.[38] Yet, how well did he work with Chamillart himself? He was not, in spite of the assertions by some historians, the de facto *contrôleur général* after autumn 1703, nor was he given a free hand in running finances by Chamillart. On many critical matters Chamillart continued to call the shots. Not until the very beginning of 1708, having become disillusioned with Armenonville, did Chamillart start handing over much more authority to Desmaretz, around the same time that his son married Desmaretz's first cousin once removed. Though Chamillart leaned heavily on him in the preparation of much of the business and for dealings with many financiers, over the years Desmaretz did not, and sometimes could not, stop Chamillart from pursuing some reckless policies. If overall Desmaretz had a positive influence on Chamillart's tenure, he cannot by any means be cleared of complicity in some of the more unfortunate policies of the period, policies whose effects he would soon afterwards have to deal with in the top job. It would be simply untenable to present a stark contrast between Desmaretz as a brilliant director general and Chamillart as a totally incompetent *contrôleur général*, and the evidence is just not there to say precisely who was responsible for every decision between 1703 and 1708. Be that as it may, one has to ask how the two men got on as colleagues. Ever one for sowing discord, Chamillart's poisonous son-in-law, the duc de La Feuillade, warned him in early 1704 that 'The jealousy of M. Desmarets, which is at the point of wanting neither an equal nor a competitor, merits real reflection', and he insinuated that Desmaretz was disloyal and might even be after his boss's job.[39] This was surely an exaggeration, as

[37] Dumas, *La politique financière*, 16–17; CCG, II, 197: Desmaretz to Bouville, 4 September 1704; II, 209: Saint-Maurice to Desmaretz, 16 October 1704; Charles Frostin, *Les Pontchartrain, ministres de Louis XIV: Alliances et réseau d'influence sous l'Ancien Régime* (Rennes, 2006), 169, 171; Antoine, *Le coeur de l'État*, 356–7; Saint-Germain, *Financiers*, 14; McCollim, 145–6; Dangeau, VI, 292; Saint-Simon, VII, 132, 137; XI, 253–5; XV, 376.

[38] Saint-Simon, IV, 271; VII, 135; IX, 17–18; XI, 256; XV, 382; Antoine, *Le coeur de l'État* , 335, 348; Pénicaut, 332; CCG, II, 196: Desmaretz to Nointel (his brother-in-law), 12 August 1704.

[39] CCG, II, 441: Desmaretz to Trudaine, 9 November 1707; Pénicaut, 139–41; Saint-Simon, XV, 360–1; Esnault, I, 309, 316–17: La Feuillade to Chamillart, 10 and 16 February 1704.

Desmaretz knew he did not enjoy sufficient royal confidence. Nonetheless, one has to ask why, several years later, so many people wanted him to replace Chamillart if he was so implicated in the appalling situation in which France found herself. One can be forgiven for suspecting that Desmaretz, perhaps through nudges and winks, had given the public the impression that he had not been master of the situation and had wearily been forced to cope with Chamillart's miscalculations.

COMETH THE HOUR, COMETH THE MAN? THE ERA OF DESMARETZ AS *CONTRÔLEUR GÉNÉRAL*, 1708–1715

Chamillart gave up the position of *contrôleur général* to Desmaretz on 20 February 1708 because he had lost authority and even, by the end, much of his remaining self-confidence. His nerves became increasingly frayed under the strain of office during 1707 and the first weeks of 1708. For some months he had repeatedly urged a peace settlement on the king and his fellow ministers because of the deteriorating financial situation which, in the autumn of 1707, looked as if it were reaching a condition where the state would be paralysed. He was, furthermore, alienating some of those who had hitherto backed him and even been his friends, such as the king's favourite, the maréchal de Villeroi. For a man who liked to please people and hated to refuse them, it is a measure of how difficult things were becoming that Chamillart had to break his word to the money markets on a number of important occasions, and that he was lashing out at generals, financiers, and the mercantile community by mid-1707. The evidence appears strong that under the pressure of the money markets defying his orders and his poorly thought-through policy announcements, between October 1707 and February 1708 Chamillart lost his nerve in the face of the financial community. Desmaretz appears to have thought Chamillart was finding the burden of fighting the markets over monetary circulation too heavy to bear. The combined pressure of running two ministries, directing the war effort against the enemy, and combatting the immoral markets was simply too much. In October 1707 Chamillart himself referred to this period as 'the most burdensome conjuncture in which I have found myself in my whole life'. When he gave up the post of *contrôleur général* it is telling that he refused the king's offer of a continued place on the Conseil Royal des finances, preferring to concentrate purely on the War Ministry from then on.[40]

After succeeding as *contrôleur général* in February 1708 Desmaretz, who scrapped the posts of directors general of finances and concentrated more power in his own hands again, worked hard to win over a still-wary king. This was rewarded nine months later with promotion to the status of *ministre d'état* and a seat on the Conseil d'En haut, though only after Chamillart and Colbert's sons-in-law, the ducs de

[40] Esnault, II, 156–7: 'Mémoire', 22 September 1707; Pénicaut, 116, 143–4; Saint-Germain, *Bernard*, 179; Saint-Simon, XV, 360; AN G[7]1780, no. 42: Trudaine to [Chamillart], 10 August 1707; G[7]1120: Chamillart to Bernard, 11 October 1707 (quotation).

Beauvilliers and de Chevreuse, urged this upon Louis in order to enhance Desmaretz's credibility and stifle court gossip that he might be removed from office. His esteem was only increased when his sons, both colonels in the army, distinguished themselves at the siege of Lille that autumn.[41] There is no doubt that Desmaretz was using his uncle's earlier tenure of office as something of a model, gathering a coterie of financier-clients around him, yet keeping all but close relatives at a greater distance than Chamillart had done. In February 1708 he added his own brother-in-law, Louis Béchameil de Nointel, to the Council of Commerce, following this in June 1715 by installing his younger brother Jean-Baptiste Desmaretz de Vaubourg on the same body. François Ogier, son of a Colbert protégé, was plucked from the receiver generalship of Montauban to become receiver general of Church finances in 1710. His most important official was Jean-Roland Malet, who came out of the naval administration to enter the Finance Ministry in 1704, and then became Desmaretz's personal *premier commis*. Desmaretz himself was not especially grasping, and might well have reined himself in after his searing experience of disgrace. He seems to have been more concerned for the re-establishment of his prestige than for wealth, securing the elevation of his land of Maillebois into a marquisate in 1706, and ensuring his third daughter married the marquis de Béthune-Orval, second in line to the symbolically important dukedom of Sully (to which he eventually succeeded). After a disgrace such as Desmaretz had endured, renewed respectability was really what the victim craved.[42]

Desmaretz's time as *contrôleur général* was a vale of tears for France. Although he by no means single-handedly brought the country through the worst period of Louis XIV's personal rule, although his policies began to backfire, and although he took a huge risk that the war could be ended in 1712–13, without his steady nerve and creativity it is hard to see how the country would have continued the war for long enough to bring about a compromise peace. On taking power he was faced with a calamitous situation in which Chamillart had all but spent France into the ground without any idea whatsoever of how the 1708 campaign would be funded. No provision had been made for food supply for the armies or for recruiting fresh men and horses. Recounting the event to the Regent Orléans in 1716, Desmaretz described the audience with Louis XIV at which he was appointed:

> He forewarned me and explained the situation plainly, telling me he knew perfectly well the state of his finances, that he was not asking the impossible of me; that if I succeeded I would render him a great service for which he could not thank me too much; if the outcome was not happy, he would not impute the ill events to me.[43]

Desmaretz's initial concerns were to arrange funds rapidly and to restore a degree of administrative order. He reorganized the appropriations, floated fresh government

[41] Dumas, *La politique financière*, 76–7; Saint-Simon, XVI, 435, 480; CCG, III, 65: Le Gendre to Desmaretz, 23 January 1709.

[42] Antoine, *Le coeur de l'État*, 365; Saint-Simon, VII, 133; XV, 381, 384–5; XVI, 436–7; DAPS, 396; Michaud, 396; Pénicaut, 313; Bonney and Bonney, *Jean-Roland Malet*, 10–11.

[43] CCG, II, 673–4: 'Compte rendu de M. Desmaretz au Régent', [1716]. On poor financial planning see SHD Ya2; AN $G^7$1780–2; $G^7$1120: Bernard to Chamillart, 11 November 1707.

annuities, levied forced loans on royal venal officials, and went in for a final large tranche of office sales. Amazingly it kept the war effort going, only for the mounting crisis in the Lyon financial market to derail the situation at the end of 1708 and in the first half of 1709. In February 1709 he probably saved France from a complete credit meltdown even greater than the one that actually occurred a month later: had he not insisted on honouring loans due for payment that year which were backed by functioning revenue sources, there would very likely have been a collapse of financial confidence of the same magnitude as in 1648 and 1787–88.[44] If this would not have caused a revolution, it would almost certainly have cost Philip V his Spanish throne. During the course of 1709 and 1710 Desmaretz appears to have sought one more big burst of financial energy from France in the hope that it would be enough to bring about an honourable peace, but the methods he used risked creating an even more disastrous financial situation had the war continued on the same huge scale into 1712 and beyond. Though he has the reputation of a financial genius, his policies also bear the hallmarks of a colossal gamble that simply could not have anticipated the series of events that saved Louis XIV's face: the downfall of Marlborough, the death of Emperor Joseph I, and the resulting collapse of cohesion in the Grand Alliance during 1712.

Desmaretz was a marked improvement upon his predecessor in his handling of the kingdom's finances and of those involved in them. At the most basic level, in part because he actually had the time, he kept a fairly close eye on the major provincial tax collectors, ensuring they paid over what they were obligated to do, and he demonstrated an informed flexibility in the way he reacted to revenue problems at provincial level. He had been involved with the *gens d'affaires*—the king's financial agents—for so long that he knew their stratagems and they feared him, even if he was also someone in whose judgement they could have some confidence. At the root of what success Desmaretz did achieve was his appreciation of the importance of the financiers' credit for the monarchy, and his firm outlook that the *contrôleur général*'s most important role was to manage the financiers as effectively as possible and enhance the circulation of money. Unlike Chamillart he seems to have fully accepted that royal credit depended fundamentally upon the credit the financiers enjoyed with the wider public, thus making it essential that they were honoured openly and that their loans to the crown were repaid promptly so as to preserve their solvency. Desmaretz allegedly told Saint-Simon that, unlike Chamillart, he would not give his word in cases where it might be impossible to keep it, and instead aimed to re-establish 'good faith, which is the soul of confidence and commerce'. In a statement that sets him firmly apart from Chamillart he argued,

> Authority forces everything that can be obtained by force, but when one requires things that depend upon opinion, one employs it uselessly.[45]

[44] Malet, *Comptes*, 115–16.

[45] Dumas, *La politique financière*, 21–2; McCollim, 154, 263; Saint-Simon, XV, 378; Saint-Germain, *Bernard*,170 (quotation).

He did take some time to build a sufficiently encompassing understanding of the money markets as they developed during the War of the Spanish Succession (as perhaps would be expected). And there is a real sense in his correspondence that he and Trudaine, the key provincial figure for much of this time as royal *intendant* of Lyon, were united during the 1700s in their struggle towards a greater appreciation of how bankers and financiers were now operating. Yet despite a sense of learning this part of the business afresh, on the job, Desmaretz kept his nerve, and he preferred measures that might secure long-term cash availability over short-term windfalls.[46] He was most concerned with securing public confidence to lend—to the crown and to its agents—so he sought to meet interest payments whenever possible and even when it might not at first sight seem an appropriate priority for scant resources. He did not aim to do without the enormous quantity of paper instruments now circulating, but he did seek to rally confidence and halt any further downward slide by substituting better paper for near-worthless paper, and rolling over loans in a reasonable and timely fashion.[47]

All this notwithstanding, Desmaretz was not always successful in his endeavours and he overreached himself when it came to some of these paper instruments and the coinage. His attempts to convert the bearer bills of the Extraordinaire des Guerres treasury were less than sure-footed, causing temporary panic in Paris and Lyon during 1708–9.[48] But his real weakness was a predilection for meddling with the currency. He had taken a close interest in these matters under Colbert, too close perhaps. He advised the government unofficially on the reminting of 1693, he was involved with all subsequent ones, and he masterminded that of 1709. On most such occasions, unusually for him, he appears to have been driven by short-term gain for the monarchy, as well as a hope that more coin would re-enter circulation for the government to borrow. He was recklessly willing to manipulate the currency in a counterproductive manner that he hoped would flush coin out in the short term, but in practice it somewhat shrank the available coinage for the government's needs since it was hoarded or exported, sometimes for a long time. This may be a harsh assessment, and there were always reasons that could be advanced to justify the manipulation of the coinage, but the fact remains that Desmaretz did not help Louis XIV in this area of policy.[49]

Running the royal finances was not, at ministerial level, a job for the *contrôleur général* alone, as we have seen, and the post of Secretary of State for War after February 1708 was once again in another pair of hands. This certainly reduced the scope for policy confusion, as long as the *contrôleur général* and the War Minister worked closely together, especially on debt emissions. For at least a few months Chamillart and Desmaretz rubbed along fairly well together, and the latter could not afford to fall out with the former, who still very much enjoyed the king's

[46] For example, AN $G^7$1093: Desmaretz to Amelot, 24 June 1708.

[47] CCG, III, 678: 'Compte rendu de M. Desmaretz au Régent', [1716]; Dumas, *La politique financière*, 56–7, 118–19.

[48] AN $G^7$1782, no. 121: [Montargis to Desmaretz], 25 July 1708; no. 147: anon. letter to Desmaretz, n.d. [1708–9].

[49] Saint-Simon, XVII, 541, 547; Frostin, *Les Pontchartrain*, 168; Dumas, *La politique financière*, 24.

support. But Desmaretz's men were developing real contempt for Chamillart, one of them in 1714 even writing of 'the errors of the previous minister' in a disdainful manner.[50] Now liberated from the contrôle général, Chamillart nevertheless still showed real incompetence in his handling of War Ministry finances, jeopardizing royal bankers' positions, and he had a poor idea of the funds Desmaretz was making available to him. In the spring of 1709 a major clash erupted between the two men over the level of disposable funds for the army, forcing Desmaretz to spell out to the king in painful detail the inadequacy of Chamillart's knowledge of war finance. Just at this time, Desmaretz was preoccupied with averting the collapse of the state's leading banker Samuel Bernard. While he approved Chamillart's ideas for a rescue, Desmaretz's irritation with his predecessor had now reached breaking point, and he waspishly rebuked the Secretary of War by stating that this bail-out was 'to prevent the collapse of a man whom you engaged in excessive advances for the King's service'.[51]

Chamillart was not long for the world of the court and the ministry. He was already an isolated figure, and his support for the duc de Vendôme, joint commander of the army of Flanders, against the king's grandson, the duke of Burgundy, at the time of their public spat during the 1708 campaign, can hardly have done much for the king's view of him.[52] The *coup de grâce*, however, came from the Grand Dauphin. Initially appointed to command the army of Flanders in 1709, the Dauphin was ready to leave for the front only to learn, to his mounting horror, of the total logistical breakdown of the army and the northern half of the kingdom. When he informed the king of the situation, Louis—fearing his son's humiliation—redesignated command to the maréchal de Villars. However much Louis liked Chamillart, it was this that sealed his dismissal on 9 June.[53] He was replaced as Secretary of State for War by Daniel Voysin, about whom little need be said at this point. Initially under the tutelage of the maréchal de Boufflers, he remained in office until the end of the reign, combining the post with that of Chancellor of France in 1714–15. Voysin's father had been one of Colbert's clients in the 1660s, and the Voysins became even closer to the Colberts: Daniel's sister married Desmaretz's brother Vaubourg in 1682, and almost certainly these long-standing ties helped relations with Desmaretz from June 1709. Daniel Voysin himself had considerable experience first as an army and then as a provincial *intendant,* before serving for another decade as a councillor of state, undertaking whatever tasks his superiors requested. But he was a cold, inflexible, and haughty figure, like Louvois earlier, a man who was neither open nor sociable, and, in diametric contrast with Chamillart, Voysin did not try to oblige people's requests—probably a good thing after the Chamillart years. As colleagues he and Desmaretz seem to have worked well enough together most of the time, especially on funding the army paymasters,

[50] AN $G^7$1124–6: note on Hogguer le jeune for Desmaretz, [1714].

[51] AN $G^7$1124–6: 'memoire pour les Sieurs Hogguer' [printed, 1710]; Saint-Simon, XVII, 186–90; SHD $A^1$2182, no. 102: Desmaretz to Chamillart, 7 March 1709 (quotation).

[52] Saint-Simon, XVII, 448–9.

[53] Pénicaut, 151–9; Saint-Simon, XI, 55; XV, 367–71; XVII, 26, 159, 392–3, 397–8, 430–5; Ars. Ms. 4494, fo. 11r.

and though at times there were hard negotiations, agreements emerged and there appears to have been no really major clash that the king had to mediate.[54] This was how the ministerial system was supposed to work.

This was the system at the centre that managed the royal finances underpinning the army's logistics, which in turn, in very large part, held up the international power of Louis XIV's France. Unfortunately for Louis, he was neither wise nor lucky in all the men he picked for ministerial office, nor in the men they, in turn, chose to support them in their tasks. The dependence upon a vast array of revenue agents, semi-autonomous expenditure agents, and supply contractors required eternal vigilance and profound insight on the part of the ministers if the weaknesses promoted by the principal-agent problem were not to handicap the state, drain its resources, and disrupt its functioning. This was far from forthcoming. So far in this book, the extent to which the state depended upon the financial resources and networks of its subjects for its wartime power, and the shape of that system, has only been alluded to. It now needs to be spelled out in order to show how the complex machinery of French finances moved towards complete seizure by the final years of the Sun King's reign.

[54] Pénicaut, 45; McCollim, 123, 184; Saint-Simon, XVII, 457–9; Malet, *Comptes*, 140; Thierry Sarmant, ed., *Les ministres de la guerre 1570–1792: Histoire et dictionnaire biographique* (Paris, 2007), 307–17.

PART II

RAISING MONEY, FINDING MONEY, MAKING MONEY: SOURCING REVENUE IN AN AGE OF CRISIS

Introduction

In the course of the two great conflicts of Louis XIV's personal rule—the Nine Years War and the War of the Spanish Succession—the state spent more and more, and became increasingly indebted. By the final decade of the reign, such was the overstretch of royal credit, the monarchy was disbursing huge amounts to less and less positive effect on the war effort. The state was turning into an uroboros, the mythical serpent that ate itself from its own tail upwards in a bid to survive, though with the danger it would not renew but kill itself in the process.

As it was, the events of the second half of the reign were set against an unfortunate context of economic stagnation, especially in the dominant agricultural sector. This made the War of the Spanish Succession much harder to fuel than the War of the Austrian Succession or the Seven Years War. Revenues from the soil for landowners, *seigneurs* (extracting feudal dues), and the crown were static, and some consolidation of holdings was required even to stand still. The 1670s and 1680s had seen some growth in foreign trade, but the personal rule as a whole was not a period of rapid advances. Leaving aside the effects of war shrinking markets, there was some underlying decline in manufacturing too, especially in fields such as cloth production where some areas of France were producing goods for export that were losing their competitive edge. Beyond Europe there was some notable expansion in French trade, largely in the final two decades of the reign, and this did help, as we shall see. But twice France was hit very hard by economic slump and demographic crisis owing to acutely disastrous climatic change and harvest failures, in 1692–94 and 1709–11. Abundant harvests carried the French to a compromise peace in 1695–97, and in 1701–4 delayed the onset of depression, but the strains were becoming ever more visible, not least through declining royal revenues.[1]

The underlying problem for the crown was that the economy was ceasing to provide the ready cash the monarchy needed for waging war on the level of the 1690s, never mind on the unprecedented scale of the following decade. This was the somewhat depressing backdrop to the crown's efforts to extract ever more revenue from its subjects and their activities. France, if not the richest state per capita

[1] Marcel Lachiver, *Les années de misère: La famine au temps du Grand Roi* (Paris, 1991), 209–406; Ernest Labrousse, Pierre Léon et al., *Histoire économique et sociale de la France. Tome 1: Des derniers temps de l'âge seigneurial aux préludes de l'âge industriel (1660–1789)* (Paris, 1970), part 2 ch. 2 and part 3 ch. 1.

in the world, was the largest economy and the most economically powerful country in Europe. But it needed to be, faced with the demands Louis XIV was placing upon it. From being a very powerful, relatively solvent country in the mid-1680s, France descended into a state of economic collapse by the end of the reign, and the monarchy was also beggared in the process.

There are several clear indices of the extent of this decline, even though the survival of only a small proportion of largely rough-and-ready financial documents makes it hard to be accurate and systematic about the financial position. As far as estimating raw royal financial power is concerned, a useful index is the gap between net revenue and expenditure, and the deteriorating position of the monarchy can be seen by comparing net and gross revenue takes. The gross headline figure was reduced by several burdens to the amount the monarchy actually had at its disposal for expenditure. First of all, French tax collection costs at the start of the eighteenth century were far higher than several decades later, and considerably greater than in contemporary England. Much more importantly, the French government had to deduct all sorts of charges on the revenues, arising from borrowing, before it could obtain its net income, the amount that was referred to as the 'parties du Trésor royal'.[2] Table 1 gives a rough indication of the growing problems in the last decades of the reign.

In the War of the Spanish Succession both net and gross revenue figures seem to have been pushed up in 1705–7, after falling in the years 1702–4, but from

Table 1

YEAR	NET REVENUE AS PERCENTAGE OF GROSS REVENUE
1661	37–38%
1683	79–80%
1690	*c.*75–80%
1697 (and previous years)	*c.*69%
1699	56%
1700	57%
1701	55%
1702	50%
1702–7	fluctuations between 49% and 60%
1714	27–28%
1715 (1 September estimate)	41%

Sources: Jean Meyer, *Colbert* (Paris, 1981), 188; Malet, *Comptes*, 101; Pierre Clément, *Histoire de Colbert et de son administration* (Paris, 1874), I, 229; Forbonnais, II, 94, 106, 112, 267, 351; CCG, II, 582: 'État', 6 September 1699; 584–5 (various documents); European State Finance Database, http://esfdb.websites.bta.com/table.aspx?resourceid=11582: 'Revenues of the French Monarchy, 1700-07'.

[2] Margaret Bonney and Richard Bonney, *Jean-Roland Malet, premier historien des finances de la monarchie française* (Paris, 1993), 23, 41.

1708—even though we do not have exact figures—the levels of each plummeted. What does this mean in terms of *livres*?

In 1683, the year of Colbert's death, it was estimated that gross revenues had stood at 116 million *livres* and net revenues at 92 million *livres*. But in 1701–7 the average net revenue fell to just 67 million *livres*. In 1714 net revenue was at a pitiful level of between 30 and 35 million *livres*, with state revenues burdened by 80 million *livres* of charges that were needed to service just the consolidated debt, never mind other short-term borrowing. Overall, between 1689 and 1714 net revenue covered only between one-quarter and one-third of total expenditure.[3] On top of all this, revenue, in terms of silver and gold, was also in decline because of monetary manipulations (which, in turn, had knock-on effects for state purchasing power and foreign exchange facilities).

Already in the early 1680s a gloomy Colbert feared that renewed war would lead to a ballooning budget deficit, excessive indirect tax pressure on the country, and credit collapse. He estimated that a future major war would push total royal expenditure up to around 110 million *livres*, and he felt that a deficit of around 35 million *livres* per annum was about as much as the country could stand for more than a year or two. It turned out France could take a much larger deficit than that, but at a huge price; and the military costs for the army alone in the War of the Spanish Succession averaged 118 million *livres*, peaking in 1705 and 1707 in the region of 148 million *livres*. The average total expenditure of around 190 million *livres* that was seen in 1701–8 proved to be far too large for the health of the state and society when the real wealth of the country was so hard to tax. Nor had the country had time to recover from the previous bout of conflict. If the burden of war were to be sustained without breakdown it was essential that any war began with the public finances in reasonable shape. The Nine Years War and the large hangover of debt it created meant, instead, that French finances on the eve of the War of the Spanish Succession were worrying, to say the least. The 1699–1700 deficits were in the region of 50 to 60 million *livres*, and it was not possible to amass funds in these years as Chamillart tried to pay down the debt, nor in the first couple of years of the ensuing conflict thanks to accelerating expenditure.[4]

Matters only got worse. The year 1703 would appear to be the one in which financial difficulties seriously started to become apparent, long before the first big defeat at Blenheim but only two years into the war, whereas it had not been until four years into the Nine Years War that financial problems had started to really bite. Bankers now became far more wary of trusting the army's treasury, the Extraordinaire des Guerres, and several of the provinces were already showing signs of exhaustion. With continued strategic overextension and the cumulative effects of defeats upon resources, morale, and market confidence, the finances by the

[3] In addition to the sources cited for Table 1, see Forbonnais, II, 172, 174–5, 178, 280; Vuitry, 29.

[4] Pierre Clément, *Histoire de Colbert et de son administration* (2nd edn, 2 vols, Paris, 1874), I, 232–4; Forbonnais, II, 100–1, 107, 112–13, 170–1, 190, 201, 224, 232, 247, 268 (on which I have based my figures for average expenditure in 1701–14); Malet, *Comptes*, 53; CCG, II, 472–3: *mémoire* by Chamillart, November 1699.

autumn of 1707 were, in the view of Desmaretz, in a 'sad situation', not least because the state 'had forced credit infinitely out of all proportion' to expenditure, as Chamillart confessed at the time. This was in the main because there had been a roughly 35 per cent leap in state spending during 1705, which was then sustained to average 230 million *livres* per annum up to the end of the war. The terrifying gulf between net revenue and spending can be seen in the size of disposable funds estimated as available for the whole of 1708 in February of that year, at the time the contrôle général was handed over to Desmaretz: a pitiful 18 million *livres*. The following year the terrible weather of January and February, and the harvest failure of that summer, wrecked agricultural revenues just at the time France was undergoing the ordeal of a complete meltdown in credit. The years 1709 and 1710 may well have seen the all-time high for *notional* taxation levels under the *ancien régime*, but the revenues from several *généralités* had totally collapsed and Allied armies were extracting contributions worth up to two years' yield through land taxes from a number of northern provinces. On top of this, in a race between total bankruptcy and keeping the war going to achieve an honourable peace, Desmaretz alienated tax revenues for upfront lump sum payments worth several years' income.[5] Desmaretz provided one important explanation for why the war was so expensive. Writing in January 1715 he confessed that the government had simply been unrealistic about what sort of a conflict it would be: aside from the geostrategic situation (see Chapter 1), constant hopes that peace was just around the corner led the king into a series of short-term expedients which brought in funds but greatly diminished the revenue base and increased interest payments. In addition, the introduction of Mint bills had also put up costs, even if he was not willing to confess to the errors of his coinage manipulations.[6]

This is the overall picture. The next four chapters will explain how the ministers tried to enhance and maintain royal funds after 1700. Their policies came at the expense of a deterioration in underlying revenue strength and monetary order, in the process worsening the principal-agent problem that was already embedded in the fisco-financier system. The gap between income and expenditure was naturally bridged by loans on a scale never previously seen, and these also began to be raised in vast quantities from the spending agents of the state, with even less financial order the result.

[5] Malet, *Comptes*, 65, 127–8; Esnault, II, 156: 'Mémoire', 22 September 1707 (Chamillart quote); II, 238: Desmaretz to Chamillart, 14 May 1714 (Desmaretz quote); CCG, III, 286: Bernages to Desmaretz, 3 May 1710.

[6] CCG, III, 621: 'Mémoire', January 1715.

3

Taxing to the Hilt? Structural Weakness and Falling Revenues

The fiscal machinery of Louis XIV's France was a highly exploitative operation, whose details cannot be explored in depth here and deserve an entire synthetic monograph in their own right. But it is important to understand the structural weaknesses of the collecting system, the mounting burdens on society, the falling revenues, and the forms of borrowing linked to the revenue system. France was not, by later standards, an overtaxed country, but the way its surplus wealth was expropriated by the state made it hard to tap its riches and impossible to service the king's enormous borrowing requirements that developed after 1688 and especially after 1701. This fiscal-political problem persisted down to the end of the *ancien régime.*

If early eighteenth-century France had a recognizably modern, though primitive, set of imposts—direct taxes, sales taxes, customs dues, tolls—the basis of the taxation system was an unequal, irrational distribution of the burdens shaped to a considerable extent by legal privileges granted to social orders such as the nobility and the Church, to corporate bodies such as clothiers and magistrates, and to whole areas such as the outlying *pays d'états*. Privileges had been conferred upon particular provinces as they were incorporated into the kingdom, and had gradually been extended to urban centres in the later Middle Ages, and to legal and administrative corporate bodies. This was often in return for considerable contributions of resources to the monarchy. Outside the Church the most privileged of all were the nobility, who had made a series of semi-explicit bargains with the crown that added up to privileges in taxation (and other rights) in return for performance of military service. They would also enjoy personal involvement in state administration while exercising little collective political power through free-standing institutions.

By 1688 France was not only riddled with privilege but built upon it. The most significant privilege of all was exemption from the principal direct taxes, the *taille* and its adjuncts. In around two-thirds of France nobles in particular were wholly or largely exempted from this onerous symbol of social subjugation, and this and other rights were extended, for a price, to commoners in the following twenty-five years on a large scale. Unfortunately, the tacit deal between crown and privileged groups would also start to unravel in the Nine Years War and the War of the Spanish Succession, as the taxability of non-privileged subjects reached its elastic limits while the scale of war expanded. Privileged groups were already subject to indirect taxation in the form of excise and customs duties, and other levies on goods, but now the crown extended crafty forms of prerogative, domanial charges upon them, and squeezed money out of the urban privileged by manipulation of venal offices. More significantly for the long term, the monarchy imposed new forms of direct taxation upon the nobility, using levies that were socially universal but were really intended to tap the privileged. Even so, this could not go too far and French taxation was very deficient in extracting the surplus wealth of the king's subjects, so throughout this period Louis XIV, certainly compared with the Dutch and British, was fighting with one hand tied behind his back. To make up some of the difference, the monarchy regularly imposed extraordinary financial and monetary levies, producing so much irregularity in government and finances that it would probably have been far less disruptive to credit, to the monetary system, to agriculture, and to commerce in general had it imposed heavier, more progressive taxation earlier in the Nine Years War and then developed this much further in the first years of the War of the Spanish Succession.[1] Taxation yields in the War of the Spanish Succession were already starting to fall because of the underlying economic effects of war, but royal policies only depressed yields further.

THE ADMINISTRATION OF DIRECT TAXATION

Over the previous two centuries the government had joined to the *taille*—the principal form of direct taxation in France—a series of lesser adjuncts that were notionally for the pay, supply, and policing of the army but in practice went into the general pot of funds: the *taillon*, the *crue des prévôts des maréchaux*, the *subsistance*, and the *subvention*. In addition to these taxes, other military-related impositions, which were properly hypothecated for the army, piggybacked on the administration of the *taille*: the *ustencile* and the *contributions des étapes* for supplying troops stationed in or moving through a province, and the *impôt de la milice*. In the *pays d'états* these were imposed in other ways, generally by the estates.[2] The *taille* and these other levies were organized on the basis of fiscal provinces known as *généralités*. From the 1660s the central government decided upon the global amount that would be demanded each year and divided this up among the *généralités*. Then a royal *intendant*, placed by the royal council at the head of the *généralité*, apportioned the amount between parishes, though much of this work was done by his subdelegates, often self-interested men drawn from local legal or fiscal officers. The actual collection of these taxes at parish level was done by the local inhabitants, who passed the funds up to a *receveur des tailles* for each district (an *élection* or *bailliage*). In turn, they transmitted the money to the *receveur général*, who was based for the most part in Paris. There were normally two such *receveurs généraux* for each *généralité*, alternating biennially, and they were often in association with other formal backers. For the *pays d'états*, there might be *receveurs généraux* but there was also a treasurer of the estates, who really performed much of this role.[3]

[1] As Desmaretz in effect conceded: CCG, III, 621: 'Mémoire', January 1715.

[2] See, e.g., Rafe Blaufarb, 'The Survival of the *pays d'états*: the Example of Provence', *Past and Present* 209 (2010), 83–116.

[3] Léon Bouchard, *Système financier de l'ancienne monarchie* (Paris, 1891), 103–18; McCollim, 44; DAPS, 47–51.

The *receveurs généraux* were essential financiers upon whom the French state relied for a regular supply of income, not just for spending on the armed forces but also for backing much credit. In the 1660s they had become the central figures in the collection of the *taille* and were remoulded by Colbert, who brought many of them within his personal orbit. After the purges of their ranks by Le Peletier in 1683–84, they settled down into a less factional and more hierarchical relationship with successive *contrôleurs généraux*. Each post was a venal office worth anywhere between 200,000 and 1.5 million *livres*, and as such the holder received *gages*—the interest on the original investment, usually around 5 per cent—and was given a rake-off known as a *remise*, worth between 4 and 11 *deniers* for every *livre* handled. The *remise* was mainly to pay administrative, staffing, and transport costs. Because of their immediate engagement with direct taxation, the *receveurs généraux* were seen as particularly creditworthy, and the crown would, in turn, borrow a great deal from them on a continual basis. Although the *receveurs généraux* were a corps of sorts, when they acted together it tended to be as coalitions of the willing rather than all together as a whole, and for the administration of their *généralité* each man worked and accounted separately, even from his colleague with whom he alternated.[4] This made them a much more atomized group than the farmers general (see below).

Whether he was an outsider to a province or not, a *receveur général* had extensive financial links to the full range of local elites, and for the *pays d'élections* in particular (covering two-thirds of the population) the *receveurs généraux* in Paris were an essential point of mediation between crown and localities. In their *généralité* a *receveur général* contracted with local venal *receveurs des tailles* to gather the funds. All, in turn, were observed by the royal *intendant*, who ensured regularity in their operations, acted to minimize friction between the demands of different taxes, and alerted Versailles to any problems in their area. But the direct management of the local *receveurs* was up to each *receveur général*, and though there were frequent legal disputes between them, many *receveurs généraux* were indulgent and protective of their underlings. The *receveurs* were under contract to pay their *receveur général* a certain amount each month, if necessary by borrowing it. Indeed, *receveurs généraux* needed their junior *receveurs* to help shoulder the burden of loans and advances to the government by feeding the main coffers of the *généralité* regularly, rather than just waiting for the taxes to roll in. A proportion of the funds remained in the locality: for this, the local *receveurs* supplied *rescriptions*—promissory notes to deliver funds—on themselves to their *receveur général*, who could then pass them to the Trésor royal for handing on to the bankers or military paymasters, for example. For the most part (less so in frontier provinces with a large military or naval presence), the local *receveurs* sent a great deal of money to their *receveur général* in Paris, and much of this was remitted using bills of exchange, which beyond a

[4] Pierre Clément, *Histoire de Colbert et de son administration* (2nd edn, 2 vols, Paris, 1874), I, 176; DAPS, 43, 46, 204; McCollim, 47; George T. Matthews, *The Royal General Farms in Eighteenth-Century France* (New York, 1958), 27–8; Mark Potter, *Corps and Clienteles: Public Finance and Political Change in France, 1688–1715* (Aldershot, 2003), 149.

certain distance from the capital was a much faster and cheaper method than sending cash by road and boat.[5] But as pressures increased, yields shrank, and local credit networks atrophied, *receveurs généraux* had to advance money to themselves and to the military paymasters on behalf of their own *receveurs*, in the case of one such *receveur général*, Galloys, in early 1709 to the tune of 1,145,000 *livres*.[6] That they could do this stems from their other unofficial function, as clearing bankers for merchants across France whose money was deposited in Paris and which they had access to.[7] They were also able to borrow vast amounts from the upper nobility and the robe magistracy.

Direct taxes were slow to roll into their coffers at the best of times. They trickled in, during good times, over a period of fifteen-plus months from the start of a duty-year—an *exercice*—but payments to the crown were due quarterly throughout that time. And it was important that these payments were regular because the pattern of tax flow did not match the expenditure needs of the army. The first two payments of an *exercice* were therefore made to the king as large advances, but because of cash-availability problems *receveurs généraux* had to borrow to meet a proportion of every payment to the crown. Typically, the costs of advances would come to about 5 per cent of the total sums due, and this—with additional charges for their own benefit—was one of the things that made being a *receveur général* so appealing. The obligation to provide actual cash to the Trésor royal was not absolute, and it suited the crown to have some cash at the centre but with the knowledge that other sources were available in the hands of the receiver system, out in the provinces. The pattern is very mixed for different periods of the reign, and for different provinces.[8] All told, though, it was a system that was open to considerable abuse and fraud, in times of peace or war. For a start, once the taxes did come in they came in fast, and when a lot of the initial loans had been paid back a *receveur général* could then start investing whatever he was able to sit on in high-yielding places. This generally meant high-interest, short-term loans to other fisco-financiers, including the *fermes générales*, windfall tax contracts, and the Extraordinaire des Guerres. On a lesser scale, *receveurs des tailles* emulated their superiors in this regard. This was risky, as it was for the crown too, and in 1707 Chamillart had to reiterate, to little apparent effect, long-standing orders that receivers at all levels should not move funds out of their chests without express royal orders. What was worse, there was a tendency to obfuscate or downright lie about costs and about the flow of taxes coming into their possession, and Forbonnais accused many *receveurs généraux* of inflating the size of arrears. This then allowed them to claim to the monarchy that they could only meet payments by further borrowing. In reality they had to borrow much less than they

[5] Potter, *Corps and Clienteles*, 154–5; DAPS, 45, 51; Clément, *Histoire de Colbert*, I, 177; AN G⁷1120: memorandum entitled 'Comté de Bourgogne 1707'; Malet, *Comptes*, 101; CCG, III, 348: Courson to Desmaretz, 27 January 1711.

[6] AN G⁷1783, no. 5: placet of Galloys, [January? 1709].

[7] Jean Meyer, *Colbert* (Paris, 1981), 196.

[8] DAPS, 44; McCollim, 47; AN G⁷1776, no. 313: Bernières to [Chamillart], 2 October 1704; G⁷1777, no. 233: Montargis to Chamillart, 27 June 1705; G⁷1120: Bernard to Chamillart, 8 October 1707; Bernard to Desmaretz, 7 July 1708.

suggested so they were simply pocketing the interest and compensation the *contrôleur général* might give them![9]

The circumstances brought about by the pressures and events of war in the 1700s provided further opportunity for graft, though some of the apparent corruption can be excused as fisco-financiers trying to protect themselves in the face of falling tax yields. By the autumn of 1706 many *receveurs généraux* and local *receveurs* were simply not retaining sufficient funds in their *généralités* nor paying up on their instruments, even when ordered to do so by Chamillart.[10] Just as damaging for the underlying financial health of the realm, receivers and their cashiers were using their slush funds to buy up various royal and para-royal financial instruments at discounts; in other words, speculating in debt using dormant royal money. There were other ways, too, to profit from the deterioration in paper instruments: at least one *receveur des tailles* was caught making a 6 per cent charge for converting the *rescriptions* of a *receveur général* into his own promissory notes, something Minister Voysin found intolerable. The government took a dim view of such corrupt diversion of funds, with Chamillart commenting, 'There is a lack of faith among men who handle money which always revolts me.'[11]

There was self-evidently an inherent principal-agent problem in the collection of direct taxation that was exacerbated by the problems and opportunities of war. That it was so hard to keep the *receveurs généraux* under tight control can be put down to the failings of the accounting system. It was not just that accounts could be delayed for years, it was the poor quality of the bookkeeping at all levels of royal government that made it impossible even for the incumbents of an office to tell in an accurate manner what the state of their affairs was at any given moment. Colbert had not managed by any means to perfect royal and fisco-financier account-keeping, but as a former financier himself he knew what to be doubly suspicious of, and he paid close attention to receipts. Not so, it seems, his successors. The disorder in the affairs of the *receveurs généraux* was prompted by a mixture of corruption, carelessness, and incompetence, as well as chaos in funding flows, which were not necessarily the fault of the receiver himself. Double-entry bookkeeping might have done something to make the fisco-financiers more immediately and transparently accountable to ministers, and the practice had its advocates at the time. Nevertheless, though the techniques had existed in France for over one hundred years and were increasingly used by merchants, little effort was made prior to 1716 to introduce double-entry bookkeeping into royal finances. Not least, this was because there were very few people who were capable of adapting its techniques to the old order of royal finances, governed as it was by often hidebound

[9] Julian Swann, *Provincial Power and Absolute Monarchy: The Estates-General of Burgundy, 1661–1790* (Cambridge, 2003), 201; Forbonnais, I, 301; II, 60; Malet, *Comptes*, 30; Eugène-Pierre Beaulieu, *Les gabelles sous Louis XIV* (Paris, 1903), 65; Clamageran, III, 88–9.

[10] AN G[7]1778, no. 146: Mongelas' note to Chamillart, 14 June 1706; no. 236: [Mongelas to Chamillart], [November 1706].

[11] SHD A[1]2504, fo. 291r: Voysin to Méliand, 22 November 1710; CCG, II, 313: D'Argenson to Chamillart, 11 December 1705 (quotation from Chamillart's marginalia); III, 89: Caumartin to [Desmaretz], [January 1709]; Forbonnais, II, 134.

rules (quite literally, given the continued insistence on using parchment for some documentation).[12] And in any case, by exposing their financial state, double-entry would erode the aura of secrecy fisco-financiers felt it was essential to preserve in order to maintain their credit if nothing else. All this notwithstanding, double-entry may well have only worked during periods when the fiscal system was not under strain. Given the failure of revenue sources, poor communication of problems, and other ways men would have tried to conceal difficulties and fraud, it is hard to see double-entry bookkeeping in the War of the Spanish Succession as the panacea the Paris brothers championed.

THE YIELDS OF DIRECT TAXATION

These immense administrative problems—in what was nevertheless the best-run branch of royal finance—only worsened the problems of returns from direct taxation. For the *pays d'élections* Colbert had reduced the proportion of total tax income coming from the *taille* and its adjuncts (as well as *dons gratuits* from the *pays d'états*) from over two-thirds of total tax revenue to around half, and the Nine Years War saw the *taille* remain at the same level as in 1682. Nevertheless, by the end of this conflict much of the *taille* collection was in arrears. In the Nine Years War the most that could be squeezed out of the *taille* was 38–40 million *livres*, but in the War of the Spanish Succession, reflecting some of the economic battering of the mid-1690s, this fell to 30–35 million *livres*. On top of this, some 15–20 million *livres* per annum was raised in the form of military taxes in cash and kind administered by the *receveurs généraux*. To increase revenues the Finance Ministry continued to iron out anomalies and regional inequalities, but it made small progress in this regard, and the sale of offices and privileges only increased the burden on the remaining *taille*-payers. More importantly, the crown added to the *taille* burden using surtaxes (often to compensate for failures to screw money out of local elites) and personal tax bills (handed to tax-dodging richer commoners), but there were also systematic increases in *taille* rates in 1705 and January 1712. There was some recognition that the burden could be too high when so many other tax demands were being made, so there were small reductions in demands during 1703–4 and 1709–11. But it was obvious that even at the higher rates a lot of money was simply not coming into the receivers' coffers, never mind reaching the monarch.[13]

By 1703 the government was facing popular resistance against the receivers, and those provinces whose *taille* yield depended upon grapes and other produce related to export were hit very hard by trade embargoes around this time too. Some

[12] Yannick Lemarchand, 'Introducing Double-Entry Bookkeeping in Public Finance: A French Experiment at the Beginning of the Eighteenth Century', *Accounting, Business and Financial History: An International Comparative Review* 9 (1999), 226, 228–41; Richard Gascon, 'Marchands et marchands-banquiers', in Pierre Chaunu and Richard Gascon, eds, *Histoire économique et sociale de la France. Tome 1: De 1450 à 1660. Premier volume: l'État et la Ville* (Paris, 1977), 314–15; Forbonnais, II, 59, 429–30.

[13] Meyer, *Colbert*, 194; Forbonnais, II, 108, 173, 195, 227; AN G[7]1788, no. 142: *arrêt*, 19 September 1713; McCollim, 49, 52; *Dictionnaire des surintendants*, 100, 103; Clamageran, III, 87.

généralités saw considerable arrears build up by 1707, and in 1709 northern French receivers had empty chests in a number of months thanks to wider economic failure. It was not uniformly bad, and some quarterly payments from receivers at that time were forthcoming, but the picture was not a happy one. Troops had to be sent into the Bourges area in 1710 to collect the *ustencile.*[14] Matters were little better in the *pays d'états*. The *dons gratuits*, grants voted by provincial estates to the king, declined in real terms during the course of the Nine Years War and War of the Spanish Succession in Burgundy, where the estates (as in Brittany) relied more heavily on indirect taxes than on the *taille*. In Languedoc, a more buoyant province, the sums peaked in 1708 before falling and then reaching a new high in 1713. Nevertheless, a measure of the difficulties in extracting such large sums here is the lament by *intendant* Bâville in 1708 that it had once been the easiest province in which to collect the *taille*, but for several years he, too, had been forced to employ troops.[15]

Somehow further sources of wealth had to be found. This began in 1695 when the government introduced the *capitation*, a graduated poll tax on all French subjects who were to be divided into 22 classes and 569 ranks based loosely on wealth rather than birth. For efficiency's sake it was collected through the *receveurs généraux*. The crown piously announced at the time that it hoped the *capitation* would allow it to do without borrowing altogether, but this was an unrealistic gloss on a levy that challenged the fundamental basis of the relationship between king and nobility. Dropped in 1698, it was reinstated in 1701, this time not on the basis of fixed national tariffs but, when applied to commoners, as a further adjunct to the *taille*. In the *pays d'états* it was paid as a lump sum supplement to the *don gratuit*. At the same time the burden was increased by one-third over that of 1695–98, with a further 10 per cent hike for commoners in 1705, while the wealthier were taxed more heavily by local *intendants* than in the 1690s. Corporations in the urban areas tended to pay lump sums. As with the Land Tax in England, the War of the Spanish Succession saw a heavier burden of direct taxation on the French landowners through 'universalist taxes'—in terms of the proportion of their revenues they handed over to the state—compared with the later wars of the eighteenth century. The burden of the *capitation* and *taille* on commoners was greater still, threatening insurrection in Roussillon by mid-1709.[16]

[14] CCG, II, 167: Lebret to Chamillart, 11 January 1704; II, 172: Julliot to Chamillart, 15 March 1704; AN G^{7}1778, nos 67–8: Mongelas: note and *état*, 10–11 March 1707; G^{7}1785, no. 51: *assignation* workbook for 1709 Extraordinaire des Guerres; G^{7}1121: Oursin to [Le Rebours?], 18 June 1709; SHD Ya2: Voysin to Foullé, 27 February 1710.

[15] Potter, *Corps and Clienteles*, 57–61; Swann, *Provincial Power*, 165, 185; James B. Collins, *Classes, Estates and Order in Early Modern Brittany* (Cambridge, 1994), 229–48; CCG, III, 18: *mémoire* by Bâville, [April 1708].

[16] Sara Chapman, *Private Ambition and Political Alliances: The Phélypeaux de Pontchartrain Family and Louis XIV's Government, 1650–1715* (Rochester, NY, 2004), 105–13; Michael Kwass, *Privilege and the Politics of Taxation in Eighteenth-Century France: Liberté, égalité, fiscalité* (Cambridge, 2000), 45, 57, 68–72, 77; Swann, *Provincial Power*, 175; *Dictionnaire des surintendants*, 101; Paul Harsin, 'La finance et l'état jusqu'au système de Law', in Ernest Labrousse, Pierre Léon et al., *Histoire économique et sociale de la France. Tome 1: Des derniers temps de l'âge seigneurial aux préludes de l'âge industriel (1660–1789)* (Paris, 1970), 270; Depping, III, 333: Noailles to Voysin, 2 August 1709.

The following year, when most financiers were no longer in a position to provide emergency assistance to the government, a desperate Desmaretz was thrown back onto the *receveurs généraux* and needed to give them additional support in the effort to roll over debts and liberate royal revenues for the final struggle in the years 1711–13. In October 1710 the king issued a declaration imposing the *dixième*, a 10 per cent tax on all private revenues, principally those deriving from the land, property (including its value if simply owned and not leased), bonds and investments, venal offices, trade, and manual work. It was based on self-assessment, although urban corporations and various *pays d'états* 'compounded' for the tax (that is, they assessed their members/citizens individually but paid the king a single agreed sum collectively). However, in demanding that French subjects declare their assets and income it struck, in theory, a huge blow against private society and the secrecy with which people surrounded their affairs. Bâville, contemplating the possibility of a similar tax five years earlier, had stressed this point. As predicted, there was a good deal of resistance and obstruction, it proved necessary to use distraint of goods, and there might have been as much as 70 per cent under-assessment! Its national yield was around 22 million *livres* per annum, and together with the *capitation* it outstripped the size of the *taille* by the end of the reign. In at least some provinces these three main direct taxes, added together, came to exceed the yields of the *taille* under Colbert, even as the actual *taille* yields alone declined.[17] This was one of the ways that the government kept going in the War of the Spanish Succession.

On top of taxing the nobility and urban elites more than previously, the king also turned to the Church, which had long since provided grants to the monarchy. Since 1660 assistance from this quarter had come most notably in the form of *dons gratuits* voted by the quinquennial assemblies of the clergy. Some five-yearly tariffs were higher than others, generally by alternation. The Church remained autonomous in terms of how it raised the money, but under Louis XIV—as in the *pays d'états*—the clergy had little choice but to agree the overall figure the king's agents proposed. The sums were raised by a mixture of direct taxation upon their own ranks and borrowing, sometimes for over half of the annual sum. The Nine Years War saw a big increase in the Church's contribution, averaging over 6.5 million *livres* per annum, through larger *dons gratuits* and royal levies on mortmained property and wood sales. The following war saw the average fall to about 4 million *livres*, but from 1705 this was obtained predominantly by borrowing. Instead of being subject to the *capitation* and the *dixième* like the rest of society, the Church compounded in various ways for additional sums.[18] Though its contribution to royal funds greatly increased in this period, it still has to be stated that the Church was grossly undertaxed, contributing at the very most about 5 per cent of

[17] CCG, II, 277: Bâville to Chamillart, 11 October 1705; CCG, III, 319: Desmaretz to all *intendants*, early October 1710; III, 357: Desmaretz to Saint-Contest, 19 February 1711; Richard Bonney, '"Le secret de leurs familles": the Fiscal and Social Limits of Louis XIV's *Dixième*', *French History* 7 (1993), 388–405; McCollim, 279–344.

[18] Albert Cans, 'L'Organisation financière du clergé de France à l'époque de Louis XIV', *Revue d'histoire moderne et contemporaine* 16 (1911), 337–8; idem. *La contribution du clergé de France à l'impôt pendant la seconde moitié du règne de Louis XIV (1689–1715)* (Paris, 1910), 3–9, 23, 28, 45, 52–66, 79–81, 97; Michaud, 369, 381–2.

royal income and borrowing, but then Louis XIV expected it to use its wealth for the great passion of his later life, piety. In this way, royal religious devotion can be said to have severely undermined the long-term viability of the *ancien régime*.

The trajectory of the tax burden was therefore generally upwards in this period, sometimes significantly so, but its need for instant cash led the government to allow corporate bodies, most notably the Church, magistrates, and outlying provinces, to buy themselves out of future years of taxation in return for large lump sums. This was something Desmaretz later came to regret, but in 1708 he forced a buy-out of the *capitation* upon the leading magistrates, in reality a forced loan. In 1709 these so-called 'rachats' provided an important chunk of royal revenue in desperate times, though it would make the war effort in subsequent years all the harder to fund. To meet the growing gap the clergy, in 1710, also agreed to pay 24 million *livres* to remove themselves altogether from the *capitation*, and in 1711 Alsace acted similarly.[19] The direct tax base was now shrinking dangerously as the war moved towards a very hazardous denouement. The patterns were similar for indirect taxation.

THE DECLINE OF INDIRECT TAXATION

For the collection and handling of the vast bulk of indirect taxes and those revenues deriving from the *domaine*, the monarchy turned towards a group of tax farmers, who contracted for these tasks in return for a cut of the total. Most *domaine* revenues will not be considered in much detail, so deserve a few words at this point. They were split into various farms much of the time, sometimes united to the general tax farm, though they were largely controlled by the farmers general by 1700.[20] They consisted of an array of sources related both to the king's own property and to his sovereign and regal rights: forests and buildings, rivers, sea roads and ports, profits from coining, temporary royal assumptions of ecclesiastical revenues, ennoblement fees, and so on. Increasingly prominent were fees for all sorts of legal registrations, especially the *contrôle des actes des notaires*: building on earlier stamp duties, in 1693 the government insisted on the compulsory registration of all notarized documents, including marriage contracts, wills, real estate titles, and leases, and added further charges for this dubious privilege. It was, in effect, a form of levy on the propertied elites who were therefore being taxed on many more of their private contracts, and the fiscal screw was tightened further: in 1703 the *insinuations* registration fees were extended and the *centième denier* tax made movable property subject to further taxation, except for transfers in the direct line of inheritance; in 1705 the *contrôle des actes* was rolled out to encompass all agreements relating to purely commercial contracts made under private seal. The *contrôle des actes* alone was farmed in 1710 for the value of 16 million *livres*,

[19] Cans, *La contribution du clergé*, 73–6; Kwass, *Privilege and the Politics of Taxation*, 110; Michaud, 374–8; John J. Hurt, *Louis XIV and the Parlements: The Assertion of Royal Authority* (Manchester, 2002), 104; Forbonnais, II, 196, 227.

[20] CCG, II, 35: Ormesson to Chamillart, 16 April 1700.

giving a sense of the mounting burden (along with the *capitation* and *dixième*) on the elites. Yet, though one should not minimize Colbert's improvements to royal *domaine* management, *domaine* revenues amounted to no more than 10–20 per cent of total revenues, even when coin manipulation, the *contrôle des actes*, and sales of noble status were at their height under Louis XIV after the mid-1690s.[21]

What mattered considerably more were the indirect taxes on commodities. These taxes, known as *impôts de perception*, consisted predominantly of various forms of the *gabelle* salt tax, which varied regionally; the *traites*, which were external and internal customs duties; the tobacco farm; and the *aides*, a series of wholesale excise duties plus sales taxes, mostly on wines and spirits. At times these were run as separate farms, especially before Louis XIV's personal rule. The actual management of each one of these sets of taxes and duties need not detain us, for what matters in the context of this study is the overall deterioration in both the yields and the contracting system in the final two to three decades of the personal rule after considerable improvements in both respects during the period 1661–89. Traditionally it is assumed that tax farming was used in a contractual form because a risk-averse government was willing to trade a certain proportion of the total revenue in exchange for the certainty of receipts. With the tax farmers paying large sums upfront for the privilege of collection, and lending the government money, farming was superficially like direct taxation as managed by the *receveurs généraux*: a form of credit directly linked to revenue-raising.[22] But this is not by any means the whole story. Indeed, the government was prepared to shoulder a certain amount of the risk itself, for it was not just credit availability and risk aversion that made large-scale farming attractive to the monarchy. It is also noteworthy that contracts specified regular and stable revenue flows from the farmers to the monarch, and the farming system could reduce the costs of accounting, accountability, and administration. The farmers answered directly as a group to the *contrôleur général* and managed their agents by providing them with an internal system of incentives to meet their targets. Legal sanctions could be invoked here, because the relationship between the farmers and their agents was a contractual, rather than administrational, one. There was also the vital matter of asymmetric information in the relationship between the king and his subjects: what the farmers and their myriad subcontractors could provide was knowledge of consumption and trading patterns on the ground, which was unclear to the government at the best of times. By using business types, familiar with mercantile practices, the state would be more likely to acquire the levels of indirect tax income it sought.[23]

[21] Meyer, *Colbert*, 203–4; DAPS, 16–17; Jean Jacquart, 'Colbert et la réformation de la domaine', in Roland Mousnier, ed., *Un nouveau Colbert: Actes du Colloque pour le tricentenaire de la mort de Colbert* (Paris, 1985), 151–9, 164; Matthews, *Royal General Farms*, 176–8; Pierre Roux, *Les fermes d'impôts sous l'ancien régime* (Paris, 1916), 270–1, 285, 289; CCG, II, 620: Chamillart to *intendants*, [8] November 1704; III, 617: 'Mémoire', [early 1715]; Rupprecht, 100; *Dictionnaire des surintendants*, 100; Saint-Germain, *Financiers*, 162–3.

[22] Noel D. Johnson, 'Banking on the King: The Evolution of the Royal Revenue Farms in Old Regime France', *Journal of Economic History* 66 (2006), esp. 964–7.

[23] François R. Velde, 'French Public Finance between 1683 and 1726', in Fausto Piola Caselli, ed., *Government Debts and Financial Markets in Europe* (London, 2008), 160; Eugene N. White, 'From Privatized to Government-Administered Tax Collection: Tax Farming in Eighteenth-Century France', *Economic History Review* 57 (2004), 641.

Nevertheless, this system needed to be policed effectively by the courts and the monarchy, the contracts needed to be very carefully drawn up, and the deliveries of the farmers needed to be closely monitored. Central to all of this was the question of indemnification of the farmers if circumstances altered, and in the final great wars of the reign the environment was indeed constantly changing. The classic form of contract known as a 'forfait' lasted for up to seven years, and it set out the amount the crown expected the farmers to deliver and the amount that they could claim as rake-off. Any losses would be borne by the farmers themselves. This was a system that encouraged rigorous application to duty and efficiency of administration. The lease, known as a *bail*, was referred to by the name of an *adjudicataire général*, a 'straw man' drawn from the ranks of junior financiers or from the *contrôleur général*'s own staff, who had ostensibly signed the contract. Somewhat different was a *régie intéressée*, a more 'controlled' form of arrangement. This was a partnership between farmers and monarchy in which remuneration for collection was proportional to receipts or was awarded at a rising rate, these contracts essentially being based upon penalties for undershooting the agreed yield and bonuses for exceeding it. A full-blown 'régie' saw farmers get commission for their management costs, the interest on any sums they advanced in the course of collections, and for the actual payments; they did not benefit from any surplus collected, but neither did they have to advance huge sums for the privilege of taking on the contract. It was a compact only to be used *in extremis*, when nobody reliable could be persuaded to take on a risky *forfait*. In the second half of Louis XIV's personal rule, for various reasons, the monarchy experimented with a series of different arrangements, but was moving towards assuming an increasingly greater proportion of the risks and potential losses itself. By the mid-eighteenth century, in fact, the crown had, as a rule, come to share some of the costs and profits of the farmers using formulae that were agreed in variations on the farming contracts described above.

During the 1660s Colbert sought to pull together more centralized syndicates of farmers who could not only be handled and monitored more easily by the Finance Ministry and the Conseil Royal des finances, but could also enjoy greater security and therefore greater credit than their predecessors, who had lived a much more precarious existence under Fouquet and the earlier *Surintendants*. The contracts for farming the king's revenues were awarded, before and after 1661, on the basis of a form of competitive tender, at least in theory, though results were largely stitched up beforehand. At least Colbert introduced an improved auction system: over the six months between the announcement of the auction and the government's decision, he worked hard to form various companies that would make bids against each other and really pressurized financiers. The government then negotiated a lease price for the various farms that were being grouped together for the *forfait*, and Colbert strenuously avoided making further concessions to lessees after the signature.[24] It took several attempts to bolt the various *fermes* together, and the pressures of the Dutch War and subsequent wars provoked further divisions of the contract again. Nevertheless, by 1683 there was a clearer line of accountability between the Trésor

[24] White, 'Privatized', 642; Clément, *Histoire de Colbert*, I, 216–18; Roux, *Les fermes*, 195–6.

royal and the *impôts de perception*, especially as the 1681 Fauconnet lease created the first recognizable 'ferme générale des droits et domaines du roi', gathering together the *gabelles de France*, the *petites gabelles*, the *cinq grosses fermes*, the *aides et entrées*, and the *domaines*, thus prefiguring the powerful *ferme générale* of the eighteenth century. The 1687 lease split the farms up, but they were reunited again in the Pointeau lease of 1691, the contract which really founded the *ferme générale* in a form that lasted pretty much up to the Revolution.[25]

The administration of the farms was increasingly passed on from one lease to the next, and by 1691 the organization was clearly established: there were now forty associates, or 'cautions', each investing 450,000 *livres*, giving a total advance of 18 million *livres*, a figure that would be demanded at each lease until 1717. Some of the farmers general would borrow and pay their investors with some of their permitted 'taxation'—the expenses rake-off totalling 6 *deniers* for every *livre* handled (i.e., 2.5 per cent). Returns on the initial investment were around 10 per cent in the era of Louis XIV, climbing to over 20 per cent by the 1730s, and there was a lot of abuse, especially by local agents of the farms. Unlike the *recettes générales*, the essential characteristic of the *ferme générale* was that it acted as a consortium, gathered together under private agreement between the participants, and the dealings amongst the directors were highly secret. By the 1690s they had central coffers and an official central headquarters in Paris, the clear mark of a para-royal outfit.[26]

The consolidation of many taxes into a single farm might have made matters more complicated, but it brought more investment in the tax system, and greater security of investment, which for a while boosted revenues.[27] But then in the 1690s those revenues started to decrease. Moreover, the government faced a serious principal-agent problem with the cartelized system that had evolved, for it was hard for central government officials to scrutinize the farmers' activity and it was equally difficult to discipline them, given that competitors for their places in the company and even for the overall contract had already been rejected as less proficient. It was even harder to keep their subcontractors and agents in line. There had thus grown up a more stable and sustainable system but one in which there was considerable asymmetry of information and rent-seeking. When the government began to adjust leases on a regular basis it gave the whip hand more and more to the farmers, producing a greater degree of moral hazard that was only restrained in practice by choosing farmers general on whom a *contrôleur général* could personally depend. Given the extreme demands of the Nine Years War and the even greater ones of the War of the Spanish Succession this was by no means always possible.

As time went on, the yields from the various farms, and the leases that were negotiated, declined from their peak of just under 70 million *livres* in 1690. By this time the farms were beginning to show signs of strain, having been unwisely divided in the 1687 lease and negotiated at that time for an unsustainable amount. Notwith-

[25] Roux, *Les fermes*, 206–14, 262, 268, 278–84; Matthews, *Royal General Farms*, 47–50, 52, 54–5.

[26] Roux, *Les fermes*, 220–7, 248–54; DAPS, 57–62; Beaulieu, *Les gabelles*, 74, 77, 117; Rupprecht, 107.

[27] White, 'Privatized', 642; Johnson, 'Banking on the King', 965–6.

standing this, in 1691 Pontchartrain scrapped the 1687 lease prematurely and took a fateful step: he awarded the lease to the Pointeau company for a still excessive 61 million *livres* per annum, but in doing so turned the *fermes* into a semi-*régie*. The lessees, anticipating declining receipts in wartime, had warned him that the price was too high for them to deliver in practice, but he insisted on this level in order to intimidate France's enemies by announcing a high lease value, and secretly promised the farmers diminutions of royal demands and additional compensation according to circumstances. But by the fifth year of the lease a deficit of over 17 million *livres* had accumulated, causing the crown to divert money from other sources to compensate the farmers general. At the same time, the use of receipts from the *aides* and *gabelles* to back the issue of more and more *rentes* on the Paris Hôtel de ville (state bonds) further depressed the amount of disposable cash from the farms that the monarchy could devote to war expenditure, and this charge on the farms continued to increase up to 1713. By the end of the lease in 1697 the crown had lost a total of 62 million *livres*, the equivalent of a whole year's revenue.[28]

It was no better in subsequent years. The shortfalls in the Templier lease of 1697–1703, the contract for which was for 55 million *livres* per annum in peacetime and 52 million *livres* in war, led the monarchy to grant 4 million *livres* of compensation and rewards to the farmers, not least because they had had to grant discounts on deliveries from their sub-farmers owing to falling yields from the *aides* and *domaines*. The tobacco farm was also removed from the lease in the course of its run. By the 1700s the farms were burdened with charges worth 59 per cent of their proceeds. This had happened because of a disastrous attempt to make the Templier lease solvent in 1698 and the drawing of funds out of the Templier lease to compensate the farmers of the previous Pointeau lease. Consequently, in 1701 France started the War of the Spanish Succession with the *fermes générales* mortgaged at an extreme level and its net revenues depressed. Just at this moment the *fermes générales* were also ordered to cover around 6 million *livres* of losses racked up by one of the military treasurers. As the war proceeded, farm takings soon fell thanks to declining domestic consumption arising from uncertainty, falling sales abroad because of currency revaluations, and Allied captures of French ships trading with the Americas. From May 1703 spending orders drawn on the resources of the *fermes générales* were bouncing regularly, and the farmers were failing to deliver funds to the bankers. This was despite, and indeed partly because of, various increases in the duties, charges, and taxes in their fiscal basket since 1701.[29]

The 1703 Ferreau lease was negotiated in the late summer and early autumn, at a time when various sub-farmers seem to have crashed, reflecting the failure of their revenue fields. The new price was set at a much reduced 41.7 million *livres*, which was only a weak 37.6 million *livres* in 1700 specie prices; the *cinq grosses*

[28] Roux, *Les fermes*, 262–3, 269–70, 274; Beaulieu, *Les gabelles*, 72. Chamillart (Esnault, I, 101: 'Mémoire...', [1694]) described the farms as already in *régie* in the mid-1690s.

[29] Roux, *Les fermes*, 273, 281; Forbonnais, II, 112, 138; CCG, II, 129: des Cassaux to Chamillart, 14 November 1702; AN G^{7}1775, no. 242: demand for payment by the company of the *vivres* of Italy, [May 1703]; G^{7}1120: Bernard to Chamillart, 27 May and 28 September 1703; *Dictionnaire des surintendants*, 103; Clamageran, III, 80–3.

fermes (main customs) were amputated from the contract; and the deal was struck for the limited time of only three years instead of six to seven. This gave the farmers, or at least those who did not intend to stay long in the *fermes générales*, little incentive to manage the business in a sustainable fashion, as the race was clearly now on to stay solvent and profit as much as possible before the clouds of war started to rain more heavily still upon their world. And Chamillart had obviously had little choice but to agree to this short, stunted lease. It was twice prolonged for another year, as a slightly different lease after 1706, because nobody could be persuaded to agree to a longer-term contract. And though this ran in the end up to September 1708, in retrospect this can only have been because Chamillart further increased all duties by 10 per cent in March 1705, at least allowing overall income to avoid complete collapse. For by 1704 the particular yields from some provinces were already in free fall, with the Bordeaux *ferme* bureau in ruins owing to a terrible vintage and moribund trade. The proto-economist Boisguilbert provided evidence of staggering contraction of consumption in the shape of the collapse of a good number of inns. Even the ruthless *gabelle* agents were taking a double hit: they had to sell salt on credit, and there was a rapidly rising incidence of salt-smuggling across internal borders. By 1710 this 'faux-saunage' had reached such gargantuan proportions that it had produced an almost total contraction of *gabelle* revenue and involved organized criminal parties of royal troops sometimes several hundred strong! By 1708 the *fermes générales* were bringing in only around 37 million *livres*, just over half the sum of the late 1680s, while the king owed the 1703–6 company 18 million *livres* in indemnities. These sorts of indemnities had become so systematic and automatic that they amounted to the king assuming nearly all of the risks and the farmers pocketing whatever they could. It was plausibly alleged two decades later that the indemnities may even have encouraged the farmers to allow their losses to build up because they could then get a more secure income from the crown in compensation.[30] The huge indemnities were almost certainly responsible for some of the fiscal slackness that pushed up borrowing and further indebted the crown.

Much as government ministers were loath to put the *fermes* under management in the form of a *régie*, by mid-1708 it made little sense to continue with the fiction of a contracted 'forfait', and in any case nobody came forward to take on the main *fermes générales* basket. This may have been because the farmers were so awash with Mint bills they could no longer use to back their debts that they decided the game was no longer—in its present form—worth the candle. Consequently the crown agreed with a fresh company of farmers that they would deliver 37 million *livres* per annum, with no liability for losses and, instead of profits, would obtain a cut of 6 *deniers* for every *livre* processed, or 2.5 per cent. But with the economic collapse of 1709 yields plummeted further. As Desmaretz despairingly reported to the

[30] AN $G^7$1775, no. 278: Pleneuf to Le Rebours, 21 October 1703; Roux, *Les fermes*, 281–5; Beaulieu, *Les gabelles*, 77; Forbonnais, II, 164; CCG, II, 172: Julliot to Chamillart, 15 March 1704; II, 538: Boisguilbert to [Chamillart?], 9 July 1704; III, 315: Desmaretz to several *intendants*, 21 September 1710.

king in late August 1709, for four months all commercial circulation had ceased and nobody was paying either the *taille* or *capitation*; the people 'are not buying any salt, they are not drinking any wine. From this the *fermes* are dropping and they are reduced this year below two-thirds of their ordinary value.' Moreover, there were a lot of disturbances surrounding the tax farmers' activity, and Desmaretz expected salt-smuggling to further depress *fermes* revenues to half their nominal target. In 1710–12 there was a further drop in yields. With little prospect of anybody now stepping in to take on a renewed farming contract the arrangements for the *régie* were renewed by Desmaretz every July until the end of the war. This undependable, short-term rolling of the contract had the great drawbacks that the farmers' credit-ratings were lower and the earmark orders on the *fermes* (now often being given several years in advance) became less dependable as instruments. But there was little alternative. Only after the conflict was over was a retrospective *forfait* lease concluded with the Nerville company, worth only 36 to 44 million *livres* (depending on the year) and dating back to 1709, but this was a formal *régie intéressée* because the king took the profits for the 1714–15 year.[31] In reality it was more a revenue-recovery 'affaire extraordinaire' contract than a normal lease.

By the War of the Spanish Succession the monarchy was therefore once again turning to some of the most hazardous forms of tax-collecting arrangements and contracts for sizeable parts of royal regular revenues. Nevertheless, hyperbolic comparisons with the era of the Thirty Years War would paint an exaggerated picture of the situation: the para-royal revenue systems were still more robust than they had been at the start of Louis XIV's personal rule, and were supported by more reliable means of securing the king's will than before. Whatever their deficiencies the revenue structures were better able, at least, to support the king's borrowing and this, in the end, is what he really needed. Even so, the limitations of the tax-gathering system as it evolved after 1690 and ministerial mismanagement—piling on the 'wrong' sort of tax increases, making reformist efforts too late, and allowing huge levels of compensation and indemnity to the main tax gatherers—pushed up the size of the royal debt and increased the costs of sustaining the war effort.

[31] McCollim, 37; Roux, *Les fermes*, 287, 291, 294; CCG, III, 603: 'Mémoire', 26 August 1709.

4

Borrowing to the Limit

The deterioration of the major revenues and their ever more unreliable collection combined with the soaring costs of the war effort to push the monarchy deeper and deeper into debt. By the end of the seventeenth century the credit mechanisms and facilities available to the French monarchy were certainly more sophisticated and robust than they had ever been, but they were inadequate for the needs of the War of the Spanish Succession. One of the characteristics of the age was a growing resort to proxy credit, owing to the monarchy's shaky credit ratings. The king squeezed as much credit, especially short-term, as he could out of his fisco-financiers, as explained in the General Introduction; however, he also demanded that major corporate bodies of the realm borrow large sums that they would then lend on to the crown. More traditionally, the *rentes* on the Paris Hôtel de ville—annuities that were the closest thing France had to state-issued bonds—were still sold on a large scale but for diminishing returns to the crown. The same can be said for the selling of offices, which reached an *ancien régime* peak in the final decades of Louis XIV's reign. Altogether, these sources could only make up some of the shortfall in royal revenues so further manipulations—especially of the currency—were considered necessary. As the global scale of royal borrowing increased, the money available for the very expenditure that was driving the reckless exploitation of the country became more expensive, not least, as we shall see, because the monarchy proved to be an unreliable debtor and financial arbitrator/regulator, with insufficient respect for the needs of all but its most indispensable creditors.

MAJOR DEBT FLOTATION BY THE REVENUE FISCO-FINANCIERS

A great deal of credit was obtained from the *receveurs généraux* and farmers general through the formal advances and stopgap credit they provided. It was an intrinsic part of their system to use credit for high proportions of the funds they handled, but as the revenue situation deteriorated their debts became larger and were prolonged. The magnitude of the formal advances to the crown can be seen in the way 72 per cent of the 1708 revenue had already been consumed in advance by September 1707. Such levels could adversely affect fisco-financiers' credit if they could not pledge sufficient collateral, and with advances totalling 65 million *livres* in July 1709 the credit of most of them collapsed. That year Desmaretz had been forced to assign over 53 million *livres* of expenditure (out of 199 million) to revenues dating as far into the future as 1717. It remained a cornerstone of his strategy in the final phase of the war to anticipate many revenues up to four years in advance. He was willing to pay 10 per cent interest to get these advances.[1] Advances from the fisco-financiers were achieved in large part by them borrowing through the issue of promissory notes or bearer bills: the *billets* on named individuals and *promesses par anticipation* on various sources. As the global size of these issues increased in a context of falling revenues, it became extremely difficult for the fisco-financiers to honour their settlements or roll them over at a modest price. There was some direct borrowing in this manner by the Trésor royal as the named debtor, particularly in 1709 when *Garde* Montargis approached merchants and currency dealers, but this was rare compared with the debts contracted by the wider fisco-financier community to feed the crown's needs.[2]

Under Colbert the evolving *fermes générales* had become something of a corporate intermediary lender to the crown, with the farmers pledging the funds from their own activities and their own wealth as collateral, issuing *promesses* and redeemable annuity bonds (*rentes*) worth 5 per cent. Such borrowing was organized by the farmers from 1674 to 1684 through the Caisse des emprunts, in which much private family money, often related to noble and bourgeois dowries, was invested. The Caisse offered an apparently excellent short-term location to park idle money for up to three months, but it became steadily less reliable at redeeming the loans and around the time of Colbert's death there had been more or less a run on its doors. Between 1685 and 1702 the farmers general continued to fund short-term state needs in a similar way, though without the formal 'front' organization of the Caisse, issuing *billets des fermes* (usually of nine to twelve months' maturity) that were tradable. One of the aims of the high 1691 Pointeau lease for the farms was to set an asset level so high it would raise the creditworthiness of the farmers, but the declining yields forced the *fermiers* into selling huge numbers of *billets* merely to meet their contractual obligations to the king! By the end of this lease in 1697 at least 50 million *livres* were owed by the farms, acting as a drag on their receipts for several years.[3]

The situation would only get worse in the next war. Chamillart tried to provide some collective solidity to the farms' credit by re-establishing the Caisse des emprunts in 1702, and there is no doubt that this was a worthy attempt to ensure the debts of the farms were seen as liabilities transcending any particular lease. But the generous 8 per cent interest on offer, if justifiable for such short- to medium-term investments, suggested that the farms were intrinsically a little unreliable. At first there was a great deal of confidence in the Caisse, but the first dent in it came in September 1704 when, to forestall possible panic after the Blenheim defeat, a seven-month suspension of repayments was imposed by Chamillart. Strangely, the

[1] CCG, II, 475: 'Mémoire' by Chamillart, 17 September 1707; III, 603: 'Mémoire', 26 August 1709; III, 454: Desmaretz to Voysin, 8 and 12 August 1712; Forbonnais, II, 196, 238; Esnault, II, 238: Desmaretz to Chamillart, 14 May 1714.

[2] AN G^{7}1098: Montargis to Desmaretz, 27 May 1709.

[3] Guy Antonetti, 'Colbert et le crédit public', in Roland Mousnier, ed., *Un nouveau Colbert. Actes du Colloque pour le tricentenaire de la mort de Colbert* (Paris, 1985), 191–8, 207, 209; George T. Matthews, *The Royal General Farms in Eighteenth-Century France* (New York, 1958), 14, 55.

unease did not turn into a collapse in confidence, perhaps because there was an increase in the interest rate to 10 per cent in March 1705, but more likely because depositors did not yet realize what a dangerous omen the stop on reimbursements had been. The wider financial public of Louis XIV's later reign was still a rather young beast with little experience of major defaults and was learning slowly. Though intended as a short-term vehicle for deposits, the Caisse after 1704 settled, through force majeure, into the role of a long-term savings bank from which withdrawals in cash were not easily made but where high rates of interest were paid regularly. Unfortunately this broke down at the start of 1709 owing to the cumulative effect of shrinking farm yields, and even interest ceased to be paid for almost two years. But the monarchy preserved the Caisse from total discredit by adding interest to the capital, and some reimbursements began again in mid-1713. That it preserved the confidence of the increasingly wary public up to this point in time is remarkable, but it did so partly because there had been no announcements of any long-term intention on the government's part to hold on to the money. In a rather circular argument that only makes sense if people were content to leave their money there for years on end, one Parisian bourgeois noted at the time that everybody trusted the Caisse and confidence had been retained because it was seen as 'the sacred depository of all the families' of Paris. Prestige seems to have trumped other considerations of creditworthiness, in an early example of fashionable society shaping market conditions. All the same, in the final years of the War of the Spanish Succession *promesses* of the Caisse were now being issued at colossal discounts of up to 80 per cent, as the farms were labouring under advance hypothecations worth well over a whole year's total revenue target. In 1715, with debts now over 140 million *livres*, the announcement of a long-term, staggered, and very limited schedule of capital repayment finally destroyed confidence.[4] For all its problems, though, the Caisse had continued to work throughout the war years because the government took very seriously the need to shore up faith in the credit of the farms by meeting interest payments without grotesque manipulations. Some sources were clearly too valuable to wreck, until peacetime at least.

Eventually, too, the burden of war debt would destroy confidence in the borrowing structures and instruments of the *receveurs généraux*, who also provided an essential component of crown borrowing, but they too weathered the actual years of conflict. As we know, the receivers as individuals, or several banded together without an official structure, had been emitting *billets* on themselves for some time before the War of the Spanish Succession, and by 1708 a large number were in circulation. So many in fact that Desmaretz had wisely been planning to allow the receivers in 1709 to keep as many of their receipts as possible to pay off these notes and maintain their credit facility (thus boosting confidence), until the economic catastrophes of that year meant this could not be allowed.[5] Later

[4] Rupprecht, 132; Vuitry, 173–4, 185–7; CCG, II, 514: 'Rapport autographe de M. Desmaretz', 3 May 1706; III, 681: 'Compte rendu de M. Desmaretz au Régent', 1716; Forbonnais, II, 141, 151, 219; Malet, *Comptes*, 110; AN G[7]655: memorandum from a Paris bourgeois to Desmaretz, [1711] (quotation); Pierre Roux, *Les fermes d'impôts sous l'ancien régime* (Paris, 1916), 301; Seligmann, 114.

[5] CCG, III, 176: Desmaretz to La Croix, 24 June 1709.

in 1709 Voysin informed Desmaretz that he needed at least 25 million *livres* to cover the winter-quarters period for the army, and to produce this the Finance Minister in November formed a consortium of twelve *receveurs généraux* who would issue interest-bearing *billets* backed by a number of revenue sources. Known by the name of its principal cashier, the Caisse Legendre began operations on 1 January 1710. It was, in part, a *régie* for several 'affaires extraordinaires'—levies on the privileged elites—with the *receveurs* in the group not receiving any profits from these sources, merely expenses and the costs of any advances made. As well as the proceeds of these revenues, their central coffers were to receive any other funds Desmaretz could pour in, including all funds from *all* the *recettes générales* for a short period of time. This accordingly turned the Caisse Legendre into both a form of government deposit bank, backed by a variety of comparatively healthy sources, and an intermediary for earmarking funds, standing between the Trésor royal and the military/naval paymasters. It was a state-organized credit syndicate based on the most solid revenues in the kingdom, collectively responsible for managing a large proportion of credit relations with suppliers and lenders. Indeed, bankers now tended to pass loans into the Caisse Legendre's coffers rather than directly to the military paymasters. *Promesses* and *billets* of the Caisse, because they enjoyed a great deal of credibility, were distributed by the Trésor royal to borrowers among the public but also to spenders such as the Extraordinaire des Guerres. Had a body like the Caisse Legendre been brought together in, say, 1702 in order to provide more solidly backed advances to the monarch—and such consortia did become a more regular feature of the fisco-financier landscape under Louis XV—then the damaging expedients of the following years might have been avoided or been undertaken on a smaller, less detrimental scale.

Altogether, the Caisse Legendre issued notes to the tune of 400 million *livres* over the next five years, and on top of this individual *receveurs généraux* inside and outside the Caisse syndicate continued to emit *billets* on themselves. Taken together with the introduction of the *dixième* in the same year, 1710, the growing reliance on the Caisse reveals a reorientation of crown borrowing away from the military paymasters and the bankers, and away from the *fermes générales* too, towards the direct taxation machinery which was under tighter political and administrative control. Desmaretz also protected the Caisse from the need to issue too many *billets*, and by the king's death the debt liabilities of the *receveurs généraux* were only one-fifth of those of the *fermes générales*. Nevertheless, their credit did not survive the reign. For the first few years the Caisse's credit and the value of its *billets* held up well, traded for discounts of only 10 per cent in 1712, and in 1713 these *billets* were considered far more reliable than specific *assignations* on revenue sources. But by January 1715 discounting had increased to 18 per cent, and there was too much reliance upon *billets* being traded in the market beyond their maturity dates for a further period of time, for the funds with which to redeem them were shrinking almost before the *contrôleur général*'s eyes. Within a matter of weeks there was a notable drop in the sums the Caisse Legendre was passing over to the military paymasters, and when the electors of Cologne and Bavaria demanded the payment of subsidy arrears in real cash in April 1715 the Caisse could no longer cope.[6] Again, though, like the Caisse des emprunts the Caisse Legendre had at least got Louis XIV through the last years of the war.

RESPECTABLE BORROWING: THE *RENTES* AND THE GREAT CORPORATIONS OF THE REALM

Although the French monarchy depended upon short-term credit, which as we have seen often became medium-term, it also needed an anchor of longer-term debt that conformed more with the cultural norms and expectations of wider propertied society, and which also had the advantage of avoiding repayment of the capital as far as possible. This longer-term credit was provided to a significant degree through the *rentes*, annuities floated on the credibility of the Paris Hôtel de ville and backed very largely by proceeds from the *gabelles* and *aides* duties that the crown funnelled—as a priority—to the city hall for paying the interest.[7] In the second half of Louis XIV's personal rule the *rentes* came in three main formats: as *rentes perpétuelles* that provided a set rate of interest and were heritable; as *rentes viagères*, life annuities, self-extinguishing on the death of the holder, which provided fixed interest; and as a variant of *rentes viagères* in the form of *tontines*. To these were added in June 1713 term *rentes* lasting thirteen years, which were, unusually, backed by the proceeds of the *taille*; and in July 1704 and December 1705 two *rentes* flotations in which the bonds were really lottery tickets, with the holders getting interest but also gambling on the possibility of being drawn for reimbursement.[8] The three main categories of *rentes* involved total alienation of one's capital, for they were reimbursable only at the will of the king. Moreover, they were very clumsy and could be surprisingly costly instruments to use as the largest component of the royal debt.

To begin with the *tontines*, these were, in the words of David Weir, 'a form of life annuity in which survivors benefit from the deaths of other participants', for as subscribers died their annuities were transferred over to, and compounded with, those of the survivors until in the end the issue was extinguished with the death of the last holder. It was a genre of borrowing that was extremely costly to the government and very lucrative for the last survivors, and in the Nine Years War, beginning with the first French state issue in 1689 and then a second subscription in 1696–97, *tontines* brought in 6.5 million *livres* of capital. This was at a cost of between 5 and 12.5 per cent to the state in interest on each purchase, which as people died off increased as a percentage

[6] Sources for this and the previous paragraph: Forbonnais, II, 213–14, 225–6, 258, 272; McCollim, 277–8, 362; AN G[7]1041: Papillon and Alleon (Paris bankers) to Desmaretz, 3 April 1715; G[7]1787, no. 281: Voysin to Desmaretz, 10 January 1712; G[7]1788, no. 18: Gallois brothers to Desmaretz, 16 August 1713; no. 271: 'Compte du S. Demeuves…', 13 January 1715; no. 215: memorandum by La Jonchère, 15 April 1715.

[7] Mathilde Moulin, 'Les rentes sur l'Hôtel de Ville de Paris sous Louis XIV', *Histoire, économie et société* 17 (1998), 625.

[8] Forbonnais, II, 228; Howard J. Shakespeare, *France: The Royal Loans—Les Emprunts Royaux, 1689–1789* (Shrewsbury, 1986), 61–79.

reaching the surviving holders (for the interest pot remained the same size). It was not surprising, therefore, that there was only a single issue in the War of the Spanish Succession, in May 1709, linked to the sequestration of private imported bullion and worth 4 million *livres* of capital. This was fairly good compensation (and costly for the crown) as a form of appeasement for an arbitrary seizure. Less expensive were the standard *rentes viagères*, first issued by the state in 1693, carrying variable interest rates depending on the age of the holder, but with even those under twenty-five receiving over 7 per cent per annum. There were only two further issues during Louis XIV's reign, in 1698 and March 1701, no doubt because like *tontines* they were expensive—holders over the age of seventy at the time of subscription got 14 per cent per annum from the 1693 flotation![9] Though *rentes viagères* became a central, indeed lethal, pillar of state borrowing under Louis XV and Louis XVI, under the *grand roi* they were small beer compared with the *rentes perpétuelles*.

Rentes perpétuelles were issued for three basic purposes: as low interest-bearing, long-term, sustained investment opportunities that were created periodically by the monarchy for the public; as higher interest *rentes* to convert various forms of short-term debt; and as lower interest *rentes* into which older, higher-interest *rentes* were transmuted. Naturally, the use of *rentes* for such conversion purposes was unpopular and did little to aid the 'crédit' of the king. Colbert had detested the tying-up of spare capital in the *rentes* and retrenched their use in his first decade in control of the finances, but he had been forced to sell more during the Dutch War and if the scale of them remained manageable until his death, it increased with a vengeance thereafter. Between 1683 and 1699 over 617 million *livres*-worth of capital was pulled in, and by 1715 the state liability of *rentes perpétuelles* had skyrocketed to perhaps nine times the size of that in 1683, representing roughly 1.4 billion *livres* of invested capital. This was double the amount of capital investment that had existed in 1699.[10] In the War of the Spanish Succession Chamillart alone launched twenty-five separate flotations we know of, and Desmaretz another twenty-four (though a lot of these were conversion operations). *Rentes* in the Nine Years War offered interest, in some cases, of up to 8.33 per cent per annum, while in the Spanish Succession war, rates were between 6.35 per cent and 7.15 per cent. This might seem an improvement, but the lower interest rates were negated by the government's failure to sell the *rentes* at anywhere near their full face value. An edict of October 1713 admitted that many fresh *rente* issues launched on the market since 1702 had brought in less than one-third of the hoped-for investment, a marked deterioration in the attractiveness of such instruments since the 1690s. Arms suppliers, whose bills the government met by giving them *rentes* to sell on, had to accept

[9] David Weir, 'Tontines, Public Finance, and Revolution in France and England, 1688–1789', *Journal of Economic History* 49 (1989), 96, 106, 115; Shakespeare, *France*, 52, 54; Philippe Sagnac, 'Le crédit de l'État et les banquiers à la fin du XVIIe et au commencement du XVIIIe siècle', *Revue d'histoire moderne et contemporaine* 10 (1908), 257–8; Moulin, 'Les rentes', 630.

[10] DAPS, 21; Moulin, 'Les rentes', 626–8; Pierre Clément, *Histoire de Colbert et de son administration* (2nd edn, 2 vols, Paris, 1874), I, 154–72; Sagnac, 'Le crédit de l'État', 259–60; Clamageran, III, 110–11. The total of extant *rentes* represented about 1.4 billion *livres* of *original* investment capital (maybe more).

55 per cent losses on them when they offered them to their own creditors or the market. In other words, to get *rentes* off its hands the government might have to accept a write-down of two-thirds of their value by speculative investors, many of whom were the government's revenue officers and suppliers! It was not surprising that it might take anything up to five years for an issue to be taken up, even with heavy discounts.[11]

That such stable bonds could be so decried needs explanation, and it can be found in an understanding of the sclerotic, cumbersome nature of the *rentes*. To begin with, the payment administration could not cope with a large number of small investors (300 *livres* was the minimum investment from 1689). The interest payment system was extraordinarily bureaucratic, and only got worse in this respect after 1706. So too was the title procedure: it was a laborious business to register ownership of a *rente* on the Hôtel de ville, involving a great deal of shuffling of documents backwards and forwards between notaries, their clients, and city hall. Furthermore, while *rentes* could be transferred or pledged as collateral for borrowing and eventually handed over, the original holders (and those who had loaned them money to buy the *rentes* in the first place) had a right of recall over them, unless they waived this right. *Rentes* were considered forms of immovable property, and thus subject to regulations similar to those for landed property (and burdensome legal fees) when it came to transmissibility. Thus the worrisome legal status of *rentes* made their resale and pledging as collateral less than easy and immobilized capital. This helps to explain why some people preferred to hold on to thoroughly discredited instruments, such as the *billets* (bills) of the Extraordinaire des Guerres in 1708, rather than see their capital disappear into perpetual inaccessibility through conversion into what, at first sight, appeared a more reliable credit device. It would not be going too far to argue that the root problem of French state credit under Louis XIV was the failure to overhaul the fundamental characteristics of *rentes* and make them a more flexible, diverse body of bonds. They remained illiquid instruments that could be traded only with difficulty, meaning that a vast proportion of French investment capital, worth somewhere around 1 billion *livres* during the War of the Spanish Succession, was tied up and could not easily be used to purchase other forms of debt or employed in exchange for cash or commodities. It is not surprising that the prospect of short-term securities being converted into such illiquid bonds spooked the financial markets on several occasions. In 1710 these conversions provoked a collapse of confidence in the government's appropriation orders—the *assignations*—since people, seeing how many other instruments were being converted into *rentes*, feared that royal revenue assignment instruments would go the same way too.[12] Nor, for similar reasons, did naturalized foreigners and well-off commoners and *anoblis* appreciate being compelled to buy or accept *rentes* in

[11] Shakespeare, *France*, 52–6, 61–79; Moulin, 'Les rentes', 626, 643; Forbonnais, II, 250–1; Esnault, I, 99: Président de Harlay to Chamillart, 4 February 1702; AN G^{7}1784, no. 34: claim by Titon, September 1709.

[12] Forbonnais, II, 190, 233; Shakespeare, *France*, 52; Moulin, 'Les rentes', 632–41.

forced loan drives in 1709–10. The effort only drove money underground as people sought to conceal their modest prosperity for when the assessors came calling.[13]

As it was, the *rentes* had become less and less appealing, even for those who would have wanted such a product. Despite having to sell most at a discount, the government still held interest rates on the *rentes* at what was an artificially low level, given their weakness as an instrument. The rate of discounting gradually worsened over the course of the war, reflecting both the nature of the instrument and the falling yields of those revenues hypothecated to the Hôtel de ville for paying the interest. Much as the government for a while had stopped paying out interest on the *promesses* of the Caisse des emprunts, half of all annuity payments were cancelled in 1709 and 1710, and by 1713 two years' worth of arrears had built up.[14] Moreover, Chamillart and Desmaretz both inflicted 'haircuts' on the holders of *rentes*—unilateral reductions in their interest-bearing capacity either through simple rate-cutting or conversion into new lower-yielding *rentes*. Prior to demobilization, in late 1713 and 1714 the army was sustained at the very end of the war partly through draconian cuts in annuity payouts totalling 14 million *livres*.[15] Nevertheless, the reduction of 1 per cent of the interest offered went down like a lead balloon abroad, especially amongst foreigners who had already chosen (for whatever reason) to convert ruined fisco-financier bills into *rentes*. The official excuse for the reductions was that usurers had been buying up *rentes* from their holders at absurdly low prices because of the stop on payments, a claim that had some truth to it, but for the most part this move hit people who had originally priced the *rentes* fairly at their true investment value in hazardous circumstances.[16]

The monarchy's failure to deal fairly with those who had had the courage to buy unreliably backed and rather illiquid instruments was one reason among many that a lot of investors preferred to lend to corporate bodies other than the Paris Hôtel de ville, the Caisse des emprunts, and the Caisse Legendre. And other corporate bodies were certainly able to raise capital at lower rates of interest. One estimate puts the loans contracted by provincial estates on behalf of the monarchy between 1689 and 1715 at some 55 million *livres*. The crown leaned on the estates to float loans as a process of pure proxy credit-raising, but the estates and urban municipalities would also borrow to pay for local logistical support for the armed forces and to cover some of the tax they owed the monarchy. This included buying themselves out of the *capitation* in late 1708 through a loan worth six times their annual obligations for this tax. Depending on the health of their provincial credit networks and head treasurer, provincial estates in the *pays d'états* could provide stable, long term borrowing on a funded basis. In the early eighteenth century they were also extending the pool of investors upon whom they could or were willing to draw. Their issues of *rentes* (like those on the Paris city hall) were largely guaranteed by

[13] DAPS, 21; Forbonnais, II, 199; Sagnac, 'Le crédit de l'État', 259; CCG, III, 293: Archbishop of Rouen to Desmaretz, 9 June 1710.

[14] Rupprecht, 128–9; Vuitry, 34; McCollim, 37; Shakespeare, *France*, 73, 79.

[15] CCG, III, 680: 'Compte rendu de M. Desmaretz au Régent', 1716.

[16] AN $G^7$1788, no. 48: Bonot to Desmaretz, at Ghent, 29 December 1713; Vuitry, 39. Similar 'haircuts' had been forced upon *rente*-holders in 1697–1700.

local revenues whose administration and levels (up to a point) they controlled, and their rights to tax their local areas might be expanded by the crown to improve their lending security. They—and the municipal authorities borrowing as the leaders of some of the bigger provincial cities like Lyon—made their payments very reliably for the most part, although by the early 1710s worries were growing about the number of years' revenue being mortgaged in advance, such was the mounting scale of their debt issues. It seems largely correct that the provincial estates could borrow at lower levels of interest than both the Paris Hôtel de ville and the fisco-financiers, at around the traditionally acceptable 5–6 per cent level.[17]

However, this was not always the case, and money became more expensive for estates too, especially in the course of the Spanish Succession war. The estates of Languedoc (and the assembly of Provence) were channels for Genoese loans to France on several occasions from 1672, though much more so from the early 1690s. But this came at a rising cost, reflecting not least Italian worries about French currency manipulations that were affecting the exchange rate of the *livre tournois*, the need for such loans to be kept secret, and Genoese hostility to France. The loans of 1702 and 1707 accordingly seem to have been contracted at 7 per cent and 7.5 per cent for a limited period of several years, though in practice the final repayment instalments of the 1707 loan, worth 1 million *livres* in total at flotation, were put off until 1755! Lyon too, with its tentacular reaches into northern Italy, borrowed as an urban corporation in Genoa (as did Provençal towns): this was most notably in 1695, 1704, 1708, and 1709, for periods of eleven, twelve, or fifteen years at 6 per cent per annum each time, a slightly better rate reflecting, no doubt, guarantees by specific Lyon merchants with strong ties to Genoa. The money was passed on entirely to the king, again for 6 per cent.[18] This gives a strong indication that proxy borrowers for the crown, at least those with formal corporate status and whose *raison d'être* was not solely as part of the fiscal machinery, were not making any money themselves by channelling loans to the king.

The monarchy also needed the Church to raise loans, again either to channel loans from other providers at the king's request or to help meet rising royal demands for *dons gratuits* and other levies on the clergy. In 1707 it also made a limited contribution to a feeble attempt to extinguish Mint bills. Like the provincial estates, the Church generally borrowed by issuing *rentes* of limited term, and these were

[17] Mark Potter, *Corps and Clienteles: Public Finance and Political Change in France, 1688–1715* (Aldershot, 2003), 14, 21, 27, 81–91, 95, 142–5, 159, 168–71; Albert Cans, *La contribution du clergé de France à l'impôt pendant la seconde moitié du règne de Louis XIV (1689–1715)* (Paris, 1910), 73; Julian Swann, *Provincial Power and Absolute Monarchy: The Estates-General of Burgundy, 1661–1790* (Cambridge, 2003), 106–7, 168–76, 186–7; CCG, III, 436–7: Desmaretz to Guynet, 26 April 1712; Rafe Blaufarb, 'The Survival of the *pays d'états*: The Example of Provence', *Past and Present* 209 (2010), 95–112.

[18] CCG, II, 85–6: Bâville to Chamillart, 26 September 1701; II, 422: various letters of July 1707; AN G[7]1775, no. 322: 'Estat', [late 1702]; G[7]1780, no. 42: Trudaine to [Chamillart], 10 August 1707; G[7]1119: *mémoire* 'Pour l'emprunt que la province de Languedoc doit faire a Gennes ...', [1707]; Giovanni Battista Cambiato to Chamillart, 1 October 1707; Giuseppe Felloni, *Gli investimenti finanziari genovesi in Europa tra il Seicento e la Restaurazione* (Milan, 1971), 525–6, 528, 539–40; Blaufarb, 'Survival', 101; W. Gregory Monahan, *Year of Sorrows: The Great Famine of 1709 in Lyon* (Columbus, OH, 1993), 65.

often bought by small investors who loaned to their local diocese at relatively low rates of interest—for the Church could not possibly countenance usurious levels. Despite the mounting demands, the Church, as argued in Chapter 3, was under-tapped by the monarchy for its war effort, so its payment of annuities was very smooth. The only hiccup came in the form of a temporary reduction of interest rates in 1709, apparently because internal Church revenues dipped as ordinary clergy felt the extreme economic pressure of the time. The result was that the Church's credit was in astonishingly good shape at the end of Louis XIV's reign, at a time when nearly everybody else's was at rock bottom.[19]

AFFAIRES EXTRAORDINAIRES, *TRAITANTS* AND EXPLOITATIVE FINANCE

The relatively low costs of borrowing through the Church represented one extreme of the crown's search for credit through elite corporate structures. The merciless use of *affaires extraordinaires* by *traitants*, which milked the elites and those who aspired to privileges, marked the other. By the end of the seventeenth century *affaires extraordinaires* meant specific contracts (known as *traités*) that were agreed between the royal council and a financier, or group of financiers, who was referred to as a *traitant*. These contracts involved advances from the *traitant* to the monarch and were, as we shall see, expensive. They were signed for the collection of windfall taxes; for the recovery of failing revenues that had not been gathered in by their normal collectors; and above all for the raising of money through the sale and manipulation of offices, a practice known as venality.

Venality was a form of patrimonial bureaucracy in which an office-holder owned his position. Over the course of the sixteenth and seventeenth centuries the state's demand for administrators grew but so did its voracious appetite for money, so it made a great deal of sense to venalize judicial, financial, and other administrative offices already in existence and create thousands of new ones for sale. By 1709 there might have been as many as 70,000–80,000 venal officials across France, a uniquely heavy density in Europe.[20] As the seventeenth century wore on, greater security of ownership and heritability was introduced into the system, with a fee of one-sixtieth of the value of an office payable to the king each year to ensure the transmission of an office on someone's death to his heirs. This charge was known as the *droit annuel* and commonly called the 'Paulette', and at the renewal of this privilege, usually every nine years, officers paid a 'prêt' of 5 per cent of their office's value. All offices enjoyed privileges or exemptions, but these could vary considerably according to status, with removal from the register of *taille*-payers and exemption from billeting troops both fairly standard rights that were accorded to a purchaser. A small proportion of offices

[19] Michaud, 346, 355–6, 367–9, 376, 380; Cans, *La contribution*, 88–91.

[20] Given the suppressions after the War of the Spanish Succession and subsequent further creations, this is not out of line with William Doyle's estimate of about 70,000 in 1789: *Venality: The Sale of Offices in Eighteenth-Century France* (Oxford, 1996), 60.

also formally endowed their holders—either immediately or gradually over two or three generations—with the status of nobility. Only a minority of venal offices existing in around 1710 paid out *gages*—a form of interest on the investment worth around 4–5 per cent per annum of the capital injected. Some offices, among the most important thousand or so, also paid out additional salaries known as *appointements* for the performance of duties associated with the office, but most did not. For most of the Grand Siècle demand for venal offices was fairly buoyant, although Colbert had tried to shrink the number of such positions until military spending forced him into a U-turn in 1671. Nevertheless, with the huge increases in numbers put up for sale in the 1690s and 1700s, a degree of market saturation was reached. Demand was not inexhaustible, especially when the likely purchasers were placed under other fiscal pressures. But while the sale of office became a much less important weapon in the monarchy's armoury for raising cash after 1715, for much of the final twenty-five years of Louis XIV's reign there was an 'archomania' abroad, a huge desire for venal office that was met with highly creative and often exploitative schemes. As Malet contemptuously remarked of his fellow countrymen,

> The Frenchman, avid for honour, for credit and for glory, is borne to clothe himself in these *charges* by a natural inclination which forces him to quit the things in which he succeeds the most capably, to satisfy his vanity at the expense of his most solid interests.[21]

But not always were people mad keen on venal purchases. The crown also thrust venalization upon unwilling subjects, including the officers of the royal artillery corps, in a form of forced loan extraction. New offices might be created simply in order to persuade existing office-holders, or corporate bodies threatened by the new arrivals, to buy them out. Furthermore, once an office was owned, it was vulnerable to the imposition of further charges upon it, particularly the enforced injection of additional capital that was handed over to the crown. The royal demand for this was accompanied by the threat, sometimes explicit, that the owners would lose their offices or not be allowed to renew the *Paulette* if they did not cooperate, while they would get additional *gages* (perhaps even at a higher rate) if they did. In an early example of Orwellian double-speak, these loans were officially known as *augmentations des gages*, and they began in earnest in 1689. The monarchy, in short, responded to demand, playing on the aspirations of the emerging 'middling sort', but it also abused the wealthy and moderately prosperous segments of propertied society, including the judicial officers of the highest courts in the land, the *parlements*. Though they reeked of arbitrary government, such levies could nevertheless be justified on the grounds that these people were under-taxed compared with less well-off commoners, something Desmaretz certainly felt.[22]

The turn away from reliance upon the usual revenue sources and supplementary taxes towards *affaires extraordinaires* under Pontchartrain involved a huge risk: that

[21] Malet, *Comptes*, 63.

[22] On the venal system from the later seventeenth century to the Revolution, see Doyle, *Venality*, esp. 7, 12, 20, 23, 36, 39–40. See also, Forbonnais, II, 227; Potter, *Corps and Clienteles*, 29–34, 74–8, 111; John J. Hurt, *Louis XIV and the Parlements: The Assertion of Royal Authority* (Manchester, 2002), 70–3, 95–8.

for collecting large proportions of its income the monarchy would depend yet again upon unscrupulous and greedy contractors whose avidity had already once contributed to political implosion at the end of the 1640s. But there were marked differences this time. During most of the period 1635–59 the proceeds of *affaires extraordinaires* had made up over half of all royal revenues, but under Louis XIV they never accounted for more than about one-third in any year, and usually far less.[23] Furthermore, in the earlier period under Richelieu and Mazarin *affaires extraordinaires* very often involved the intrusion of *traitants* into the normal revenue-collecting arrangements, with the king alienating big chunks of royal income to *traitants* for years in advance in return for rather measly instant windfall payments. On a much smaller scale, Colbert had also used favoured *traitants* to collect controversial new taxes in the Dutch War.

However, in the 1690s and 1700s well over four-fifths of all *traités* signed between the council and financiers were related to venal office. There was very little alienation of taxes to contractors.[24] For all the problems of the final wars of the reign, Louis XIV and his ministers did not make the fatal mistake of parcelling out the collection of back taxes on a large scale to *traitants* as replacement contractors. The king thus avoided truly massive decreases in net yields. Four factors allowed Louis to avoid the perils that the regency government of the 1640s had fallen into: first, Colbert's reorganization of the financial officials and farmers made their operations more sustainable when their revenue sources lagged; second, the provincial *intendants* were keeping a much closer eye on revenue collection and could more easily take action when problems appeared on the horizon; third, the senior fisco-financiers had accumulated much more capital and extended their credit options since the 1660s; and fourth, with the mushrooming of paper instruments, tax collectors of all kinds could keep themselves afloat through speculating and acquiring substitute financial assets they could subsequently employ. These together produced a far more robust structure just about capable of weathering the extreme demands of the Nine Years War and the War of the Spanish Succession. When tax yields did decline, instead of giving up on the normal revenue officials and farmers, and substituting *traitants* for them, Chamillart and Desmaretz preferred to pressurize them into drawing ever deeper on their own credit with appropriate if rather flimsy royal guarantees of support.

All this notwithstanding, *affaires extraordinaires* did play a big role in royal financial tactics after 1689, and the monarchy was heavily reliant upon *traitants*. Many of the *traitants* were drawn from the ranks of senior financiers already holding tax-collecting offices, from among the farmers, and from among military suppliers, notably those running the bread (*vivres*) companies. This was especially the case when it came to those who were backing the principal *traitant* for a contract. *Traités* were indeed frequently awarded to support the activity of military suppliers and at their direct sugges-

[23] Alain Guéry, 'Les finances de la monarchie française sous l'ancien régime', *Annales ESC* 33 (1978), 230, 236–7.

[24] On earlier *affaires extraordinaires*, see Julian Dent, *Crisis in Finance: Crown, Financiers and Society in Seventeenth-Century France* (Newton Abbot, 1973), 33–91. On the background after 1661, see Vuitry, 42; Clamageran, III, 23; Forbonnais, II, 108; DAPS, 163–4; Doyle, *Venality*, 30–1.

tion: for example, one bread supplier (for the Pyrenees forces in 1706–7) was given the contract to sell new offices in the chancelleries of all the Superior Courts of the realm in order to support his activities. Conversely, men who were predominantly *traitants* might try to give themselves more stable foundations by taking on middle-ranking financial offices. There was thus a lot of intertwining of financial and army-supplying activities.[25] Leaving aside François Mauricet de La Cour, who will appear in the final chapter of this book, the most remarkable case was that of Paul Poisson, who styled himself de Bourvallais in an attempt to increase his respectability. After enriching himself through a massive number of *traités* after 1689, Poisson even penetrated the heart of government, one of a number of men we shall encounter whose conflicts of interest did not preclude them from achieving solid second-tier power in the state central apparatus. In February 1710 Desmaretz procured for him the office of *secrétaire garde des minutes* of the King's Council for over 600,000 *livres*. It gave him the right to conserve all archives of the royal councils and extraordinary commissions (many of which concerned financial operations); to sit in on some councils; to *alone* sign leases for farms, the *vivres*, *traités*, and so on; and to act as commissioner for the adjudication of works or supplies for the farmers general, sitting in committee with them. It would be a mistake to see this as a mere sinecure in such a pair of hands. Poisson came to have as much power and influence in government in the field of *affaires extraordinaires* as Mauricet had over the *vivres*, as Samuel Bernard had concerning banking, or as treasurer general Montargis had as an army paymaster.[26]

How and why did people like him become so indispensable for the implementation of *affaires extraordinaires*? For venal-related fund-raising, various other sales of privileges and status, and windfall taxes for the confirmation of rights it made sense to use a separate contract not directly associated with the normal tax-collecting infrastructure. In the case of the venal offices, they could in theory have been marketed and sold directly by the office of the *receveur des revenus casuels*, but this had two disadvantages: his staff and network were far too small to do this across the whole kingdom, and the crown would not have received the large advances that they could demand from the *traitants*. Instead, the system worked roughly as follows. A contract would be awarded for a 'forfait', the gross amount to be collected. The *traitant* would then give an advance to the monarchy, based upon credit made available to him by associates and through issuing bearer bills on himself and his company. He would then deduct from the global proceeds of the contract interest upon this advance, known as the *remise de dedans*, normally around one-sixth of the value of the contract. He would also take a cut of the sums he actually collected, known as the *remise en dehors*, usually worth around 10 per cent. The capital collected was ideally delivered in instalments over a period of a year or two, but in practice it could take much longer even to bring in a proportion of the target. In the case of income from venality it would be given to the *Parties Casuelles*, otherwise it was placed at the immediate disposal of the Trésor royal.[27]

[25] Potter, *Corps and Clienteles*, 140; Saint-Germain, *Financiers*, 111; DAPS, 212; AN G^{7}1497: *arrêt*, 26 April 1707.

[26] Saint-Germain, *Financiers*, esp. 171–2.

[27] Doyle, *Venality*, 4, 6, 28–9; Clamageran, III, 22; DAPS, 60–3, 206.

In all, it was a rapacious system. Many of these *traités* were not dreamed up by disinterested administrators in the Finance Ministry but by men who were eyeing up prospects for making fast money and who touted themselves as the natural contractors for their schemes. Once a contract was under way, they behaved like some of the *receveurs généraux*, dragging their feet about handing over sums due, stringing out deliveries to the crown as long as possible, and using the funds they had accumulated to make profitable loans to other people. They also loaded additional administration costs onto the final bill, and were almost unregulated by the state and its officials. They were a byword for the ruthless extraction of money from the propertied classes, having no compunction about billeting troops on defaulters to obtain payments. As Chamillart lamented to the prince de Condé, they were loathed not only for what they did but the way they did it: their 'most ordinary fault' was to make themselves blameworthy and odious in even the most simple and legitimate matters 'by their too harsh and excessive ways of behaving'.[28] In some cases they also charged a lot more than the state was comfortable with. This might be justified by the risks of a contract failing in whole or in part, and *traitants*' own creditors had to be satisfied, but it still might add up to a considerable profit. Most historians agree that the combined cut they obtained (if one joins together the *remise de dedans* with the *remise de dehors*) was in the region of about one-third of the gross total in the 1650s under Fouquet. It is also largely accepted that for the later period 1689–1715 it averaged about 23 per cent, and that Pontchartrain's tenure saw generally higher rake-offs than those of his two successors. The evidence also suggests that Chamillart's management of *affaires extraordinaires* was the least successful of the three later *contrôleurs généraux*, pulling in a smaller average sum per contract than did Pontchartrain and Desmaretz.[29]

But matters may well have been worse than we think. The table of *affaires extraordinaires* for the years 1700–7 set out in the monumental work by Boislisle, and based on a contemporary manuscript list, indicates that cuts of 36.3 and 23.8 million *livres* for the *remises* out of a total sum of 259 million *livres* contracted represent a notional rake-off of 36 per cent, a figure just as bad as in the 1650s.[30] If this was also happening in the Nine Years War it would explain very well why in spring 1700 Chamillart embarked on an effort to claw back excessive profits made by *traitants* in the period 1 January 1689 to 1 September 1699. Threatening them with a possible insistence by the king that they reveal the detail of their activities, including the names of their investors, Chamillart got them to cough up some of their gains. It was, however, a modest effort, bringing in around 14–18 million *livres* in the end, for Chamillart was well aware that if he pushed the financiers too far he would harm the state's future ability to use *traités*. The way the process was conducted might also cause modern eyebrows to be raised: Chamillart handed the job of fine-collector to François Mauricet de La Cour, one of the greatest *traitants*

[28] Saint-Germain, *Financiers*, 108–9; Vuitry, 79–80; CCG, II, 46: Chamillart to Condé, 16 July 1700.

[29] DAPS, 63; Forbonnais, II, 275; Clamageran, III, 23.

[30] CCG, II, 605.

and supply contractors of the reign, who would in the following years become one of Chamillart's most favoured lieutenants.[31] This was, in effect, a smaller, less judicial version of the Chambre de justice of the 1660s, and in retrospect it was not necessarily wise, with the troubled Spanish inheritance in the offing. But something clearly had to be done about the excessive profiteering that had gone on.

Affaires extraordinaires were big business. An average of twenty-nine contracts were signed each year between 1689 and 1697. After a sluggish start in the early years of the War of the Spanish Succession, matters picked up in 1703, not least under pressure from some of the financiers. There was an average of fifteen contracts per annum in 1701–3, soaring to seventy-two in 1704, before tailing back to an average of forty in 1705–7, climbing to fifty-eight in 1708, and then averaging twenty a year for the rest of the reign. The total signed for reached a peak of 93.8 million *livres* in 1704, before dropping quickly to the low 20 millions, followed by two bigger efforts in 1708 (66.8 million) and 1709 (49.1 million). It never got above 18 million in any year for the rest of the reign. Nevertheless, *affaires extraordinaires* brought in a great deal of income for the monarchy in the final two wars of Louis XIV's reign: in terms of gross capital value, the total contracted has been estimated at between 750 and 850 million *livres*, of which the king received in the end perhaps two-thirds.[32]

An honest case could be made for greater resort to venality: as one treasurer of the Extraordinaire des Guerres pointed out, greater revenue from *affaires extraordinaires* was a useful way of compensating for the reduced income from the *fermes générales*, whose takings always declined in wartime.[33] However, the use of *affaires extraordinaires* was being taken to extremes in this period. One of the hallmarks of these contracts from 1689 was the increasing venalization of more and more minor positions. Venal offices had traditionally existed in the judiciary and the financial administration, but, with the first stirrings in the Dutch War, venality was extended after 1689 to positions related to industrial products, food products, transport and communications regulation, vanities and luxuries, municipal positions, and posts involving public health. The monarchy also venalized the right to sell certain goods in fields where an oligopoly or monopoly existed. The intrusion of venality into these fields took off after 1702, but there is very little evidence that venalizing any of the hundreds of regulatory positions did very much good at all, except to the *traitants* collecting the purchase payments and to the king at the brief moment he received some badly needed extra money.[34] On top of this, the Spanish Succession war saw new offices created, or mooted, in order to exert financial pressure on existing institutions and office-holders, threatening them with a dilution of their authority, prestige, or income if they did not buy out the new posts or otherwise advance more money to the crown.[35]

[31] Germain Martin and Marcel Bezançon, *L'histoire du crédit en France sous le règne de Louis XIV* (Paris, 1913), 141; Depping, III, 319: Chamillart to Achille de Harlay, 8 April 1700; DAPS, 230, 747.

[32] For different estimates, see DAPS, 167; Doyle, *Venality*, 51; Potter, *Corps and Clienteles*, 13.

[33] AN G^{7}1775, no. 109: memorandum on 1702 Extraordinaire exercice, 20 February 1703.

[34] Saint-Germain, *Financiers*, 68–70; Malet, *Comptes*, 412–13; Vuitry, 68–71; Forbonnais, II, 166, 185; Eugène-Pierre Beaulieu, *Les gabelles sous Louis XIV* (Paris, 1903), 128–34; Doyle, *Venality*, 34–5.

[35] DAPS, 25; Doyle, *Venality*, 33–4; Hurt, *Louis XIV*, 98, 102.

Not as important, but still making a vital financial contribution, were the *augmentations des gages*: up to 200 million *livres* were levied through these additional capital demands after 1689 in an oppressive and much-resented manner. In addition, December 1709 saw a break in the tradition of renewing the *Paulette*, with office-holders now given an exemption from its payment in return for a one-off contribution (worth sixteen years of *Paulette*) to royal coffers. The money was slow to come in but it appears to have raised 24 million *livres*, compared with the 13.2 million *livres* raised through the *Paulette* and *prêt* in the whole of the previous cycle of 1700–8. This certainly helped at a desperate time, but as with other drastic measures in 1709–10 it reduced the amount of money for the years 1711 onwards, and nobody could foresee what those years would bring. The most prominent victims of these manipulations were the magistrates of the *parlements* and other Superior Courts, who may have been given greater security of position and social status under Louis XIV and who, in some cases, may have been investing in fisco-financiers' activities; but venal demands from the king exhausted, and to a degree immobilized, their personal and corporate credit by 1709.[36]

Ministers did not relish selling more offices, as this would usually shrink the pool of *taille*- and other charge-payers; however, a desire to reduce dependence on *affaires extraordinaires* ran up against the uncomfortable truth that, despite the *traitants'* rake-offs, most alternative ways to raise money would probably not squeeze resources out of the propertied strata of society so efficiently. Moreover, the crown was using venal officers, and particularly the corporate bodies of which they were members, as proxy sources of credit. The demands the crown made on them usually forced people to borrow, perhaps by issuing private *rentes* on themselves and certainly by pledging some or all of their venal office and its revenues as collateral. Like the provincial estates and the clergy, the more senior *corps* could indeed borrow at more favourable rates than the king or most of his fisco-financiers, and then pass the funds on; but to maintain their credit and service their own debts the venal office-holders depended more and more on the king paying their *gages* on time. This by no means always happened in the War of the Spanish Succession.[37]

By 1704 it was already becoming evident that the extension of venality since 1689 had severely eroded the tax base, as too many cheaper offices, worth less than 10,000 *livres* capital, had been endowed with tax exemption. This provoked the move by Desmaretz in 1709 to suspend this exemption for three years, an unfortunate arbitrary attack on stable property rights that venal offices were supposed to represent. Moreover, it has been estimated that whatever the actual loss to the taxpaying capacity, the capital received by the monarchy through venal sales or extensions was typically absorbed within twelve years by *gages* and other payments, after which the crown was making a loss on the transaction. By 1715 *gages* payouts had increased in thirty-two years from 16.4 to 37.6 million *livres* per annum, a near-doubling in amount after allowing for currency depreciation. This squeezed disposable crown revenues even

[36] Potter, *Corps and Clienteles*, 12–13, 37–41, 130, 156–7, 182; Hurt, *Louis XIV*, 105–16; Doyle, *Venality*, 43–4; Saint-Germain, *Financiers*, 224–9, 241; DAPS, 415, 789.

[37] Potter, *Corps and Clienteles*, 12–14, 128–30; Doyle, *Venality*, 37.

more. Furthermore, in a circular process *affaires extraordinaires* were also competing with indirect taxes: the *traitants* focused their attacks so much on the consuming classes that this depressed demand for luxury goods after 1689, thus necessitating yet more *affaires extraordinaires* to compensate for weaker indirect tax revenues.[38] In 1702 Chamillart acknowledged frankly that the market for new offices and further capital injections was saturated, and a year later it was painfully obvious that new capital was rolling in at a decelerating pace. The government nevertheless ploughed on with venality as a tool, even though the failure of *assignations* already issued in advance upon anticipated income from *traités* was beginning to disrupt the military paymasters' arrangements. By 1704, the peak year for contracts, the stage had been reached where the king was signing new contracts with the sole purpose of supporting old ones to sustain the credit of the *traitants* concerned. When he thought he had pushed things too far, Chamillart in 1705 expressed a determination to rely upon straightforward credit much more, but the problems his broader policies were generating, destabilizing the monetary system in particular, made this a pious but forlorn hope.[39]

When the king eased off on venality in 1705 and 1706 the *traitants* got a breathing space to allow for bigger pushes again in 1708–9, but the government was creating a vicious spiral: too many *traités* had depressed revenues and tempted the ministers into clawing back some privileges and rights, in turn sapping confidence in venality among potential buyers and their creditors, which in turn forced the government into more desperate squeezes on this sector of society. By the time Desmaretz took office in February 1708 bigger new contracts were finding neither signatories nor guarantors, because potential contractors considered the target sums too large. Several contracts had to be reduced in size or scrapped altogether. Moreover, the heavy involvement of many fisco-financiers in failing *traités* contributed to the shrinking of credit as the 1700s wore on and saturation point in the venal market was reached, just at the same time as the 1709 economic crisis and the banking sector's credit crunch. As the contractors had found it harder and harder to recover the monies they had invested as advances in a *traité*, they found themselves under-resourced for their other activities. In short, their slush funds were shrinking thanks to the petering out of venal negotiations. And from January 1709 *assignations* issued (as earmarks) on the *affaires extraordinaires* could not be traded for a song. It was not a surprise, then, that later that year many *traitants* came close to bankruptcy or, in a few cases, stepped beyond that fateful line, becoming either illiquid or insolvent. There was some attempt to rescue contracts by reworking their obligations and easing the negotiations of these men's promissory notes, and Desmaretz was determined to keep as many individual financiers afloat as he could. But the king was only willing to help those who found some additional cash to help him through his own difficulties, and this pressure continued into 1711 when, in a delicious irony, many *traitants* were forced to purchase 12 million *livres* of *rentes* on the Hôtel de ville. This abuse of the

[38] Potter, *Corps and Clienteles*, 71; Saint-Germain, *Financiers*, 30; Malet, *Comptes*, 47–8; CCG, II, 536: Boisguilbert to Chamillart?/Desmaretz?, 1 July 1704.

[39] AN G[7]1776, no. 72: Dalon to Chamillart, 15 April 1703; no. 410: memorandum, [January 1704]; DAPS, 21, 212; CCG, II, 565: Boisguilbert to Chamillart, 5 November 1705, latter's marginalia.

abusers, however, was highly dangerous and probably contributed a great deal, along with other measures around this time, to depressing credit even further, just when France seemed in maximum danger. What it certainly did was reveal how, by 1710, *traités* as a serious source of reliable revenue had had their day, even if some *traitants* survived to fight another.[40]

The French monarchy's essential core taxing and borrowing activity was thus sluggish, exploitative, involved alarming conflicts of interest, generated intrinsic principal-agent problems that became even greater as the pressure of war mounted and increasingly dubious expedients were tried, and encouraged (if not necessitated) reckless behaviour by financiers if they were to profit (or even survive). The government failed to organize the *receveurs généraux* into the backbone of state credit until far too late in the war, instead ordering and permitting far worse expedients that destabilized the war effort and financial world, and increasing the debt considerably. For all the desire of king and ministers to rein in the excesses of their financial contractors—whether officials, farmers, or *traitants*—the monarchy depended upon their work, their networks, and their credit far more than during peacetime, and because they were poorly marshalled by the government for most of the period, certainly up to and including 1709, they could very largely name their price. That so many were also investors in army supplies and in the military paymasters only entrenched their position. The failure of the crown to pay *gages* to the venal officers, in some cases for over a decade after 1709,[41] while regularly rescuing the farmers general, *traitants*, and even some *receveurs généraux*, is but one indication of the way the upper echelons of finance were prioritized over those lower down the financial food chain. This privileging of the great financial and supply facilitators of the realm over most other subjects is even more glaring in the cases of the military paymasters. Before we turn to the funding of the armies, however, the final pieces of the revenue-raising picture need to be put into place: the monetary manipulations arising largely from ministerial attempts to ease revenue difficulties but which succeeded in making the war effort harder to manage and the financiers even harder to control.

40 DAPS, 165, 216; CCG, III: Desmaretz to Ormesson, 23 May 1709; McCollim, 271–3, 348–50.

41 Forbonnais, II, 195; Hurt, *Louis XIV*, 115–16.

5

Manipulating the Coinage

The greatest financial concern of governments in the late seventeenth and early eighteenth centuries was not so much the raising of money through taxation but ensuring there was sufficient cash in the country that could be available for borrowing and for tapping in the places where the state needed it. It is a truism that the ensuring of monetary stability and confidence in the markets is the most desirable way to achieve good levels of circulation, and this is certainly the case over the medium to long term. But in a period when most European economies remained somewhat undermonetized the temptation to undertake expedient manipulations of the money supply, in order to achieve short-term monetary boosts, was strong. Between 1689 and 1726 the French currency was to experience considerable upheaval, as coins were gradually revalued upwards against the *livre* and the *livre* was consequently devalued against gold and silver. The details of this period are extraordinarily complex, and must very largely be skirted over in this book. What this chapter will attempt to do is to show how the French government tried to boost monetary volume and its revenues through the manipulation of the coinage. When this proved insufficient, the government resorted to the printing of Mint bills, as we shall see in Chapter 6. Such attempts to inflate the money supply, generate more disposable revenue, and prevent a seizing-up of lending activity nonetheless had the potential to be seriously counterproductive, even in the short term: it created opportunities for financiers and bankers to manipulate the government's needs for their own ends, either for profit or to help keep themselves afloat. The manipulations over the final twenty-five years of Louis XIV's reign put up the costs of credit and the war effort.

Bills of exchange and other financial instruments were vital for large-scale remitting across long distances, but what was ultimately needed was cash: cash in the armies to pay the ordinary troops and prevent desertion and marauding; cash for suppliers so they could purchase food, transport services, labour, and so on for their operations; cash for arms manufacturers so they could pay their artisan workers and their raw-material suppliers; and cash to lubricate the credit markets on which the early modern state became so dependent. Yet while cash was ultimately doled out in lower-denomination coins to troops and workers, the greatest concern, both on the part of the government and the paymasters and suppliers of all hues, was reserved for gold and silver. Not only were these metals culturally essential for backing paper instruments in this era of bullionism and as a measure of wealth and credit, but also bulk payments usually had to be conducted in gold and silver for simple practical reasons, particularly when the state's military and naval activities were involved.[1] Any government of the time in every country pursuing bullionist approaches to the state and the economy found it hard to control the money supply and the values of the means of exchange. State officials found it particularly difficult to judge the international market ratio of gold to silver when setting values on coins, causing big waves of imports or exports of coins as the markets responded. France, unlike eighteenth-century Britain, was weakly supplied with gold and for practical reasons (namely the links with the Spanish economy and New World) silver was the principal precious metal for France.[2] Unfortunately, and there were drawbacks to any set of arrangements at this time, shortage of gold coin was inconvenient for the necessary bulk movement of cash for the armies, and therefore may have put up the cost of bills of exchange and of acquiring silver as a substitute.[3]

There were several methods of expanding or protecting the money supply. Successive French kings and ministers sought the expansion of trade first and foremost to increase the amount of specie available in the kingdom which could then be drawn on through taxation and loans, largely for war expenditure. On the whole, Louis XIV's regime tried to avoid imposing heavy windfall levies on specie inflows into the kingdom in order to incentivize people to bring gold and silver in and thereby increase the pool of monetary resources, but they did not always judge this well. Moreover, rather too often after 1688 the *contrôleurs généraux* of finances felt they had to manipulate the rules, frameworks, and official values of gold and silver coins in order to fill short-term revenue gaps. Government behaviour was accordingly arbitrary and unpredictable. The results, as we shall see, were not happy and as time went on, fewer and fewer returns were achieved. Coin was hoarded or exported on a vast scale, many transactions were driven underground on the basis of the market valuations of both coins and monetary instruments, and there were major problems in ensuring money was delivered to suppliers and the armies in legal form. The manipulations pushed up the costs of waging the war as the price of limited short-term success in flushing out coin.

FRENCH MONETARY STOCK IN THE ERA OF THE SPANISH SUCCESSION

Space, and the need for a clear focus, precludes a detailed discussion of the state of France's monetary stock during the period 1688–1715, but, as the damaging monetary manipulations stemmed in part from an inadequate coin resource for the needs of the war, some outline of the situation must be provided. It is widely held that France's stock of hard specie was declining throughout this period, and to the extent that this is true it had more to do with the needs of war and people's reac-

[1] DAPS, esp. 33, 175–6.

[2] Spooner, 194, 199–201; Forbonnais, II, 128.

[3] SHD A[1]1613, no. 197: Montargis to Chamillart, 2 November 1702; Claude-Frédéric Lévy, *Capitalistes et pouvoir au siècle des Lumières* (3 vols, Paris, 1969–80), I, 249.

tions to government manipulations than with the imperatives of trade.[4] There were both acute and chronic reductions in specie volume. Whatever the cause of sudden coinage retreats, these could prove very damaging. Even if they did not amount to more than a few hundred thousand *livres*, retreats could threaten transactions and the Lyon clearance system, and thus put in jeopardy the supply of coin to the armies. A chronic drain on top of this would gradually sap the ability of France to mobilize specie and credit, and worsen the exchange rates with other parts of Europe. The debate is customarily framed in terms of the national stock as measured in silver. Estimates vary, but the most reliable suggest that in 1689–90 France had around 18,000,000 *marcs* of silver, worth some 500–550 million *livres*, while by 1715 this had dropped to around 13,500,000 *marcs*, or roughly 474 million *livres*. These figures are essentially derived from official estimates of the processing of coin through the mints, and other measures. What matters is not the moderate loss in *livre* terms but the much larger apparent loss in terms of silver mass, measured in terms of the *marc*. Most of this chronic decline, perhaps three-quarters of it, seems to have taken place during the Nine Years War. The figures estimated around the time of the periodic recoinages make the situation look even worse: one highly placed contemporary in 1705 estimated that the government had found over 530 million *livres* of specie during the 1689 reminting, but only 95 million *livres* during that of 1704! And in the spring–summer of 1709, at the time of the great recoinage, only 215 million *livres* of coins were brought into the mints.[5] But within the overall downward trajectory of silver stock there were periods of relatively plentiful coinage availability, and this has to be remembered.[6] Why the monetary stock should apparently be in severe decline remains a matter of debate about details, but broadly speaking there was a certain amount of hoarding around the times of recoinages and remintings, and a great deal of fraudulent underground coining either at home or abroad. This was combined with a greater degree of speculative and fraudulent coin movement in and out of the kingdom than is often acknowledged by historians.

France had an underlying problem of specie export in any case, whether the government tinkered with coin values or not. Specie flowed out in conjunction with the rhythms of trade, particularly with the burgeoning of Levant commerce. The drain of coinage from France through the armies was just as disturbing, and the ministers constantly fretted over it. In the Nine Years War, when French troops were operating beyond the country's borders on nothing like the geographical and numerical scale of the War of the Spanish Succession, perhaps as much as 8–9 million *livres* of specie were being exported each year, much of that into Alsace with its separate currency system. It got far, far worse. *Intendant* Le Bret wrote in July 1703 of 'the extreme rarity of money that the distant war forces us to carry abroad

[4] AN $G^7$1777, no. 91: 'Memoire contenant les moyens de retablir le commerce en France...', by Macaire, 21 November 1705.

[5] DAPS, 175, 182–3; Lüthy, I, 96; AN $G^7$1119: 'Memoire touchant les finances de France que le S^r. Huguetan a donné au mois de Juillet 1705'.

[6] For example in 1697: AN $G^7$1774, no. 12: *receveurs généraux des finances* to Pontchartrain, 30 January 1697.

these days'. Huguetan, who had been one of the key figures in French remittances abroad in 1703–4, estimated that France was exporting between one-quarter and one-third of its strong specie *every year* to make war payments of various kinds.[7] This hair-raising assessment was made at a time when there were serious coinage manipulations going on, and these could intensify the flight of coin from France, for reasons we shall see later. Had outflows of such a magnitude occurred year in, year out throughout the war, it would have been totally impossible for France to have kept going, as the inflows of fresh bullion and coin could not have made up for the losses. Rather than coin physically moving abroad on such a scale, international compensations were arrived at in part through a markedly deteriorating set of exchange rates for the *livre* on the various French and international marketplaces. Nevertheless, there may well have been quite a lot more coinage exported than some historians have allowed for. Extensive smuggling operations were organized by merchants and bankers, especially the Swiss and Genevans who were central to Louis XIV's army remittances abroad, as well as official currency dealers. This smuggling aimed to achieve a profit that might be enjoyed by keeping the coin abroad (depending on exchange rates and balance of payments). However, gains could really be maximized at a time of royal monetary manipulation by buying up and then moving coins abroad for false reminting/recoining before sending them back into France to go back into circulation once they had been processed.[8]

Coinage therefore could leave France in large quantities, but the essential thing to remember is that this tended to be episodic, coinciding with monetary uncertainty or government manipulations. It may well have been the case that several hundred million *livres* of coins (in 1689 prices) went abroad over roughly twenty-five years, and some of it would have been melted down into other currencies, or become trapped abroad because the smugglers' logistical deficiencies could not get them back into France. Nonetheless, in net terms the drop was far smaller than this: coin influxes and considerable repatriation mean that we can merely guess at an overall long-term net drop (in 1689 prices) of at most 100 million *livres* or so, one-fifth of the monetary stock of the 1680s, by the end of Louis XIV's reign. We will never know by how much the total French monetary stock decreased during the period, because there was a lot of false-coining and recoining that went on beyond the knowledge of the state. Fortunately, it was generally in the interests of false-coiners to put revised coins back into circulation. Aside from in Lyon and (from 1708) Marseille, the failure of most French merchants and places to weigh coins to ensure their legitimate status helped sustain fairly high levels of circulation, except at crunch moments when coins were held back by their holders.[9] This surely helps to explain why French financiers were often able to find large sums, even when the official figures for monetary stock suggest a massive drop in available specie.

[7] DAPS, 184–5; CCG, II, 145: Le Bret to Chamillart, 16 July 1703; AN G[7]1119: 'Memoire touchant les finances de France que le S[r]. Huguetan a donné au mois de Juillet 1705'.

[8] Lévy, *Capitalistes*, I, 23–4, 43; Lüthy, I, 128; CCG, II, 64: Herbigny to Chamillart, 18 December 1700; II, 184: Montézan to Chamillart, 30 and 31 May 1704.

[9] CCG, II, 247–8: Bâville to Chamillart, 12 May 1705; III, 44: Bâville to Desmaretz, 18 August 1708.

Counterbalancing any outflows of specie from France were imports of coin and metal. The scale of this almost certainly did not make up for the losses of coin that occurred, but some metal, especially unformed bullion, did stick and could be exploited for the war. Luckily timed injections of fresh bullion and specie into the French economy could be essential at difficult moments for the government, and France (and her antagonists) was very fortunate that the period 1698–1700 saw the start of a renewed serious inflow of gold and silver into Europe from the Americas. Though privateering played its part, most of France's specie windfalls came through the Spanish monarchy from both Iberia and its extra-European empire. By 1700 the 'carrera de Indias' was in an advanced state of decay, helped towards its demise by English, French, and Dutch interloping which was growing as Habsburg rule in Madrid entered its final excruciating years. And after November 1700, when Philip V ascended the Spanish throne, the French were able to break into the Peruvian economic zone, the so-called South Seas, bringing Spanish silver and other goods and raw materials back to Europe while using the slave trade as a cover. There was thus continued interloping by French ships, especially those connected with Saint-Malo, and from 1701 there was a considerable increase in the amount of American treasure being landed in Europe at non-Spanish ports. Among the backers, direct and indirect, for these ventures were some of the greatest financiers of the kingdom, including Samuel Bernard and the Crozat brothers, who were essential to the royal war effort, and Etienne Landais, one of the army paymasters.[10] It is not surprising that they received a lot of tacit support from the Finance Ministry.

The pattern of goods and cargo coming from the Americas was not steady, but sometimes the hauls were relatively big and the total amount brought back did make a difference. This was notably so in 1709 when fortuitous arrivals probably had the effect of saving the Spanish crown for Philip by preserving the French monarchy from total financial meltdown. Greater Franco-Spanish cooperation, necessitated by the military crisis in Iberia, increased the influx of silver and other goods from the New World after autumn 1707, with one official French estimate of January 1709 putting the amount of metal and cargo imported since 1701 at over 180 million *livres*. Most important of all, because of its timing, was the arrival of a number of ships, individually and in small convoy, three months later: a reasonable estimate is that Chabert's flotilla brought a total benefit to France of over 16 million *livres* in metal and foreign coin that could be converted in the mints. The overall cargo value of the inflows of March–April 1709 was even evaluated as high as 30 million *livres*, and this was only a guesstimate. Throughout the war there was considerable smuggling.[11]

[10] Geoffrey J. Walker, *Spanish Politics and Imperial Trade, 1700–1789* (London, 1979), 1–13; Saint-Germain, *Bernard*, 123, 131–5; Michel Morineau, *Incroyables gazettes et fabuleux métaux: Les retours des trésors américains d'après les gazettes hollandaises (XVIe–XVIIIe siècles)* (Cambridge/Paris, 1985), 321.

[11] Lévy, *Capitalistes*, I, 400; Henry Kamen, *The War of Succession in Spain 1700–15* (London, 1969), 175, 179–81, 186; Walker, *Spanish Politics*, 32–3; E. W. Dahlgren, *Les rélations commerciales et maritimes entre la France et les côtes de l'océan Pacifique (commencement du XVIIIe siècle). Tôme Premier: le commerce de la Mer du Sud jusqu'à la paix d'Utrecht* (Paris, 1909), 474–5.

The South Seas trade was dashing and buccaneering, but most of the Spanish silver that came into France made a less glamorous entrance via Iberia, much of it through the Pyrenees and the port of Bayonne. Cadiz became a major French trading centre in the next two reigns, but outside Spain it is little appreciated how important it was in the War of the Spanish Succession too, both for trade between France and Spain and for the movement of bullion between the Americas and Italy (to benefit the Bourbon empire there). As a group of French Cadiz merchants told Desmaretz in 1714, 'this trade is the principal source of our riches, and the French traders who are established at Cadiz the channels by which such wealth reaches us [in France]' in the shape of gold, silver, wool, cochineal, indigo, and other goods. And Lyon—so essential for banking loans and for remittances to Louis XIV's armies—was, more than any other, the French city that interacted with Spain.[12] Nevertheless, the French government made itself uncompetitive at attracting foreign metal: not only did excessive regulation deter ingot and bullion imports, but also, from 1689, the king imposed duties on all foreign specie presented at French mints, unlike in Genoa, Holland, and England.[13]

All in all, we can never be certain about how much bullion and specie came into France from the Spanish *monarquía* during the War of the Spanish Succession, not least because of huge clandestine importations that were spirited away before officials could venture aboard docking vessels.[14] Those who have looked at the detailed evidence, both contemporaries and historians, have come to different conclusions, with Dahlgren reckoning that anywhere between 250 and 400 million *livres* worth of precious metals came into France, while Morineau, examining the Spanish evidence as well, puts the figure at around 150–180 million *livres*. It was probably somewhere in the region of 200–250 million *livres*.[15] But however much it was, that which remained in France for at least a few months was occasionally useful for windfall taxation (generally avoided), but was absolutely vital for the lubrication of the French fisco-financier system and the credit and exchange markets.[16] More generally, the big increase in British and French involvement in the extra-European world after 1698 helped turn the War of the Spanish Succession into the titanic, draining struggle it became: the British war effort was sustained in large part by increased interloping in the East Indies, while the French prevented their war effort from collapsing by interloping in the Americas. Nevertheless, it was not enough to bring in fresh metal and foreign coins. Ministers therefore continued to follow a

[12] Louis Dermigny, 'Circuits de l'argent et milieux d'affaires au XVIIIe siècle', *Revue historique* 212 (1954), 245–6; CCG, II, 376: Trudaine to Chamillart, 18 January 1707; II, 383: La Bourdonnaye to Chamillart, 16 February 1707; AN G^{7}1094–5: Chauvin, Moreau, Piou, Le Baillif, and Gilly to Desmaretz, 3 September 1714 (quotation); BNF Ms. Fr. 16756, fo. 158r: 'Memoire sur la Generalité de Lyon dressé par Mr d'Herbigny Intendant en l'année 1698'.

[13] CCG, II, 158–9: *mémoire* by Mesnager, October 1703.

[14] Saint-Germain, *Bernard*, 155–6; Marcel Giraud, 'Crise de conscience et crise d'autorité à la fin du règne de Louis XIV', *Annales. Histoire, Sciences sociales* 7(2) (1952), 174–5, 178.

[15] Dahlgren, *Les rélations commerciales*; Morineau, *Incroyables gazettes*, 317. See also Saint-Germain, *Bernard*, 140, for a 1715 estimate of 300 million *livres* over the previous fifteen years.

[16] AN G^{7}1094–5: Amelot to Louis XIV, 17 April 1709; CCG, III, 156: Desmaretz to Bernage, 22 May 1709; III, 369–70: Desmaretz to Jérôme de Pontchartrain, 23 and 24 April 1711.

pattern of manipulation of the French coinage, begun in 1689, to try to make more out of what France already possessed.

MAKING MONEY OUT OF MONEY, OR, THE MANIPULATION OF THE COINAGE

The importation of fresh bullion and specie was a slow and undependable method of increasing the velocity and volume of monetary circulation, and in the late 1680s and 1690s it had in any case been of little help. The government had therefore begun regular manipulations of the coinage, varying the value of the *louis d'or* and the *écu* against the *livre*; in other words, altering the 'rating' of the coins in terms of the unit of account. The monetary policy of the successive *contrôleurs généraux*—Pontchartrain, Chamillart, and Desmaretz—reveals more than anything the hand-to-mouth approach of the government, with regular reratings and even full recoinages creating a remarkable degree of instability in the world of finance and trade. Because the ball was already rolling, Chamillart and Desmaretz, after 1700, probably had no choice but to go in for at least some periodic readjustments, but the cumulative effect was a bruising experience and one that the later governments of Louis XV and Louis XVI were anxious to avoid.

Upon taking office in 1689 Pontchartrain was certainly faced with an unsatisfactory coinage situation and any *contrôleur général* would have needed to rerate the major coins. Colbert had bequeathed coin values that were badly judged in relation to older coins and ingots, and were out of step with circulation values practised in interior and international markets. Trade patterns had been altering quite rapidly and high volume trade was increasing, so the government would need to react at some point, but it was hard to do so in a precisely targeted manner to achieve the desired aims. Throughout the period, governments lacked the necessary information about the exact reasons for fluctuating exchange rates and for different values placed upon coinage, both at home and abroad. Not only the markets but foreign governments and institutions might price French coins (in *livre* terms) at rates different from those of Louis XIV. In part this depended upon the different gold to silver ratios prevailing in different places. The best a government could do, if it wanted to maintain a healthy amount of currency in the kingdom, was to set the values of coins as close as possible to the market circulation rates for gold and silver, and ensure that the precious metal content (the 'intrinsic value') related appropriately to the legal *fiat* value of the coins and the current price of the basic metal.[17] This was a tall order, and Louis XIV and his ministers were deeply frustrated that they could not force the financial world to accept the *fiat* value as the market value of French coins. From 1689 the government began a series of at least forty-three reratings aimed, in large part, at bringing in extra revenue to the monarchy in the form of 'seigniorage' (a charge at the mints for reprocessing coins)

[17] Seligmann, 2–3, 24.

and at reducing the king's debt liabilities (contracted in *livres*).[18] Even if the scale of the alterations paled into insignificance compared with the monetary chaos unleashed in the Hundred Years War, in a very different world of much greater trade and international exchange it was still a sorry step towards inflated credit costs and a more expensive war effort.

It was certainly fair to say, as Desmaretz suggested, that when setting coin values a whole series of considerations, some of them incompatible, had to be weighed up, especially the trade-off between a weak *livre* producing costly exchange dealings and the amount of coinage available in the kingdom.[19] But the government often seems to have been somewhat unclear about exactly what it was doing and why. Even when it was sure of its aims, by moving away from using rerating as a bullionist tool for ensuring adequate money supply and turning it into a revenue scam the *contrôleurs généraux* created huge unpredictabilities for traders and the credit markets. This helped drive the cost of loans upwards, and produced periodic acute shortages of cash. In turn, the king then had to react to downward revenue pressure or further monetary instability with another augmentation of coin values, which would be preceded by staged diminutions that dried up credit, ultimately producing more expensive foreign exchange. Desmaretz in particular was too confident in his ability to read the market values and behaviour of coinage, and he had something of an itch to tinker with official values as a short cut to extra revenue and as a way to flush out cash in order to increase the amount available for borrowing. It is hard to escape the conclusion that ministers simply did not appreciate how much damage their coin policies would do to France's economic power over the medium term in a context of prolonged, increasingly demanding warfare.

Most of the augmentations of the coins did not involve full recoining (and sometimes a change in intrinsic value) but merely an alteration by the mints of the faces of the *louis d'or* and the *écus*, which would be overstamped with fresh symbols to represent the latest coded value. A full recoinage was much harder work and was rarely employed, though in 1709 it was needed in part because the coins were so overstamped that their faces were becoming a mess.[20] The aim, in most cases, was to get cash into the mints, restamp it, cream off some profit for the king, and get it back out into circulation. This cycle could take months, if not several years, to complete. The first rerating of the coinage in the Nine Years War was in 1689–90, undertaken partly to get *écus* back in circulation again in France in greater numbers, but also done in such a way as to produce a benefit of 40 million *livres* for the king. Initially the seigniorage rake-off was high, and—after a further augmentation in 1693—it may have reached a peak in 1694 of 24 million *livres*, dropping back before another, slightly lower peak of 20 million *livres* was reached in 1697. In total, the benefit to the king in the Nine Years War may have been as high as 95 million *livres*, an average of 10.5 million *livres* per annum. The eighteenth-century

[18] Seigniorage was the gross levy, out of which 'brassage', the cost of the operation, was deducted.
[19] CCG, II, 194: Desmaretz to Barentin, 23 July 1704.
[20] Vuitry, 153.

historian of the monarchy's finances, Forbonnais, thought, not unreasonably, that this success produced mirages in the minds of ministers who believed they could see riches ahead by pursuing the same course in the War of the Spanish Succession. The 1701–3 augmentation process might have produced up to 29.2 million *livres* in seigniorage, and that of 1704–6 another 29 million *livres*, but this last amount only kept up with the 1701–3 tally because the king was now taking one-sixth of all the coins, whereas previously he had taken only one-eleventh. This was a heavier levy on the economy, and it was clear that this source of easy cash was declining. If the three augmentations of 1701, 1704, and 1709 did only bring in a total of 69 million *livres*, then this was an average, for the whole war, of only 5.3 million *livres* per annum, half the rate of the 1690s.[21] One of the reasons for this was the declining amount of money that was brought into the royal mints, a major reason being that augmentations were very tempting for traffickers, who would buy up coins and have them falsely restamped or re-created.

There were other benefits to the crown from augmenting the official value of the *louis d'or* and the *écu*. As a memorandum of early 1715 noted, the stronger the value of the coins the less the king had to physically give out in specie to pay off his debts, while Le Rebours, in the Finance Ministry, argued in 1708 that a further augmentation would help discharge more state and para-state debt, there being no way 'more gentle' to achieve this because it especially affected the under-taxed members of noble and bourgeois society. The real benefit would—superficially—come in the shape of paying out fewer coins in interest on the *rentes* and in repaying short-term loans, especially paper devices that were clogging up trade and the military supply system. A new coin value set high above the previous low-point legal circulation value of coins, certainly more than a few percentage points, nullified any interest earned on providing short-term loans to the king's agents. Lüthy also pointed to the opportunity the king had to meet his other expenses in fewer coins.[22] But against this one should note that serious disadvantages would arise: credit might dry up if an augmentation was set at too greedy a rate, future loans would come at greater expense as lenders anticipated likely further augmentations of the coinage, and subsequent taxes paid to *receveurs généraux*, *traitants*, and so on would be in fewer coins.

As well as the immediate relief an augmentation might bring to the monarchy, there was a more direct benefit the government hoped to get: the deterrence of coin export and the promotion of coin/bullion importation. It needs to be stressed that devaluations of the *livre*—that is, augmentations of the coins—were also a tool of government to manipulate the availability of money in the country for borrowing by the state, its agents, and society at large, and this contributed to the nature of the augmentations of 1689 and 1693.[23] The stronger the coin values in France, the

[21] Seligmann, 32; Forbonnais, II, 75, 80, 85, 93–6, 112, 129, 139, 172; Vuitry, 163–4.

[22] AN G^{7}1119: 'Mémoire', [first months of 1715]; CCG, III, 652: 'Mémoire', [spring 1708] (quotation); Lüthy, I, 101.

[23] CCG, II, 77: Le Bret to Chamillart, 20 June 1701; CCG, II, 293: Trudaine to Desmaretz, 18 December 1705; AN G^{7}1777, no. 91: 'Mémoire...' by Macaire, 29 November 1705; SHD A^{1}1525, no. 63: Ferrand to Chamillart, 10 October 1701; Saint-Germain, *Bernard*, 164.

more there would be available. However, international exchange, and exchange for remitting money to French frontier zones with different currency systems from most of the kingdom, would come at a higher price as bankers and currency brokers built in 'insurance' against further manipulations.[24] And, given the geostrategic situation in the War of the Spanish Succession, demanding more foreign exchange than ever before, this mattered. Nevertheless, this was a war in which long-term financial planning was not a priority because of the scale of the demands, and what mattered—for good or ill in the long run—was stop-gap expediency: the augmentations of 1701, 1704, and 1709 eased revenue and credit problems in the short term and thus allowed funds to be made available to, for example, the treasury of the Extraordinaire des Guerres. But it was not a recipe for winning a long war of attrition.

The government would typically prepare an augmentation by decreeing diminutions—or 'abatements'—of the coins in circulation, a decision that did not require coins to be restamped or re-created. This was not primarily so the king could pull in more coins through taxation (denominated in *livres*),[25] as any such gain would be cancelled out: a diminution would in fact also force the king to compensate his fisco-financiers and bankers for losses on their contracts and on the coins they held at the time. The main reason was so there could be huge leaps upward in the value of the coins to the level decreed by the subsequent augmentation, thus bringing in more seigniorage to the king. The government also hoped that a diminution, generating fear of further diminutions, would flush coin out into circulation, particularly for lending to the fisco-financiers. That is why diminutions were announced in advance, with weeks or even months before the new, lower values would come into effect. This gave people a window in which to lend out their assets. There were indeed often several diminutions in a row: prior to the 1693 augmentation, the values of the coins were diminished four times; and prior to the great recoinage of 1709, diminutions were announced in March and November 1708 and on 16 March 1709. The state never brought the coin values back down to the level they had been before the previous augmentation, and this was important to ensure the public did not think the bottom of the valuation had been reached.[26]

This was because there needed to be careful assessment of the market. The military treasurer Montargis, in 1703, stated clearly that abating coin values did put money into circulation but once a diminution started then there had to be several progressive drops; if there were not then money would become rare again, but if society was hit with another and another diminution it would take fright at the possibility of further losses incurred by sitting on coin instead of lending it out. Montargis reckoned that the moment when money was at its rarest was the time to strike with an augmentation. In other words, the public anticipation of an aug-

[24] Forbonnais, II, 210; SHD A[1]1525, no. 179: Mongelas to Chamillart, 29 November 1701; Ya2: Voysin to Saint-Contest[?], June 1710; CCG, III, 80–1: *maire-échevin* and the 'gens des trois ordres' of Metz to Desmaretz, 22 December 1708.

[25] As Dessert (DAPS, 180) and Saint-Germain (*Bernard*, 163) argued.

[26] Forbonnais, II, 181–2, 203; Seligmann, 40, 56, 134–5.

mentation could lead to hoarding of cash, depending on whether people thought the new lower ratings were the lowest the government would go. When available coins were very hard to get, *that* was the moment to announce an augmentation. Desmaretz argued, with some justification, that the diminutions since his arrival at the financial helm in February 1708 had been so well judged they had forced coin out into circulation. Diminutions had certainly produced up to another 5 million *livres* of loans to the Extraordinaire des Guerres back in 1703.[27] The tricky thing was that if the public did not believe there would be another diminution it could really dry up cash fast across the country, since people preferred to wait for an expected augmentation. In March 1712, on the back of observing multiple diminutions over the previous two decades, Samuel Bernard observed that the only way he knew to get people to lend was to announce two or three abatements at once, every couple of months, 'in order to give a cruel uncertainty to those who hold back their money'. Diminutions did flush money out for investing in financial instruments, but this would be limited, especially after a second or third diminution, by fear among lenders that they would be reimbursed in fewer gold and silver coins after an augmentation. Sometimes diminutions simply failed to flush out coin, or threatened not to do so, causing real problems for the bankers and military treasurers.[28]

Moreover, if the legal value of coins in France dipped below the values put on them in neighbouring territories it could cause a flight of coin abroad, the very thing the government wanted to avoid. All governments, indeed, wanted to suck in foreign coin and bullion from abroad, but some were better than others at doing so, and a particularly insidious problem—as far as the French were concerned—was the tendency of some enemy governments in the War of the Spanish Succession to inflate the prices at which French coinage could be received and circulated within their territories. Although other governments had to be careful not to debase their own currencies in international exchange in consequence of this, the British and various Italian territories were engaged in this practice to acquire the highly prized *louis d'or*. Foreign governments could also make their own currencies more exchange-competitive by keeping the value of their unit of account high against their own coins.[29] There were thus floors set by the international market regarding how low the king could go in any coin abatements, and therefore on the ultimate potential for seigniorage that the king might enjoy. These were some of the many trade-offs involved in monetary manipulations and judging their timing.

[27] AN G[7]1775, no. 109: memorandum [by Montargis] on 1702 Extraordinaire des Guerres *exercice*; G[7]1777, no. 230: Montargis to Chamillart, 17 July 1705; CCG, III, 488: Desmaretz to d'Aguesseau, 6 May 1713.

[28] AN G[7]1122: Bernard to Desmaretz, 5 March 1712 (quotation); G[7]1775, no. 315: Pleneuf to [Le Rebours?], 18 December 1703; G[7]1785, no. 128: Renouard to Boutin, 5 August 1709; CCG, II, 91: Des Cassaux du Hallay to Chamillart, 1 November 1701; Forbonnais, II, 191.

[29] AN G[7]1121: 'Memoire a observer sur la Conduitte qu'on tenûs ou tiennent ceux qui ont esté & sont chargé en France de faire remettre les fonds . . . ', [1709–10]. On, e.g., Lorraine, see CCG, II, 180: Saint-Contest to Chamillart, 30 April 1704.

GETTING THE PRICE RIGHT: THE STRUGGLE BETWEEN THE STATE AND THE PUBLIC OVER COINS

The success of the entire interlinked augmentation–diminution process hinged, of course, on the official price of the coins, particularly at the cash booths of the royal mints. But to understand this, the basic 'reformation' process needs some general explanation in a fictitious manner. During the course of one or a series of diminutions, the value of the *louis d'or* (or *écu*) would decline from X *livres* to, say, X – 10. The government would then announce an augmentation—to take place a few days or weeks later—and an end-date—several months into the future—after which unreformed coins would cease to be legal tender. At the same time, the government would announce that during the reformation process the royal mints would accept *louis d'or* at a price of X – 5. This should have given an incentive to people to bring their coins into the mints. After the mint workers had done their work the freshly stamped or recoined *louis d'or* would be returned to the depositors, this time with a value of, say, X + 15. For example, the *louis d'or* might be brought down from 15 *livres* to 12 *livres*, then received in the mints at L13:10s, and released again worth L16:10s. In such a scenario the crown would get a gross profit, before costs, of some 3 *livres* on each *louis d'or* presented.

The depositors would have been given receipts to the value of their coins in *livres*, *sous*, and *deniers*, and coins would be disgorged to the public on the basis of that value, meaning that after the mint work had been done they would receive fewer coins back than they had deposited. The augmentation reformations were initially supposed to take a few months, but—depending on the pace at which coins were brought in—numerous extensions to the end-date of the process could be made. In consequence, for example, the reformation begun on 13 December 1689 actually lasted until the spring of 1693, and that announced in September 1701 went on for over two and a half years. During those periods, the deadlines for bringing old coins into the mints were repeatedly extended to try to maximize seigniorage revenues for the king, and to give enough time for coins that had been exported to be brought back into the country (should any holders want to put them through the mints).

The price the government set for the royal mints to accept old coins, or foreign coins or bullion for that matter, is what we might call the 'mint specie point' or the 'bullion price'. To ensure maximum seigniorage gains, on paper, the king needed to set a mint specie point way below the *fiat* value of the new coins that would be disgorged, but this might well not produce optimal gains in reality. So, the public could make a small notional gain from handing in coin if the legal circulation rate was X – 10 and the mint specie point was X – 5, while the government could make a big profit if it then disgorged coins at a new legal circulation rate of X + 15. Alternatively, if the government set the mint specie point at X – 2 the public would reduce its losses in this reformation while the government's seigniorage profit (the difference between X – 2 and X + 15) would be less. Setting the rate was a matter of trial and error, and one cannot escape the thought that ministers were acting intuitively. With the government having its own interests in the price offered, the mint specie point did not necessarily reflect the market value of the coins, either in terms of their intrinsic value or in terms of the relationship between the old coins and the new ones that the market would try to set. This caused the failure, or limited success, of most of the manipulations of the French coinage undertaken in this period.

Neither Chamillart nor Pontchartrain before him seems to have had clear ideas about what level the mint specie point should be set at: in March 1706, for example, Chamillart reduced the mint specie point, thinking that the government could get more of a profit from the silver being brought in, but it rapidly became evident that people were simply not going to deposit silver, *écus*, or *piastres* in the mints at all. The duc de Noailles, shortly after assuming control of royal finances during the regency for Louis XV, noted that many people holding coins or precious metal had wanted to get far higher prices for bringing them to the mints, and had been deterred from doing so by the ungenerous official rates offered. But policy changed over the course of the war, since Desmaretz and those high up in the state who had dealings with the Spanish monarchy do seem to have come to appreciate this problem. Indeed, as early as autumn 1708 Desmaretz pretty much settled for a policy of getting bullion into France through attractive rates, rather than trying to get a profit on it for the king, and this approach continued for the rest of the war.[30] From *existing* French coins, however, the government continued throughout the period 1689–1715 to seek seigniorage profits, and this did a lot to produce false-coining and the export of French coin. Several *intendants* back in 1704 had already warned Chamillart and Desmaretz of the effects of a badly judged set of mint specie points and reissue values that benefited the crown too much at the expense of the public.[31] In essence, the amount of seigniorage the crown was willing to settle for could determine how many coins were brought in for reminting: too high a profit for the king and too high a specie loss for the public (based upon the difference between the new circulation rate and the mint specie point) could act as a major deterrent to public cooperation with the state's monetary alterations. The high rates of seigniorage extracted in the 1693 and 1704 reformations produced a serious drop in the number of coins processed by the mints, when compared with those of 1689 and 1701 (as well as 1709) in which the state had sought fewer profits. Taking these several reformations together, it would seem that anything more than a one-tenth seigniorage gain for the king was likely to provoke the presentation of less coin and bullion at the mints than the government had hoped for.[32]

Instead, people would hold on to the old coins, in the expectation that the government would have to blink first and offer better prices, and there is a lot of evidence in this period that people simply did not believe the government when it gave people 'final chances' to convert money or paper devices. Amnesties for old

[30] CCG, II, 308: *mémoire* by Trudaine, 11 March 1706; III, 49: duc de Gramont to Desmaretz, 1 September 1708; AN $G^7$1787, no. 290: memorandum on Bayonne finances, 19 January 1712.

[31] For example CCG, II, 187: Béchameil de Nointel [brother-in-law of Desmaretz, no less] to Chamillart, 11 June 1704.

[32] Forbonnais, II, 46, 96, 129, 139.

coin, in the shape of enhanced legal circulation values and an acceptance that unreformed coins could continue circulating for some time to come, were issued by the government (e.g. December 1709). Such long-term hoarding in the hope of a better deal would also account much later for very old coins often being accepted under the counter, for a cut, by mint workers.[33] Alternatively, if people thought the government would not give in, the money would go underground. If the royal mints were not offering a competitive price—in terms of *livres* per *marc* for bullion and foreign currency; and *livres*, *sous*, and *deniers* for French coins—then many holders would sell coins to others, who would then either export them to somewhere that would value them more highly or put them into the murky world of false-coining workshops. The falsely reformed coins would then be placed back into circulation at the new official rate. Anecdotally, it would appear that for bulk acquisitions traffickers might have to offer 10 per cent or more over the official mint specie point for old coins (though this could be much lower if the little people were the sellers), and then they had to have a margin of another 3–4 per cent at minimum to make it worthwhile. The forgers were happy with a smaller profit than the king was seeking. In the Nine Years War, the government initially does not seem to have expected this. Ironically, by setting the augmented coin values much higher than the current low circulation values, the state was not only creating the possibility of a large profit for itself, it was also creating just such an opportunity for organized fraudsters. The scope for such fraud, then, depended upon where the mint specie point was set. Too far below the reissue value and fraudsters could offer a more competitive 'deposit' price, but the closer the mint specie point was to the reissue value the less seigniorage the crown would get; a difficult trade-off to judge. The long lead-in times for both augmentations and diminutions, however necessary for practical reasons, had the disadvantage that they also gave time for crooks to buy up coins in competition with the state. The unreformed coins would be bought up either with bills of exchange on a foreign source denominated in *livres* which people could later cash for falsely reformed French coins, or with foreign coins that had no officially fixed circulation value inside France.[34]

By the War of the Spanish Succession, the French authorities knew that they had a serious problem on their hands. According to D'Honneur, one of Chamillart's principal advisers, in February 1702 (when an augmentation was ongoing) some dishonest financiers were seeking out unreformed *louis d'or* and giving to ordinary people 1, 2, or 3 *sous* more for them than the mint specie point price, with the purpose of making a profit:

> It appears that this is to pass them to the frontiers where they are given to those who make remittances to the troops, or into foreign lands to get them reformed and then sent back into France, where they will circulate [at the new augmented rate], even though light weight.

[33] AN $G^7$1775, no. 95: *arrêt*, 27 September 1701; CCG, II, 191: Chamillart to all *intendants*, 5 July 1704.

[34] Lévy, *Capitalistes*, I, 22–3, 207; CCG, II, 77: Le Bret to Chamillart, 20 June 1701; Forbonnais, II, 205.

Short of finding evidence for a big operator being caught red-handed, D'Honneur's view should be taken with the utmost seriousness: some of the biggest players in the currency reformation scams were men intimately connected with the supply of money to the French armies. One such character, Joseph Planchut, was *receveur général* of the *généralité* of Toulouse and a Lyon banker essential for the remittances to the king's armies abroad: he was apparently at the centre of an elaborate coin-assembling and transport operation from Languedoc to Geneva whenever a monetary diminution was in view.[35] This would indicate that at least some people wanted to get shot of coin as soon as a first diminution occurred, and the fraudsters wanted to get the coins into storage ready for releasing to the forgers once it became clear what an augmented, reformed coin would look like. For obvious reasons, it only made sense to start the faking of the new or reformed coins once the mints started disgorging examples, but depending on anticipated coin values—and here men like Planchut reveal their speculative nature—it also made sense to start collecting the old coins as early as possible for practical reasons.

The government needed to do something to try to counteract this assault by its own war suppliers on one of the key marques of royal sovereignty, the right to mint and set values on coin. One way was to go in for a diminution of new, reformed coins quickly, as this would shrink the profit margin of forgers who would have to put their fraudulent coins back into circulation at a lower-than-expected value. But this would only work if the government was resigned to getting few more coins for restamping into the mints anyway. Another way was to continue with further diminutions of the legal circulation values of unreformed coins:[36] this would increase the costs traffickers would incur in buying up coins, while hopefully forcing coin-holders to bring them to the mints for fear of further diminutions. The first such extra diminution was usually enough to kill traffickers' carefully calibrated profit margins, but, depending on other factors such as the acceptance rate of unreformed French coins abroad, this might not produce the deposit of more coins at the royal mints. This was tried in 1709 with only limited success. Eventually the government would abrogate the legal tender status of unreformed coins, but those who still held them by this stage were probably people who could either get them melted down and completely recast, or thought they had some influence over government now or in the future to get the mints to take their holdings.

Alternatively, if he really desperately needed to get more coin circulating in France, the king could swallow hard and simply pay a premium for coins brought into the mints in bulk by his own bankers, financiers, and supply contractors, people who would naturally be amassing lots of coin anyway and who could thereby disguise their involvement in coin buy-up operations that undercut the government's profit. Although a lot of the money found in this way had been abroad, one suspects a great deal of it had not, and the men involved might try to sell it to the government at a preferential rate, higher than the mint specie point and sometimes even in excess of the market value of the coins. In the Nine Years

[35] SHD A[1]1613, no. 178: D'Honneur to Chamillart, 22 February 1702; Chaussinand, 44.

[36] Lévy, *Capitalistes*, I, 359–60; Vuitry, 141–5.

War the government had shown, as its ministers later realized, some naïvety about buying coin or bullion from such money men at higher rates than the mints would offer to the rest of the public. Within two years the government had learned that such people were buying up more and more coins in anticipation of augmentations, so the king stopped giving contracts to 'repatriate' coins to the mints. Alas, speculators switched back to simple false-coining, thus still reducing the amount of seigniorage gains the government might make. In the War of the Spanish Succession Chamillart and Desmaretz did all they could to avoid repeating the use of contracts for bringing unreformed French coins into the mints.[37]

If the government were to accept bulk deposits of specie and bullion from big financial players, it was better to do so on an ad hoc, unadvertised basis. This method was used to acquire bullion and foreign coins that the government could be more certain were entering the country from abroad. The government set differential acceptance prices at the mints between gold and silver coming in from abroad and that of domestic origin. The exact terms had to be kept as secret as possible not only to reduce fraud by other big financiers, but also so as not to stymie the hand-in of unreformed French coins by the rest of the population, who would then see just what price the government was really willing to pay. Mints would pay the standard rates to anyone contracted to bring in coins, while the additional premiums were paid secretly through the Trésor royal. Bankers such as Lullin agreed to bring Spanish *piastres* to the mints in return for cashing an equal value of depreciated paper instruments there. After the great 1709 financial crisis, Samuel Bernard and his associates, the Saladin brothers, were charged with bringing into France as many guineas, ducats, *pistoles* and, placing temptation in their way once again, old *louis d'or* as they could find.[38]

The government did continue to be very flexible towards favoured French and Spanish merchants, and some financiers, about the rates at which bullion would be received in and paid out from mints, but sometimes the hallmark of policy was less adaptability and more sheer confusion about costs and market behaviour. Mint specie points for Spanish *piastres* might be set without sufficient regard for the transportation costs of getting them to some mints, especially at Paris and in eastern France. The bankers Samuel Bernard and Daniel Hogguer on several occasions warned the government that mint prices (especially those offered to traders in gold and silver finery for cloth) had to be higher than market prices if *piastres* were to be sucked into France. But the government sometimes reduced the mint specie point in a misguided effort to get more seigniorage profit.[39] Only in 1709 did Desmaretz set realistic and very favourable prices for bringing foreign coin and metal into the mints, producing steady results for over two years. *Intendant* Méliand, in March

[37] Lüthy, I, 44, 117, 128; Lévy, *Capitalistes*, I, 46–7, 55–61; AN G[7]1119: La Closure to Desmaretz, 9 June 1709; CCG, II, 237: Desmaretz to Saint-Maurice, 24 October 1704.

[38] Lüthy, I, 129, 132, 190, 232; CCG, III, 247: Bernage to Desmaretz, several letters between December 1709 and March 1710.

[39] AN G[7]1123: 'Memoire des freres Hogguer', [late 1705–early 1706]; Daniel Hogguer to [Le Rebours?], 2 September 1706; G[7]1093: note from Amelot (unsigned memorandum-placet), 10 September 1708; SHD A[1]1699, no. 322: Bernard to Chamillart, 13 October 1703.

1714, reported that over the previous five years the massively elevated value of *louis d'or* and *écus* in France, and the rates at which coin and metal were received in the mints, had sucked all old French gold and silver coins, and a great deal of foreign metal too, back into the country, with very little leaving France. Though Méliand exaggerated, this improvement was helped along a great deal when, in December 1712, Louis XIV finally gave up attempts to get any profit on coin conversion at the mints, settling instead for simply having enough coin in France on which the state and its agents could draw.[40]

Had the king and his ministers taken this approach to coin valuation from the start of the Nine Years War, instead of pursuing the chimera of increased revenues from seigniorage, the king and his ministers might have had better credit opportunities and terms at their disposal. Instead, leaving aside the effect on non-agricultural wages,[41] manipulations ensured credit became more expensive (threatening, for example, a 2 per cent rise in interest rates in February 1703), and the techniques and instrumentation of credit were arguably stunted. At the same time, supply and banking contracts became uncertain and required greater guarantees.[42] This was particularly the case for foreign exchange dealings, where actual costs diverged significantly from what the government wanted and hoped to pay to move money abroad to its troops and allies. Diminutions of coin values should in theory have brought exchange rates down but they did not, because of the uncertainties about an ultimate leap upwards in values during an expected coin augmentation.[43] More generally, volatile monetary periods—regardless of whether coins were officially valued higher or lower than their market value—could even lead to a shortage of parties willing to issue bills of exchange and therefore also produce more expensive foreign exchange, because people were uncertain how many coins they might ultimately receive in final redemption of such bills.[44] General instability could also produce exchange charges and market values for French coins based upon speculative hopes (held by the *vivres* companies, for example) of estimated gain after a future augmentation.[45] Stronger *louis d'or* and *écus* would certainly dampen imports and thereby improve the balance of trade, but this would come at a cost to the overall volume of trade and therefore reduce the availability of cheap exchange for France on foreign marketplaces.[46] It was fortunate that the policy of the very weak *livre* after 1709 came at a time when the state's demand for foreign

[40] E. Levasseur, *Histoire du commerce de France: Première partie: avant 1789* (Paris, 1911), 328; AN G[7]1787, no. 244: *mémoire* by Mesnager, [1711]; CCG, III, 529: Méliand to Desmaretz, 25 March 1714; III, 678: 'Compte rendu de M. Desmaretz au Régent', [1716].

[41] Upward: see Forbonnais, II, 248.

[42] AN G[7]1775, no. 109: memorandum on Extraordinaire, 20 February 1703; Philip T. Hoffman, Gilles Postel-Vinay, and Jean-Laurent Rosenthal, *Priceless Markets: The Political Economy of Credit in Paris, 1660–1870* (London, 2000), 3, 22, 56–7; Mark Potter, *Corps and Clienteles: Public Finance and Political Change in France, 1688–1715* (Aldershot, 2003), 113, 169; Forbonnais, II, 247–8.

[43] SHD A[1]1965, no. 230: [Note on exchange] by David Vittafano [of Venice], [October 1706]; AN G[7]1119: Bernard to Chamillart, 19 June 1706.

[44] For example CCG, II, 64: Herbigny to Chamillart, 18 December 1700.

[45] For example AN G[7]1782, no. 18: *mémoire* by Galloys on the *munitionnaires*, [February 1708].

[46] AN G[7]1119: 'Mémoire', [first months of 1715]; SHD A[1]2409: Pleneuf to Tourton, 8 October 1712.

exchange was much reduced, after French forces had very largely retreated behind the kingdom's frontiers.

If the pattern of market reactions to the coinage manipulations, and to official prices set for bullion and foreign coin, appears mixed and extremely complicated—reflecting, as markets always do, myriad interests, calculations, and circumstances—the effects of the manipulations can be seen with real clarity in the sums emitted by the mints, which heavily declined between 1689 and 1715. According to Forbonnais' figures, across the whole period there was a drop in success of 40 per cent in real terms between the 1689 and 1709 reformations. Most of that fall came with the second great reformation of 1693, but one should also note the disastrous product of the 1704 reformation, which processed a mere 38 per cent of the amount done by its 1689 precursor. Royal income from this process, as we have seen, was limited, the benefits were shared with forgers—among them the crown's own financial contractors—and what benefits were accrued, at most 6 million *livres* per annum on average, were more than outweighed by the extra costs that the monarchy's arbitrary monetary policy imposed on its war effort. Forbonnais estimated that coin enhancements in the years 1688–99 increased the cost of supplies bought by the state during this period by 5 per cent, or around 6 million *livres* per annum, owing to the unfavourable exchange rates this produced.[47] One can safely reckon the additional costs this generated were even greater in the years 1701–14, when vastly more funds and supplies from abroad were acquired and the coinage enhancements were much larger. The manipulations also led the crown into the most dangerous expedient of all, as the sheer pressure the monarchy put on its mints, even with the disappointing amount of coin processed, forced it into permitting the issue of Mint bills. These began as stopgap receipts but gradually became supplementary currency, thus setting up yet another monetary device that could be manipulated for short-term revenue. The temptation became extreme and the monarchy was unable to resist it, with disastrous results.

[47] Forbonnais, II, 76, 97, 106, 129, 134, 139, 209, 221.

6

Paper Money and Absolute Monarchy

In the first two decades of the eighteenth century France undertook a series of experiments in the use of paper money that would culminate in the Mississippi Bubble. Without the debt problems bequeathed by Louis XIV, and the steps taken in the use of paper instruments, however shambolic they were, there would have been little receptivity in government circles for the schemes that John Law gradually rolled out after 1715, at the centre of which stood his bank notes. It was a highly volatile two decades, and the atmosphere was markedly different from even the 1690s. That decade had seen the rapid spread in the use of bearer bills, promissory notes, and the like, to which we have already been introduced, and the most significant form of these devices that came into widespread use in the War of the Spanish Succession—the bills issued by the Extraordinaire des Guerres—will be examined in Chapter 9. This chapter, however, will focus on the Mint bills that came to flood the markets in the 1700s, instruments to which the government gave limited legal status in an effort to encourage their use, up to a point, as supplementary official currency. As the economic thinker Boisguilbert put it in an ecclesiastical metaphor, Mint bills became 'a coadjutor for specie'.[1] This chapter will accordingly try to explain how the Mint bills functioned, why they were needed, how they very largely escaped the government's control within a few short years, and how this all related to the war effort.

MONETARY KNOTWEED: THE RISE AND RISE OF THE MINT BILL

However fast and smoothly the French state managed (or did not manage) to get bullion and specie into the royal mints for restamping or recoining, the mint workers still needed time to revise the metal before spewing it out into society again. If the mints as a group across the kingdom were usually operating a little below capacity, periodically there were months if not years of acute pressure.[2] The Paris Mint had the greatest problems of them all: Paris was the financial capital that drew coin like a Newtonian occult force. Yet the number of men who had the requisite skills to be mint workers, even there, was insufficient for the amount of

[1] CCG, II, 537: Boisguilbert to Chamillart, 4 July 1704.
[2] Spooner, 113–14.

specie that had to be processed during the organized remintings and recoinages of the Nine Years War and the War of the Spanish Succession.

The mints had traditionally provided receipts known as 'récépissés'—denominated in *livres, sous,* and *deniers*—for deposits made with them, and these could be cashed after a very short amount of time when new specie was ready. From 1683 these were put into circulation, though they traded in a very limited fashion, and from 1693, at the time of a major recoining, the first 'billets de monnoie', or Mint bills, were issued, valid for periods of a month and for larger deposits of coin. In hindsight this step was clearly taken in order to 'bridge' the period we should call a 'hiatus of specie', when the volume of coins in circulation was temporarily reduced by mint activity, and the government, in the midst of a war and (in 1693) economic crisis, needed to keep supplies and pay flowing to the armies and navy. This was moderately successful, so, with a further augmentation and calling-in of the coinage at the end of the first campaign season in the War of the Spanish Succession, on 19 September 1701 the government repeated the trick. It now stressed in an edict that these Mint bills could be used as a cash substitute in private transactions. These Mint bills were issued only by the Paris Mint, the Hôtel de Monnaie. Just over a month later it was becoming clear that the newly stamped coins were being reissued at a slower than hoped for rate, so these bills—known eponymously as 'billets Euldes' after the master of the Paris Mint—were transformed into title deeds bearing 4 per cent interest per annum.[3] The Mint still aspired to redeem them within a month, and for the first six months of this reminting episode monetary discipline was preserved: Mint bills were issued to exactly the value (in *livres*) of the gold and silver deposits. But in the first quarter of 1702 it became clear that the government was supplying the military treasurers with *assignations* (appropriation orders) on revenue sources (such as the *taille*) which had a term date stretching too far into the future for the money to be realized when needed. Under pressure from the banker Samuel Bernard and the treasurers general of the Extraordinaire des Guerres, Chamillart therefore authorized the mints to pump out more bills than the specie and bullion deposits justified, handing them to the king's spending officials. It was the first of several occasions when the government reacted to pressure from its most important financial remitters and payers with a multiple increase in Mint bills, bringing inflationary potential for the war effort.[4]

From this point on, the number of Mint bills in circulation continued to rise, reaching a value of 6.6 million *livres* at the end of 1703. This was still a very small proportion of overall monetary volume, but if they were mishandled the Mint bills could nevertheless plunge a country that depended on tight margins of circulating cash into crisis. In September of that year the government reiterated that Paris Mint bills would continue to circulate as cash substitutes, and further decreed that only bills equal to or less than 600 *livres* would be reimbursed with coin; those of

[3] Spooner, 203; Seligmann, 70; Vuitry, 169–70; DAPS, 185.

[4] SHD A[1]1613, no. 183: Montargis to Chamillart, 29 March 1702; Esnault, I, 94–6: 'Mémoire', probably by Desmaretz, [January 1702]; I, 97: 'Mémoire' by Bernard, 27 January 1702; Michaud, 359.

a higher value would be replaced by new Mint bills reimbursable in 1704. This was tantamount to admitting that reimbursement of coin was on a go-slow or was even partially suspended. Until autumn 1703 the Mint bills had retained the confidence of the public because they were being turned over and reimbursed on a limited but noticeable basis, but in October the first crisis over the Mint bills struck. Despite the September edict, even small Mint bills were not being reimbursed as they should have been, so coin availability was drying up as people feared reimbursement for their business transactions in dubious instruments that could not be cashed or easily transferred. This coincided with the time when the financial public were becoming increasingly aware that revenues from the *fermes générales*, used *inter alia* to back the *rentes* on the Paris Hôtel de ville, were also in rapid decline. The government consequently succumbed to this pressure to find further sources of extraordinary revenue.[5] Without waiting for additional old coins to come in for reminting, the government, in May 1704, started yet another augmentation of the coinage. Predictably this would mean the emission of yet more Mint bills even before the old ones (stemming from the 1701 reminting episode) had been redeemed. Furthermore, some larger Mint bills had had their redemption dates pushed back to July 1704, and all were now carrying an enhanced interest rate of 8 per cent per annum.[6]

The great crisis broke in early August 1704, some time *before* the defeat at Blenheim. The Lyon money market was overloaded for the first time by the need to remit money at once to Spain, Italy, Flanders, and Bavaria on an unprecedented scale, and this coincided with several other major problems: Lyon itself was suffering from a shortage of specie thanks to the coin augmentation; revenues from the *fermes générales* and the *receveurs généraux* had continued to shrink and some *assignations* had totally failed; and Samuel Bernard, tasked with much international remitting, was owed over 4.3 million *livres* by a variety of people. On 6 August Bernard therefore pressured Chamillart to allow him to deposit *assignations* and other instruments he had received with the Paris Mint. In return he would get Mint bills redeemable three to four months after the *assignations* matured, and these sleeping *assignations* could even be used to postpone the redemption of Mint bills should Chamillart wish. Although it is not clear exactly when Bernard's proposal was adopted, this siren song was, in essence, a proposal to decouple completely Mint bills from coin deposits, and to gamble upon the eventual realization of royal revenue instruments to back a far larger number of Mint bills than had so far been issued. Up until then Mint bills had remained in essence bridging instruments whose interest-bearing character served to try to maintain the favour of the public, but now they were becoming a bizarre new hybrid. Mint bills mutated into long-term money substitutes, which might never be turned into cash at the Mint, *and* which carried interest as a form of government short-term debt. In the words

[5] 1704 was the peak year for financial expedients, and a huge number of contracts were also signed for *affaires extraordinaires*.

[6] Vuitry, 171–3; Saint-Germain, *Bernard*, 165; AN G[7]1775, no. 278: Pleneuf to Le Rebours, 21 October 1703; no. 283: Pomereuil to Chamillart, 31 October 1703; no. 425: Fabert[?] to Chamillart, 20 October 1703.

of a memorandum four years later, Bernard came to be seen as the 'author in Mr de Chamillart's circle of the multiplicity and abuse of the *billets de monnoye*'. The practice of bankers, military paymasters, and others depositing dangerous paper instruments with the Mint and getting Mint bills in return therefore began in the second half of the summer of 1704, and was critical to maintaining liquidity until the summer of the following year. Moreover, by October, if not far earlier, the *Garde du Trésor royal* was negotiating various bearer bills drawn on the *fermes générales* for cash (at discounts), and putting the cash into the Paris Mint, the said cash then being parcelled out to Bernard for other paper he deposited with the Mint. Other depositors found themselves being propelled further back in the Mint queue for getting their cash back.[7] The acute financial crisis of July–August 1704 certainly required some drastic action to raise short-term loans, but the consequences of doing so through a mutant form of money that became a fixture of the scene were to bedevil French royal finances and the availability of credit for the next decade and even, indirectly, for longer.

No sooner had Bernard offered his plan for expanding the money supply available to royal remitters than the money markets suffered further upheaval. On 21 August news reached Paris of the rout of the Franco-Bavarian armies at the hands of the Duke of Marlborough and Prince Eugène of Savoy at Blenheim on the Danube eight days earlier. This provoked a run on the Caisse des emprunts prompting an edict on 17 September suspending payments on its *promesses* until 1 April 1705, which in turn did nothing to shore up confidence in other paper instruments. With the Caisse now temporarily closed off as a source of fresh credit, the government turned elsewhere. While 1704 had seen another 7 million *livres* of Mint bills put into circulation, during March 1705 alone another 43 million *livres* were issued. Meanwhile, in January that year, it had proved impossible to redeem Mint bills in specie. They were therefore made exchangeable for fresh Mint bills that were renewable and carried 7.5 per cent interest per annum—a reduction from the previous high of 8 per cent that must surely have unsettled holders.[8]

All this notwithstanding, it was only in April 1705 that confidence in Mint bills slumped, when the government reimbursed matured Caisse des emprunts notes half in Mint bills and only half in cash. It was now quite evident that huge numbers of Mint bills had been specifically created, unbacked, to stave off the collapse of other paper instruments, so the tradable value of the Mint bills themselves fell by three-quarters in a matter of a few days. The government declared they would be accepted for up to half of the value of any fresh deposit made in the Caisse des emprunts or in the purchase of *rentes* on the Paris Hôtel de ville, hoping this would

[7] Victor de Swarte, *Un banquier du Trésor Royal au XVIIIe siècle. Samuel Bernard. Sa vie—sa correspondance (1651–1739)* (Paris/Nancy, 1893), 27; AN G^{7}1120: Bernard to Chamillart, 6 August and 6 October 1704; G^{7}1011: memoranda entitled 'Le S^{r}. Euldes 1708' and 'Copies des ordres de Monseigneur Chamillart', [both June 1708]. Also, 'Memoire sur les billets de monnoie', 1708, printed in appendix to André-E. Sayous, 'La crise financière de 1709 à Lyon et à Genève', *Revue d'histoire économique et sociale* 24 (1938), 170.

[8] Dangeau, X, 101; Michaud, 359, 365; Seligmann, 76; Saint-Germain, *Bernard*, 165; BNF F-21056: *déclaration*, 6 December 1704.

prop up their value. But to try to keep cash circulating it was also decreed that a maximum of only one-quarter of any deal or payment in Paris could be made using Mint bills. These announcements were really made not to support the Mint bills for their own sake so much as to support the king's war entrepreneurs: the Mint bills deposited in the Caisse des emprunts were parcelled out to suppliers of finance and *matériel* for the armies for use in paying off their own debts, and the king was giving them moral support in their efforts to force such discredited instruments on their creditors. Even so, it was a decision that was misguided, probably because it had never been attempted before: royal suppliers needed cash to pay their own suppliers, or at least cash was needed further down the supply chain, so either the first or second pair of hands into which the Mint bills passed would have to try to trade them for cash, which meant accepting a huge discount. In turn, they would then insist on further compensation from a government that was ill-inclined to give it but in the case of its biggest suppliers had to do so to retain their essential services.[9]

Surprisingly, at this stage the markets did not react by reducing the status of Mint bills to lavatory paper, and this needs explanation. As the disgraced rogue banker Huguetan observed in July 1705, 'although there are no funds to back them, the daily benefit [in the form of interest] and the ease [of use] has ensured they have been received up to now with all sorts of confidence'. Inertia also aided the state during these months: if Mint bills were on hand for paying royal debts and suppliers, they would be accepted simply because they were available; by contrast, Samuel Bernard revealed, if a particular financial bureau said it had nothing and directed people to the Paris Mint then this caused people to demand cash. It was, of course, far easier to print more Mint bills than produce the coins. Bernard also did what he could (and why would he not, given his dependence on Mint bills?) to steady the nerves of his correspondents against Allied attempts to discredit French paper altogether, though he could only continue to get huge amounts of foreign exchange at a heavier price. Furthermore, it was not yet suspected that the government would let Mint bills increase in volume even further to the astronomical heights they would reach in 1706–7. All this notwithstanding, the royal decision to give aid to the state's main financial suppliers in the form of unbacked Mint bills in the late summer and autumn of 1704, and again on a far greater scale in the spring of 1705, came at a serious cost: trading relations were disrupted, with knock-on effects for tax revenue; foreign exchange was made far more expensive, especially for Bernard; and creditors did not want to be paid by, or enter into transactions with, Parisian debtors if it meant accepting Mint bills.[10] Were this to continue over months, it would only promote volatility in the market value of Mint bills.

Moreover, the very structure of the Mint bills, and the still limited use of them that could be made, did not help in their circulation and credibility, and for this

[9] BNF F-21058: *déclaration*, 24 October 1706.

[10] AN G[7]1119: 'Memoire touchant les finances de France que le S[r]. Huguetan a donné au mois de Juillet 1705'; G[7]1120: Bernard to Chamillart, 1 April 1705; Forbonnais, II, 152.

the government was also responsible. To receive interest on a Mint bill, it would have to be presented at the Paris Mint for renewal: after July 1706 bills worth 1,000-plus *livres* needed to be presented every month, with the consequence that their circulation and their general attractiveness for use in high-volume foreign exchange were diminished even further. Smaller bills needed to be renewed after six months, which meant interest flowed even more slowly towards their holders.[11] Even more of a problem were the high values in which Mint bills were denominated, which meant there was relatively little additional monetization brought to daily economic life in France, something John Law criticized. Samuel Bernard actually wanted to set the minimum size at 1,000 *livres* so as to maintain Mint bills as the preserve of high-volume financial trading, but with Chamillart already committed to using them for artificially supporting the war effort this was simply impractical. As it was, the smallest value of a Mint bill in the earlier years appears to have been 500 *livres*. Relatively high values such as this meant that bulk suppliers could not pay many of their smaller suppliers in Mint bills, nor could the Extraordinaire des Guerres easily pay army officers and small-scale regimental suppliers in this manner. It was also very hard for the Extraordinaire des Guerres to use them to discharge some of its short-term bearer bills, which had been parcelled out to cover smaller sums. Moreover, by 1706 there were too few Mint bills worth 500 *livres* for the needs of paper financial reimbursements and bills of exchange emitted by the Extraordinaire des Guerres. In February that year this led Chamillart, under pressure from the military paymasters, to issue many more 500-*livre* bills, again unbacked by coin or even *assignations*. By this time, though, it appears the crown had grasped the problem of Mint bill size: the smallest value had been reduced to 400 *livres* by May and to 200 *livres* on 6 July, but policy veered wildly with the permitted size of the smallest bill fluctuating between 100 and 500 *livres*. However, even 100-*livre* bills did not overcome the problem that families, army officers, smaller suppliers, and others needed to make a lot of transactions below this level, so their purchasing power dropped if they came to hold such instruments.[12] These people would need to sell their Mint bills for discount rates, thus contributing to the discredit in which they were held.

On top of this, there was a real problem of convertibility with the Mint bills. Not only were they not redeemed as expected, but the government's own lack of enthusiasm for accepting them from the public in royal fisco-financiers' coffers was severely detrimental to their credibility. As early as January 1705 *intendant* Trudaine of Lyon warned Chamillart that this was one of the reasons the Lyon market, not as yet directly exposed to the Mint bills, was so worried about their growing use: the king's refusal to accept Mint bills 'in any of his bureaux [...] makes [the public] suspect the worth of this form of money, since the King, who

[11] Seligmann, 75, 79; BNF F-21058: *déclaration*, 6 July 1706.

[12] Richard Bonney, 'France and the First European Paper Money Experiment', *French History* 15 (2001), 257; AN G⁷1120: Bernard to [Le Rebours?], 19 December 1705; G⁷1775, no. 277: Pleneuf to Chamillart, 13 October 1703; G⁷1778, no. 15: note on 'Reassignations', 24 January 1706; BNF F-21058: *déclaration*, 6 July 1706; *déclaration*, 24 October 1706; Forbonnais, II, 162; CCG, II, 203: Montrevel to Chamillart, 26 November 1707.

creates it, in no way wants to get it for himself'. Unfortunately, the logic that led Chamillart to expand the use of Mint bills—the needs of the war effort—also insisted that they should not be accepted as a form of taxation. In reply to Trudaine, Director General Desmaretz accepted that Mint bills would have more credit if they were accepted in the king's coffers, but then all the king's revenue-gathering financiers would be inundated with them. One can see the point of view of the Finance Ministry: for the government's fisco-financiers to receive Mint bills in tax or in venal payments from the king's subjects was to add even more to the costs of the war effort at some point further down the supply chain, once these additional Mint bills had been paid out. The king wanted cash. Only in October 1710 did Desmaretz decide to use tax payments as one pathway for the gradual extinction of Mint bills altogether.[13]

Nevertheless, government policy—irresistibly driven by short-term fiscal-military needs—became inconsistent about accepting Mint bills in payment of obligations to the state. A number of fisco-financiers with interests in handling the king's expenditure, as well as bankers like Bernard, lobbied from December 1703 for Mint bills to be accepted by revenue officers, not least, so Bernard argued, 'in order to make it known that the King regards them himself as extremely good instruments'. Not all of a transaction needed to be in Mint bills, and—he suggested—the king could set a ceiling on the proportion that could be included in a single fiscal payment or loan deposit. But it took the crisis of the Caisse des emprunts in April 1705 for the first breach in the dyke to be made, when the government agreed to accept Mint bills for up to half of each deposit made at this institution. As Desmaretz had predicted a few weeks earlier, the volume of Mint bills being pressed on the various 'caisses publiques' now increased. For the rest of the War of the Spanish Succession Mint bills were received in royal coffers inconsistently, sometimes for a proportion of a payment, sometimes in certain branches of the revenue and credit system, and sometimes not at all.[14]

Governing circles remained split between those who championed greater circulation for Mint bills and those who worried that this would produce a sharp and potentially disastrous reduction in coin availability for the armies and navy. The contrast with England could not be greater: though England did not have Mint bills it did have Bank of England notes, and these were received in all payments made to the state and its agents.[15] It was consequently far easier to use them as coin substitutes, whereas in France the anxiety about insufficient gold and silver coin led the government into an incoherent Mint bill policy that further shrank these forms of specie, pushed up the cost of getting them, and increased the price of

[13] CCG, II, 228: Trudaine to Chamillart, 18 January 1705; II, 229: Desmaretz to Trudaine, 11 February 1705; AN G[7]1031: *arrêt*, 27 January 1711.

[14] AN G[7]1775, no. 249: [Two *trésoriers de France*] to Chamillart, 20 December 1703; G[7]1779, no. 198: Dupille's memorandum for Chamillart, [May 1707]; Bernard, *mémoire* of 30 December 1703, in Swarte, *Un banquier*, 22; Forbonnais, II, 152; Seligmann, 81; CCG, II, 441: Trudaine to Chamillart, 29 October 1707; BNF F-21058: *déclaration*, 24 October 1706.

[15] 'Mémoire au sujet de l'établissement d'une banque en France' [by John Law], 1702, in Paul Harsin, *Crédit public et Banque d'État en France du XVI*[e] *au XVIII*[e] *siècle* (Paris, 1933), 110.

supplying the war. Chamillart and his advisers were in uncharted waters, and obviously did not know how markets or local economies would really react if faced with a full-scale use of Mint bills alongside cash, but with hindsight we can see that their half-hearted and inconsistent use of Mint bills, coupled with the emission of ever greater quantities of them, was the worst of all worlds.

And the numbers kept on climbing, diminishing confidence further. The major source of the discrediting of the Mint bills was the insufficiency of resources devoted to their redemption, a failure of appropriations that was the hallmark of Chamillart's tenure of the contrôle général.[16] He simply allowed more and more debt to pile up and instead devoted available revenue resources to the armies. He failed to see that he could have better sustained the war effort through borrowed money that could have been obtained more easily had more of the tax revenues been devoted to rolling over the debts and Mint bills in as timely a fashion as the financial vagaries of the period allowed. Trudaine, who as *intendant* of Lyon was the government's canary down the financial mineshaft, was not taken seriously enough when he stressed in January 1705 that two of Lyon's greatest fears were: one, that the interest on Mint bills would be paid in yet more Mint bills, and two, that the bills would never be redeemed with cash. He would repeat these points, Cassandra-like, over the coming years, contrasting France with the governments of Venice and Holland which enjoyed excellent credit because they repaid their creditors in cash upon demand at the maturity of a loan. The historian Philippe Sagnac, not unreasonably, suggested the government needed to have immediately available only a quarter of the capital value of all Mint bills to meet likely demands for reimbursement. Although Chamillart did try to redeem a lot of the Mint bills, he renewed far too many of them by *fiat*. And while a lot of coins were needed for the bankers Bernard and the Hogguer brothers, and for the Extraordinaire des Guerres, Chamillart short-sightedly channelled too many straight to them. He also handed them more and more unbacked Mint bills, in effect simply printing money.[17]

By January 1706 Mint bills to the value of 100 million *livres* were circulating, and by October this had reached the catastrophic total of somewhere between 173 and 180 million *livres*. It is no coincidence that this happened in the *annus horribilis* for French arms, when the war could not be snuffed out in Iberia, Marlborough inflicted another heavy defeat on France at Ramillies, and the Franco-Spanish were compelled to evacuate northern Italy all but entirely after the disastrous routing of their siege army below the walls of the Savoyard capital Turin. Chamillart had been intending to give a lot of funds to his principal bankers, the Hogguers, that year, but the lifting of the siege of Barcelona by Philip V and the battle of Ramillies led the *contrôleur général* in May–June to switch funds over to more pressing needs. The Hogguers were told to carry over their debts in Lyon for several more months and continue to pay the army in Italy (which at that point still

[16] Forbonnais, II, 211; BNF F-21058: *déclaration*, 29 May 1706.

[17] CCG, II, 228: Trudaine to Chamillart, 18 January 1705; II, 302: Trudaine to Chamillart, 2 February 1706; Philippe Sagnac, 'Le crédit de l'État et les banquiers à la fin du XVIIe et au commencement du XVIIIe siècle', *Revue d'histoire moderne et contemporaine* 10 (1908), 263.

seemed on the brink of a great victory of strategic moment). Accordingly, the Paris Mint was ordered to print vast numbers of fresh Mint bills. In a classic case of somebody promising to reform their ways but not yet, on 29 May Chamillart formally pledged not to create any further Mint bills after 1 July, but the numbers continued to grow. What made matters far worse was that Chamillart also announced that Mint bills would not be reimbursed until quite some time after the outbreak of peace.[18]

By July 1706, just when the government needed to make huge payments, cash had dried up thanks to the accelerating quantity of Mint bills. One solution was to compel people to use Mint bills, and since late 1703 Chamillart had even been urged to give the bills 'force' status in Paris, not least by Bernard who had a vested interest in people accepting Mint bills the king was already giving him. But other considerations made for an alternative policy: an attempt to *encourage* people to use cash. Under advice that the public needed to feel Mint bills were safe instruments, on 6 December 1704 the king had given them legal status, though nobody was to be compelled to use them in payments, but unfortunately the government allowed them to be used too much in transactions: from April 1705 it was permitted for up to three-quarters of a deal to be honoured in Mint bills. When the volume of Mint bills was small this mattered little, but with a larger quantity in circulation this rule came to prove Gresham's Law: the bad money (Mint bills) began driving out the good (coin). The government had to react, but many contemporaries (and even some historians) misconstrued the change of policy owing to the ambivalent language of the royal declarations: from 1706 the government was not trying to force people in Paris to use Mint bills as much as possible, but instead wanted to restrict the *maximum* proportion of Mint bills that could contribute to a payment. In other words, in the minds of Chamillart and Desmaretz in the spring and summer of 1706, the aim was in fact to make people use cash as much as possible, to flush cash out into circulation; as cash became more plentiful again then one could even increase the proportion of a transaction that had to be conducted in cash. Alas, this approach merely contributed to the discrediting of the Mint bills.

A declaration on 6 July 1706 laid down a series of maximum amounts that Mint bills could make up in private, Paris transactions. The maximum ratios of Mint bills to cash were set on a sliding scale according to the overall size of the deal: with effect from 15 July, transactions under 400 livres in value were to involve no Mint bills at all, while large transactions over 1,000 *livres* were allowed to use up to seven-eighths of the total in Mint bills, not least because it was appropriate to use such paper instruments for high-value transactions. In late October the proportion to be paid in cash for medium-sized payments was even increased from one-half to three-quarters of each transaction. One can only construe this measure as a serious effort to force more cash into circulation. However, by November treasurer general Mongelas of the Extraordinaire des Guerres was discharging bills of exchange on

[18] Seligmann, 89; AN G[7]1124–6: 'Memoire pour les Sieurs Hogguer', [printed, 1710]; Saint-Germain, *Bernard*, 169–70; Bonney, 'France', 256; BNF F-21058: *déclaration*, 29 May 1706.

Paris with only one-fifth cash and the rest in Mint bills, and was flooding the market. Furthermore, contemporaries reacted to the declarations in two ways: some who understood what was going on (especially the biggest players in the market) were alarmed by the failure to give Mint bills equal status with cash, while others (typically those on the receiving end) mistakenly worried that they were being forced to use these infernal devices. In a curious form of pincer movement it seems that the Mint bills were being discredited from both sides, by those who wanted to use them more and by those who did not. Realizing what was happening, the government, from 1 January 1707, once again allowed transactions to be agreed with liberty of stipulation—a contract could state freely that payment would be made in coins or Mint bills or a proportion of each. This produced some rallying in the value of Mint bills, but the problem was not going to go away. The money markets were absolutely flooded with the wretched things.[19] By mid-1707 all the *receveurs généraux* were paying out half of their dues to the Extraordinaire des Guerres and bankers in Mint bills. These men, in turn, passed them on in such huge volumes that in late October the *intendant* of Lyon remarked, 'the Extraordinaire des Guerres is the great source of the largest number of Mint bills'.[20]

The war effort was now dependent upon a financial instrument that was apparently out of control, and the public had known this for quite some time. The trading value of Mint bills had plummeted to 25 per cent of their face value during the spring of 1705, but they rallied remarkably to par value by the end of the year, and in February and March 1706 were negotiable for discounts of only 5–8 per cent. This was the calm before the storm. As the markets slowly noticed that the Paris Mint was churning out somewhere between 4 and 8 million *livres* of bills each month, a ridiculous sum at the tail end of a coinage reformation, they reacted accordingly, if slowly at first. Then in the final four months of 1706 there was a vertiginous drop in the market value of Mint bills. Of course, we have to recognize that our data is extremely anecdotal, and the price at which people might be willing to take on Mint bills could vary significantly according to their needs and circumstances. Nevertheless, there is evidence of discounting of up to 53 per cent.[21] This was producing a great deal of speculation that government officials castigated as 'a commerce of usury pernicious to the public'. There were also enormous knock-on hikes in prices for those buying foreign exchange in Paris.[22] These prob-

[19] For this and the previous paragraph, see René Dumas, *La politique financière de Nicolas Desmaretz, Contrôleur Général des Finances (1708–1715)* (Paris, 1927), 32; BNF F-21056: *déclaration*, 6 December 1704; F-21058: *déclaration*, 6 July 1706; *déclaration*, 24 October 1706; AN G[7]1778, no. 250: Mongelas to [Le Rebours?], 24 November 1706; G[7]1120: Bernard to Chamillart, 24 June 1704; CCG, II, 512: 'Mémoire', 30 January 1706; II, 515: 'Rapport', 3 May 1706; Forbonnais, II, 170.

[20] AN G[7]1120: 'Recette gñalle de Franche comté', note, 22 July 1707; CCG, II, 440: Trudaine to Desmaretz, 29 October 1707 (quotation).

[21] AN G[7]1778, no. 85: Titon to Chamillart, 8 March 1706; G[7]1123: 'Estat pour compter par les freres Hogguer...', [November 1706 or later]; Legohérel, 238; SHD A[1]1990, no. 784: Pleneuf to Chamillart, 1 November 1706.

[22] BNF F-21058: *déclaration*, 24 October 1706 (quotation); AN G[7]1120: Bernard to [Le Rebours?], 18 September 1706.

lems did not get any better for years to come: in Lyon Genevan merchant and banking houses in 1707 were buying up Mint bills at low prices, waiting to sell them on for higher prices, and then spreading rumours to discredit them so as to monopolize them again. Royal revenue receivers and farmers, by 1709, were, in a calculated fashion, refusing to accept Mint bills in their offices, thereby discrediting the bills and thus giving themselves the opportunity to buy them up at colossal discounts, before using them to discharge their own obligations where they could. Far more surprising is the way that Samuel Bernard was able to exploit his indispensability in 1706–9 in order to persuade the government to permit him to undertake what can only be described as insider trading using coins and Mint bills in the expectation of a coin revaluation—for the benefit of the king's remittances, naturally.[23]

Speculative behaviour inflicted great damage on the war effort and financial stability over the long term, even if the men involved were reacting in a thoroughly rational way to the situation brought about very largely by the government. In the short term, 1706–7 saw a terrible contraction of business in Paris brought about by the discrediting of the Mint bills, the massive increase in their volume, and the counterproductive efforts of government to reduce the amount of Mint bills that could be used in transactions. Prices in the capital fell—in turn depressing the revenues of the *fermes générales*—as people sought to minimize their use of Mint bills and to retain as much cash as the market (in their particular sphere of business) would allow. Moreover, the Mint bills had reduced the availability of cash generally, thereby forcing the government and its agents to issue more and more paper in a race to the bottom.[24] On 16 October 1706 Chamillart offered the king the following grim, realistic assessment of the situation:

> I took the liberty of informing Your Majesty that the [evil of Mint bills] would become irremediable, if the war obliged us to make such a large number that paper trumped money. What I foresaw has happened; the disorder that they have produced is extreme; far from seeing them as a new means by which we can draw aid, it is absolutely necessary to think of reducing their numbers, yet at a time when resources are lacking everywhere…

A week later Chancellor Pontchartrain, whom Chamillart had turned to for advice, declared he was at a loss to know what to do about the Mint bills. Both men were bewildered that everything the government had tried in order to boost their credibility had only made matters worse, and both now feared further drastic action would provoke a 'frightful catastrophe'.[25]

[23] AN G⁷1778, no. 195: Du Bois to Chamillart, 21 August 1706; no. 146: note from Mongelas, 14 June 1706; Saint-Germain, *Bernard*, 177; Colonel Herlaut, 'Projet de création d'une banque royale en France à la fin du règne de Louis XIV (1702–1712)', *Revue d'histoire moderne* 8(NS2) (1933), 154, citing a memorandum from 7 January 1709 in AN G⁷715.

[24] Paul Harsin, *Les doctrines monétaires et financières en France du XVI*ᵉ *au XVIII*ᵉ *siècle* (Paris, 1928), 92.

[25] CCG, II, 474: Chamillart to Louis XIV, 16 October 1706; Esnault, II, 140: Pontchartrain to Chamillart, 23 October 1706.

REDUCING THE LOAD, SPREADING THE PAIN

The drastic action Chamillart announced on 24 October 1706 was the first of several serious attempts to convert Mint bills into other financial instruments. In September the government began the first of a series of opportunities for people to invest in *rentes* on the Hôtel de ville (or *promesses* on the *fermes*) using Mint bills, as long as half the payment was made in cash.[26] Now the government decreed that from 1 November six leading farmers general and four *receveurs généraux* would provide 50 million *livres*-worth of five-year-maturity bearer bills on themselves—known as 'billets à cinq ans'—carrying 5 per cent interest from 1 January 1707, and people could present their Mint bills for conversion into these instruments. On top of this, another 6 million *livres* of Mint bills would be reimbursed, at the rate of half a million a month, from one year later, 1 January 1708. But in the second half of the autumn the lack of public confidence in this scheme made itself plain. According to the well-placed chronicler of Louis' court, the marquis de Dangeau, in December 1706 the king and Chamillart were continuing to work on ways to withdraw the Mint bills, with the *contrôleur général* putting on a brave face in his private pronouncements that they would all be gone by the following July. On 2 January the period for converting Mint bills into 'billets à cinq ans' was extended until the end of March. On top of this, by October 1707 over 14 million *livres* were withdrawn by the Extraordinaire des Guerres and replaced with its own bearer bills.[27] But the overall process fell short of expectations, not least because people did not believe that the 'billets à cinq ans' would ever be repaid, that the interest rates would be honoured in full, or that the government would amortize the bulk of outstanding Mint bills from 1708.[28] The conversions that did occur, reaching 84 million *livres* by October 1707, had ambivalent results: from the early summer the market value of Mint bills rallied somewhat, and apparently fluctuated for the rest of the year between a 25 per cent and 40 per cent discount. On the other hand, turning Mint bills into illiquid *rentes* was going to bury assets, and the instruments on the *fermes générales* or the Extraordinaire des Guerres were simply not credible for those who hoped for rapid reimbursement of their money or for those who could avoid shedding their Mint bills in such a way at this time. Trading losses on the five-year bearer bills issued by the *fermes générales* actually reached 80 per cent! One contemporary thought the conversions had actually ensured that only one in four commercial transactions were actually carried through, and if so this was bad news for the economy and for the war effort.[29]

Between February and April 1707 additional efforts were made to persuade corporate bodies (including the Church) to buy up Mint bills with credit instruments issued on themselves, but these schemes were generally a failure, mainly

[26] BNF F-21060: *déclaration*, 18 October 1707; Forbonnais, II, 169.

[27] BNF F-21058: *déclaration*, 24 October 1706; F-21060: *déclaration*, 18 October 1707; Dangeau, XI, 262; Seligmann, 85.

[28] Forbonnais, II, 170.

[29] Dangeau, XI, 344; AN $G^7$1780: nos 38, 40, 43: Ollivier to Chamillart, 30 July, 9 August, and 4 September 1707; Saint-Germain, *Bernard*, 179; Swarte, *Un banquier*, 41; Vuitry, 177–8.

because the interest rates on offer were too miserly for the bulk holders of Mint bills: most of them were speculating bankers or fisco-financiers (like the Crozat brothers) who—one can surmise—preferred to keep their Mint bills in the hope of either achieving greater profits through passing them on in the market or forcing full-value redemption from the crown at some point in the future. The government tried another tack. On 24 May 1707 it announced that new-style Mint bills would be issued, replacing 72 million *livres* of old ones: they would be in a single form of 1,000 *livres* each, be guaranteed by the Paris Hôtel de ville, and carry 7.5 per cent interest per annum from their maturity date. The remaining old Mint bills would be altered: three-quarters of them would be turned into 'billets nonreformez' and the final batch into special 'Billets reformez', though unfortunately the latter involved a unilateral rescheduling of debt and they came to be particularly feared by financiers. These old bills would eventually have to be converted into 'billets à cinq ans' or *rentes* on the Hôtel de ville or the Church by 30 November, or they would be annulled. This plan was carried through, though many old Mint bills were still not brought into any office for conversion.[30]

All the while the government was toying with conversion schemes, it was also mulling over an extremely dangerous step: the extension of the Mint bills to the rest of the kingdom so that Paris merchants could meet their debts elsewhere with these instruments. As it was, it cost Parisians a great deal to persuade correspondents and contacts elsewhere to accept payment in Mint bills, in February 1707 up to 71 per cent of the value of a transaction![31] From the moment they were first issued there had been a great deal of trading and speculating involving Mint bills outside Paris, especially in the Lyon clearance system, although they did not enjoy legal status in any transactions beyond the capital. It was, however, a big leap to making them legal tender nationally, and this move would pose an enormous threat to the availability of foreign exchange at a reasonable price. This was because so many foreign exchange transactions were now being put through the Lyon system, where hitherto those selling foreign exchange had no obligation to accept Mint bills in final return payment. If the weak Mint bills were introduced as legal tender this would inevitably spread the contraction of coinage to Lyon and other cities, and would surely force foreign bankers and foreign correspondents of French bankers to accept Mint bills as payment, if only as an alternative to going bankrupt. Over the medium to long term this would pile on the costs of foreign exchange as additional exchange premiums were built into agreements to cover 'insurance risks'. It would generally make it far harder to get foreign exchange within France on foreign marketplaces.

Nevertheless, when it suited the king's biggest bankers they did beseech the *contrôleur général* to extend the legal use of Mint bills beyond Paris. To accompany the expansion of the Mint bills from the spring of 1706, and to spare Paris the entire pain of supporting their circulation, Chamillart told the Hogguer brothers

[30] Forbonnais, II, 169; BNF F-21060: *déclaration*, 18 October 1707; AN $G^7$1780, nos 145–6: notes on Mint bills.

[31] AN $G^7$1120: note on exchange costs, [early February 1707].

he intended to let the bills circulate in Lyon from 1 September. Evidence from that summer suggests that the Hogguers, who were the biggest financial and banking operators in France that year, were pushing extremely hard for this move, even claiming mendaciously that Lyon merchants secretly wanted this too in order to regularize the situation. Desmaretz, who as Director General of Finances under Chamillart had special responsibility for monetary policy, was also genuinely worried that without the extension of Mint bills to Lyon all trade between that city and the capital would cease; inevitably the burden of Mint bills would have to be shared by the rest of France, and the later this happened then the worse things would be. But the flexible Desmaretz was soon convinced by Trudaine, *intendant* of Lyon, and others that however problematic the situation was, it would become disastrous if the Mint bills were given legal circulation outside Paris. Trudaine had already expressed worries back in May that this step would completely destabilize the Lyon clearance system, and by the end of August rumours in Lyon of an extended circulation of Mint bills were causing panic flights of cash into bills of exchange to withdraw money from the kingdom. This firmly convinced Desmaretz that Lyon had to be preserved in order to support the king's armies operating beyond the frontiers. This was the priority, surely.[32] From then on, it was Chamillart who was driving the policy of extending legal status.

It would not be going too far to say that by spring 1707 Chamillart was hell-bent on extending Mint bill use to Lyon, despite severe warnings from the likes of Samuel Bernard—who wanted to be able to draw on foreign exchange through Lyon for months if not years to come—that money would simply dry up there. He even ventured an ominous prognostication:

> Paris is under the sun's gaze. It contents itself with murmuring often inappropriately but it is very much to be feared that the frontier provinces might go further.[33]

Chamillart received entreaties not to implement this policy from as far afield as Madrid, from the French army *intendant* there. But so adamant was he that Paris' pain should be shared across France that on 12 April he just went ahead and announced the extension: with effect from 20 May up to one-third of each payment in Lyon and elsewhere could be made in Mint bills. Despite other concessions, such as allowing Mint bills to be paid in at some royal fiscal agencies, his action set off a rash of alarmed but very well-reasoned pleas for a rethink from across France, and protests from the major cities. Amongst other reasons for the opposition was a fear that the government was simply going to print even more Mint bills if it could increase the market into which they could be dropped, beyond Paris to the whole kingdom. Hair-raising stories of a complete disappearance of specie and huge hikes in interest rates reached Chamillart's ears, but he only backed down after lobbying from the Lyon, Bordeaux, and Rouen deputies on the Coun-

[32] CCG, II, 345–6: Desmaretz to Trudaine, 9 and 27 August 1706; II, 402: *maire, échevins* and *députés de commerce* of Marseille to Chamillart, 2 May 1707; AN G^{7}1124–6: 'Memoire pour les Sieurs Hogguer', [printed, 1710]; G^{7}1778, no. 195: Du Bois to Chamillart, 21 August 1706.

[33] AN G^{7}1120: Bernard to Chamillart, 11 March 1707.

cil of Commerce: they persuaded him that instead of extending Mint bills beyond Paris he should try to shore up public support for them by injecting greater transparency into the market and announce how many were circulating. The disastrous declaration was withdrawn on 10 May. Although the king and Chamillart saved some face by claiming this was done to allow the provinces time to accommodate themselves to a future extension, it was probably the most humiliating domestic climbdown Louis XIV had been forced into since the 1650s, and was a measure of the growing power of markets when the fiscal-military state needed their services. This seems to have been the moment when Chamillart began to lose his grip on the royal finances and on reality. The day after the declaration was rescinded he lashed out, in a letter to all provincial *intendants*, against wicked speculators for whipping up a storm against his policy, blaming the protests rather than the policy itself for bringing foreign exchange to a halt. In remarkably petulant tones he exclaimed that he was even willing to risk terrible exchange rates in order to enforce the circulation of Mint bills on disobedient subjects. He was clearly just biding his time before making a second attempt.[34]

Two weeks later the declaration of 24 May set out a plan to reduce the number of Mint bills by issuing 72 million *livres* of new-style Mint bills and by reissuing the remaining older bills.[35] This stabilized the situation again, but Mint bills continued to sell with a considerable markdown on their face value. The general failure of these conversion efforts contributed to Chamillart's return to the charge, but the reasons for the second attempt at extending Mint bills across France later in 1707 had altered since the spring. There was huge pressure on the state in the summer and early autumn to liquidate war debts incurred in Spain during the crisis years 1706–07. Although extending Mint bills to Lyon would deeply damage future trading, the situation was so abysmal that those associated with the finances of the Spanish theatre seem to have felt there was no choice: the alternative, their complete failure to discharge their debts at Lyon, was simply too awful to contemplate. On 18 October Chamillart responded, without much agonizing, to their cries for help and, in a step wholly coloured by extreme short-term thinking, he declared Mint bills would circulate almost everywhere from 1 December. That this measure was directly linked to the needs and self-serving arguments of the war-related financiers and bankers has not been properly acknowledged, but the detail of the extension makes this even more obvious: Mint bills would still not circulate in Flandres, Alsace, the Franche-Comté, the Trois Évêchés, or Roussillon, precisely because it would disrupt the use of coin in those areas dominated by the army (or, one might add in the case of the Franche-Comté, the war-related iron industry). It was also the case that while only one-quarter of a payment could be made up of Mint bills, this was not uniformly the rule: for discharging bills of exchange and bearer bills issued by the Extraordinaire des Guerres, Mint bills could account for up to half a transaction's value. Once again, the military paymasters and some of

[34] AN G^{7}1092: Méliand to Chamillart, 1 May 1707; CCG, II, 409: Mesnager, Anisson, and Fénelon to Rouen traders, *c.*11 May 1707; II, 411: Chamillart to all *intendants*, 11 May 1707.

[35] Forbonnais, II, 170.

the international war bankers would enjoy privileged treatment denied to others in the French financial and commercial system.[36]

Predictably, though, none of this was enough to forestall a credit crisis in Lyon, whose merchants were outraged by this second unwelcome attempt to introduce more Mint bills into their city. Even before the declaration was announced, rumours that Chamillart would try again caused enormous difficulties for Ollivier, the key banker for the Extraordinaire des Guerres for its Spanish business, who could not get nervous Lyon businessmen to lend him money. Money only got scarcer. In a graphic demonstration of how he had misread market behaviour, Chamillart had expected that the stipulation that three-quarters of a transaction had to be in cash would stabilize lending and give some confidence to people that the government valued cash three times as highly as Mint bills. However, it only served to encourage people to see Mint bills as worth only one-third of the equivalent in cash! In the face of all this Chamillart became more and more intemperate, and increasingly antagonistic to anyone and anything related to Lyon. He even warned the Lyon city provost Montézan, the head of the municipality, that if he did not use duress on traders then Versailles would send in troops in December to force people to use cash and Mint bills in the proportions now ordered. Never before had the absolute monarchy been so defied by mere traders and money-grubbers, and it did not know how to deal with the situation except by threatening them with prison without trial and proscription from business activity for life. Trade only declined further. With expedients failing and royal revenues now exhausted through excessive future anticipations, by the end of the year it looked as though the war would soon have to be brought to a humiliating end, such was the collapse of credit.[37]

DRAINING THE SWAMP

Lying low in this final stage of the war between Chamillart and the markets was Nicolas Desmaretz, who had quietly absented himself from Paris in October 1707 at the time of the disastrous declaration, and who ensured that Lyon, through his confidant Trudaine, knew that he had not wished this false step upon France. Cryptic notes written at the foot of their correspondence in Desmaretz's own hand, acknowledging he was going behind his boss's back, also suggest that as far back as the summer he had suspected Chamillart's tenure as *contrôleur général* might very soon come to an end.[38] If Desmaretz had really supported Chamillart's Mint bill policy, then why did the mercantile and financial world greet his elevation to the contrôle général with such relief, even joy, on 20 February 1708? Just a week after

[36] Seligmann, 94; AN G[7]1780, no. 53: Stalpaert to Chamillart, 17 July 1707 (from Cadiz); no. 65: memorandum by Ollivier, [July 1707]; CCG, II, 440: Trudaine to Chamillart, 29 October 1707.

[37] AN G[7]1780, no. 101: Stalpaert to Chamillart, 16 October 1707; CCG, II, 441: Trudaine to Chamillart, 18 October 1707; II, 447: Chamillart to Montézan, 14 November 1707; II, 451: Chamillart to Desmaretz, 1 December 1707; III, 674: 'Compte rendu de M. Desmaretz au Régent', [1716].

[38] CCG, II, 345, 441: Desmaretz to Trudaine, 9 August, 9 November 1707.

his promotion an edict rescinded the October declarations, and instead made it clear that any amount of Mint bills—or cash—could be used in transactions in the kingdom, without compulsion from any party to a deal. Chamillart could not and would not have done this, but Desmaretz rushed to do so.[39]

However, this was a palliative measure. The bigger problem was how to get rid of Mint bills altogether, not promote the weak and devalued circulation of such an excessive amount of them. Back in 1706 the possibility had been raised of making Mint bills convertible on demand into cash at a new emitting bank, and minds now turned towards the possibility of such a bank being set up to retire Mint bills altogether. Desmaretz was entirely open to the suggestion, but it was only in 1707–10 that minds were applied to the idea of creating what is nowadays called a 'bad bank': a bank that would take in Mint bills in exchange for issuing interest-bearing notes; and the said notes could, in turn, be exchanged for cash with a deduction of 5 per cent. The closest such a project got to realization was in the winter of 1708–9, and the prospect of it coming to fruition had a marked effect on Mint bills, which rallied from a roughly 30 per cent to a less than 15 per cent discount.[40] But the chances of establishing such an institution, even with full royal backing against vested interests and sceptical voices, faded rapidly in the harsh climate of early 1709, when the weather wreaked a terrible toll on the economy and the Lyon clearance system collapsed. As it became known that the bank would not be launched, Mint bills dropped in value again, to trade by late March 1709 at nearly 40 per cent below par.[41] In the meantime, the crown had become so unable to service interest payments on surviving Mint bills (of various hues) that it had contracted the job to two arch-*traitants*, no doubt for significant rake-offs.[42] Clearly the government had to do something to exterminate this disastrous monetary instrument.

Other, rather more traditional methods of withdrawal were now tried. From early 1708 Desmaretz was weighing up the possibility of using another major coin augmentation, whenever circumstances allowed, to try to withdraw a large number of Mint bills. Knowing that he had to enhance the credibility of financial instruments if borrowing was to get the state through the rest of the war, he seems to have become determined that the king should forgo any seigniorage income on a coin reformation and devote the profits to retiring Mint bills. What he lacked until the spring of 1709 was an opportunity. Then, providentially, on Easter Sunday, 26 March, a seven-strong merchant convoy escorted by a single royal vessel under the command of Michel Chabert put into Port Louis from the South Seas, and a handful of other ships also arrived in France laden with bullion and Spanish specie. Desmaretz reacted with a decree on 22 April ordering the manufacture of new gold and silver coins at a higher rate than previously. Then, as it became clear just how large a windfall the ships had brought, the government changed its approach and

[39] CCG, III, 674: 'Compte rendu de M. Desmaretz au Régent', [1716].

[40] Saint-Germain, *Bernard*, 183–4, 188; CCG, II, 346: Desmaretz to Trudaine, [August 1706]; Harsin, *Crédit public*, 43.

[41] AN $G^7$1784, no. 278: Le Bartz to Desmaretz, 25 March 1709.

[42] AN $G^7$1782, no. 194: Le Mesle and Baudry to Desmaretz, 19 November 1708.

ordered a complete recoinage on 14 May, announcing that all newly created *louis d'or* and *écus* would be put into circulation with values of 20 *livres* and 5 *livres* respectively. The intrinsic values were only 16 *livres* 4 *deniers* and 4 *livres* 1 *sol*, so the extra value could be used partly to pay the merchants who had brought in the money for their costs and partly to withdraw Mint bills. The government announced that one-sixth of each deposit at the mints would have to be in Mint bills, which could be 'cut' into smaller denominations to allow ease of presentation and conversion.[43]

Desmaretz averred, for years to come, that his actions had saved the country and the operation had been a great success: it procured funds to pay the armies, engaged possessors of Mint bills to do all they could to find coin worth five times their bill holdings, got circulation going, and over a matter of a few months extinguished 43 million *livres* of Mint bills and other paper instruments. Others were less convinced of the efficacy of his project. Certainly the big hike in the rating of French coins caused specie to come back into the kingdom or otherwise come out into circulation, and Desmaretz must take credit for the courage of this move, which risked a ruinous foreign exchange situation for years to come. Aside from this, one might doubt just how successful he really was. The aim had been to withdraw all 72 million *livres* of new-style Mint bills then in circulation, but only 43 million *livres* were taken in. Forbonnais later argued that many people were in fact duped by the financial wizard of Versailles, failing to understand that because of the augmentation of the coins they would bear a loss of one-fifth, in *livre* terms, on their total deposits when they received new coins back. Moreover, in yet another case of the government prioritizing the war effort's financiers, these men were given much of the coin whereas lesser mortals who had deposited their money, and Mint bills, in good faith were given back untradable receipts on the mints at the moment they were supposed to receive their new coins. On the other hand, others surely did understand what was happening and still cooperated with the coinage reform. The banker Tourton, who certainly knew what he was talking about, complained that people would not part with their coin because of the profit they could get by turning it in at the mints. He was probably referring to people who had bought up lots of Mint bills at usurious rates and who consequently might even profit overall. One can also suggest that Mint bills were so discredited that many holders would have wanted to get rid of them for any reasonable price, and there is testimony that agents were stationed on the outskirts of towns to solicit coin from country-dwellers, for a very small profit to the peasant, precisely so that a big player could make up enough coin to get rid of the Mint bills he held. For some people a 20 per cent overall loss would be a necessary price to pay to maintain their cash flow. After all, this was at a time in June when no less a figure than the treasurer general of the Extraordinaire des Guerres could only trade Mint bills with a 57 per cent loss in the marketplace. Forbonnais was, nevertheless, probably right when he thought that others preferred to send money to forgers in the hope of a higher profit, or, if

[43] Saint-Simon, XVII, 542–5 (Boislisle essay); Forbonnais, II, 193, 203–4; Lévy, *Capitalistes et pouvoir au siècle des Lumières* (3 vols, Paris, 1969–80), I, 338, 384.

unusually powerful, held on to their money and their Mint bills in the expectation of pushing the government into better terms in the future.[44] All told, despite the stronger coinage and the necessary withdrawal of the Mint bills, the overall results of Desmaretz's policy were nothing to celebrate. Saint-Simon spoke of it bringing 'a ruin to individuals, and a disorder in trade which ended by destroying it'. Even the surviving Mint bills continued to trade into the summer of 1710 at discounts of around 40 per cent, though it is a measure of how bad so much other paper was that people preferred to receive them rather than be lumbered with bearer bills on many fisco-financiers.[45]

Knowing more needed to be done, between June and December 1709 the government made further, erratic efforts to get coin moving, bring more Mint bills in, and get more old coins reminted; but all these measures seem to have done was drive coin underground or abroad. Further opportunities were given to the public, sometimes through the intermediation of corporate bodies like law courts and towns, sometimes through tax offices, to present the remaining Mint bills for liquidation over the following years. In the meantime, on 7 October 1710 the king gave fair warning that from 1 February 1711 all remaining unconverted Mint bills—whether old- or new-style—could no longer be used. Predictably, the grace period was extended more than once, and it was only on 1 October 1712 that Mint bills were finally killed off.[46]

Desmaretz's ingenious efforts to suppress Mint bills, if they came at a heavy price, were probably unavoidable, and the least problematic way of proceeding. He certainly thought so. A memorandum attributed to him and written several years later gave a strong sense that he believed the introduction and handling of Mint bills had been little more than a disaster for the French state, which had no longer appeared in control of its own finances or the country's financiers.[47] His policy of putting the monarchy back in charge of finances, or at least re-creating that illusion, required the king to restrict the financial instruments he or his principal agents could employ, and to that end Desmaretz was also set upon retiring the bearer bills issued by the Extraordinaire des Guerres and converting bad paper into more stable, if illiquid and unwelcome, *rentes*. All this notwithstanding, his 1709–12 policies for withdrawing the Mint bills and converting other paper were more of a gamble than perhaps we realize, and it relied on peace arriving before complete collapse finally occurred. He was also only able to pursue the policies he did because France needed far smaller foreign remittances after 1708 than a few short years earlier. Had Louis XIV still been trying to defend large chunks of the Spanish

[44] CCG, III, 675: 'Compte rendu de M. Desmaretz au Régent', [1716]; Seligmann, 103–4; Forbonnais, II, 205–6, 221; AN G^{7}1783, no. 120: Tourton to Desmaretz, 24 May 1709; G^{7}1785, no. 128: Renouard to Boutin, 5 August 1709; no. 62: note by de La Garde, 15 June 1709.

[45] Saint-Simon, XVII, 212 (quotation); AN G^{7}1121: Bernard to Desmaretz, 21 May 1710; G^{7}1784, no. 102: placet of Delabelle, [October 1709]; SHD A^{1}2409: Pleneuf to Haillet, 10 August 1710.

[46] Forbonnais, II, 206–9; McCollim, 313–15; Dumas, *La politique financière*, 73; AN G^{7}1031: *arrêt*, 27 January 1711; CCG, III, 357: Desmaretz to all *intendants*, 21 February 1711.

[47] Saint-Germain, *Bernard*, 180, citing a 'Deuxième mémoire sur les billets de monnoie'.

Netherlands, half of Italy, and Bavaria at this time, he would have been far more dependent upon maintaining good foreign exchange, and Desmaretz's room for manoeuvre would have been narrower. As it was, military remittances on a vast scale had already forced the king into growing reliance upon international bankers, his military paymasters, and suppliers, who had between them played an important role in persuading the government to undertake exploitative *affaires extraordinaires* and disastrous monetary manipulations. To understand how and why France's finances deteriorated so badly in this period we must therefore turn to this world of army finance.

PART III

THE DEGENERATION OF MILITARY FUNDING AND THE RISING COSTS OF WAR

Introduction

The history of French finances in the era of the pre-Revolutionary Bourbon monarchs has hitherto been predominantly the history of taxation and borrowing that ultimately bore so much responsibility for bringing the *ancien régime* to its knees in the 1780s. But royal finances were very largely expenditure-driven, as the monarchs to a greater or lesser extent prioritized international goals over the husbanding of the kingdom's social and economic resources, pursuing disputes by whatever means necessary through a variety of arms races, cold wars, and full-blooded conflicts. It is, then, somewhat surprising that so little attention has been devoted to the systems of expenditure that the monarchical state operated, and that little attempt has been made to integrate discussion of the naval and military treasuries with borrowing and revenue-raising. The largest impediment to a detailed understanding of the Extraordinaire des Guerres and the other smaller military treasuries is the semi-private nature of these organizations which have, with considerable justification, been termed 'para-royal' or 'para-state' operations. The archives and papers retained by their treasurers general, and those they presented to the government and courts, have very largely disappeared, despite the Extraordinaire des Guerres being nothing less than the behemoth of military finances in the western world of the seventeenth and eighteenth centuries. A treasurer general of this organization, during one of his years 'en exercice' (on duty), was the single most important fisco-financier in France, responsible in Louis XIV's reign for handling at times well over 100 million *livres* of the king's money and up to three-quarters of all royal war expenditure.

By looking at the channelling of money to the military paymasters and the armies in this final part of the book it becomes possible to provide a fuller picture of royal finances in one of the key periods of the *ancien régime* than has hitherto been attempted. It should make it easier to understand why and how royal finances degenerated in the War of the Spanish Succession. Fundamentally, the state was throwing more and more resources at the same expenditure engagements thanks to indemnities, compensations, and exchange costs, which all rose as revenue sources failed, the appropriations system crumbled, and monetary instability became a chronic feature of the period. These deficiencies encouraged speculative manipulation and trafficking in financial instruments that were used for the war effort, and this, too, played a part in inflating costs and pumping up royal liabilities. Chamillart in particular allowed something of a military-industrial complex to develop, as a small group of financiers and bankers encouraged him into more expensive forms of credit, contributed to the mismanagement of royal finances, and pushed up prices for military logistics. It is only through looking at the fisco-financiers working within the royal financial system for the army that we can gain a rounded picture of just what was going wrong and why. Indeed, the *billets de l'Extraordinaire des Guerres*, in their manifold forms, provide the perfect case study for understanding not only how fisco-financier debt worked, and how far bearer bills had come to dominate short-term credit, but also how such debts could be allowed to build up and remain undischarged at unsustainable levels during the final war of Louis XIV's reign. The developments of this period can even be taken more generally as a warning to states about the need to exercise strict control over appropriations, and about what can happen when semi-autonomous government agencies are allowed, if not forced, to take on enormous liabilities. As essential background to this, Chapter 7 introduces the military treasury of the Extraordinaire des Guerres and the problems in managing the military paymasters.

7

The Treasury of the Extraordinaire des Guerres in the Era of the Spanish Succession

Under Louis XIV the military treasury of the Extraordinaire des Guerres handled more money on behalf of the king and the Trésor royal than any other body in France, and this made the monarch, whose character was so martial, reliant at the best of times upon the operations of the military paymasters. As a result of the expansion in debt that the Extraordinaire took on in the course of the Nine Years War and the War of the Spanish Succession, its treasurers general, and their associates, became even more indispensable than their offices would suggest.

From the 1530s French military finances were reorganized, reflecting the rapidly changing nature of warfare in this period: the more senior treasury of the Ordinaire des Guerres dealt with the small, core, permanent forces in peacetime and their funding during wartime. It and several other minor treasuries continued to fund many of the household forces and other elite troops until the 1780s. But the Extraordinaire des Guerres grew in importance as it funded the growing volume of additional troops, especially infantry, who remained on a footing during both war and peace. At the head of the Extraordinaire were placed several venal treasurers general, sometimes two but a lot of the time three or four such men, who rotated on duty on the basis of annual 'exercices'. Alternation in office between treasurers general made sense because they needed time off duty in order to sort out their accounts and assemble backers for their next year on duty. Below them stood a number of agents in a very rough and ready hierarchy. Although their roles changed over the course of the Bourbon monarchy, all of these subordinates continued to fulfil the same essential tasks: they acted as the agents of the treasurers general, receiving money from them directly and from other sources, and disbursing it under orders.[1] This, very approximately, was the system that survived for nearly 250 years, from the reign of François I to the Revolution. For the financial problems of the French state to make sense an exploration is now required of the nature and roles of the Extraordinaire, and how it related as an early manifestation of

[1] Henry Germain-Martin, 'Le financement des guerres de Louis XIV et les trésoriers de l'extraordinaire des guerres', *Revue des travaux de l'Académie des sciences morales et politiques* 126 (1973), 21; P. J. M. R. Frémont, *Les payeurs d'armées: Historique du service de la trésorerie et des postes aux armées (1293–1870)* (Paris, 1906), 37–49; and, for an exploration of the system in the period *c.*1680–1701, Rowlands, 109–34.

semi-private 'agency government' to the newly matured sovereign state. This chapter will therefore describe how this para-royal agency functioned and was, ostensibly, managed, and will end by examining the financial power of the treasurers general and the range of associates they used.

WHOSE JURISDICTION? MINISTERIAL CONTROL AND CONFUSION OVER THE EXTRAORDINAIRE DES GUERRES

After 1661, when the position of *Surintendant des finances* was mothballed, the Extraordinaire des Guerres came firmly under the authority of the Secretary of State for War, a position held by three generations of the Le Tellier family from 1643 to 1701.[2] It was the Secretary of War, not the *contrôleur général des finances*, who installed and removed the treasurers general, directed the orders for the payments they were to make, worked with them on their accounts, and protected them when they got into difficulties. In keeping with the still very personal nature of administration at this time, there was also some crossover of personnel between the bureaux of the War Ministry and those of the Extraordinaire des Guerres, reinforcing the notion that the Extraordinaire was in a strong sense a shadow ministry itself.[3] This close collaboration was necessary because, in a situation of fragmented government dependent upon private fisco-financier and patronage networks, the interests of the spending arms of the state—the army and navy—were by no means always coincidental with those of the principal revenue-raisers who answered to the *contrôleur général*.

Unlike the English Treasury, the French Finance Ministry was below the secretaries of state in the status pecking order. This could produce financial incontinence, especially when dynastic stakes of the highest international order were being played for. The likelihood of overspending was therefore built into the system. Given this was the set-up, it was consequently all the more essential that good order was preserved: the distinction between primary revenue receivers and secondary receivers (like the Extraordinaire treasurers) had to be preserved as much as possible. It was also vital that spending ministers defended their departments as part of an orderly system. If this did not happen, the chances of a well-managed flow of finances to the armies, an accountable system of financial contractors, and control of the royal debt were much diminished. At the very top of government the king held the ring between the various ministries, and under Louis XIV it was he who made the spending decisions with the Secretaries of War and the Navy. Although the secretaries of state were supposed to channel the detailed spending orders ('ordonnances de paiement') through the *contrôleur général* for the king to sign, the *contrôleur général* was by no means always consulted or allowed to discuss the wisdom of an order, and this could cause him difficulties in organizing the required appropriations that were provided (for the most part) in the form of *assignations*. As a leading diplomat noted,

[2] Rowlands, 115–16. [3] Pénicaut, 257–8.

> As it is for the Secretary of State for War to resolve the roll of expenditure for the armies, it is for the Minister of Finances to provide the revenues for it, and to assure their payment.[4]

Unfortunately in the War of the Spanish Succession this system unravelled.

The division of responsibility between the Finance Ministry and the War Ministry was brought to a temporary end when Chamillart succeeded Barbezieux in January 1701 as Secretary of State for War while retaining the office of *contrôleur général*. As a consequence of this dramatic move, the Extraordinaire des Guerres came more and more under the influence of the Finance Ministry, which might have made affairs smoother, but because this involved neither a blending of specialist bureaux nor the evolution of a clear financial hierarchy (as Necker tried to realize under Louis XVI), it did not, alas, help matters. Chamillart was severely overburdened and this had a number of effects on army funding: most notably he failed to manage effectively the financial allocations to the Extraordinaire (see Chapter 8), and at times he failed to liaise properly with the treasurers general, much to their frustration. What was worse, with Chamillart as both *contrôleur général* and Secretary of War for over seven years there was nobody to stick up for the legitimate interests of the Extraordinaire des Guerres.[5] This weak guardianship by the War Ministry under Chamillart in 1701–8 almost certainly allowed the debts contracted by the Extraordinaire to be hugely inflated as it mutated from a spending body and now took its place in the credit-raising orbit of the *contrôleur général* among several sets of fisco-financiers who were all seeking out larger and larger short-term loans to meet their obligations.

After Chamillart passed the contrôle général to Desmaretz in February 1708 (while retaining the War Ministry until June 1709) the old chain of accountability was in theory restored, as a separate Secretary of War once again issued the king's specific orders to the treasurers general. In practice, the situation did not revert to the arrangements of 1661–1701, as the Finance Ministry continued to play a more significant role in managing the Extraordinaire. Nevertheless, in the final seven years of the reign, with Desmaretz committed to stabilizing Extraordinaire debt, the enhanced influence of the Finance Ministry at least prevented the total collapse of military funding. Instead of just delivering batches of *assignations* to the Extraordinaire treasurer general on receipt of the king's payment orders, the Finance Ministry now actively and much more carefully tried to pair the myriad needs of the Extraordinaire with appropriate revenue sources. Furthermore, Desmaretz, not Chamillart, would deal with bankers, *agents de change*, and other financiers for covering advances to the Extraordinaire des Guerres. Despite this encroachment onto War Ministry territory Desmaretz had some sense of the limits of his authority, refusing to get involved with Extraordinaire spending details once he had allocated funds to it, and he still regarded the Extraordinaire des Guerres and the artillery financiers as being under the War Ministry's protection.

[4] AN G[7]1093: Amelot to Desmaretz, 16 November 1708.

[5] AN G[7]1782, no. 27: note, ostensibly from 1707 by Chamillart, [30 March 1708 in reality]; G[7]1778, no. 81: note from Mongelas to Chamillart, 18 March 1706.

Unfortunately Chamillart was not a good protector, even when he was responsible for the War Ministry alone, remarking to Desmaretz on 7 December 1708, 'you know the condition to which I have reduced the Extraordinaire de la Guerre with a view to helping you'.[6] If the Extraordinaire had suffered in 1701–8 because it lacked a protector against the Finance Ministry and against the temptation to use it as yet another large-scale credit machine, the situation had not altogether improved thereafter. The next Secretary of State for War after June 1709, Daniel Voysin, was a firmer defender of his patch than Chamillart had proved to be. He was now determined to regain and retain a grip on the Extraordinaire. Despite a bit of friction, he and Desmaretz generally did work in a cooperative fashion to keep the funds flowing and to control the treasurers general as much as possible, but Voysin may have been insufficiently protective of his treasurers general, and many soldiers and financiers turned to Desmaretz, perhaps even more than to Voysin, when they had a problem with the personnel of the Extraordinaire des Guerres.[7]

Of course, the two ministries had teams of secondary officials to handle the detailed management of the Extraordinaire des Guerres, in particular to oversee the processing of pay orders, the assignment of revenues, and accounting and auditing. There had long been a bureau inside the War Ministry dealing with the Extraordinaire, but if it had some questionable practices and less than expert administrators this was counteracted from July 1701 by the placing of a high-ranking *commis* of the Ministry, François D'Honneur, inside the bureaux of the Extraordinaire. A highly diligent and scrupulous individual, D'Honneur was given the special responsibility of signing off all the borrowing undertaken by the treasurers general (a form of 'visa'). How far D'Honneur was able to undertake another of his key tasks—preventing unauthorized use of temporarily spare resources by the treasurers general—is not known, but his presence certainly steadied public confidence in this treasury.[8] Somewhat less comforting were the Finance Ministry's arrangements for monitoring the Extraordinaire. Chamillart's closest adviser on the Extraordinaire was Jacques Poulletier, but so problematic is his position that it will be considered separately in Chapter 10. Desmaretz, who inherited Poulletier as an *intendant des finances*, seems to have been less than confident in his trustworthiness. Fortunately, Desmaretz's own former secretary-turned-*commis* in the Finance Ministry, Gilbert Clautrier, had once been a *commis* of the Extraordinaire des Guerres, so there was at least one person in his department he felt understood the issues of military funding well. In February 1709, with the secret blessing of Chamillart, Desmaretz had also ordered another of his *commis* to monitor the delivery of funds to the Extraordinaire to ensure revenue officials were doing their job, but he also charged him with observing whether the treasurer general was

[6] AN G[7]1785, no. 2: Chamillart to Desmaretz, 4 March 1709; Pénicaut, 186–7 (quotation).

[7] Thierry Sarmant, ed., *Les ministres de la guerre 1570–1792: Histoire et dictionnaire biographique* (Paris, 2007), 310; McCollim, 123–4, 192–3; AN G[7]1783, no. 307: Mongelas to [Le Rebours?], 16 August 1709; G[7]1786, no. 381: prince de Birkenfeld to Desmaretz, 5 December 1710.

[8] Pénicaut, 234–5, 246; SHD A[1]1613, no. 178: D'Honneur to Chamillart, 22 February 1702; Ya2: Chamillart to Desmaretz, 27 December 1708; Claeys, I, 1104–5.

distributing the funds across all parts of France as he should.[9] As the affairs of the Extraordinaire des Guerres became more and more complicated and burdensome after 1688 it was probably inevitable that, whoever was in office, the Secretary of War and the *contrôleur général* were going to have to share responsibility for the Extraordinaire. But there were right ways of doing this, as in 1709–15, and wrong ways, as in 1701–8.

THE STRUCTURE OF THE EXTRAORDINAIRE DES GUERRES, 1682 TO 1716

The military campaigns of the Sun King in the 1660s and 1670s suggested that the Extraordinaire des Guerres badly needed to be overhauled and regularized. Bringing it under the firm jurisdiction of the Secretary of State for War after the chaos of the Richelieu and Mazarin era had not been enough to create a smoothly functioning army treasury. Two of the treasurers general of the 1670s and 1680s had allowed a culture of waste to take hold in which the perversion of resources was common, and one of them, Louis Jossier de La Jonchère, went bankrupt in 1683. Unlike Chamillart later, the then War Minister Louvois protected his treasurers general from outside interference. But his insistence that Jossier compensate the king with half a million *livres* for fraud committed by his agents and underlings suggests strongly that Louvois felt any weakness shown by ministers towards financial contractors—including compensating them for monetary manipulations and for malfeasance committed by their underlings—would worsen the already chronic principal-agent problem. As far as he was concerned the big financial contractors had to accept the threat of losses as well as the prospect of gains, and they had to accept responsibility for the operations of their entire network.[10] Whether Louvois could have adopted such a firm attitude during an era of burdensome war (which the 1683–4 conflict was not) is an open question. And as so often with Louvois, he was not being entirely fair. The treasurers general were saddled with underlings whom even the most adept of them could not have managed well. By 1684 Louvois and the king had come to realize that they had to give a stronger structural shape to this organization, so in the next two years a series of reforms were rolled out, in particular the scrapping of autonomous venal offices of junior treasurers below the rank of treasurer general. This meant the treasurers general could now, with more justice, be held to account for their organization's performance, and this new system would generally work fairly well for France through the Nine Years War.[11]

[9] McCollim, 181–2; CCG, III, 99: Bernage to Desmaretz, 16 February 1709, marginalia by Desmaretz.

[10] Claeys, II, 765–6, 968; Robert Challe, *Mémoires. Correspondance complète*, ed. by Frédéric Deloffre and Jacques Popin (Geneva, 1996), 378; Guy Antonetti, 'Colbert et le crédit public', in Roland Mousnier, ed., *Un nouveau Colbert: Actes du Colloque pour le tricentenaire de la mort de Colbert* (Paris, 1985), 202–3, 206; AN G^{7}1774, no. 38: extract of council registers, 24 May 1683.

[11] SHD X^{1}2: *édit*, February 1684; AN G^{7}1774, no. 33: extract of council registers, 21 April 1684; Saint-Simon, VIII, 303.

Evidence from the 1680s and 1690s suggests that the treasurers general were now running a network from their various Paris headquarters that was much more under their control than previously. The personnel at the centre were not numerous, comprising in 1726 a general cashier, twenty-four *commis*, and two bookkeepers. There would have been few more in the War of the Spanish Succession.[12] For the *commis* beyond Paris, who numbered some 150–200 during wartime, the treasurers general adapted their own internal hierarchy, as they now had a flexibility previously denied them when other venal officials had been present in their system. The treasurer general would employ a *commis* in every *généralité* (and at Genoa to amass cash for Italy). Sometimes there were several in one area, with a *commis général* at their head, and they could be moved around from province to province. In the armies there was similarly a principal *commis* under whom several other *commis* worked. While *commis* were often selected in consultation with the Secretary of War and other associates of the Extraordinaire, they could be sacked summarily by the treasurer general alone. Although the king established a rule that the same man should not be employed in the same post for more than two years in succession (in order to prevent the diversion of funds into local financiers' hands), the limited availability of competent men throughout the reign, and the need to keep on men with good credit ratings, sometimes for seven or more years in a row, compromised this ideal.[13] These subordinates were by no means all paupers or even commoners. The senior *commis*, especially the most important treasurer stationed with each field army, needed to have sufficient financial stature to be able to take out loans, and this became more the case as the War of the Spanish Succession ground on. For example, it was fortunate that treasurer general Sauroy kept the Paris brothers on with the army of Flanders in 1708: during July–August he sent them only 28,000 *livres* when 1.5 million *livres* were needed, forcing them to borrow the rest locally in the Spanish Netherlands. This need for financial heavy-lifting also explains why Philippe, duc d'Orléans took Antoine Crozat, the outgoing *receveur général* of Bordeaux, as the treasurer of the French army he was commanding in Spain in 1707.[14]

In the entrepreneurial system that was a standard feature of *ancien régime* France financial control over underlings was as important, if not more so, than patronage control and playing upon their ambitions. To reduce the temptations for fraud the remuneration of the *commis* was proportional to the amount of money they could prove they had handled, at the rate of 2 *deniers* for every *livre* (0.83 per cent). The treasurer general's hold over them was enhanced by the requirement that they provide surety (a 'caution'), which was often raised by loans from others, but as one *commis* noted in 1701, it was 'certain that there are many *commis* currently employed who have no cautions at all worth solidly 20,000 *livres*'. Should their subordinates fail in their duty, or pervert funds, then the king generally left the

12 Saint-Simon, XVI, 668; CCG, III, 21: La Houssaye to Desmaretz, 30 April 1708.

13 SHD A[1]1519, no. 187: Aubert to Chamillart, 12 July 1701; A[1]1594, no. 23: Bouchu to Chamillart, 9 January 1702; Ya2: Voysin to Mongelas, Duplessis, and Girangy, 18 November 1709; CCG, II, 438: Bâville to Chamillart, 23 December 1707.

14 Ars. Ms. 4494, fo. 20r: 'Discours de M[r]. Paris de la Montagne', n.d.; Claeys, II, 268–9.

treasurer general to pursue his *commis* in the courts, sometimes employing the full panoply of legal action.[15]

Notwithstanding the considerable improvements in the performance and administration of the Extraordinaire since the early 1680s, the collapse of two sets of treasurers general in the course of 1701 caused the government to look again at restructuring this organization, but in doing so the door was opened to some retrograde policies. There is strong suspicion that Maximilien Titon, the arms entrepreneur and financier, was pushing for the creation of fresh venal offices in the Extraordinaire with the prospect of taking on the lucrative contract for collecting the capital investments. This is just one of many instances of a major figure with the ear of the minister, and possessing a vested interest in supplying the armies, lobbying for damaging financial alterations to the state's apparatus.[16] In July 1701 Titon suggested a wholesale restructuring of the Extraordinaire to save money, and it was surely not a coincidence when the Extraordinaire's *commis* based at Titon's manufacturing centre of Charleville, Mairon, only a month later submitted a detailed proposal to recreate venal offices inside the Extraordinaire. Mairon also proposed that they could organize themselves as a separate corporate body and offer proxy credit to the king independent of the treasurers general; the lesser venal treasurers would, furthermore, be able to delegate their responsibilities to anyone they wished. Mairon's plans would have wrecked the accountability structure built up in the 1680s. He even explicitly made a virtue of the fact that the treasurers general would no longer, under his scheme, have to bear responsibility for the faults of their agents. At this stage the king was not sufficiently desperate for money to heed this insidious counsel. However, nine years later, in March 1710, when royal finances were near breaking-point, proposals were again made to convert many of the *commis* into venal *trésoriers*, and this time they were carried through. The new system was bitterly resented by the treasurers general, who knew they would now find it far harder to control the organization over which they held responsibility. The fact that many of the proceeds of these office sales would be channelled to the treasurers general indicates how far ministers were prepared to sacrifice long-term order for costly short-term cash injections.[17]

It was quickly apparent that the new system was a mistake. By September 1711 many offices were still not sold, it was proving hard to prevent charlatans who had bought such offices from taking up their responsibilities, and the treasurers general were having to bypass many of their venal officials and install their own trusted agents as *commis* with commissions again. Aside from the disruption this all caused, and the casting aside of reliable, experienced men in some places in

[15] SHD A[1]1285, no. 33: Bagnols to Barbezieux, 17 April 1694; A[1]1526, no. 259: [*mémoire* by Mairon], August 1701 (quotation); AN G[7]1775, no. 283: Pomereuil to Chamillart, 31 October 1703; no. 34: *mémoire* on Extraordinaire for 1699 and 1701, [June 1703]; G[7]1787, nos 393–4: draft *arrêt*, [December 1712].

[16] The same problem led to the venalization of the artillery officers in 1703.

[17] SHD A[1]1526, no. 171: Titon to Chamillart, 6 July 1701; no. 258: *mémoire* by Mairon, August 1701; A[1]2272, no. 18: Mongelas to Voysin, 7 June 1710; BNF F-21054: *édit*, October 1701; F-21063: *édit*, March 1710.

favour of neophyte or merely titular office-holders, there was also the problem of insubordination and corruption which revenalization enhanced. Furthermore, by reducing their direct responsibilities and thus the amount of commission they received, this revenalization move damaged the creditworthiness of the treasurers general and did little to maintain an orderly system for channelling money to the armies. This, as the duc d'Orléans realized when he rescinded the venalization in 1716, was deeply damaging.[18] The fact that this and similar venalizations were proposed by men who were involved in military supply of one kind or another, who had influence in the corridors of power, and who had a financial interest in *affaires extraordinaires* more generally is a good illustration of the pressures now being brought to bear on the ministers, pressures that even Desmaretz and Voysin succumbed to.

THE FINANCING AND RESPONSIBILITIES OF THE EXTRAORDINAIRE DES GUERRES

There were two main revenue streams for getting money to the Extraordinaire des Guerres: there was indirect funding supplied from the taxpayers and from loans that were channelled via the Trésor royal; and there was direct funding by the Extraordinaire itself collecting revenues or floating loans. The treasurers general of the Extraordinaire were the most important of the secondary receivers of revenue, getting the bulk of their resources in almost all years of Louis XIV's personal rule from the primary receivers such as the *receveurs généraux* and the farmers general. But they also collected some revenue themselves directly from the king's subjects. The army budget was set at the start of the year and was adjusted according to need during the campaign season and winter quarters.

On the basis of the *ordonnances de paiement* they received from the War Ministry, the treasurers general would be allocated funds by the Finance Ministry through the Trésor royal, generally in the form of *assignations* issued with the king's approval on an astonishing variety of revenue sources. The stream of funds was unpredictable and erratic, and typically could vary in any one month between a few thousand *livres* and over 14 million *livres*. At any given moment, a treasurer general would have dozens of *assignations* in his 'portefeuille', with varying maturity dates and worth perhaps millions of *livres*, which he would juggle and deploy as seemed best.[19] This reflected the multiple revenue streams of the monarchy and the presence of the Extraordinaire across the entire territory of the French monarchy. Some of the funds would be obtained from, say, a *receveur général* in Paris; other *assignations* might be cashed with a bureau of the *fermes* out in a provincial town. On several occasions the proceeds from contracts for *affaires extraordinaires* were hypothecated for the Extraordinaire des Guerres, most notoriously when the crown

[18] AN G[7]1787, no. 403: Morands des Cours to [Le Rebours?], 23 July 1712; G[7]1788, no. 131: Sauroy to Desmaretz, 26 April 1714; CCG, III, 399: La Houssaye to Desmaretz, 5 September 1711.

[19] AN G[7]1777, nos 252–334: weekly *états* of funds, December 1703–February 1706.

revenalized many of the Extraordinaire's own officials in 1710.[20] Those funds gathered by the Extraordinaire in Paris could either be carted to where they were needed or the treasurer general could draw a bill of exchange upon somebody in a place where he wanted to transmit money. Out in the provinces, on the frontiers, or with the armies, one of his *commis* would then take delivery of the funds. Colbert had laid down guidelines that primary receivers were supposed to pay up within two weeks of an *assignation*'s maturity date, failing which the ministers would get involved. Primary receivers might also be forced into giving additional guarantees of payment.[21]

The treasurer general was expected to cover any temporary shortfalls but at least the difficulties he faced securing money were now explicitly recognized in a systemic way. They needed to be. Starting in the Nine Years War, *assignations* began to be given with maturity dates further and further into the future, while primary receivers began to delay payments. During the War of the Spanish Succession these problems were rampant. Bankers could also channel funds to the Extraordinaire either inside France or abroad by assembling bills of exchange and handing them to the treasurers general for transmission through the network, or sending bills of exchange directly to Extraordinaire *commis* elsewhere. A third way was for bankers to send bills of exchange to their own correspondents abroad who would, in turn, pass on the money to the Extraordinaire's agents. Either the bankers (or other issuing financiers) could accept final liability for a bill of exchange, or the treasurers general of the Extraordinaire might do so themselves.

Although the Extraordinaire was heavily dependent upon primary receivers to provide it with the money for military expenditure, it did act as a primary receiver itself on a small scale. This was particularly the case in some frontier and recently acquired provinces where the Extraordinaire, rather than the normal *receveurs généraux* or farmers general, might collect tax revenues or handle monetary movements.[22] By the 1690s the Extraordinaire also took in the proceeds of contributions extracted from enemy territory, managed confiscations from Huguenot exiles and enemy subjects, and levied some forced loans, including on Jews. All in all, the total sums acquired directly by the Extraordinaire could vary enormously, but very rarely exceeded 10–15 per cent of its total annual income. The Extraordinaire was also permitted to deposit silver matter in the mints on preferential terms.[23] The final source of revenue the Extraordinaire sought out for itself was credit, raising money in large part through bearer bills (see Chapter 9).

What was the Extraordinaire des Guerres expected to do with these funds? The single largest set of payments were those made to the regular infantry, cavalry, and

[20] SHD A[1]2504, fo. 269v: Voysin to Thibault, February 1710.

[21] Legohérel, 115; AN G[7]1774, no. 12: *receveurs généraux* to Pontchartrain, 30 January 1697.

[22] AN G[7]1774, no. 30: *assignation* payments lists from 1698, 11 July 1699; CCG, III, 81: Bernières to Desmaretz, 19 September 1708; Darryl Dee, *Expansion and Crisis in Louis XIV's France: Franche-Comté and Absolute Monarchy, 1674–1715* (Rochester, NY/Woodbridge, 2009), 67, 155.

[23] SHD Ya2: Chamillart to d'Angervilliers, 22 February 1709; CCG, III, 427: Roujault to Desmaretz, 13 February 1712; II, 39: *nouveaux convertis* of Montauban to Chamillart, 6 June 1700; Saint-Simon, XVII, 545 (appendix III).

dragoon regiments for the wages of the troops and the salaries of the officers. After 1688 the Extraordinaire also paid the provincial *milice*, a set of auxiliary conscript battalions, once they assembled and then left their home province.[24] The detail of pay distribution need not be spelled out here, except to say that by the end of the seventeenth century it was overseen more carefully than before: the *commis* of the Extraordinaire would deliver pay to the regiments and companies on the basis of muster rolls certified by agents of the War Ministry. The Extraordinaire coffers and accounts would quite separately hold further sums—mainly derived from off-reckonings on the soldiers' pay and known as 'retenues'—that were distributed under strict supervision to support recruitment, equipment, and clothing in line with the franchise nature of the French regimental system. In addition, the Extraordinaire paid out further allowances several times a year in the shape of the *ustencile* tax, gathered after 1689 by the *receveurs généraux* and passed on to the Extraordinaire to support the additional logistical needs of military units during winter quarters and the campaign season.[25] The Extraordinaire made a further series of payouts related to logistics on behalf of French regiments. Arms and equipment would be ordered by regimental officers or inspectors, but because the Extraordinaire held their funds—as a sort of regimental banking system—the treasurers general or their *commis* would pay those entrepreneurs who delivered the *matériel*, for example Boucher of the Franche-Comté for cavalry armour or Titon for the supply of firearms to the infantry.[26] On top of all this, the Extraordinaire supported all the costs of bread supply outside the campaign season, and paid for bread for garrison forces in the interior provinces at all times of the year.[27]

Somewhat more complex were the arrangements for meeting the costs of bread supply to the field armies, the 'vivres' system. In nearly all the years of Louis XIV's personal rule bread supply to the armies was contracted out to private consortia of so-called 'munitionnaires', dominated by some of the most powerful fisco-financiers. These companies established agents across France and with the forces in the field to raise financial advances, buy up grain, mill it, bake the bread, and distribute the supplies. It was an enormous operation, so big that separate contracts were usually signed for the armies of Flanders and Germany together and the armies of Italy and Catalonia together. At times, further contracts were signed for just a single army. The contracts were negotiated jointly by the Secretary of War and the *contrôleur général*, signed by the former and ratified in the royal council. Once a contract was under way the Finance Ministry assigned revenues to the Extraordinaire des Guerres to pay for bread needed by the field forces during the campaign season, and the treasurer general then passed funds to the *munitionnaires* in Paris. The *munitionnaires* then distributed funds down through their network of agents and suppliers. For frontier garrisons, the local Extraordinaire *commis* would pay

[24] SHD OM15: *règlement*, 29 November 1688.

[25] Rowlands, 200–18.

[26] SHD Ya2: Voysin to Le Guerchois, 17 January 1710; A[1]1990, no. 1413: Pleneuf to Le Fer d'Aulton, 21 September 1706.

[27] Louis André, *Michel Le Tellier et l'organisation de l'armée monarchique* (Paris, 1906), 306–8; CCG, III, 236: Desmaretz to Voysin, 30 October 1709.

the local *vivres* agents in appropriation notes drawn on the treasurer general, which were then sent back to Paris for cashing. Furthermore, if the *vivres* was struggling then the Extraordinaire—as a more powerful financial organism with much larger funding streams—would advance even more money to the *munitionnaires* or perhaps go even further by undertaking the purchase of food and fodder (for transport) on their behalf. In 1710, at a time when the *vivres* contracts had collapsed and food supply was being run directly as a semi-*régie*, the Extraordinaire appears to have taken on the job of running the majority of the financial operations for bread on the ground. To support them in this task the treasurers general were given a small rake-off for all sums handled for this business. The only problem throughout the Spanish Succession war was that the treasurers general were wont to provide the *munitionnaires* with long-dated *assignations* on themselves that they regarded as a low priority for cashing.[28]

Additional financial responsibilities came and went over the course of Louis XIV's personal rule.[29] These were largely related to the empire-building of the marquis de Louvois, who was determined to subordinate the technical branches of the war machine (artillery and fortifications) to his direct administrative and financial oversight through his favoured financiers. From 1683 to 1696 Louvois' trusted Extraordinaire treasurer general Jean de Turmenyes also managed the finances for the Hôtel Royal des Invalides, an institution that was funded through a kind of insurance deduction from all military-related payouts at the rate of 3 (or 4) *deniers* per *livre*. But this arrangement was altered in March 1701 when two posts of treasurer general of the Invalides were created for a price of 300,000 *livres* each, while in 1705 the artillery treasurer general also regained some autonomy from the Extraordinaire des Guerres.[30] If there was some greater streamlining of the Extraordinaire's roles in the early years of the War of the Spanish Succession, the burden of responsibilities nevertheless failed to shrink. The Extraordinaire was used as a distribution channel for a great deal of the funding of Philip V's forces in the Spanish Netherlands, while it also made advances to Spanish troops in Milan because the revenue system was so weak in this duchy. Moreover, Philip used the Extraordinaire as a pipeline for remitting money to where he wanted it, in particular to meet suppliers' invoices.[31] With the acquisition of the Spanish empire by the Bourbons the Extraordinaire evidently had to widen its horizons, much to its discomfort.

The greater geographical spread of military operations in the 1700s consequently led the Extraordinaire to work with remittance bankers and merchants on a far

[28] AN G[7]1776, no. 483: request by Charpentier, [1704]; G[7]1778, no. 56: 'Etat' by Mongelas, 16 January 1706; G[7]1802, no. 130: *munitionnaires* of Italy to Pontchartrain, 16 April 1691; no. 233: *état* of *assignations* held by *munitionnaires*, 7 April 1694; CCG, III, 284–5: Voysin to Desmaretz, 25 April 1710; Iung, I, 23–4, 29, 71, 87.

[29] Including payments of pensions in newly conquered territories, and assisting with the paperwork for the military route network with its allowance and supply distribution system (the 'étapes').

[30] AN G[7]1788, no. 110: note on Turmenyes, 14 April 1706; no. 148: 'Memoire…', [1714]; SHD A[1]1894: Pleneuf to Lieureville, 27 August 1705.

[31] See numerous accounting documents and notes from 1705–13 in AN G[7]1777–88 and G[7]1092.

greater scale than ever before. This involved not only receiving funds from bankers (as outlined above), and being aware of funds that the Trésor royal was directly supplying to bankers to purchase remittances sent to the Extraordinaire's agents; just as much it required the treasurers general to hand funds to bankers to back their remittances. Rather more unexpected is the use the Extraordinaire made of more straightforward mercantile networks to move funds, arrangements that were apparently as little known by ministers as they are by posterity. Usually only when things went wrong do these people make an appearance in the archives, one such case being that of the Moreau brothers. They were Parisian clothing suppliers who had a large network of outsourcing agents across France for small-scale manufacture, and who in 1703 supplied the Extraordinaire with remittances and credit worth over 3 million *livres*.[32]

The crucial thing to remember is that there was no single way of managing the flow of remittances, but such was the need for them that in the War of the Spanish Succession the Extraordinaire was heavily dependent upon banking, and domestic and foreign exchange, in a way it had not been for any of Louis XIV's earlier wars. In consequence the treasurers general had to maintain a good credit rating not only with French fisco-financiers but also with the international banking community. This meant punctual, reliable provision of *assignations* to bankers either as prepayments or in reimbursement of agreed debts. Here, the treasurers general were somewhat at the mercy of the primary receivers, such as the *receveurs généraux*, and when such *assignations* failed the bankers would often turn back to the Extraordinaire in expectation of alternative compensation. By 1705 the mercantile community was beginning to sense that earlier understandable lapses in discharging bills of exchange were giving way to a systematic failure by the treasurers general to pay up on bills that had been drawn on them by army officers for the payment of suppliers.[33] In the 1700s and 1710s the Extraordinaire's relations with the banking community were obviously a fraught business, made worse by the unpredictable and often unfathomable nature of exchange dealings. Compensation to royally contracted bankers for excessive exchange rates and currency losses they suffered also became vital to uphold crown international exchange credibility, and here too the Extraordinaire was involved, sometimes handing over additional monies (see Conclusion).[34]

In the end, such dealings were a means to an end: the king's money physically had to get to the troops, the suppliers, and the *commis* of the Extraordinaire. In some ways the most uncomplicated way of doing this was to send money from

[32] AN G[7]1123: Daniel Hogguer to Chamillart, 28 May 1705; G[7]1775, no. 321: 'Bordereau...jusqu'au der[er]. Octobre 1703', [November 1703]; G[7]1777, no. 40: Mongelas to Chamillart, 28 November 1705; G[7]1776, no. 151: Moreau *frères* to Chamillart, 20 January 1704.

[33] Forbonnais, II, 179; AN G[7]1120: 'Memoire au sujet des Remises de l'Extraord[re]. des guerres dans les païs estrangers', [1703]; G[7]1776, no. 43: Vieuxcourt to Chamillart, 29 January [1705]; no. 269: D'Honneur to Chamillart, 25 November 1704.

[34] SHD Ya2: Voysin to Nointel, 24 December 1709. See also, by contrast, SHD A[1]1594, no. 9: Chamillart to Bouchu, 8 January 1702, when the Trésor royal paid compensation directly to bankers instead.

Paris by carts. At times the gates of the city saw tens of thousands of *livres* passing through each day en route to the frontiers. Nevertheless, to move money this way was time-consuming and risked unexpected delays caused by environmental conditions and even enemy seizure in front-line areas.[35] Ministers felt that coin should be moved only when it was not possible to send bills of exchange. Since 1676 those sent by the treasurers general were supposed to be very swiftly cashable. But in a sign of things to come, there were already delays in meeting obligations with bills of exchange and similar instruments sent by the treasurers general in the crisis year of 1694. This would happen many more times in the War of the Spanish Succession, when the treasurers general would also face further pressures to pay up on more and more instruments issued by their agents across Europe to desperate army officers and suppliers.[36]

ACCOUNTS AND ACCOUNTABILITY IN THE EXTRAORDINAIRE DES GUERRES

With so many of the Extraordinaire's activities involving bills of exchange, dealings between private individuals, and the use of complex and shadowy networks, the French monarchy had a major principal-agent problem with this organization. To police this treasury the means at the king's disposal were also inadequate: War Ministry staff were overstretched with a multiplicity of duties, and even the Secretary of State for War only had time to go through the final, end-of-year accounts closely. In any case, accountancy practices tended to obfuscate as much as they shed light on operations. Poor accountancy typically means weak accountability, and this was a characteristic of the Extraordinaire from the top to the bottom. For a start, many of the *commis* were incompetent at keeping books, while in some places accounts were in a hopeless muddle or non-existent in any meaningful form because the hierarchy of *commis* inside the Extraordinaire was in fact far from linear and straightforward, and was sometimes completely confused. Besides this, the geographical dispersal of military units could cause considerable delays in the processing of muster rolls and payments.[37] War Ministry officials in the provinces were also palpably not checking the accounts properly, or were even corrupt. They certainly colluded in sharp practices. Even some *intendants* themselves were suspected of self-interest, cronyism, or complaisance.[38] This gives a sense of how hard

[35] SHD Ya2: Chamillart to Sauroy, 4 August 1708; AN $G^7$1783, nos 305, 307: Mongelas to [Le Rebours?], 14 and 16 August 1709.

[36] SHD $A^1$1285, no. 227: Le Bret to Barbezieux, 21 June 1694; OM 13: *ordonnance*, 16 August 1676; Ya2: Voysin to Barillon, 26 May 1710.

[37] SHD Ya2: Chamillart to several frontier *intendants*, 8 February 1707; Voysin to Mongelas, Duplessis, and Girangy, 18 November 1709; $A^1$1526, nos 258, 259: *mémoires* by Mairon, August 1701; AN $G^7$1787, no. 236: memorandum by widow and heirs of Arnauld, [late 1711]; $G^7$1775, no. 31: memorandum on the Sauvion-Terrat case, n.d.

[38] AN $G^7$1778, no. 291: 'Extrait du livre de recepte de... Sr Jean Roson...', 22 July 1711; Ars. Ms. 4494, fo. 8r: 'Discours de M^r. Paris de la Montagne', n.d.; CCG, III, 19–20: Chamillart to Bagnols, 20 April 1708.

it was for Versailles to check the Extraordinaire's agents out in the field, and why it was necessary to wring surety payments out of *commis* and punish severely those who were caught wilfully abusing the system.[39] Inside the Extraordinaire the internal auditing and accounting procedures were really no better. By the 1690s the various *contrôleurs* (auditors) of the Extraordinaire, who were supposed to check documentation produced by *commis*, were utterly useless and the positions had descended into venal sinecures that merely provided steady investment income for their owners, people who were otherwise occupied as army officers or in other walks of life. These posts were reformed in 1701, but it is unclear whether this made the *commis* more accountable in reality. Voysin certainly made little progress with efforts to improve auditing.[40]

With problems such as these going on throughout their networks, what chance did the treasurers general have of maintaining a grip on their own accounts? These men were not paragons of bookkeeping virtue struggling with a mass of chaotic underlings and overburdened government servants. They themselves only loosely followed the rules by which they were supposed to maintain their *registres-journaux*.[41] Treasurers general regularly failed to send sufficient funds to their agents, either through negligence because their offices were in disorder, or through deliberate fault. And sometimes funds were sent without any accompanying instructions for their employ, with the result that they were used for unintended purposes.[42] This did not matter much to the treasurers general, as long as they stayed afloat and perhaps managed to prosper. One might conclude that many financiers thought accounts would take care of themselves. Besides, if the systems the treasurers general operated did inflate the king's costs then the additional funds they had to process would bring additional rake-offs under the remuneration system. Furthermore, opaque accounts also had everyday advantages for them, allowing the delay and diversion of funds, although better auditing under Louis XIV (for all its manifest imperfections) prevented outright perversions reaching disastrous proportions. In the end, as one of them candidly admitted, it was impossible to undertake a full audit of the business of a treasurer general, and nobody had ever tried it, because

> no Treasurer of the Extraordinaires des Guerres has yet been sufficiently orderly in his affairs to be able to reveal the work of all his exercises in a single operation of arithmetic.[43]

At the end of each 'exercice' year a treasurer general had to present an 'état au vrai'—an interim statement of the year itemizing receipts, expenditure, revenue sources not realized, and clawbacks—to the royal council. Soon afterwards the Paris Chambre des Comptes was supposed to receive a full-blown set of accounts

[39] BNF F-23621: *édit*, June 1717.

[40] AN G⁷1775, no. 398: placet of de Joüy, [1702]; SHD A¹1613, no. 176: D'Honneur to Chamillart, 14 February 1702; Ya2: Voysin to all *intendants*, 30 June 1709; BNF F-21054: *édit*, October 1701.

[41] SHD A¹2272, no. 85: Quesneau to Voysin, 21 June 1710.

[42] McCollim, 124; Ars. Ms. 4494, fo. 18v: 'Discours de Mʳ. Paris de la Montagne', n.d.

[43] AN G⁷1775, no. 33: memorandum by Arnauld, [1704].

within three years of the end of a duty-year (or two years during peacetime).[44] Various things conspired to prevent this from happening. First of all, a duty-year was not over at the end of the nominal year: especially in the War of the Spanish Succession the Extraordinaire might not receive many funds for a year or more after they were supposed to be delivered; and it might take several years to retire the bearer bills issued by a treasurer general.[45] Second, it proved extremely hard to bring in all the local accounts and receipts to the Extraordinaire headquarters in Paris. As one *commis* put it,

> the way of withdrawing the *acquits* & discharges [...] is so burdensome that it is well-nigh impossible that a treasurer general after several years of exercise does not fall into a type of chaos.[46]

In a context of year upon year of exacting war after 1689, it followed that the amount of time it took to provide full accounts grew longer and longer: in the summer of 1715 treasurer general Mongelas had still not fully presented even his *summary* accounts for the 1706 duty-year![47] Faced with all this, nobody could be sure where a sizeable amount of the king's money might end up and in what form. It did not help that after 1701 the monarchy turned up the flow of expenditure, mismanaged the appropriation of funds to the Extraordinaire des Guerres, and came to rely more and more on the credit of the treasurers general and their associates.

THE FINANCIAL POWER OF THE TREASURERS GENERAL

To sustain the huge payments to the armies and arms suppliers and to maintain borrowing—in an era of interrupted and inadequate cash flow—the treasurers general of the Extraordinaire des Guerres needed to be resilient both psychologically and financially. Not only were financial emoluments and liquidity critical for a man to exercise the office of treasurer general successfully but also personal credibility. They also needed to have co-investors in their positions and, just as importantly, associates to back their debt issues, such was the burden of office by the 1700s. Some idea of who these men were, and the nature of their financial situations, therefore needs to be provided.

In 1695 the treasurers general of the Extraordinaire des Guerres, like everybody else in the kingdom, were assessed for the new *capitation* tax: they appeared in the first class (out of twenty-two), and at the eighteenth rank, two ranks above that of the *receveurs généraux des finances* and the farmers general, and only two ranks below the king's *contrôleur général des finances* himself.[48] The general esteem for the

[44] AN G[7]1774, no. 1: representation by La Touanne, [1690–1]; BNF F-21054: *édit*, October 1701; F-23621: *édit*, June 1717.

[45] BNF F-21054: *édit*, October 1701; SHD Ya2: Chamillart to all *intendants*, 25 March 1708.

[46] SHD A[1]1526, no. 259: *mémoire* by Mairon, [August 1701].

[47] AN G[7]1788, no. 237: 'Extrait...', [*c.*25 June] 1715.

[48] Germain-Martin, 'Le financement des guerres', 20.

treasurers general, formally confirmed in the *capitation* assessment, was reflected in the prices paid for the post, which were also affected by market conditions, the responsibilities of the moment (which did vary a bit), and the solvency of the Extraordinaire. Generally, though, the prices increased in the second half of Louis XIV's personal rule: one of the posts had changed hands in 1683 for 900,000 *livres*, another for 1.4 million *livres* in 1709, and one for as much as 2.12 million *livres* in 1695–6. By contrast, an office of *receveur général* usually only sold for somewhere between 150,000 and 700,000 *livres* in this period. Much of the capital would be raised through borrowing (usually by floating personal *rentes* on oneself), and this was repaid slowly or only when the post was sold on again. The investors had prior claims over any income derived from the *office* as the interest on their loans.[49]

The official income came in two major forms. First, there were the *gages*, the interest paid out by the crown for the capital investment in this venal office: the edict of October 1701 fixed this at 30,000 *livres* per annum. Second, there were the permitted rake-offs on all sums that flowed through the hands of the Extraordinaire des Guerres, the so-called 'taxations'. These were awarded to cover the costs of a treasurer general's entire operation, and in 1726 such expenses—notably the wages and expenses of *commis*, accounting, and transport—were estimated at around 400,000 *livres* for a complete 'exercice' of one year on duty and one year off. This was for handling around 60 million *livres*. The expenses would have been far larger in wartime, owing to the increased expenditure and the more problematic distribution of troops; and whenever the Extraordinaire dealt with money for the artillery, fortifications, or elite troops then further rake-offs would be forthcoming. The *taxations* were also supposed to provide a cushion for meeting the costs of any advances a treasurer general had to make to the king's forces, including the interest on any loans he raised. From the 1680s, if not slightly earlier, a treasurer general received *taxations* at the rate of 4 *deniers* for every *livre* processed (or 1.66 per cent), except for a brief time in 1710. There was also a supplement to the *taxations*, known as the *droit de rolles*, a payment based on the number of horse and foot companies in the army in any given month and which could generate up to another 100,000 *livres* a year.[50] If a treasurer general was handling, say, 130 million *livres* for the king in the War of the Spanish Succession, he was therefore drawing for his income and costs somewhere around 2.25 million *livres* in a three-year cycle that treasurers operated at this time. The administrative costs were perhaps 1 million *livres*, excluding the servicing of loans which, as we shall see, grew as an obligation in this period. This might leave several hundred thousand *livres* for the treasurers general to employ, after paying those who held a share in their office.[51]

[49] DAPS, 146–9; AN G[7]1775, no. 233: Arnauld to Chamillart, April 1703; G[7]1778, no. 110: note on Turmenyes, 14 April 1706; G[7]1787, no. 8: placet of Sauroy, [January 1711].

[50] Saint-Simon, XVI, 668; AN G[7]1782, no. 27: note by Chamillart, 1707; BNF F-21054: *édit*, October 1701; F-21063: *édit*, March 1710; F-21064: *édit*, November 1710.

[51] The treasurers general were also making money by lending to courtiers, ministers, and all sorts of lesser officials at interest: e.g. AN G[7]1775, no. 28: 'Debet du Compte… 1699', [1702]; G[7]1776, no. 144: *mémoire* on the marquis de Béthune, [July 1704].

In the early eighteenth century it remained the case that the Extraordinaire des Guerres was a significant magnet for financiers and for financial investment because ultimately, although the job got harder as the War of the Spanish Succession wore on, the agency and its heads could not be permitted to fall.

THE PERSONAL POSITIONS OF THE TREASURERS GENERAL

Dealing with the treasurers general in a thematic way, while illuminating, gets us only so far in understanding the strength, power, and resourcefulness of these men, which made them so essential and so valued by the king in the 1700s. Each treasurer general of the Extraordinaire needs to be considered as the leader of a consortium of financiers: of those involved, some were formal investors in the purchase and ownership of a treasurer general's office, others merely associated themselves on an ad hoc basis for one or more years at a time. It was not by any means a free-floating set of arrangements devoid of factional considerations, nor, given the private interests involved, would one expect it to be. There were in fact four basic networks that held the formal offices in our period: Turmenyes–Arnauld–Mongelas–La Jonchère; La Touanne–Sauvion–Le Bas de Montargis–Le Bas Duplessis; Durey de Vieuxcourt–Durey de Sauroy; and Berthelot de Pleneuf.[52] There was some rivalry between these groups but generally speaking this concerned matters of business rather than inherent antagonism. Space precludes an examination of all these men here, but their weight can be seen by looking at the two most important: Mongelas and Montargis.

Romain Dru de Mongelas was one of the titans of French finance in the last decades of Louis XIV's reign. He was the son of a magistrate in the *Parlement* of the tiny sovereign principality of Dombes north of Lyon, controlled until 1681 by the 'Grande Mademoiselle', who was Louis XIV's first cousin, and which then came into the possession of the duc du Maine, the king's favourite bastard. These were friends in high places for the family, and in the shape of Maine a potential source of investment from the 1690s. The Dombes was also one of the centres of false coining in the French isthmus. In 1694 Mongelas could be found as the principal *commis* of the Extraordinaire in the Sarre region, and two years later he bought one of the offices of treasurer general of the Extraordinaire, providing a small share of the capital and exercising the post jointly with Jean-Louis Arnauld de La Perrière, the main financial investor. After performing two duty-years Arnauld was more or less sacked in May 1701, and the responsibilities for the remainder of that year were handled by Mongelas. However, it rapidly became clear that he was in difficulty, despite his serious financial backers. When Chamillart reorganized the treasurer general positions into three posts that autumn it was made clear to Mongelas that he was not wanted: in May 1702 he was obliged to sell half his office to

[52] Pleneuf was also on good terms with Mongelas, and through his other associates was connected directly with the Durey brothers. For a table of the treasurers general, see page xviii of this book.

Pleneuf and finish washing up his 1701 *exercice*. From this low point, however, Mongelas bounced back. By December 1703 Chamillart was thinking of bringing him back as the leader of a future *exercice*, surely because the team of backers Mongelas could assemble was formidable. In 1706 and 1709 he once again headed the Extraordinaire before selling on his share of the treasurer generalship to La Jonchère. Arnauld and Mongelas had had further co-owners of their office, most notably François Mauricet de La Cour, who ploughed 350,000 *livres* into the treasurer generalship, before taking on the newly created office of treasurer general of Les Invalides in 1701. His influence over Chamillart will be considered in Chapter 10.[53]

Then there was Pierre Thomé, and here we cross the line between office co-owners and mere associate investors in duty-years' finances. Thomé was Mongelas' cousin, and was treasurer of the Galleys between 1692 and 1699 before becoming a farmer general from 1703. With Vincent Maynon and Antoine Crozat, Thomé became an associate of Arnauld and Mongelas for the 1697 and 1701 *exercices*. What this means is that Mongelas had the support of the three key figures in the Compagnie de Guinée, which in the summer of 1701 was formally granted the *asiento* to bring slaves into the Spanish New World by Philip V. Even if this special contract did not bring much money it was a visible anchor and generator of confidence for a bunch of financiers who, in this time of opportunity and uncertainty surrounding the Spanish empire, could expect to pull in considerable loans. Three years later Thomé made the transition from investor in an Extraordinaire *exercice* to holding a formal share in the post of treasurer general, coming in with Mongelas for half the value of the office. On Thomé's death in 1710 his widow sold this share to Mongelas. Mongelas then appears to have become a sleeping partner of La Jonchère, the man who formally succeeded him as nominal treasurer general. With Pierre Thomé's death, Mongelas confessed to Voysin that his affairs had become greatly disturbed.[54]

Formal co-owners and associates were obviously needed more than ever, and many of them stuck together, with beneficial effects. It is surely no accident that in 1710 Mongelas became one of the two *secrétaires des commandements* to the duc de Berry, Louis XIV's youngest grandson, when Vincent Maynon, his associate, was the head of Berry's personal administration, as *surintendant* of the duke's finances, lands and buildings, and director of the household and finances of Berry's wife.[55] These arrivistes were now moving beyond the private offices of dukes and peers, whose affairs they often ran, to colonize the *maisons* of members of the royal family.

[53] AN G[7]1775, no. 233: Arnauld to Chamillart, April 1703; no. 306: Chamillart to [Le Rebours?], 9 December 1703; G[7]1787, no. 236: memorandum on Arnauld's widow and heirs, [late 1711]; SHD A[1]1285, no. 46: La Gourpille to Barbezieux, 10 April 1694; Claeys, I, 226, 728–9.

[54] AN G[7]1780, no. 181: *mémoire* on Extraordinaire after 1695, [1707]; G[7]1775, no. 32: *mémoire* on Arnauld, [*c.*1701–2]; no. 233: Arnauld to Chamillart, April 1703; G[7]1783, no. 358: Sabatyer to Thomé, 5 October 1709; Claeys, I, 729; Chaussinand, 32, 111; SHD A[1]2272, no. 196: Mongelas to Voysin, 18 July 1710.

[55] AN G[7]1786, no. 327: Mongelas to Desmaretz, 6 October 1710; G[7]1787, no. 393/394: draft *arrêt*, [October 1712]; Joseph Sevin, comte de Quincy, *Mémoires du chevalier de Quincy*, ed. Léon Lecestre (3 vols, Paris, 1898–1901), III, 55; Claeys, II, 373.

We should not overlook the fact that in 1712–14 Berry was second in line to the French throne (if one excludes Philip V of Spain). Maynon and Mongelas, the latter not dying until 1737, could easily have become courtier-ministers had Berry succeeded as king.

Only one other set of financiers in the realm became as powerful as Mongelas, and they represented an even more essential cog in the wheels of the Extraordinaire: the Le Bas family in the shape of the two treasurers general Claude Le Bas de Montargis, marquis de Bouchet Valgrand, and his brother Michel François Le Bas Duplessis. Montargis in particular became completely indispensable to the government. François Le Bas, seigneur de Lescheneau, father of the two men, had been a *commis* of the Extraordinaire des Guerres before moving into the artillery corps under Richelieu. When he died his wife remarried in 1670 to Charles Renouard de La Touanne, who became treasurer general of the Extraordinaire from 1685 until he died, his affairs in ruins and under investigation, in June 1701. Meanwhile, Montargis and Duplessis took full advantage of their stepfather's power and influence. For ten years after 1691 Montargis was a major official of the Extraordinaire out in the field. In February 1693, aged thirty-two, he married Henriette Catherine Hardouin-Mansart, daughter of Jules Hardouin-Mansart, who was already *premier architecte du Roi* and only six years away from elevation to glory as Superintendant of the King's Arts, Buildings, and Manufactures. Montargis is known to have supported his father-in-law's career financially. Hardouin-Mansart's children in fact provide a key set of links between financiers involved in funding the war effort directly: another of his daughters, Catherine, married Vincent Maynon in 1699, while his son Jacques, comte de Sagonne, married Madeleine Bernard, daughter of the banker Samuel Bernard in 1701. The Le Bas connections with the powerful and influential did not, however, stop there. The brother of Montargis and Duplessis was Claude Louis Le Bas de Girangy, seigneur de Claye, the treasurer general of the king's *Gardes du Corps*, inside the household military corps, between 1702 and 1716. In October 1706 Girangy married Marie Catherine Quentin, who was first lady of the bedchamber to the duchess of Burgundy, destined (it seemed at the time) to be queen in due course. She was also daughter of the first valet of the *Garderobe du Roi*.[56] This gave the Le Bas brothers an influence at the court, a higher status in the eyes of the public (however resented this might have been), and a level of credibility that no treasurer general had possessed in the first half of Louis XIV's personal rule.

Considered the most reliable and accommodating of all the Extraordinaire treasurers general of the era, Montargis nevertheless found himself under such a burden of debt that he had to step aside in 1708, not least because he had taken up a duty-year twelve months early, out of turn, in 1707. Like Turmenyes in 1696, he made an upward move, buying the post of *Garde du Trésor royal*, and was succeeded at the Extraordinare by his brother Duplessis. Duplessis, however, was seen by ministers as a guarded, foot-dragging incompetent, whom Voysin thought, as early as April

[56] La Chesnaye, II, 32–3; Lüthy, I, 145; Claeys, I, 1086; II, 108–11; Chaussinand, 60.

1710, 'wanted very much to be relieved of his position'. His accounts were a complete mess, according to other officials. Despite this, he continued in office until 1716, and even undertook another duty-year in 1713, the final year of fighting. His tenure says something about the extreme difficulties facing treasurers general in the final years of Louis XIV's reign, but also about the reluctance of ministers to fire them or seriously discipline them. To take a hard line would not only have caused trouble with the immediate entourages of leading members of the royal family, but would also have threatened the credit of the Extraordinaire as a whole and the Trésor royal, and by extension the financial credibility of the entire war effort.[57]

Almost all of those who became treasurers general of the Extraordinaire des Guerres in the War of the Spanish Succession, or took formal shares in ownership of the office, had entered the post with some family or personal experience of this organization or of one of the naval treasuries, while Pleneuf had worked with it a great deal as a supplier of all manner of goods and services to the army. It follows that they were very familiar with the Extraordinaire's roles, structures, methods, and problems, and—at least until serious difficulties suggested otherwise—they were of sufficient stature to be credible with the wider public. Some of them enhanced that stature in the course of the war, either in the Extraordinaire or after leaving it. Joseph Durey de Sauroy, whose family also dominated the finances of the Franche-Comté, succeeded his brother Vieuxcourt in 1708 and continued in office until 1741. This is a real indication of the financial stamina of some of the treasurers general and the resources they could call upon.[58] Nonetheless, at the very start of the War of the Spanish Succession it became clear that the hangover of debt from the Nine Years War and the crisis of the treasurers general in mid-1701 required the crown to provide additional assistance. This came partly through attaching a range of associates, backers, and lenders to the treasurers general.

THE PAYMASTERS' AUXILIARIES: ASSOCIATES AND BACKERS OF THE EXTRAORDINAIRE DES GUERRES

The treasurers general could draw financial support not only from those who co-owned their prestigious venal offices but also from a range of other investors. These included leading courtiers, robe magistrates, and military commanders, for example the prince de Rohan-Guéméné who placed 45,360 *livres* with La Jonchère in 1712 at 6 per cent annual interest.[59] Important as such people were, those who

[57] AN $G^7$1098: Montargis to Desmaretz, 11 March 1710; $G^7$1787, no. 73: Duplessis to Desmaretz, 21 April 1711; Claeys, II, 112; CCG, III, 284–5: Voysin to Desmaretz, 25 April 1710 (quotation); III, 287: Le Guerchoys to Desmaretz, [August 1710]; SHD $A^1$2272, no. 261: Quesneau to Voysin, 2 August 1710.

[58] Claeys, I, 787, 795; AN $G^7$1775, no. 182: memorandum on Montargis' and Vieuxcourt's 1704 *exercice*, 7 March 1704; no. 306: Chamillart to [Le Rebours?], 9 December 1703; $G^7$1776, no. 208: memorandum, 17 August 1704.

[59] CCG, II, 310: *premier président* Morant (Toulouse) to Chamillart, 5 March 1706; AN $G^7$1787, no. 300: memorandum on the prince de Guéméné, 13 February 1712.

mattered more for the purposes of regular, swift cash flow and public reputation were those other fisco-financiers who were prepared to stand behind the treasurers general. Whoever the backers were, there were several ways of supporting a treasurer general: one could become an official associate for a particular duty-year and sign any credit notes for it; one could be a publicly acknowledged backer who in reality had secret royal exemption from any liability; one could be a private backer not officially known to the public but with legal documentation setting out the relationship to the treasurer general; or one could be a top-secret backer so only a very small number of people would know of your involvement.[60] The grandees and army officers fitted largely into the last category, while the fisco-financiers could act in all the ways described above, as well as co-owning the office of treasurer general.

It is to these fisco-financiers who acted as helpmates to the treasurers general that we need to turn, for while there had been earlier backers for the Extraordinaire using formal, legal associations, the public associates and secret investors were invaluable in the War of the Spanish Succession. Much like the treasurers general themselves, associates enjoyed greater protection from the vagaries of the war than most members of the financial and social elites. They had such a privileged position because they were considered inherently strong and solvent. This was mainly, but not exclusively, through their diverse interests in the king's financial affairs. Before the nature of the associations and the reasons for the shape they took can be fully understood a picture of some of the most important associates and big lenders needs to be provided. Some of the associates, such as Vincent Maynon, drew their strength from being active as *receveurs généraux*, as farmers general, or as financial managers for grandees and even royals. One man who combined all three roles was Pierre Delpech, who had the *recette générale* of Riom (Auvergne), was a full member of several *fermes générales* consortia, and was, like Chamillart, one of a team who oversaw Madame de Maintenon's pet project, the *Maison royale de Saint-Louis* at Saint-Cyr. Delpech was so trusted she tasked him with managing her marquisate too. He was therefore a remarkably prestigious and useful associate for treasurer general Montargis in 1702, and it may be no accident that Delpech was involved in this particular year, when Maintenon's husband the king, unusually, had a direct financial share in the running of the Extraordinaire des Guerres.[61] Others were even more useful to the treasurers general, but the stronger they were the more likely they were also to behave like *prime donne* who put their own interests above those of the king. This was particularly the case with the greatest financier of the period 1700–30, Antoine Crozat, who until 1707 was a *receveur général*.

Antoine's formal role of associate to the treasurers general—designated with signing bearer bills and acting as public guarantor for loans—was confined to the *exercices* of 1695, 1697, 1701, and 1704; however, he also took on a much more active role at times. Far from being confined to Paris, Antoine was the principal *commis* of

[60] AN $G^7$1780, no. 181: *mémoire* on the Extraordinaire after 1695, [1707]; $G^7$1775, no. 306: Chamillart to [Le Rebours?], 9 December 1703.

[61] AN $G^7$1776, no. 200: *édit* for Poulletier, 30 December 1701; Claeys, I, 661; DAPS, 572.

the Extraordinaire des Guerres for the French army of Spain in 1704, 1705, and 1707. Not coincidentally, during this last year the commander-in-chief of French forces in Spain was the duc d'Orléans, in whose household Antoine was entrenched by virtue of marriage connections and acting as the duke's banker.[62] Whether in Paris or abroad, the ties of Antoine and his brother Pierre with the territories of the Spanish monarchy, in particular their trading links inside Iberia itself and the financial connections they could exploit between Languedoc and Genoa, were essential for remitting money to the Extraordinaire agents with the French forces in Castile, Aragon, and the duchy of Milan, either through bankers or through merchants. In the multilateral world of international remittances they also raised loans in Amsterdam for the Extraordinaire.[63] In all this, Antoine was working directly with several treasurers general: Turmenyes, his own brother-in-law Vieuxcourt, Montargis, and, until relations had become venomous by 1706, with Mongelas.[64]

By 1701 the assistance of associates like Maynon and the Crozats was vital, particularly for the issuing of debt on the Extraordinaire. Be that as it may, the arrangements with associates were not an unalloyed benefit for either the crown or the Extraordinaire des Guerres. While the associates were supposed to bolster the credit of the Extraordinaire, ironically they may have encouraged the already casual approach to accounting, as several men working together could, for a while, get away with being less exact in their affairs than a single treasurer who needed to keep much more on top of his business to preserve his own creditworthiness.[65] Moreover, securing the necessary support of individual financiers involved big concessions, as we shall see. The problems began with getting together and holding together a 'société' of financiers behind a treasurer general. The details of the agreement to form a 'union' could be tricky to negotiate, meaning some duty-years started without the full array of expected associates in position. Associates could also get cold feet, and withdrawals and deaths happened, sometimes in the middle of a duty-year.[66] But for all that *ad hominem* considerations for association or dis-investment were important, they do not tell the whole story of the problems of creating companies for Extraordinaire duty-years.

As far as investors were concerned, a big obstacle to formal association was that a treasurer general, upon leaving office, technically remained liable for the finances of the Extraordinaire in the period in which he had been in post, sometimes, as it turned out, for a very long time indeed. To compound the risk, when there was confusion over accounts because the Extraordinaire was handling the monies for

[62] Claeys, I, 73; SHD Ya2: Voysin to Blécourt, 30 May 1710; Voysin to Méliand, 17 July 1709; AN $G^7$1092: *bordereau* entitled 'M. de Moriana', 15 May 1704; $G^7$1787, no. 426: Mongelas to Desmaretz, 30 December 1712; Lévy, *Capitalistes et pouvoir au siècle des Lumières* (3 vols, Paris, 1969–80), I, 117–19, 420.

[63] AN $G^7$1778, no. 77: [note by Mongelas], 7 March 1706; $G^7$1775, no. 223: Mongelas to Chamillart, 5 October 1701; Lévy, *Capitalistes*, I, 173, 176; Michaud, 681; Chaussinand, 85.

[64] AN $G^7$1778, no. 35: Mongelas to Chamillart, 8 February 1706; no. 124: list of non-cooperating *recettes générales*, [May 1706]; no. 159: Mongelas to [Chamillart], 13 July 1706.

[65] Legohérel, 290, citing a *mémoire* of January 1704 (AN $G^7$1828).

[66] AN $G^7$1775, no. 34: *mémoire* on the Extraordinaire years 1699 and 1701; $G^7$1780, no. 181: *mémoire*, [1707].

other branches of the service, such as fortifications, there was a danger of litigation that could drag on for years. It was not surprising that some associates therefore preferred to remain in the shadows, but around the start of the War of the Spanish Succession a ruling by the Paris Cour des Aides, the major taxation tribunal of the realm, exacerbated uncertainties surrounding financial associations. Examining a case involving the management of fortification funds by the Extraordinaire, this court seemed to decide that private investors in a fisco-financier could no longer shelter behind some form of non-liability, but were exposed to actions for compensation against the principal holder of an office.[67]

None of this amounted to encouragement for financiers or others to invest in the activities of the Extraordinaire des Guerres, just at the moment when it was clear this treasury was struggling to fund the very limited military operations of 1701–2. Renewed efforts had to be made to bring in associates. For the 1702 *exercice* treasurer general Montargis enjoyed the ultimate of backers, the king himself. Montargis had taken on the role so late in the day after the collapse of his stepfather La Touanne that there was little choice but to run this year as a *régie*, in which 'His Majesty profited from one-half of the benefits'. To help Montargis further, the king provided associates in the form of three *receveurs généraux*, who were to be guarantors only of those bearer bills used by the Extraordinaire to borrow money and which they had signed; for any bills they discharged they would be compensated out of normal Extraordinaire income.[68] Chamillart had also come to realize the need to protect investors in key royal financiers. However, instead of imposing strict limited liability, protection took somewhat arbitrary and unstable forms that benefited associate investors who possessed muscle, at the expense of the crown and the public. An associate could be publicly declared as such, by the crown, to bolster confidence in a treasurer general, but there might be a secret agreement with the king that this associate would have zero liability for the finances of the duty-year. Following on from this, the crown had to protect these men from all kinds of legal pursuits by creditors as time wore on.[69] In legal terms the system of associates for a treasurer general was to all intents and purposes a fiction, nothing more than an exercise in confidence-generation among the wider public. Rewards were also joined to legal protection, with each member of the 1702 association getting, all told, the very generous sum of 70,000 *livres*. The persistence of similar financial rewards in subsequent years, when non-liability agreements had much diminished the risks for the associates, made association with the Extraordinaire a very good deal.[70]

67 AN G^{7}1774, no. 40: *mémoire* for Nicolas Leclerc, [post-1703]; G^{7}1775, no. 30: placet of Sauvion, [*c.* late 1701–3].

68 AN G^{7}1775, no. 102: memorandum, [1703] (quotation); no. 103: memorandum, [1703], uses the term 'régie'; G^{7}1776, no. 200: *édit* for Poulletier, 30 December 1701; G^{7}1782, no. 27: note from 1707 by Chamillart.

69 SHD A^{1}1613, no. 199: Pleneuf to Chamillart, 14 November 1702; AN G^{7}1775, no. 306: Chamillart to [Le Rebours?], 9 December 1703; G^{7}1776, no. 318: 'Coppie de la deliberation des S^{rs}. de Carqueville et Lallemant…', 23 November 1702; BNF F-23619: *déclaration*, 4 December 1708.

70 AN G^{7}1775, no. 32: *mémoire* on Arnauld, [*c.*1701–2]; G^{7}1776, no. 317: 'Projet', [late 1703]; G^{7}1776, no. 198: note, 24 August 1704.

These were the men who ran the military finances, or who supported them, and they needed to be resilient, drawing support from across the range of para-royal financial activities and operators. It is no accident that Chamillart preferred to attach prominent *receveurs généraux*, usually from the wealthiest provinces, to the Extraordinaire formally as associates. Increasingly, the Extraordinaire was supporting the credit of the *recettes générales* and the farms, and the *recettes générales* that of the Extraordinaire, in a loop that became more and more perilous for the credibility of all concerned as royal income deteriorated, expenditure rose, and more and more credit had to be raised to sustain the king's armies.

8

The Crisis of Spending and Appropriations in Louis XIV's Personal Rule

At times of insufficient revenues the mounting of front-line military effort by the French war machine became progressively harder. But it was not just a matter of inadequate revenues for the jobs in hand, as historians so often content themselves with noting when explaining military disappointment (if they bother with financial affairs at all). It was a question of getting money to where it was needed. In the course of the War of the Spanish Succession the system for appropriating revenues to expenditure, which had worked tolerably well in the Dutch War and the Nine Years War, crumbled and made the job of the military paymasters even harder. This made no small contribution to the gradual decline of France as the superpower of the age, and is a key index of the degeneration of royal finances. Before the deterioration of appropriations can be explained some sense of the magnitude of the sums allocated through the Extraordinaire des Guerres needs to be given.

THE GENERAL PATTERN OF WAR REVENUE AND WAR EXPENDITURE, 1701–14

Because of the random survival of royal accounts, and the opacity of those that remain in the archives, it is well nigh impossible to derive accurate information about the amount of expenditure the king pushed through the military paymasters. The best set of figures seem to be those given by the mid-eighteenth-century historian of French finances, François Véron de Forbonnais, even with their inconsistencies, as they seem to fit reasonably well with all sorts of sums suggested in the surviving original documents.[1] They also appear to include large sums that were spent on behalf of the War Ministry, much of it ultimately by the Extraordinaire, but were channelled through bankers and supply contractors. Some expenditure was also accounted for by the servicing of debts incurred by the paymasters. There seems to be no better way to proceed in order to obtain a reasonable, if vague, picture of the situation.

[1] Those provided by Arthur de Boislisle, in tables and lists at the back of his source volumes on the *contrôleurs généraux* (CCG, II, 600–1, 604), do not match up so well with what can be gleaned from various archival documents in AN $G^7$1774–1789 and $G^7$1119–26.

Some expenditure was fairly consistent between 1689 and 1714: 3–4 million *livres* per annum was spent on the troops of the royal household and the Gendarmerie de France in the 1690s, and about 4–5 million *livres* in the 1700s. Most of this was disbursed through the Ordinaire des Guerres and other smaller treasuries for elite forces. Fortification spending was generally 2–3 million *livres* per annum in the War of the Spanish Succession but at times in the Nine Years War had been much higher. The biggest fluctuations were with artillery spending—which oscillated between 1 million and 6.7 million *livres*—and with the sums paid out to the *vivres* contractors to supply bread to the armies, which in 1707, for example, stood at some 11–12 million *livres*, but which reached as high as 45 million *livres* after 1709! Throughout most of the War of the Spanish Succession the amount spent on troop pay and regimental allowances—excluding upkeep for the transit system of military *étapes* and around 4–6 million *livres* of subsidies for Spanish troops—was some 70–80 million *livres* a year. There was not much change in this respect between 1704, when France was engaged in far-flung theatres of war across western Europe, and 1710, when Louis XIV's armies (incidentally, much shrunken in size) were very largely stationed on the country's frontiers and inside the kingdom. Only in 1705–7, when France was at its most stretched, do the costs of basic troop upkeep appear to have grown to between 80 and 90 million *livres*. The years 1705 and 1707 saw the peaks of overall military expenditure: much of the excess can be attributed to additional supply and transportation costs, the negotiation of financial instruments, and commission and compensation for various financiers. Table 8.1 sets out the figures, as supplied by Forbonnais, for total expenditure related to the wars on land, whether channelled through the Extraordinaire or not. For all its imperfections it at least provides a powerful sense of how war expenditure was kept within manageable boundaries in the Nine Years War but ballooned after 1701–2.[2]

To carry out this expenditure the crown was supposed to provide sufficient funds to the bankers, the suppliers, the Extraordinaire des Guerres, and the other military treasurers, but it did not do so. In retrospect the 1680s and 1690s—for all the funding bottlenecks that were encountered—seem to have been a golden age for army funding. There were some moments of acute funding difficulties throughout the Nine Years War, building from 1692 into a more serious crisis in 1694, a time which shared many of the characteristics of most years after 1702: monetary shortage, supply failure, financial overstretch, rejection of bills of exchange, ministerial bewilderment, and defensive warfare.[3] The effects lasted into 1695, and ensured Louis XIV would have to make painful sacrifices in peace negotiations, but there was some recovery in 1696–97. However, the breakdowns of the 1690s

[2] Sources informing the discussion of expenditure are: Forbonnais, II, tables on pages 100–1, 170–1; and on pages 190, 194, 201, 214, 224, 232, 237, 247, 268; AN G[7]1776, no. 294: 'Compte du Roy…', 12 December 1704; G[7]1777, no. 83: 'Estat', 13 August 1705; G[7]1780, no. 129: basic Extraordinaire des Guerres 1707 expenditure statement, [1708]; SHD A[1]1594, no. 9: Chamillart to Bouchu, 8 January 1702; Ya2: Voysin to Bâville, 20 December 1710.

[3] AN G[7]1774, no. 14: *mémoire* by Turmenyes, 9 March 1697; SHD A[1]1285, no. 7: de Sève to Barbezieux, 4 April 1694; nos 25, 31: La Fond to Barbezieux, 13 and 16 April 1694.

Table 8.1 War expenditure, 1689–1714

YEAR	TOTAL ESTIMATE (millions of *livres*)	YEAR	TOTAL ESTIMATE (millions of *livres*)
1689	81.98	1702	89.18
1690	84.8	1703	109.58
1691	83.93	1704	98.77
1692	89.13	1705	148.69
1693	85.16	1706	127.61
1694	78.97	1707	147.94
1695	78.31	1708	118.7
1696	77.85	1709	128.5
1697	74.65	1710	130.94
1698 (peace)	62.27	1711	122.01
1699 (peace)	55.09	1712	116.95
1700 (peace)	51.88	1713	116.74
1701	79.68	1714	93.48

Source: Forbonnais, II, tables on pages 100–1, 170–1; and on pages 190, 194, 201, 214, 224, 232, 237, 247, 268.

(and their consequences) pale in comparison with the difficulties of the early eighteenth century. As early as December 1701, after a few months of campaigning in northern Italy—the sole theatre of war at that time—a *commis* in Lyon for the Extraordinaire was so overstretched he could not send a mere 200,000 *livres* in bills of exchange to Mantua. The next campaign season in 1702, this time on a far bigger scale with the entry of the British and Dutch into the war, buffeted royal finances. By mid-1703 some funds were producing cash sixteen or more months late. So far, credit was holding up quite well, but the build-up of arrears for resources going to the Extraordinaire was beginning to take its toll of the treasurers general's operations. December 1703 was something of a milestone in the deterioration of army funding: for the first time in this war a treasurer general (Pleneuf) admitted he could no longer provide money for recruitment and the replacement of horses to officers who came calling at his Paris headquarters for their dues. The War Ministry's man inside the Extraordinaire, D'Honneur, appears to have agreed that things were taking a turn for the worse: up to then officers had been paid regularly, he noted. Within a year the Extraordinaire treasurers general were regularly complaining that not even negotiable paper instruments were making their way into their hands on anything like the scale needed, and by the end of 1704 money for recruiting fresh troops to the army had completely dried up.[4] To maintain payments to the field armies and arms suppliers the treasurers general appear to have

[4] AN G[7]1775, no. 315: Pleneuf to [Le Rebours?], 18 December 1703; no. 316: D'Honneur to Chamillart, 19 December 1703; G[7]1776, no. 307: Colonel de Curzay to Chamillart, 22 December 1704; SHD A[1]1525, no. 221: Guyet to Chamillart, 24 December 1701.

reduced the flow of funds they despatched to the interior provinces or allowed to remain there. Meanwhile, the revenue yields produced by the *receveurs généraux* were deteriorating, to such a point in the summer of 1706 that they too were not making funds available in the provinces for the Extraordinaire's *commis.*[5] Why this should be so is worth a brief digression, for there were some underlying structural problems with the way the main revenue collectors operated, or were being told by government to operate, which made their activities mesh less than perfectly with those of the Extraordinaire.

The government had long been aware of the dangers of moving too much coin to Paris from the sticks. The capital was well known to be a magnet for silver and gold as the centre of luxury commerce and consumption, and was the place that received the vast majority of the interest payouts on the *rentes*, in cash. It also housed the headquarters of most of the largest fisco-financiers of the realm who needed to deliver funds promptly to the Trésor royal, funds sent up from the provinces to a large extent in bills of exchange as well as in cash. Because large numbers of bills of exchange needed to be cashed in the capital it gave financiers an additional incentive to centralize coin there to help meet such demand. Thus there was a vicious spiral in which more and more coin flowed into the capital (further depressing provincial business, consumption, and indirect tax revenues), while the volume removed from the provinces was not sufficiently replaced by recirculation of coin out of Paris.[6] In the mid-1700s the capital was to become so powerful a specie magnet that it hampered the war effort. In part, this was because incoherent government policy made it so. In 1704 the king forbade financiers with funds in the provinces from giving any to the Extraordinaire agents there in return for bills of exchange drawn on the treasurer general in Paris. However, this policy forced the treasurer general to cart far more money than usual around France, creating difficulties the Finance Ministry simply failed to understand.[7] On top of this, somewhat inconsistently, by August 1705 the Finance Ministry had allowed some provinces to be regularly denuded of coin by the likes of the farmers general, *traitants*, and *receveurs généraux*. These and other powerful financiers, sensing a rise in the price of money in the capital as demand for it grew and Mint bills became increasingly dubious, were instructing their agents to pump coin into their offices in Paris as much as possible, either through bills of exchange drawn on merchants and other financiers there or by carting cash up from the country. Sometimes the bills of exchange would be handed straight to the Extraordinaire treasurer general, who then had to try to negotiate whatever he could get for it. In early 1706 this problem seems to have become particularly inflated, so much so that in August Chamillart had to order financiers to keep some cash in their provincial coffers, rather than bringing it all to Paris. It did little good, and Desmaretz even tried to

[5] Darryl Dee, *Expansion and Crisis in Louis XIV's France: Franche-Comté and Absolute Monarchy, 1674–1715* (Rochester, NY and Woodbridge, 2009), 155–6; AN G[7]1776, no. 292: Bouchu to Chamillart, 5 December 1704; G[7]1097: Mongelas to Chamillart, 22 August 1706.

[6] AN G[7]1774, no. 12: *receveurs généraux* to Pontchartrain, 31 January 1697; CCG, III, 348: Courson to Desmaretz, 27 January 1711.

[7] AN G[7]1776, no. 91: note, [April 1704].

replace cash in provinces particularly stripped of it, like Périgord in 1708, by buying what he could there for the war effort (in this case pigs). In subsequent years Desmaretz still had to order halts to excessive coin shipments from the provinces to Paris.[8]

The shortfalls in money sent to the armies or given to the officers, and the difficulties in obtaining cash in the provinces, could be very disruptive for ordinary soldiers, artisans in the arms industry, local suppliers, and others. The growing funding gap would also force the Extraordinaire des Guerres into contracting more and more debt to fulfil the obligations it was under. Shortages of funds could also have an effect on the strategic situation. In 1702 the sudden appearance of alarming funding problems in the Extraordinaire and the banking networks acted as a brake upon operations. It was hard to defend France's ally the Archbishop-Elector of Cologne, and in the upper Rhineland the maréchal de Catinat could not follow orders to engage the enemy because he lacked money. As Margrave Ludwig of Baden laid siege to Landau, the gateway to both the Palatinate and lower Alsace, Catinat was paralysed. Landau fell.[9] Over the following three years the fortunes of the army's finances ebbed and flowed, as did the war effort as a whole, though money alone did not determine the course of the conflict. However, in 1706 came a whole series of signs that all was far from well with French logistics, and that this was beginning to shape Bourbon fortunes quite dramatically. What concerns us here are the first signs, in February 1706, of pay for the ordinary troops in Hainaut not materializing. This was a time of year when the Extraordinaire des Guerres could normally depend on a healthy intake of resources. In the following year lending to the Extraordinaire des Guerres, which had reached enormous proportions in 1705–6, dropped and then began to seize up, because of the adverse cash-flow situation and the inability of the treasurers general to redeem their debts across France. As a result, troops were beginning to go for several weeks without pay. The situation continued to deteriorate and the campaign of 1708 was the last in which the Extraordinaire des Guerres was able to meet the funding needs of the main armies, in part by ceasing to pay the invoices of provincial suppliers. Thereafter, though it kept going, it was an exhausted network that struggled even to provide resources on a hand-to-mouth basis to the armies.[10] For this a great deal of the blame must rest with the central government for placing too much of a load on its shoulders, for destabilizing the currency, and for mismanaging the allocation of resources, all of which escalated the costs of the war. How the money was misdirected and the flows mismanaged needs close scrutiny.

[8] CCG, II, 268: merchants of Amiens to Chamillart, 1 August 1705; II, 298: Le Blanc to Chamillart, 22 January 1706; III, 10: Bishop of Périgueux to Desmaretz, 23 March 1708; AN G[7]1778, no. 191: Chamillart to Le Bret, 11 August 1706; Dee, *Expansion and Crisis*, 164–5.

[9] Thierry Sarmant, Hervé Lemoine, and Marc Boulanger, *Guerre, pouvoir et finance dans l'Alsace du Roi-Soleil: La famille Dietrich de 1681 à 1715* (Vincennes, 2000), 80–3.

[10] AN G[7]1778, no. 51: Roujault to [Chamillart], 13 February 1706; no. 52: memorandum by Mongelas, 17 February 1706; Ya2 (various letters indicating halts to payment of suppliers); CCG, II, 423: Chamillart to Le Gendre, 16 July 1707; III, 63: Desmaretz to Vendôme, 17 October 1708; III, 127: Desmaretz to d'Angervilliers, 23 May 1709.

THE DEGENERATION OF APPROPRIATIONS UNDER MICHEL CHAMILLART

In the War of the Spanish Succession there was a general decline in the system for appropriating revenue sources to expenditure, since *assignations* in particular failed altogether, or failed to yield sufficiently, or had to have their maturity dates put back. The *assignation* allocation system had more or less worked during the Nine Years War, though there had been serious problems in 1693–94 and, according to the financial official Malet (who was a *parti pris* Colbertist), all three *contrôleurs généraux* after 1683 but before Desmaretz neglected to maintain pressure on the primary revenue receivers to deliver their funds properly. If so, it would appear that the problem became very serious only in the War of the Spanish Succession. Already by 1704 the issuing of a straightforward *assignation* was often not enough to ensure the funds would be released at all by mint directors or mainstream primary receivers of taxes and loans, so on repeated occasions the treasurers general of the Extraordinaire had to get the Finance Ministry to issue supplementary orders. This caused delays, ill-feeling, and more paperwork for all concerned, but was a minor irritation compared with the chaos into which appropriations would sink in the years to come.[11]

In part this happened because even the strongest revenues—such as those on income from Languedoc, the Church, and the postal system—were struggling at times.[12] Far weaker revenue sources were beginning to fail from as early as 1701, notably *affaires extraordinaires*, a source the government was coming to rely on but whose success was in every case unpredictable and becoming more so. By 1703 treasurer general Pleneuf was complaining about delays of four to five months beyond the maturity dates of many *assignations* before he got his money. In spring of that year two *assignations* sent by the Extraordinaire to the *vivres* (bread) company of the army of Italy, worth 300,000 *livres*, bounced, while in Pleneuf's chest in November, out of a total of 10.8 million *livres* of *assignations*, over 6.7 million were 'de non valleur', that is, write-offs, at least for the time being. The year 1704 saw only a deterioration of the situation regarding funds earmarked for the Extraordinaire. The customs and consumption receipts were squeezed under pressure from the Anglo-Dutch commercial interdicts in the first half of the year; contracts to collect *augmentations des gages* (even from magistrates in the highest law courts) were seriously in arrears; and the salt taxes became almost unemployable in late 1704 and 1705 owing to their priority use to prop up the Caisse des emprunts and other borrowing by the *fermes*. These were all identified at various times as the weakest *assignations*. In August 1704 the general failure to produce funds for the banking operations of Samuel Bernard, through non-realization of *assignations*, led several of Chamillart's deputies to intervene directly to try to negotiate *assignations*

[11] Malet, *Comptes*, 102; AN G⁷1776, no. 78: Vieuxcourt to Chamillart, 11 May 1704; no. 436: Du Barbier to [Chamillart], 6 November 1704.

[12] Michaud, 366–7; Forbonnais, II, 111; AN G⁷1778, no. 35: Mongelas to Chamillart, 8 February 1706.

with anyone who would supply credit, but the meagre results pushed Chamillart (at Bernard's behest) into expansion of the money supply through an increased generation of unbacked Mint bills. In 1704 even the *receveurs généraux* were falling behind, perhaps by as much as 50 per cent, in their *ustencile* payments to the Extraordinaire; and by mid-1707 *rescriptions* (general promises to pay from any *caisse* in an individual's charge) even on the likes of Jacques Dupille, *receveur général* of the normally reliable Lyon *généralité*, were failing completely. In northern France increasingly importunate Allied demands for contributions from exposed French territory were diminishing revenues from these provinces, at a rate that accelerated after autumn 1708. At this hour Samuel Bernard was now reporting that he had a severe backlog of unpaid *assignations* drawn on *receveurs généraux* all over France.[13]

The straightforward shrinking of revenue had knock-on effects and was in any case not the only cause of the deteriorating appropriations situation. There was also severe mishandling of revenue assignments by the Finance Ministry during the War of the Spanish Succession. First of all, too much expenditure was being authorized by Chamillart as Secretary of State for War, but too little revenue to back these orders was actually being ordered by Chamillart as *contrôleur général des finances*, or by Alexandre Le Rebours, who was in charge of the appropriations for most of this era. They forgot to put items of expenditure—for which *ordonnances de paiement* had been issued—on the distribution list of *assignations*, or the ministry simply did not get round to doing this for months or even years. The *vivres* company directors—the *munitionnaires*—constantly feared their allocations would be forgotten about when the lists of fund distribution were drawn up, with the result that the Extraordinaire treasurers general might not pass them the resources they needed. All this had detrimental effects on credit repayments and therefore the cost of borrowing for the Extraordinaire (and for the *munitionnaires*). At times the gap between payment orders and fund allocations could add up to millions of *livres*. By October 1707 Chamillart had failed to assign funds to the value of 34 million *livres* to the treasurer general of the 1706 duty-year. These huge gulfs could not easily be filled by credit, precisely because the treasurer general had been given too few revenue sources he could trade or use to back such sums. The longer delays in assigning revenue sources to expenditure were not just producing ever more borrowing on the part of the Extraordinaire but also more and more non-payments.[14]

[13] AN G^{7}1775, no. 223: Mongelas to Chamillart, 5 October 1701; no. 242: demand for payment by the *vivres* of Italy, [May 1703]; no. 288: 'Estat…', [November 1703]; G^{7}1776, no. 83: memorandum on the *ustencile*, 20 April 1704; no. 84: Montargis to Chamillart, 21 April 1704; no. 265: D'Honneur to Le Rebours, 10 November 1704; no. 345: 'Reponse', [mid-November 1704]; no. 398: note on the 'Caisse d'emprunts', 23 September 1704; no. 410: memorandum, [January 1704]; G^{7}1120: Bernard to Chamillart, 6 and 22 August 1704; G^{7}1777, no. 42: note, 9 August 1705; G^{7}1779, no. 198: memorandum by Dupille, [May 1707]; G^{7}1119: Montargis to Chamillart, 18 June 1707; Saint-Germain, *Bernard*, 197.

[14] AN G^{7}1775, no. 202: 'Estat…', 16 December 1705; no. 276: 'Estat…', 14 October 1703; G^{7}1778, no. 326: balance sheet for 1706 *exercice*, 2 October 1707; SHD A^{1}1699, no. 261: [Mauricet] de La Cour to Chamillart, 30 January 1703; Iung, I, 71–2.

At the same time as Chamillart failed to allocate enough *assignations* to expenditure orders, he was assigning a growing proportion of funds from sources that would not mature until further and further into the future. This began in 1702 when the Extraordinaire was in effect being told to use such *assignations*, with maturity dates more than three months away, as security for loans, or to trade them—still at this time for nearly their face value. But, if nobody was willing to cash them, or the Extraordinaire could only cash them for an excruciating discount, then no immediate funds might be found. With the Extraordinaire holding more and more of these very-long-dated *assignations* on unreliable sources, potential creditors became unenthusiastic about accepting them as collateral or security, thus hitting the income of the treasurers general. Already treasurer general Montargis was warning Chamillart of the consequences of this. Though it smacked of special pleading he was not wrong when he said that it was vital to prioritize the Extraordinaire's payment demands ahead of the *vivres* and *étapes* (march-route) suppliers in the allocation of short-dated *assignations*, for the Extraordinaire 'cannot without risk be a single day unable to meet its payments in Paris, and as long as this chest maintains itself the other affairs will jog along'. The next retrograde step was for the Finance Ministry to channel *assignations* to the Extraordinaire that were long-dated *beyond the end of the current duty-year*. In other words, the government began the wholesale anticipation of revenues on future years, at the suggestion of, among others, Montargis. In February 1703, seeing few other remedies to close the growing funding gap, he recommended that henceforth the *assignations* of future calendar years should be issued and anticipated for up to 10 per cent of total army expenditure. Such a modest proportion was not held to, far from it: from 1706 the crown was issuing *assignations* that were long-dated two whole fiscal years into the future. Since at least 1703 Chamillart had tended to allocate reliable funding sources to those who were willing to accept long-dated *assignations* upon them. As time went on and Mint bills increased in volume, these would be payable in paper and in Paris. In turn he expected the holders to retain them until their dates of maturity and not trade them, in order to avoid a general depression of *assignation* values. However, by mid-1706 the Extraordinaire had no choice but to trade such *assignations* for whatever they could get for them, suffering large discounts. This was done either with those men upon whom the *assignations* were drawn or with other financiers in the market. A dismaying state of affairs, certainly, but it was still a less damaging way of proceeding than issuing even more Mint bills.[15]

The failure to allocate enough sound *assignations* was symptomatic of a generally very poor oversight of the whole of royal finances by Pontchartrain and Chamillart successively. Throughout the latter's tenure of the contrôle général, the *premier commis* of the Finance Ministry responsible for monitoring the inflows and outflows of the Trésor royal was not given proper information about what this treasury

[15] SHD A[1]1613, nos 183–4: Montargis to Chamillart, 4 April 1702 (quotation); AN G[7]1775, no. 109: memorandum [by Montargis], 20 February 1703; G[7]1778, no. 49: 'Estat abregé...', 22 February 1707; CCG, II, 475: 'Mémoire', 17 September 1707.

should expect. He was being failed by his colleagues in the ministry, by the Trésor royal itself (which was most reticent about what it was actually receiving), and by the financiers who were supposed to be depositing sums with it. This is despite the fact that one of the two *Gardes du Trésor royal*, Jacques Poulletier, had been explicitly charged with following the payment of all *assignations* in 1705, 1706, and 1707, receiving a further 12,000 *livres* a year for this role. Alas, Poulletier (whom we shall encounter in Chapter 10) was Chamillart's general 'Mister Fixit' for finances, a man who undertook all sorts of distracting (and self-serving) random tasks on Chamillart's behalf. The lack of proper supervision of the Trésor royal was manifested in a failure to keep detailed registers of receipts and expenditure in the ways Colbert had insisted upon. Moreover, Colbert had personally paid very close attention to the flow of funds, while it appears that Chamillart engaged in little scrutiny of the allocation of finance to spending, leaving matters to the likes of Le Rebours and Poulletier. Unfortunately these junior ministers had an insufficient overview of what the state needed and were incompetent.[16]

The chaos was exemplified in a number of ways. As early as May 1702 the Extraordinaire treasurer general was not receiving *assignations* he was expecting, and was even being deprived of others he had been allocated. Funds from the *capitation* in 1703 were not being realized because the *assignations* were dated to a point when collection had hardly begun! *Assignations* were being given for sums far greater than those actually expected or collectable, and in 1706 the Finance Ministry even issued *assignations* on *augmentations des gages* to be paid by the corps of *maîtres des requêtes*—when no such forced loan had been ordered! As Bernard put it, as far back as August 1703:

> In truth, Monseigneur, it would be much better not to give me any *assignations* at all than to give me them on people who do not owe money or who are not going to pay up.

As if this were not bad enough, precious documents and receipts were lost in the chaos of Chamillart's offices.[17] Consequently it was not at all uncommon for revenue sources to be assigned to more than one expenditure purpose. These were known as 'doubles assignations', which were cropping up as early as the summer of 1703. They left the Extraordinaire, the artillery, and arms suppliers with empty hands, just when they were expecting revenues to help them pay off debts or pay their workers. The buck for this stops with Le Rebours, who was repeatedly sending out double *assignations* under Chamillart and continued to do so under Desmaretz after February 1708. This maladministration not only left people short of funds, it also eroded confidence in royal *assignations* as an entire genre of financial instrument and payment guarantee. It worsened the credit rating of the king's

[16] CCG, II, 610: 'Projet', [late summer/early autumn 1710]; AN G[7]1098: memorandum on checking *assignations* of the Trésor royal, by Malet, [1710?]; SHD A[1]1894: Pleneuf to Ferrand, 3 June 1705; McCollim, 111–12; Forbonnais, II, 133.

[17] SHD A[1]1613, no. 187: Montargis to Chamillart, 15 May 1702; CCG, II, 144: Le Bret to Chamillart, 16 July 1703; AN G[7]1120: Bernard to Chamillart, 13 August 1703 (quotation); G[7]1784, no. 15: *état* of *assignations*, 1 September 1709 [re 1706].

fisco-financiers and accordingly increased the cost of the war. It also made it easier for fraud to be perpetrated, with a fair chance that it would not be detected for a long time to come, if ever: Desmaretz was sure that bearers of *assignations* were managing to get interest on delayed funds paid twice over, because Le Rebours and his clerks were not monitoring the situation properly.[18] The Finance Ministry should not necessarily be blamed for the simple failure of revenue sources or the anticipation of revenues years in advance—which was indeed the best form of floating debt—but it had precious few excuses for manifest incompetence in managing the paperwork for the *assignation* system as a whole. There is, moreover, a suspicion that Chamillart was adding to the chaos by reallocating *assignations* to his favoured inner circle of financiers and suppliers, notably the Berthelots and Mauricet de La Cour (see Chapter 10).

While this was happening, the treasurers general of the Extraordinaire des Guerres found themselves in competition with the revenue-raising financiers: as revenues slumped the latter, especially the *traitants* collecting forced loans and venal office sales, were anxious to hold on to as many of the proceeds of their collections for as long as possible, not least to maintain their own solvency and pay off their creditors. Some primary receivers had made so many loans to the Extraordinaire des Guerres—which were not repaid—that by 1708 they either could not or would not cough up further advances. The divergence of interest between revenue collectors and spending officials became glaringly obvious in the course of 1706, and there was even outright disobedience of Chamillart's orders by the *receveurs généraux* and farmers general. As well as one or two cases of overt defiance, which were quashed, the Finance Ministry discovered that it was not easy to persuade fisco-financiers to issue *rescriptions* upon themselves as back-up guarantees for the payment of the *assignations* that were drawn upon them. In May 1706 as many as seven *receveurs généraux* refused to cooperate by handing over *rescriptions* to the Extraordinaire treasurer general, Mongelas. Mongelas countered with a nuclear option, proposing that Chamillart disrupt the entire *assignation* system by allowing the Extraordinaire itself to issue *rescriptions* upon the *commis* of the *receveurs généraux*, and these *rescriptions* would have priority for payment over any other instruments drawn upon these men. Chamillart agreed, but it did little good in the coming months, not least because the *receveurs généraux* moved their available provincial money to Paris in even greater proportions than before—consequently, *rescriptions* were regularly protested as undischarged. Chamillart now moved to give even higher priority to the Extraordinaire, in November 1706 allowing that year's treasurer general, Mongelas, to strip the *receveurs généraux*, treasurers of provincial estates, the receiver general of the clergy, and all *traitants* of all the funds they would hold in their coffers in March 1707.[19]

[18] CCG, III, 30: Desmaretz to Le Rebours, 1 July 1708; III, 616: 'Mémoire', [start of 1715]; AN $G^7$1775, no. 439: Pleneuf to Chamillart, 19 July 1703.

[19] CCG, II, 424: Roujault to Chamillart, 31 July 1707; AN $G^7$1778, no. 123: memorandum by Mongelas, 8 May 1706; no. 124: list of non-cooperating *receveurs généraux*, [May 1706]; no. 146: Mongelas to Chamillart, 14 June 1706; no. 236: [Mongelas to Chamillart], [November 1706]; no. 239: [Mongelas to Chamillart], 13 November 1706.

With such difficulties involved in getting fisco-financiers to pay up their revenues, those people holding *assignations* upon them resorted to negotiating them, at discount rates that steadily worsened as the War of the Spanish Succession wore on. Until early 1704, it seems, royal financiers had found ways to avoid having to negotiate heavy discounts on *assignations* they held: the *commis* of the Extraordinaire in the provinces would issue bills of exchange, for discharge by the treasurer general (in Paris), to local agents of, say, a *traitant*, who would advance them the funds they were seeking; the treasurer general would then pay off his bill of exchange by handing over *assignations* drawn upon those very same men who were at once the payers of those *assignations* and the creditors of the Extraordinaire *commis*! This avoided the discrediting of *assignations* generally, but it disrupted the *assignations* system and ironically Chamillart found this intolerable. He evidently had no clear set of ideas about how the appropriations system should be managed to keep discounting to low levels. In any case, the top primary receivers quickly became wise to the Extraordinaire's use of bills of exchange, and their increasing transfer of cash to the capital militated against the continuation of this improvised way of getting *assignations* paid.[20]

The game in the marketplace turned quickly against the Extraordinaire des Guerres. The treasurers general had some muscle, and could, with more vulnerable fisco-financiers, force them to pay up an advance *assignation* with only a small discount. Unfortunately, most of the time the holder of an *assignation* wanting to realize it prematurely, or after it had failed to transmute into money upon maturity, took a sizeable hit if he wanted to avoid receiving Mint bills. In November 1706 Mongelas had to accept losses of 76 per cent on *assignations* he held in order to get cash! Moreover, many of the new owners seem to have insisted upon a right to return an *assignation* if subsequently they could not obtain its proceeds. There was also the problem that many *assignations* were sold to *agents de change*, who may have been in cahoots with the men upon whom they were drawn—by buying an *assignation* up at a discount they were in effect withdrawing it from circulation and might then even make a profit on the final yield, splitting the gain with the tax collector. Many *assignations* simply could not be negotiated at all, usually when their term date was too far into the future to be reliable. As advance *assignations* grew more common, people might refuse to buy *assignations* on the *fermes* because nobody knew who the farmers might be by the time the maturity date was reached. This was also the case with *affaires extraordinaires* when the company of *traitants* for a contract was considered to be incomplete. Furthermore, the discount rates for *assignations* reflected not only the chances of a successful delivery of the funds but also the market for such instruments: there might be nothing wrong with a particular *assignation* or *rescription*, but if a large number of people were trying to trade them this would depress their prices and could produce a downward spiral in their market value. If the Extraordinaire des Guerres was the body trying to sell *assignations* in such circumstances, then this would produce a further shortfall in the treasurers general's revenues and a further increase in the costs of war, either

[20] AN $G^7$1776, no. 91: note, [April 1704].

because the government provided more *assignations* to cover the gap or because the Extraordinaire borrowed extra money. As Montargis bemoaned, in April 1707,

> For lack of cash funds one is not in a position to resist the bad proposals of lenders, who either do not want to give their cash, or only want to do so on conditions which fruitlessly devour the largest part of the money that one can hope to get from instruments and immature *assignations*.

By now the Extraordinaire had become dangerously reliant not just on Mint bills (themselves heavily discounted) but also upon the negotiation of *assignations* for heavy discounts. The worst situation was when an *assignation* was discounted *and* discredited Mint bills were handed over, with the Extraordinaire then taking a further loss when trying to use these bills. At first ministers had been very loath to countenance such downgrading of royal funds and tried (without success) to stop it altogether in early 1707, but by February 1709 the government, in desperation, was telling the treasurers general to sell any *assignations* for whatever the market would offer.[21]

The general deterioration of the appropriations system led royal officials to emergency actions that made immediate sense to get cash for the Extraordinaire but in the medium term only contributed to the chaos. From 1701, as had happened in the Nine Years War, *intendants* were raiding the coffers of local revenue agents in order to help out the Extraordinaire, mainly on the frontiers, but until the end of 1706 this was sporadic and on a limited scale.[22] Thereafter we can find instances of *intendants* totally denuding even the main chest of their local *recette générale* of all its cash and paper to support the Extraordinaire in that area, forcing bills of exchange drawn on the treasurer general onto the hapless local *receveurs* and *fermes* agents. When good reasons could be provided for such violent steps, Chamillart tended to give retrospective approval. Indeed, just before Christmas 1706 Chamillart told a number of *intendants* that although he had hitherto forbidden them to release any funds arising from *affaires extraordinaires* in their provinces, they must now hand them to agents of the Extraordinaire whose credit depended upon them: treasurer general Montargis had issued bills of exchange worth 510,000 *livres*, and, in a case of the tail wagging the dog, Chamillart was now having to adapt his system accordingly.[23] Chamillart continued to authorize *intendants* to divert funds in their provinces in case of dire necessity, and several *intendants* thought this a blanket permission to do so whenever it was necessary. After Desmaretz succeeded as *contrôleur général* in February 1708 he therefore found total disorder in the local coffers of many tax collectors and *traitants*, but in a measure

[21] AN G^{7}1778, no. 233: [Mongelas to Chamillart], 10 November 1706; G^{7}1776, nos 239, 380: Titon to Chamillart, 12 November and 8 October 1704; no. 134: note, 19 February 1704; G^{7}1775, no. 288: 'Estat...', [November 1703]; G^{7}1779, no. 43: Montargis to Chamillart, 15 April 1707 (quotation); SHD Ya2: Chamillart to Mongelas, 17 February 1709.

[22] For example, SHD A^{1}1525, no. 171: Chevalier to Chamillart, 26 November 1701; AN G^{7}1776, no. 81: memorandum on Châlons, April 1704.

[23] AN G^{7}1779, no. 222: Brunet de Rancy to Chamillart, 18 June 1707; G^{7}1778, nos 266–70: Chamillart to various *intendants*, 19 December 1706; CCG, II, 423: Chamillart to Le Gendre, 16 July 1707.

of how disjointed and dysfunctional the Finance Ministry had become, he seems to have been ignorant of the scale of the problem while he had been Chamillart's number two.[24] Unlike in England, where the system of earmarking and delivering funds to army paymasters was carefully managed, in France the entire appropriations system was falling apart. Something needed to be done.

THE STRUGGLE TO RE-ESTABLISH CONTROL OF SPENDING UNDER NICOLAS DESMARETZ

In the autumn of 1707 Chamillart had penned a memorandum in which he acknowledged the obvious crisis of appropriations for funding the armed forces. He could see no way of getting funds available during 1708 without annulling all *assignations* on that year that had already been alienated in advance. Within days of taking office as *contrôleur général* Nicolas Desmaretz adopted a variation on this policy: all *assignations* on 1708 revenues that had already been issued were reassigned to 1709, and Desmaretz was even able to persuade the holders of some 10 million *livres* of *assignations* to put their claims back to 1714–16. This liberated the Trésor royal at a stroke, freeing up around 50 million *livres*, and Desmaretz accompanied this move by a serious attempt to restore order to the appropriations system. He was acutely aware that under Chamillart the Trésor royal had lost its near-monopoly on channelling resources between revenue-raisers and the king's spending agents, and he determined to restore its place as the receiver of all net royal revenues (after deductions): once again it would either take in cash from most primary receivers, or it would accept reports of cash available on which *assignations* and *rescriptions* could be issued. Additional *commis* were installed in the offices of the Trésor royal and, remarkably, some double-entry bookkeeping was introduced. Apart from bringing some order to cash flow again, this would have the dual advantage that Desmaretz himself would enjoy a much clearer picture of the state of the king's finances, receiving a weekly and monthly tally of incomings and outgoings, and the financial public (which was, one should remember, still small) would once again see money circulating in the king's own coffers. Though it took several weeks, if not months, for primary receivers to start paying up again upon simple presentation of an *assignation*—still preferring for the most part to receive an additional order from the Finance Ministry—in the spring and summer of 1708 *assignations* were honoured much more than in the previous year and were not too difficult to negotiate. However, the combined effects of Mint bills, Chamillart's loss of expenditure control, further revenue contraction, and Desmaretz's reassignment of earlier 1708 *assignation* claims onto future years ultimately took their toll: by late October *assignations* were failing again, too many were being long-dated too far into the future, and payments were increasingly being delayed. *Assignations* on *affaires extraordinaires*, and even on less suspect sources, could not

[24] For example, CCG, III, 4: Bâville to Desmaretz, 6 March 1708; III, 31: Bernières to Desmaretz, 11 July 1708.

be negotiated at all from the start of 1709, notably because of the uncertainty over the future of Mint bills and the continued use of Mint bills by the *receveurs généraux* and the *fermes* to pay out on *assignations*. Moreover, one-third of all spending orders from 1708 did not have *assignations* allocated to them, which was still enormous by historical standards, if not quite as bad as in 1707.[25] By early February 1709 the French government's spending was again on the brink of total collapse, and it did not help that Chamillart seemed to have little idea of what had been assigned to the Extraordinaire des Guerres.[26]

This time, despite being in a minority of one on the council, Desmaretz persuaded the king that the last thing they should do was repeat his 1708 trick of shunting *assignations* forward onto future years. He was adamant that this would precipitate a total shutdown of lending and the reduction of royal *assignations* to worthless paper. Instead, on 19 February the council announced that all *assignations* drawn on sources for 1709 would be honoured. Alongside this, and to ensure a smoother release of resources, Desmaretz established a 'visa' system over the *assignations*: from February to June his trusted *commis* Malet monitored the state of all *assignations* and checked on how much had already been anticipated. The aim was to minimize the amount of double assigning, and give the financial public the confidence that this problem had come to an end. The move was quickly derailed by the mounting chaos in the banking sector and at Lyon that very nearly brought France to complete defeat in the spring and summer of 1709. The virtual standstill in negotiations for *assignations* in the spring seemed to indicate that the government was reaching the end of the road. Nevertheless, the steps taken by Desmaretz almost certainly allowed the country to struggle through the darkest financial days of the war. While they did not restore easy credit, they did prevent an irretrievable collapse of public confidence in the crown's ability to honour its debts at this time, and there was just enough cash flow to enable Louis to refuse extreme Allied demands later that year to drive his own grandson off the Spanish throne. Indeed, many of those who held *assignations* dated for 1709 ended up relending their money to the government and other fisco-financiers, if only for want of surer places to invest in.[27] For a while this worked just enough to help the state get through the catastrophic financial situation of 1709. From the summer of that year, on a selective basis, Desmaretz began demanding *rescriptions* from the *receveurs généraux* and farmers general, as guarantees that the funds from *assignations* were paid up. But generally Desmaretz and Voysin tried to avoid this and concentrated on forcing these men to deliver the *assignation* proceeds on time. The *contrôleur général* also worked hard to prevent

[25] Esnault, II, 163: 'Projet', [autumn 1707]; Forbonnais, II, 180–1; Malet, *Comptes*, 101; Seligmann, 56; AN $G^7$1098: memorandum on checking the Trésor royal *assignations* by Malet, [1710?]; Mongelas to Desmaretz, 31 January 1709; $G^7$1011 (various documents on failing *traités assignations*); $G^7$1119: Sacerdotti brothers to Desmaretz, 18 March 1708; $G^7$1120: Bernard to Desmaretz, 25 October 1708; $G^7$1782, no. 267: summary accounts of Extraordinaire, 22 December 1708.

[26] Saint-Simon, XVII, 186–90.

[27] Malet, *Comptes*, 115–16; Forbonnais, II, 192; AN $G^7$1098: memorandum on checking the Trésor royal *assignations* by Malet, [1710?]; $G^7$1784, no. 278: Le Bartz to Desmaretz, 25 March 1709; Margaret Bonney and Richard Bonney, *Jean-Roland Malet, premier historien des finances de la monarchie française* (Paris, 1993), 13.

good *assignations* being traded for less than their value or for discredited paper, and to reduce the scope for financial disorder by increasing the amount of resources (such as forage) delivered in kind to the army's regiments.[28]

But despite his efforts Desmaretz was powerless to prevent tax and venality yields shrinking still further as the months passed by, and many sources were failing altogether. By October 1709 a number of *receveurs généraux* were no longer paying out on their *taille* or *capitation* funds, while much expenditure was being covered again by *assignations* anticipating long-dated future revenues. Even D'Honneur, *receveur général* of La Rochelle and the man who monitored all Extraordinaire expenditure for the War Ministry, could deliver 'nothing' from his *généralité*. Advances to the *receveurs généraux* by local communities for their tax payments had now built up so much that the receivers were running out of tax sources altogether. In fact, over the winter of 1709–10 the *recettes générales* were making so many advances for food and forage for the troops in winter quarters that their chances of meeting their normal funding obligations of handing money to the Extraordinaire des Guerres in the coming campaign season were depressed further.[29]

Chaos persisted also because of central actions. The Finance Ministry was continuing to issue more *doubles assignations* under Le Rebours' direction, and this persisted for the rest of the war, if on a lesser scale than before 1709.[30] Money was not replaced in the provinces either. There was a continued and continuous transport of specie out of the provinces to Paris by fisco-financiers, now at the direct (and reluctant) orders of Desmaretz. Not least this involved the treasurers general of the Extraordinaire, whose *commis* were under instructions to send on any coin they managed to acquire so it could then be passed to the army of Flanders, the equal top priority by the spring of 1710. The other great priority for Desmaretz was restoring payments of the *rentes* on the Hôtel de ville, unsurprising in view of his desire to convert floating debt into these bonds. This too required a big transfer of coin from the provinces to the capital. These significant coin flows contributed, to no small degree, to the continued failure of *assignations* across the kingdom. Further disorder flowed from the practice of *intendants* insisting that a *receveur général* pay the Extraordinaire des Guerres from any source of funds they held in a province, regardless of what a presented *assignation* said the source should be.[31] At least this was through the *intendants*. What was worse, in the second half of 1709

[28] AN $G^7$1784, no. 43: memorandum on *rescriptions*, 21 September 1709; no. 173: Trudaine to Desmaretz, 5 December 1709; $G^7$1786, no. 141: Herlaut to Desmaretz, 4 April 1710; SHD Ya2: Voysin to Poirier, 2 March 1710; CCG, III, 272: Desmaretz to all *intendants*, 12 December 1709.

[29] AN $G^7$1784, nos 149–50: Le Guerchoys to Desmaretz and Voysin, 22 October 1709; $G^7$1121: Oursin to [Le Rebours?], 18 June 1709; SHD $A^1$2182, no. 134: D'Honneur to Voysin, 20 June 1709 (quotation); Ya2: Voysin to Ogier, 24 January 1710; Voysin to Chauvelin, 26 January 1710; CCG, III, 246: Desmaretz to all *intendants*, 3 December 1709.

[30] SHD $A^1$2504, fo. 263v: Voysin to Titon, 10 May 1710; AN $G^7$1783, no. 59: Moreau to Desmaretz, 12 March 1709; $G^7$1788, nos 110–24: various documents on assignment problems in 1713 *exercice*, June–October 1714.

[31] AN $G^7$1784, nos 149–50: Le Guerchoys to Desmaretz and Voysin, 22 October 1709; SHD $A^1$2272, no. 6: Duplessis to Voysin, 3 June 1710; no. 128: Quesneau to Voysin, 1 July 1710; no. 207: Voysin to Le Guerchoys, 23 May 1710; CCG, III, 348: Courson to Desmaretz, 27 January 1711; III, 287: [various *intendants* and others to Desmaretz, Le Rebours et al. in 1710].

desperate generals were using funds they had seized from convenient coffers to prevent mutinies and even the wholesale disintegration of the army of Roussillon.[32]

Desmaretz now found himself lurching into the very expedients he had so set his face against in 1708–9. In May 1710 he announced that those *assignations* on 1709 that had not yet been realized would be annulled and reissued as *assignations* on 1711 revenues; *assignations* issued on 1710 would similarly be pushed back to 1712. This was the polar opposite of his stance in February 1709, and predictably confidence in the *assignations* fell. In July 1710 the treasurer general of the Extraordinaire was so short of funds that Desmaretz had no choice but to approve shocking levels of discounting on *assignations* he was selling. Even the highly suspect Poulletier called the discount offers 'exorbitant and ridiculous', and they were having an effect on the price of the best *assignations* too. This, in turn, threatened the Caisse Legendre, the consortium of *receveurs généraux* whom Desmaretz had brought together to, among other things, supply and negotiate *assignations* with the Extraordinaire des Guerres—and upon whom the solvency of the monarchy now as good as depended.[33] When France was blessed with a decent harvest Desmaretz then overreached himself. Believing confidence would return, in autumn 1710 he completely annulled all *assignations* drawn on 1711–13, and converted them into sluggish and illiquid *rentes* on the Hôtel de ville; alternatively they could be handed in to the mints for receipts with interest. Public confidence in the entire system of *assignations* now collapsed altogether. This profound error, not some brilliant foresight, was what led Desmaretz to then channel all sums from the *taille* and *capitation*, and as many other *assignations* as possible, through the Caisse Legendre, in 1711 and 1712. Moreover, these were often in the form of advances from the *receveurs généraux* as individuals. Only this body, representing the most solid *receveurs généraux*, could hope to negotiate *assignations* (often with each other behind closed doors!) with any chance of moderate discounts.[34]

As Desmaretz admitted to an *intendant*, the traditional *assignation* system now had to be scrapped altogether because it fell into such chaos in 1710. On 7 October all revenue collectors were forbidden to issue or honour *assignations*. Instead they were to provide coins to the Trésor royal for what they currently owed, and for funds that needed to be spent in advance they were to furnish the Trésor royal with *rescriptions* on themselves; the Trésor royal would then parcel out the *rescriptions*, to the Extraordinaire des Guerres for the most part. If any *assignations* were given out through the Caisse Legendre (or very occasionally the Trésor royal), then they were only to be cashed at the due date—they were emphatically not to be paid off earlier or for any discount. The *rescription* system meant that instead of

[32] AN G^{7}1783, no. 350: Grandchamp to Desmaretz, 19 August 1709; G^{7}1784, no. 28: duc de Noailles to Desmaretz, 12 September 1709; no. 114: maréchal de Chamilly to Desmaretz, 31 October 1709.

[33] CCG, III, 222: Desmaretz to La Houssaye and other *intendants*, 6 October 1709; SHD A^{1}2272, no. 168: Duplessis to Voysin, 9 July 1710; no. 241: Poulletier to Voysin, 28 July 1710 (quotation).

[34] CCG, III, 608: 'Projet', [late summer/early autumn 1710]; III, 677: 'Compte rendu de M. Desmaretz au Régent', [1716]; III, 618: 'Mémoire', [start of 1715]; Forbonnais, II, 215, 225, 233.

tax collectors sitting on funds from one fully collected source while refusing to honour *assignations* on another incomplete source, they would be forced to pay up from any source they possessed. Credit should therefore carry on flowing. There was also to be no negotiation of *rescriptions* in the provinces.[35]

To summarize, prior to October 1710 the Trésor royal gave *assignations* to the Extraordinaire on current and future revenue sources; the Extraordinaire would then cash them in early for a discount or trade them away for cash or Mint bills, also for a discount. The failure of many revenue sources and the continual trading of *assignations* depreciated the value of these paper devices, encouraging speculation and reinforcing the existing trail of chaos inside the Trésor royal and Finance Ministry. After the October 1710 reform the Trésor royal would take in cash or *rescriptions* from the revenue collectors, and provide *assignations* to the Caisse Legendre. The Caisse would then sit on them until their maturity dates, at which point the Trésor royal would parcel out *rescriptions* on the fisco-financiers in question, for payment on sight; or the Caisse would issue its own promissory notes, backed by the *assignations* it held, to anticipate funds and get them to where they were needed. These *rescriptions* or notes were then presented in the provinces to be cashed. Although it was bureaucratic to do so, Desmaretz also placed a second lock on the stream of funds: even when *rescriptions* were presented to them, the revenue collectors were paying out only on further explicit orders from Desmaretz. He wanted to be sure that, however sluggish this made things, there would be fewer refusals and fewer despairing people turned away from fisco-financiers' bureaux entirely empty-handed. By this point Desmaretz and War Minister Voysin had also agreed the postponement of around half the monarchy's payments as part of a drastic prioritization programme, thus ensuring fewer appropriation orders were sent out.[36] The entire system was designed to bring an end to the colossal devaluation of *assignations*—that is, the public depreciation of royal revenue sources—and to keep the market out of this arena of royal prerogative. As with his efforts to withdraw Mint bills, Desmaretz had come to realize that French royal sovereign authority was too weak to maintain control over some financial instruments when they circulated in society during periods of crisis.

Alas, the best laid plans often go awry, especially in circumstances of chronic revenue failure. Notwithstanding all Desmaretz's efforts, by the end of 1710 Voysin reckoned that most of the time the armies were now getting only one-quarter of the funds they were notionally allocated. During the winter quarters of 1710–11 Desmaretz now bypassed his own new system in an implicit admission that it was too cumbersome to deal with the army's needs when the troops were scattered and the field armies not gathered. Reversing his earlier strict stance that only in the most dire emergencies should funds in the provinces be diverted to immediate purposes, Desmaretz now authorized the provincial *recettes générales* to hand sums

[35] CCG, III, 364: Desmaretz to Le Guerchoys, 21 March 1711; III, 327: Desmaretz to the *Gardes du Trésor royal*, 23 October 1710; III, 404: Lescalopier to Desmaretz, 26 December 1711; III, 610: 'Projet', [late summer/early autumn 1710]; McCollim, 316; AN G[7]1031: *arrêt*, 7 October 1710; SHD A[1]2504, fo. 291r: Voysin to Méliand, 22 November 1710.

[36] AN G[7]1787 (numerous documents).

directly to *commis* of the Extraordinaire des Guerres for paying troop wages—in other words, he was now actually cutting out the Trésor royal and the Caisse Legendre from this process.[37] Behind the scenes the Caisse Legendre, and Desmaretz's own staff, were striking deals all the time with *receveurs généraux*, farmers general, and *traitants* for these financiers to advance funds on their own *rescriptions*, for up to a 10 per cent discount. At least this was conducting discounting in a compartmentalized and fairly closed manner, such that the public at large might not realize the extent of what was going on. Moreover, by late 1712 the government had reverted to the parcelling out of a mixture of cash and advance *assignations*, some long-dated to 1715, to the treasurers general of the Extraordinaire des Guerres, to forage contractors and to others, with 10 per cent interest as an inducement to accept such shaky instruments. All these problems notwithstanding, the *assignations* were under greater control than at any time since 1701, and at least in 1711 Desmaretz was able to pay off advances that were made on the orders of provincial and army *intendants*.[38]

Yet this was because there was by this time much less expenditure, and in any case the wider appropriations system was now on the edge of final disaster. The finances, like the gunpowder industry, were on their last legs in 1712: in order to get a mere 1.23 million *livres* for the troop wages in January–March (a pitiful sum compared with a decade earlier), some 900 separate *assignations* had to be earmarked by the Trésor royal. That is to say, a huge number of very small *assignations* on multiple sources were now being used to keep the war effort going, far more than would have been necessary for 1.23 million *livres* in the Nine Years War. This reflected the inability of most of the monarchy's primary revenue receivers to do more than pay up their receipts in dribs and drabs.[39] The decisions of autumn 1710—including the introduction of the *dixième* tax—had staved off a seizure of credit and a complete halt in expenditure long enough for the death of Emperor Joseph I and court manoeuvres in London to bring about Britain's withdrawal from the war. Be that as it may, the price of calamitous decisions in 1701–10 that had crippled the appropriations system, and the cost of Desmaretz's attempts to correct the worst of them, was ruinous: in the final years of the War of the Spanish Succession France faced a rapidly shrinking military capacity, high interest rates, weak confidence, battered markets, and the mortgaging of the future well into the next reign (as things turned out). And in the year after the end of the war, 1715, the collapse of both the Caisse des emprunts and the Caisse Legendre meant that sums reaching the Extraordinaire des Guerres dropped precipitously.[40]

It was just as well the fighting ended when it did, with Allied scouting parties already able to get as far south as Versailles. Virtual history is a risky business, but

[37] CCG, III, 246: Desmaretz to all *intendants*, 3 December 1709; SHD Ya2: Voysin to Bâville, 20 December 1710; Voysin to various *intendants*, 8 December 1710.

[38] AN $G^7$1787, no. 281: Voysin to Desmaretz, 10 January 1712; CCG, III, 454: Desmaretz to Voysin, 8 and 12 August 1712; III, 679: 'Compte rendu de M. Desmaretz au Régent', [1716]; III, 390: Desmaretz to Trudaine, 21 August 1711.

[39] AN $G^7$1787, no. 252: La Jonchère to Desmaretz, 3 January 1712.

[40] AN $G^7$1788, no. 215: memorandum by La Jonchère, 15 April 1715.

it is not unreasonable to conjecture that a complete collapse of appropriations in 1712–13, with a British government still committed to the war, when combined with a final crisis of credit that, as we shall see, was just around the corner, might have led the Allies to do more than dip their toes in the Paris region. Such a collapse in appropriations was indeed on the cards, and it would have happened without the winding down of the war theatres in the Low Countries and the southern Alps. France would certainly have been defeated, in part through a failure of revenues and a failure to manage appropriations over the longer term. This mismanagement did not just put up the costs of war, it very nearly cost France the war altogether.

9

The Overdraft of War: Short-Term Debt and Military Finance

The widening gap between royal revenues and spending needs was filled to a very large extent by borrowing through *rentes*, the Caisse des emprunts, *affaires extraordinaires* in the form of disguised forced loans, and proxy loans through intermediary corporate bodies. Far less stable, though, was the credit derived from the issuing of bearer bills—*billets*, *promesses*, and so forth—by a multitude of fisco-financiers. By the end of the 1690s bearer bills in France were far more transferable and negotiable than they had ever been, and this helped monetary circulation during the War of the Spanish Succession, producing a larger and larger volume of such bills in circulation. On the down side, far too many of them, worth far too much, began to linger instead of being extinguished swiftly. The most secure bearer bills were anchored on revenues collected directly by the issuer and his team, but as the distance grew and the number of stages increased between the ordinary taxpayer and the issuer of a bearer bill, then the more dangerous a risk of default or prolongation this bill carried. The Caisse Legendre set up in 1710, one of the largest issuers of bearer bills, was unusual in the stability it evinced for a few years, but in this case its credit was anchored in a pool made up of some of the best revenue sources of the kingdom. For the other fisco-financiers, even acting in ad hoc associations, it was a riskier business—just as it was for those who took on their debt instruments. Both because it had few direct revenues of its own in relation to the volume of its expenditure, and because of the sheer quantity of bearer bills it emitted, the Extraordinaire des Guerres provides the most extreme case of *billet* use in this period.[1] Examining these notes also shows the desperate, flailing attempts by the government to convert short-term debt and reveals the reactions of the financial community to these moves. What is more, it indicates how much of the *rentes* issues were closely connected with the military treasuries.

The Extraordinaire had issued credit notes and 'IOUs' in the Dutch War and the shorter conflicts of the first half of Louis XIV's personal rule, but there were two significant differences between the period before *c.*1690 and the period after: first, by 1700 the *billets* were far easier to trade and prolong, a characteristic of the wider genre of negotiable bearer bills; and second, the advances that these instruments represented became much larger and built up to the point where redemption became a very serious problem. Despite the reservations of many in government

[1] It is also the only viable case study of bearer bills as a phenomenon in this period.

circles, in the course of the War of the Spanish Succession the Extraordinaire des Guerres was turned into what some contemporaries loosely referred to as a 'banque', and it cost the government a lot of money. On the one hand, everyone knew that the crown's prioritization (by and large) of its war machine entailed a serious commitment to the Extraordinaire. As an anonymous memorandum stressed,

> It is so important to sustain the credit [of the Extraordinaire], because this treasury is the one in the Kingdom which puts the most money into circulation, and which interests the King and the good of his service the most.[2]

On the other hand, most people did not want to be paid in bearer bills by the principal organization that was supposed to be delivering cash. And while around 1700, people could assume that the government would try to service and repay Extraordinaire loans without too much delay or manipulation, by the middle years of the War of the Spanish Succession it was evident that the government was developing the Extraordinaire gradually into something like the Caisse des emprunts, though with less sense of discipline and fund hypothecation. Furthermore, it may not have helped that the treasurers general did not have to issue their bills through *agents de change*, who were deputed to certify bearer bills emitted by *traitants*. Although this made it faster to put Extraordinaire bills into circulation, it meant junior officials in this agency had more freedom to issue *billets*, increasing the amount of money borrowed throughout the system and for which the treasurers general then became liable.[3]

As it was, using *comptables* as short-term lenders to the crown through their bearer bills and other instruments may not have been as costly as the rake-offs taken by *traitants* in *affaires extraordinaires*, but such short-term loans floated by secondary receivers like the Extraordinaire involved higher interest rates than other forms of proxy borrowing or *rentes*; and perhaps marginally higher rates than those attached to short term instruments issued by financiers who were closer to the original revenue sources, such as the *receveurs généraux*. In a declaration of 1708 the king, somewhat unconvincingly, sung the virtues of the enormous loans contracted by the Extraordinaire, for they had 'dispensed Us from having recourse to other means which could have burdened our Subjects'.[4] If he meant more Mint bills, monetary manipulations, and *affaires extraordinaires* then one could agree, but the way the Extraordinaire bills were being managed was proving a very expensive way to proceed.

Given the decline of net revenues and the regular failure of revenue sources in an era of economic stagnation, a higher 'stopgap' borrowing requirement was without question necessary for the Extraordinaire des Guerres. The mess in the appropriations system contributed to this higher debt requirement. But because it was so hard to keep this organization under political and administrative control it was vital to hold down its borrowing levels and ensure regular redemption of its paper.

[2] Bib. Maz. Ms. 2626, fo. 58v: 'Memoire. Billets et decomptes de l'extraord. de la guerre', n.d.

[3] *Manuel des agens de change et des courtiers de commerce*... (Paris, 1823), 15–16 (*édit* of December 1705).

[4] BNF F-23619: *déclaration*, 4 December 1708.

Payment with *rentes* by the Extraordinaire was infeasible because such devices were too illiquid, so there had to be some form of short-term credit issuance by this treasury in the form of *billets*. The danger was when these already expensive short-term instruments were prolonged and prolonged, with the effect of driving down their market value, driving up their interest rates, and pushing up prices demanded by suppliers, who wanted to build in a level of insurance against their invoices being paid in under-par Extraordinaire *billets*. What this chapter will therefore try to do is explain how and why the Extraordinaire des Guerres, the most important financial agency in the kingdom, became such a bad debtor.

THE CREDIT INSTRUMENTS OF THE EXTRAORDINAIRE DES GUERRES: BILLS OF EXCHANGE AND BEARER BILLS

To cover a hiatus of revenue, the Extraordinaire des Guerres could raise funds by drawing bills of exchange—*lettres de change*—on correspondents. The Extraordinaire also had to use bills of exchange because of the pattern of remitting funds abroad, and this on a notably large scale to get money for the French forces in Spain in 1706 and 1707. It is worth showing how the treasurers general used bills of exchange unscrupulously in order to buy themselves time (at quite a price) through forcing more credit out of their existing creditors. It was perfectly standard for the treasurers general or their *commis* to meet their payment obligations to suppliers using bills of exchange, in large part because many such suppliers were not based in Paris. The treasurers general were supposed to discharge these instruments at, or shortly after, the moment of maturity and presentation, but they might fail to do so. This was possible without irritating creditors as long as the delays were only of the order of four to six weeks and payments were then met in full. But partial defaulting began to happen systematically from the autumn of 1704, when officers bearing bills of exchange called on the treasurer general in Paris but were given only one-quarter of their due as interim payments. The problem was compounded at this time by the practice of *commis* out in the field issuing small numbers of bills of exchange worth large sums (instead of lots of smaller bills worth less than 500 *livres*)—as with larger Mint bills, this was making it harder to discharge at least some of these bills of exchange entirely with cash, and harder for the holders to trade them. From January 1705 widespread worries across France that bills of exchange on the Extraordinaire des Guerres would be refused and then protested diminished enthusiasm for these instruments.[5] Nevertheless, with Extraordinaire bearer bills at their elastic limit by early 1707, the treasurers general turned towards greater use of bills of exchange to obtain funds across France. And from 1706 the treasurers general were paying suppliers with bills of exchange drawn on their *commis*—a way of delaying payment that they spun out for longer

[5] AN G[7]1776, no. 269: D'Honneur to Chamillart, 25 November 1704; no. 454: request from Vieuxcourt, 23 October 1704; no. 43: Vieuxcourt to Chamillart, 29 January [1705].

by not providing the sums to discharge such bills. But the banking and exchange crises of 1707 and then 1709 gradually led the treasurers general to reduce their use of bills of exchange, and caused the Extraordinaire's staff in general to reduce the average size of each bill of exchange: by May 1710 some were for as little as 10 *livres*, a reflection of both the collapse of cash flow in the Extraordinaire and the smaller and smaller sums that were available for discharging these bills. By this time treasurer general Duplessis was extremely reluctant to allow his *commis* to draw bills of exchange upon him to pay army officers and suppliers, and had to be forced by War Minister Voysin into accepting these liabilities. With few other ways of keeping 'money' flowing there was little choice but to do this.[6]

If bills of exchange were vital credit (as well as exchange) instruments for the Extraordinaire des Guerres, far more important was its use of its own bearer bills as instruments for paying what it owed to suppliers and soldiers. For convenience these will be referred to generally as 'War bills'. There were two basic ways of doing this: either it could issue bearer bills of varying kinds in order to raise funds (in the form of cash or other tradable instruments) from others; or it could pay its obligations not in cash or Mint bills or bills of exchange but in its own bearer bills. In effect, the first method was borrowing on behalf of the king from voluntary lenders; but the second method was a form of forced loan on army suppliers and military men, who had to accept deferred and discounted payment of what they were already owed. Given that logistical and equipment contractors usually supplied on credit already, this also provided an increase in the credit period that the Extraordinaire was enjoying.

By the War of the Spanish Succession the War bills came in several forms as a substitute for cash to meet specific obligations: *billets de subsistance*, with which army officers were paid; and *billets de masse*, *d'ustencile*, *de remontes*, *de recrues*, *de retenue*, and *de fourrages* for the various other payment obligations to the troops, officers, and suppliers. These seem to have been given different labels as a useful way for the Extraordinaire to keep track of why they had been issued, and in the case of the second group of *billets* above they were supposed to be hypothecated to specifically earmarked revenue sources and expenditure.[7] On top of this, military units themselves might issue what were known as *billets de troupes*, paying their obligations in localities and to equipment/clothing/food suppliers in credit notes on the unit's future income from the Extraordinaire. If they were legitimate expenses then they were turned into *reconnaissances* ('recognitions') of the local Extraordinaire *commis*, for him to redeem directly with the suppliers and host communities. If this seems orderly, it is best to think of it as organized chaos.[8] The size of such payment bills could vary considerably from a few *livres* to several thousand, and maybe even more.[9]

[6] AN G[7]1779, various documents, notably no. 117: note, 11 April 1707; SHD Ya2: Voysin to Barillon, 26 May 1710.

[7] Seligmann, 99.

[8] AN G[7]1782, no. 48: duc de Noailles to Desmaretz, 29 April 1708; CCG, III, 226: *maire* and *échevins* of Caen to Desmaretz, 5 September 1709.

[9] AN G[7]1775, no. 26: 'Estat de payements…', [March 1700]; no. 277: Pleneuf to Chamillart, 13 October 1703.

It is perhaps not surprising that these were used as ad hoc devices for payments, but it was a very different situation with the other War bills, the *billets d'emprunts*, with which the treasurers general and their agents raised actual cash as loans. Accounts from September to December 1703 reveal that loans were taken out by treasurer general Pleneuf on most days, and the sums ranged between 1,000 *livres* and 1,708,935 *livres*, reflecting the spread of lenders from small investors to consortia of financiers. By this stage War bills had been officially convertible for at least six years: they could be used by holders to meet the annual venal *Paulette* levy and some tax payments at the Trésor royal (meaning the *receveurs généraux* could use them to meet their obligations to the king). The War bills therefore enjoyed something of a privileged status among para-royal instruments and other paper money devices, not unlike Mint bills. But there were limits to convertibility, and treasurers general often refused War bills as payment from others. No other financiers seem to have enjoyed such privileged rights and status for their bearer bills during the War of the Spanish Succession, at least before the Caisse Legendre's foundation in 1710. From 1706 the crown, in advance, now officially and publicly authorized the Extraordinaire to receive sums from individuals, delivering in return bills of exchange drawn on Lyon or bills 'payable to the Bearers'.[10] Such public support by the monarch had become essential.

Bearer bills were supposed to mature within a matter of a few short weeks or months, but as the War of the Spanish Succession ground on the volume of undischarged War bills mounted. This was not just because revenues were inadequate or delayed, the reason why, say, *receveurs généraux* issued bearer bills in growing numbers. It was also because the appropriations system was breaking down, the Finance Ministry was poorly coordinating the primary receivers' credit methods (if at all) before 1710, and the credit instruments pressed as cash substitutes upon the treasurers general of the Extraordinaire by, for example, the farmers general were simply not large or reliable enough to act as adequate funds for meeting obligations. This forced the treasurers general themselves to borrow: this was, of course, not on the guarantee of revenues they collected but on those collected by other men and agencies who were one, two, or even three steps removed from their own *caisses*. As the situation of the fisco-financiers and the Trésor royal worsened, the bearer bills issued by the Extraordinaire changed from being short-term stopgaps to medium-term and open-ended borrowing instruments. It took longer and longer for the crown to pay off the debts of a treasurer general's *exercice* year, forcing these men to take out loans beyond the end of the duty-year to cover their liabilities in the meantime, even as they discharged older debts. This, in turn, had an impact on the amount and price of credit available to the other treasurers general taking up their duty-years.[11]

[10] AN G[7]1775, no. 108: 'Etat des billets d'emprunts... 1703...', [1703–4]; no. 249: [two *trésoriers de France*] to Chamillart, 20 December 1703; no. 277: Pleneuf to Chamillart, 13 October 1703; SHD Ya2: Voysin to prince de Rohan, 16 March 1710; BNF F-23619: *déclaration*, 4 December 1708 (quotation).

[11] AN G[7]1775, no. 107: memorandum on 1702 Extraordinaire *exercice*, 3 August 1703; no. 144: 'Estat...', 14 July 1703.

What makes the War of the Spanish Succession very unusual among *ancien régime* conflicts is that between 1701 and 1708 such monumental and risky loan flotations were approved by the *contrôleur général des finances*. In the War Ministry prior to 1701 the Le Telliers had sought to maintain the solvency of the Extraordinaire treasurers general and keep their borrowing as low as possible by leaning on the *contrôleurs généraux*. As a matter of preference the war ministers of Louis XIV's reign wanted the credit risks in wartime to be shouldered as much as possible by men like the *receveurs généraux* and the *fermes*, answerable to the Finance Ministry and close to the tax revenues. Michel Chamillart's cumulation of the office of Secretary of State for War with that of *contrôleur général* in January 1701 changed the situation dramatically: he appears to have regarded the treasurers general of the Extraordinaire as yet one more group of financiers he could use as sources of credit and as channels for loans from wider society. By this means the government could also defer the payment of suppliers, army officers, and others. Yet Chamillart's approach—which at best was to acquiesce in the treasurers general meeting their expenses through issuing more and more bearer bills—was not considered sound by some of his underlings. In a surprising statement of Gladstonian fiscal rectitude, the artillery's director general Pleneuf (a former Extraordinaire treasurer general) noted pointedly in 1705 that 'after all, the true function of a treasurer is to receive before paying out'.[12] After February 1708 Desmaretz (and Voysin from June 1709) tried to bring the War bills back under control, but it proved very hard to repair the damage that had already been done.

RAISING LOANS FOR THE EXTRAORDINAIRE DES GUERRES, 1701 TO 1708

Throughout Louis XIV's personal rule it was not at all uncommon for minor cash-flow problems to force the Extraordinaire into issuing short-term mandates maturing after two to three months upon either the treasurer general or upon one of his agents, and the number of such instruments multiplied during difficult times. During 1694 the holders of these bills found they had to accept discounts of 8–10 per cent if they wanted to realize them in cash.[13] The Extraordinaire also raised funds through borrowing during emergency situations, usually because the generals or army *intendants* could not wait for funds to reach the local Extraordinaire *commis* in the usual ways. After 1706 the volume and intensity of this lending increased. During his defence of the city of Lille in late 1708, the maréchal de Boufflers borrowed on behalf of the Extraordinaire, from within the city community and authorities, 494,288 *livres* which were to fall due fifteen days after any capitulation.[14] Similarly, when funds dried up in those French

[12] SHD A[1]1894: Pleneuf to d'Esgrigny, 17 March 1705.

[13] For example, SHD A[1]1285, no. 77: Vaubourg to Barbezieux, 1 May 1694; no. 208: de Sève to Barbezieux, 11 June 1694.

[14] SHD Ya2: Chamillart to Desmaretz, 14 November 1708; AN G[7]1783, no. 14: 'Etat des sommes avancés...', [1709].

provinces that enjoyed little priority, their *intendants* and provincial governors also borrowed heavily to fill the coffers of the local Extraordinaire agents. A high proportion of such loans was drawn from local sources, through city magistrates or—in the north-east—Jews in Metz. If credit was arranged directly with the treasurer general of the Extraordinaire at the centre then specific revenue streams might be pledged for repayment. Alternatively, the effort sometimes involved loans gathered together by local Extraordinaire agents, depending on the circumstances.[15] The other channel for loans was the royal bankers: not only were they involved in remitting money for the king to the armies, but from time to time they acted to procure straightforward loans in France or abroad. Although they did this on a fairly regular basis after late 1709 (after their international remittance operations slowed dramatically), the bankers were also vital during earlier emergencies: the loans Samuel Bernard could obtain in and through the Spanish Netherlands provided the last prop of financial support for the French army of Flanders as it wandered the Low Countries after the battle of Oudenarde in the late summer of 1708.[16]

Most such emergencies could and did happen in any war, but in the Nine Years War both the navy and the Extraordinaire des Guerres began running an underlying structural deficit in their finances that grew at an alarming rate. By his 1695 duty-year Extraordinaire treasurer general Turmenyes was supporting advances and loans that had now reached 10 million *livres* per annum. At the point at which they collapsed, in spring 1701, treasurer general La Touanne and his colleague Sauvion—who had been in office sixteen years—owed individuals 9.8 million *livres* they had borrowed through *billets d'emprunts*, much of it in peacetime since 1697. Only 6 million *livres* of this were covered by funds, and then only theoretically, as the yield of some sources would be disappointing.[17] Nevertheless, this was nothing compared with what was to come. Shortly after the outbreak of hostilities in the summer of 1701 First President Harlay of the Paris *Parlement* could speak of War bills as 'this sort of commerce which has become so important' both in terms of the volume of trading and in terms of the state's need for it; but he might not have anticipated just how big this would soon get.[18] For the 1701 *exercice* alone, when hostilities were almost entirely confined to northern Italy, the Extraordinaire borrowed over 28 million *livres*, including in the period beyond the duty-year after 1 January 1702. The 1702 *exercice* borrowed a total of 27 million *livres*, while for the 1703 *exercice* the sums raised through loans (over several years) exceeded 46.5 million *livres*. Well might that year's treasurer general, Pleneuf, exclaim, 'I did not believe it was possible for anyone to support such an excessive burden.' Delays of four to five months in the realization of assigned

[15] Esnault, II, 197: duc de Gramont to Chamillart, 6 June 1708; SHD Ya2: Chamillart to La Houssaye, 26 January 1707; A[1]1613, no. 172bis: Montargis to Chamillart, 4 January 1702; CCG, II, 366: D'Argenson to Chamillart, 2 December 1706.

[16] Esnault, II, 204–8: Bergeyck to Chamillart, 22 and 24 July 1708; Lévy, *Capitalistes et pouvoir au siècle des Lumières* (3 vols, Paris, 1969–80), I, 356–8.

[17] AN G[7]1788, no. 148: 'Memoire...', [1714]; BNF F-21054: *déclaration*, 3 June 1701.

[18] CCG, II, 77: Harlay to Chamillart, 18 June 1701.

revenues were driving up the amount of borrowing, but the *assignations* were not easy to trade, except for expensive credit, because many were starting to deliver considerably less than their face value. The total loans for the 1704 *exercice* seem to have been lower but this was the calm before the storm and it was already a costly situation.[19]

The borrowing that took place through War bills throughout the 1700s was expensive, in the region of or exceeding 10 per cent per annum: 6,000 *livres* were borrowed at 10 per cent by the Extraordinaire *commis* in Besançon in April 1708 to pay the troops, even though official rates were around 6–7 per cent.[20] Nor were loans easy to come by, though they were periodically given a boost by anxiety: coin-value diminutions provided a negative incentive for people to loan to the Extraordinaire. Indeed, apprehension about such diminutions seems to have induced even such powerful figures as *receveurs généraux* to place surplus money at the disposal of the Extraordinaire.[21] Nevertheless, by the end of 1704 the War bills were not discredited. This was in large part because the treasurers general were able to discharge their debts in reasonable time, and without forcing creditors into extensions too often. By May 1703 over 99 per cent of the debts from the 1701 *exercice* had been cleared; and by December 1703 some 90 per cent of the 1702 *exercice*'s debts had been paid off, with the remainder scheduled for clearance by May 1704. With pressure from the treasurers general themselves, determined efforts were at this time still being made to ensure resources were found to repay debt capital from these *exercices* at the moment a particular loan fell due. The government was stoking up the underlying deficit level of the treasurers general but it was still making a priority of upholding their creditworthiness.[22]

However, the handling of the debt from the 1703 and 1704 *exercices* deteriorated, a consequence not only of falling revenues but also of a growing tendency to treat the Extraordinaire des Guerres as an intermediary, proxy credit body. It was already obvious that the Extraordinaire was contracting debts that considerably exceeded the usual two- to three-month short-term duration, but now even these medium-term debts were in danger of not being extinguished. By November 1704 the remaining debts from the 1702 *exercice* were being prolonged and repayments strung out: even though it was a matter of only just over 1 million *livres*, the failure to devote funds to meet the final capital repayments was threatening to impede the raising of credit for the forthcoming 1705 *exercice*. As for the 1704 *exercice*, worries about the solvency and strength of Vieuxcourt, that year's treasurer general, appear to have induced Chamillart to prioritize his credibility, pushing back a minority of

[19] AN G[7]1775, no. 60: memorandum on 1701 Extraordinaire, 12 May [1703]; no. 107: memorandum on 1702 Extraordinaire, 3 August 1703; no. 315: Pleneuf to [Le Rebours?], 18 December 1703 (quotation); G[7]1782, no. 105: *mémoire* on Extraordinaire debts, 21 July 1708.

[20] AN G[7]1775, no. 321: 'Bordereau...', [early November 1703]; G[7]1787, no. 143: *mémoire*, [November? 1711].

[21] AN G[7]1776, no. 434: Pleneuf to Chamillart, 3 September 1703; G[7]1777, no. 230: Montargis to Chamillart, 17 July 1705; CCG, III, 21: La Houssaye to Desmaretz, 30 April 1708.

[22] AN G[7]1775, no. 115: memorandum on 1702 Extraordinaire, 13 December 1703.

Pleneuf's 1703 debts for later redemption and piling up larger and larger debts for 1705 and 1706 instead.[23]

The government was entering dangerous waters. Treasurers general were determined to prioritize the repayment of their debts for the very good reason that they needed to maintain their credit over the medium to long term, and this was indeed a respectable stance considering they had relatively few revenue sources to back their debts other than those given them by the Trésor royal. Yet they had to plead with Chamillart—even in early 1703 when funds were still flowing quite well—to ensure that they had enough revenues to maintain a steady flow of uninterrupted interest payments and capital repayments. Treasurer general Montargis had to spell out in simple terms to Le Rebours, the *premier commis des finances*, that

> the funds from all those [1702 *billets*] that I discharge will return to the current [1704] *exercice* [...] If I found myself completely unable to satisfy [my debts] two years after an *exercice*, which is something that has never yet been seen, that would be to give a defiance to the public that is very necessary to avoid.

But the Finance Ministry was beginning to set its face against such reasonable wisdom. Instead for some debt discharges it damagingly assigned funds that were to mature only a year or more later, well into the next year of *exercice* Montargis undertook.[24] The Extraordinaire des Guerres was creeping ever closer towards the edge of a precipice. Either through poor control or deliberately (to expand the state's use of medium- and long-term proxy creditors) Chamillart was slowly and unwittingly imperilling the position of the treasurers general and thereby jeopardizing future military performance. Back in September 1703 Pleneuf had already warned him that 'the credit of the bills [...] has been pushed further than in any previous *exercices*', and the *assignations* backing them were becoming difficult to trade for fair sums.[25]

All this notwithstanding, the value of the Extraordinaire bearer bills was still holding up: throughout 1704 and 1705, according to the banker Tourton (writing several years later), these were being negotiated remarkably at only a 1 per cent loss (actually up from about a 5 per cent discount in 1702). The same applied to bills of exchange on treasurer general Vieuxcourt. The Trésor royal itself was not just accepting them in payments but was also immediately putting them back into circulation, a reflection of the confidence these bills then enjoyed. To preserve this credibility the treasurers general were using Mint bills to retire some of their own bearer bills (at least when the Mint bills were not in a period of discredit); they were extinguishing their debts if people did not wish to renew them; they were carrying forward the debts of one treasurer general to the *exercice* of another (not

[23] AN G^{7}1776, nos 265–6: D'Honneur to Chamillart (plus list), 10 November 1704; G^{7}1777, no. 195: request from Vieuxcourt, 1 August 1705; Michel de Gouberville, 'Armes et argent: les Berthelot, munitionnaires du Roi Soleil', *Annales de généalogie et d'héraldique* 53 (1994), 11.

[24] AN G^{7}1775, no. 109: memorandum on 1702 Extraordinaire, 20 February 1703; no. 162: Montargis to Le Rebours, 3 January 1704 (quotation); no. 169: list of 'assignations qui sont ez mains du Sr de Montargis', 29 January 1704.

[25] AN G^{7}1776, no. 434: Pleneuf to Chamillart, 3 September 1703.

without tensions among the colleagues); and they were doing their level best not to delay bill of exchange payments by more than two to three weeks. But to achieve this, Vieuxcourt and his colleagues were having to trade *assignations* or Mint bills for discounts of 10 per cent or more, and accept penal interest rates on loans they contracted. Or they were buying Mint bills at discounts and then hoping to pass them on for a higher amount.[26] The treasurers general of the Extraordinaire were clearly sacrificing the interests of the revenue machine (by driving down the market price for *assignations* and Mint bills) in order to meet their own cash-flow requirements, and, harsh though this was, it was probably a better way of proceeding than loading themselves up with more and more medium-term debt. It at least preserved their personal credibility for the essential task of sustaining payments to the armies.

Had Chamillart tried hard not to allow the volume of War bills in any given year to exceed the levels of 1702–4, and instead tried for a few more years to burden the main revenue collectors or even significantly increase the tax load on the privileged, then the credibility of the Extraordinaire might have remained high for longer. But instead the government adopted a 'smoke and mirrors' approach: it reinforced the treasurers general by persuading them to cooperate in backing each other's debt issues and giving them publicly known associates of standing who would co-sign their bearer bills, all the while increasing the volume of debt carried by the Extraordinaire. By failing to provide enough *assignations* and funds, and failing to access more credit and taxes through the *receveurs généraux* and their bearer bills, Chamillart now left the military paymasters with little choice but to raise their capital and interest liabilities. With most of these liabilities now covered by secret guarantees from the king, the treasurers general and their associates had little incentive to resist a further downward descent into debt. Sooner or later the burden was going to become unsustainable, and the credit margin the Extraordinaire traditionally held in reserve for real military and logistical emergencies was no longer going to be there, or at best it would become exorbitant to use. The state was risking a paralysis or even total breakdown of military campaigning.

For the 1705 *exercice* Montargis ran up debts of 62,855,447 *livres* (over a period of three to four years), of which perhaps some 20 million *livres* were contracted *after* the end of the calendar year. Unsurprisingly, at the start of April 1706 a crisis moment arrived. The king owed Montargis 27.8 million *livres*, plus nearly the same amount again to cover untradable or long-dated *assignations*. Interest on this was costing the Extraordinaire 10 per cent per annum, if not more. By now the insufficient funds reaching the treasurers general meant that they were staring at the option of using bearer bills to pay interest on their borrowings, thereby adding further interest charges onto the interest payments! Instead, they preferred to carry the 1705 debts onto 1706 and 1707, nominally at least. Montargis and Mongelas

[26] SHD A[1]1613, no. 203: Mongelas to Chamillart, 11 December 1702; AN G[7]1011: 'Reponse du S[r]. Tourton au memoire du s[r]. de Ville', [February 1708?]; G[7]1777, no. 31: memorandum, 25 March 1705; no. 42: Vieuxcourt to Chamillart, 6 August 1705; no. 142: report by Vieuxcourt on the 1704 *exercice*, 7 July 1705; no. 181: request from Vieuxcourt, 13 June 1705; no. 195: request from Vieuxcourt, 1 August 1705; G[7]1778, nos 101, 114: notes of Montargis, 1 and 22 April 1706.

(the 1706 duty treasurer general) agreed that Mongelas would accept up to 5 million *livres* of Montargis' *billets*, with the agreement of the creditors. This was considered essential to achieve an orderly rolling over of debt that now simply could not be withdrawn on time. Both men planned to get the lenders 'imperceptibly' to carry the rest of the 1705 debts over into the 1707 *exercice*, by which they presumably meant they would undertake very secret negotiations with each creditor to avoid a mass panic and open realization of what was going on. This, in April 1706, was the moment of first, serious default. The treasurers general were fortunate that few people at the time wanted to receive capital repayment in Mint bills, and accordingly they planned to maintain the level of the 1705 debt (in the form of its carry-overs) at 27 million *livres* for three years to come. Above all, they stressed the need to prevent the public becoming aware that the debt of a single *exercice* would remain at such a level for over three years, the triennial cycle of the treasurers general. This was because Mongelas and Vieuxcourt (for 1707) were secretly not, in fact, taking on legal liability for Montargis' debts but merely pretending to do so, and the risk that the public would realize this worried them greatly. If it became known a treasurer general (Montargis) was entering his next *exercice* (1708) with such an enormous liability it would render him useless and provoke a complete collapse in the credibility of the Extraordinaire des Guerres. Faced with equally unpalatable options forced on them by Chamillart, they probably chose the right way forward, but this was a very dangerous and certainly very costly strategy. In 1706 and 1707 this move to roll over the 1705 debts added further to the debt-servicing liabilities for Montargis, and contributed to enormous liabilities piling up for the subsequent duty treasurers general. For the plan to work Mongelas had to issue bearer bills on himself in 1706 that would not be redeemable before New Year 1707, undoubtedly increasing the price of such credit, even if he used many funds to redeem 1705 debts and thereby kept loans flowing into his own coffers.[27]

All those involved in this conspiracy were banking on a successful or quiet set of military campaigns in 1706. What nobody predicted was how large the debts of the 1706 *exercice* would become, as military disaster was piled onto enormous logistical efforts in Flanders, the Pyrenean region, and the southern Alps and Piedmont. By the end of the year, the king owed Mongelas 58 million *livres*, causing his colleague Thomé to exclaim to Chamillart that 'there has never been any treasurer in such advances'.[28] By October 1707 a colossal 40 million *livres*' worth of *billets d'emprunts* and another 8.4 million *livres* of other *billets* from 1706 remained outstanding. Further loans were also contracted subsequent to this, and one estimate put the total borrowing of the 1706 *exercice* at 108,367,228 *livres*! It is not impossible that these *billets d'emprunts* were being sold by the treasurers general for less than their face value (as was happening with *rentes* on the Hôtel

[27] AN G[7]1782, no. 105: *mémoire* on Extraordinaire debts, 21 July 1708; G[7]1120: 'Etat des fonds deubs a l'Extraord[re]. des Guerres 1705…', 26 October 1705; G[7]1778, nos 101, 112: notes of Montargis, 1 and 22 April 1706.

[28] AN G[7]1778, no. 48: Thomé to Chamillart, 22 February 1707 (quotation); no. 271: *état* of 1706 *exercice*, 30 December 1706.

de ville), thereby pushing up the real interest rate. Certainly, many of the Extraordinaire's liabilities were met by discounting a variety of instruments, given by the king to the treasurers general, for around one-third of their value if not more. As for the 1707 *exercice*, Montargis had to come in to take over the duties a year earlier than he had anticipated, out of turn. In doing so, he agreed to advance 28.5 million *livres* (including 15 million *livres* of debts he was still carrying from 1705), and to borrow a further 20 million *livres*. As one document put it drily, 'This is an arrangement that it is believed one could propose without being able to answer for its success.'[29] The costs of the 1707 borrowings mounted up, and only worsened as the credibility of the Extraordinaire declined; even the towns in Flanders, through which a lot of cash flowed, were loath to lend it money. By the middle of 1707 the failure not merely to repay capital but also to pay interest on the 1706 *exercice* loans made it far harder to get new loans for the Extraordinaire, and in 1708 some of the Extraordinaire's *billets de subsistance* were being traded by desperate army officers for as little as 17 per cent of their face value. If one assumes such instruments were officially bearing 7 per cent annual interest (possibly more), this meant the new holders of such bills were really accruing interest of 41 per cent![30]

By the autumn of 1706 the excessive issuing of Extraordinaire bearer bills, and indeed the gradual discrediting of many paper instruments, was already causing the credit of the treasurers general to dry up in Paris. At best they were having to pay heavy interest rates, or accept loans in Mint bills while agreeing to provide capital repayment in cash (an expensive deal).[31] This forced them to turn to other financial centres outside the capital for short-term loans, meaning greater use of bills of exchange drawn, most notably, upon Lyon. The use of bills of exchange to get credit opened the possibility of prolonging debts by touring these instruments around various financial centres and passing them through various sets of hands before ultimate discharge. In 1706 and the first few months of 1707 the cost of doing this was actually less than that of raising straightforward credit in Paris, which says a lot about the credibility of the treasurers general's instruments in the capital. Unfortunately the combination of an accumulating volume of bills of exchange drawn and sent *from* Spain *on* the treasurers general and *on* their Lyon agents, with bills of exchange drawn *by* the treasurers general in Paris on their Lyon correspondents, produced a liability so great that the international exchange credit of the treasurers general began to crumble. This was, not coincidentally, at a time of discredited Mint bills and excessive circulation of Extraordinaire bearer bills. By July 1707 merchants were pleading with Chamillart to order treasurer general Montargis to meet his bill of exchange obligations, and his colleague Mongelas' failure to do the same for exchange liabilities left over from 1706 was adding to the

[29] AN $G^7$1778, nos 326, 332: [balance sheets for 1706 *exercice*], 2 and 27 October 1707; $G^7$1779, no. 228: list of 'Fonds à fournir par mois…', 31 March 1707 (quotation); $G^7$1780, no. 156: Montargis to Chamillart, 14 July 1707.

[30] AN $G^7$1779, no. 202: De Pomereuil to Chamillart, 7 May 1707; $G^7$1780, no. 156: Montargis to Chamillart, 14 July 1707; Seligmann, 99.

[31] AN $G^7$1779, no. 43: Montargis to Chamillart, 15 April 1707.

problem and producing a further lack of confidence in Montargis' bills of exchange. People in Lyon began panic-selling Extraordinaire bills of exchange for 15 per cent losses, despite offers of 6 per cent annual interest for renewing them. By mid-September the discounting on Montargis' bills of exchange was 45 per cent in Lyon and only (if that is the right word) 30–35 per cent in Paris. Paris was still outrageously expensive, but now it had again become cheaper than Lyon as a source of credit. In turn, the new Mint bills that were being issued were, by August, already trading in Lyon at a 30 per cent loss because Montargis was defaulting on his bills of exchange: this discounting occurred because his creditors became increasingly desperate to get cash to meet their own obligations and therefore sold their new Mint bills for what they could get. The success of new Mint bills was therefore directly tied to the Extraordinaire des Guerres and its debt instruments, but they were going down together and in the process driving prices that the state had to pay for its war effort and for its credit ever higher. The 1707 crash of Extraordinaire instruments at Lyon increased the price of credit there and yet the Extraordinaire needed to continue borrowing through this centre for another two to three years for armies abroad. This made the riding out of the much bigger 1709 banking crisis even costlier, according to one of the co-treasurers of the Extraordinaire, Pierre Thomé.[32]

THE EFFORTS TO REGAIN CONTROL OVER THE DEBT OF THE EXTRAORDINAIRE DES GUERRES, 1708–15

Back in 1704 the government had not envisaged that short-term borrowing by the treasurers general would cover such a high proportion of an entire *exercice*—around 85 per cent of the 1706 *exercice* and one-third of 1707's expenditure obligations. The debt burden had risen to the point where in January 1708, at a moment when no preparations had been made for the financing of the forthcoming campaign, the treasurers general were unable to pay off their bills of exchange or trade any of their own bearer bills. There was almost no cash circulating within the royal and para-royal financial system and the state was staring into the abyss.[33] Desmaretz, stepping up to the office of *contrôleur général* on 20 February, had to act quickly, but his efforts, outlined below, had limited success. This was because discounting was done in each place—whether small locality or Paris or Lyon—by a small number of people with liquid assets to spare. By now, because of bearer bills passing through their hands and through awareness of cash-flow problems in general, they had gained enough of a sense of the magnitude of the War bill issue to bring the process to a halt, even if they had little idea of the exact figures involved. It is

[32] AN $G^7$1779, no. 132: Méliand to [Desmaretz?], 4 July 1707; $G^7$1780, no. 59: placet of Jean Contard and associates, [July 1707]; no. 65: *mémoire* by banker Ollivier, [July 1707]; $G^7$1780, no. 64: Ollivier to [Chamillart], 5 July 1707; $G^7$1781, no. 47: Barescut to Chamillart, 16 September 1707; $G^7$1783, no. 357: Thomé to Desmaretz, 19 October 1709.

[33] AN $G^7$1782, no. 4: Mongelas to Chamillart, 28 January 1708; CCG, III, 616: 'Mémoire', [early 1715].

indeed not possible to say exactly what the outstanding War bill liabilities were in January–February 1708 (not least because of varied labelling in the accounts), but we can estimate them closely enough to suggest a picture of a system that had slipped control. There were 61.7 million *livres* of bills outstanding that had been issued by the military paymasters as a group, and the interest owed on this was somewhere in the region of 5–9 million *livres* more. There were also at least another 18 million *livres* of arrears owed in other ways to the troops and suppliers. At best, then, the Extraordinaire des Guerres owed around 80 million *livres*. This was brought down by the end of 1708 to around 64 million *livres* of arrears and credit notes, of which *billets d'emprunts*—used to raise cash—amounted to at most around 47 million *livres*. This does not include further borrowing during 1708, which seems to have been largely undertaken through bills of exchange and loans from bankers and big merchants, as in subsequent years. At this point the efforts to bring down Extraordinaire debt through repayments and rollovers seem to have stalled. By March 1709, when the deepest financial crisis of the king's personal rule began to emerge, the Extraordinaire des Guerres still owed its various creditors some 63,932,060 *livres*.[34]

Desmaretz's general approach was that debt repayments had to be made, or, if not, then rolled over on advantageous terms for the creditors. He also preferred the Trésor royal and the most solvent primary revenue receivers, rather than the state's spending treasurers, to shoulder the flotation of the bulk of short-term loans. On this basis he did work with the treasurers general to try to reduce their debts. Between 22 February 1708 and 24 October 1709 the volume of *billets d'emprunts* was brought down quite sharply, from 61.7 million to 26.9 million *livres*, through a combination of repayments by the treasurers general and the Trésor royal stepping in with additional funds they handed directly to the creditors.[35] However, the pace of repayments slowed down from March 1709 and although the reduction helped the personal credit of the treasurers general somewhat, it took no account of the 30 million *livres* or more of other bills forced on hapless suppliers and soldiers by the Extraordinaire des Guerres and regimental administrators. During 1708 Desmaretz's liberation of anticipated revenues had allowed treasurer general Sauroy to avoid issuing *billets d'emprunts* at the centre for getting voluntary cash loans, but the Extraordinaire instead borrowed that year on a rolling basis on the frontiers using bills of exchange drawn on the treasurer general in Paris in order to pay the field armies. Alas, not all these bills of exchange were paid off. Matters got worse the following year. As Mongelas noted later, in 1709 the Extraordinaire had only functioned out in the provinces at all through loans procured locally thanks to the intervention of the *intendants*. Local *commis* may also have been issuing *billets d'emprunts* on an ad hoc basis to those who were forced into lending them

[34] CCG, III, 673: 'Compte rendu de M. Desmaretz au Régent', [1716]; AN G^{7}1782, no. 105: *mémoire* on Extraordinaire debts, 21 July 1708; G^{7}1782, no. 267: summary accounts of Extraordinaire debts and assets, 22 December 1708; G^{7}1784, no. 2: 'Bordereau' for several Extraordinaire *exercices* 1706–9, [March? 1709]; no. 7: *bordereau* weekly account, 30 March 1709.

[35] AN G^{7}1785, no. 54: 'Etat des billets d'emprunts…', 24 October 1709.

money. Moreover, *commis* and army officers continued to force a variety of bearer bills on people—in effect, deferred and devalued payments.[36]

In 1709–10 Desmaretz's determination to use more and more long-dated *assignations* and advances from primary revenue receivers had a lot to do with his desire to pass such instruments on to the Extraordinaire des Guerres to reduce the latter's need to issue credit notes. It was then up to the treasurer general to use them to meet his obligations, or to trade these *assignations* for whatever price he could get, until the Caisse Legendre took on the responsibility for this. But the treasurers general still needed to obtain credit owing to poor cash flows and the depreciation and delayed realization or failure of *assignations*. Unfortunately, thanks to the credit crunch, *assignation* policy, drastic reorganization of War bills (see below), and the currency reform, by mid-1709 the treasurers general were finding it very hard to raise fresh credit, prompting a serious clash between a frustrated Desmaretz and treasurer general Mongelas.[37]

In spite of the *contrôleur général*'s good intentions, the process of debt reduction was not smooth, even during 1708. A week before Desmaretz's promotion in February 1708 the government, all too aware it was facing a crisis in the Extraordinaire, allowed holders of its *billets* to convert them into *rentes* on the Hôtel de ville bearing 6.25 per cent annual interest, or into *promesses* of the Caisse des emprunts (for one-quarter of a deposit), or to use them to pay up to one-quarter of any transaction involving venal offices. Unfortunately—as with Desmaretz's efforts in 1710 to convert a variety of instruments—this held little appeal for the public because it meant swapping liquid, if discredited, instruments for immobile and illiquid ones, so War bills continued to be the subject of usurious trading.[38] Further steps would have to be taken. By the end of February 1708 Desmaretz had promoted treasurer general Montargis to *Garde du Trésor royal* to enhance the credibility of all treasurers general and encourage lending, but this had only limited positive effects.

That summer Desmaretz took the dangerous step of forbidding the treasurers general to renew their bearer bills, presumably to encourage people to convert them to *rentes*. This caused consternation in Paris 'in such a manner that the largest part of the people believe that all is entirely lost'. Montargis recommended instead the compulsory conversion of such bills into bearer bills on the *fermes générales*, to allow (in effect) their renewal for a further year to eighteen months.[39] It was a counsel of despair but it had the merit of shifting the burden back onto the primary receivers and preserving this money in liquid, negotiable instruments. At this

[36] AN G^{7}1782, no. 92: Sauroy to Chamillart, 21 June 1708; G^{7}1783, no. 21: Desmaretz to Le Blanc, 25 February 1709; no. 59: Moreau to Desmaretz, 12 March 1709; G^{7}1784, no. 52: Agniel brothers to Desmaretz, 1 October 1709; G^{7}1785, no. 124: de La Garde to Desmaretz, 10 August 1709; G^{7}1786, no. 218: memorandum, 19 June 1710; no. 261: Sister de Leuvargue to Desmaretz, 11 July 1710; G^{7}1788, no. 102: [Mongelas] to Desmaretz, 6 May 1714.

[37] AN G^{7}1784, no. 319: de La Garde to Desmaretz, 23 August 1709; G^{7}1779, no. 179: note, 7 March 1709.

[38] Forbonnais, II, 190; BNF F-23619: *déclaration*, 4 December 1708.

[39] AN G^{7}1782, no. 121: [Montargis to Desmaretz], 25 July 1708.

point in mid-1708 financial trading in Extraordinaire instruments came to a grinding halt throughout the country, as all awaited some government announcement about how to break out of the impasse. Over the coming months, government circles wrestled with the problem of how to improve the Extraordinaire's situation, while continuing to pay down some of its debt. In the meantime, suppliers in important areas would not accept War bills. One anonymous person around this time dared to tell Desmaretz that everyone had rejoiced when he had been seconded to help Chamillart (in 1703), but that since his elevation to the contrôle général the situation with the Extraordinaire des Guerres bills had only got worse.[40] In September the treasurers general petitioned for Desmaretz to uphold the legal protection they claimed their affairs were supposed to enjoy: the right to have all civil cases against them heard by the military tribunal of the *Connétablie et Maréchaussée* that sat at the 'table de marbre' of the Paris palace of justice, with appeals only to the Paris *Parlement*. This seems to have been agreed, but while it helped ease the legal pressure on them such protection only increased the discredit and price of debt instruments and bills of exchange issued by the Extraordinaire des Guerres.[41]

Desmaretz followed this with a decision to renew all Extraordinaire bills en masse, *faute de mieux*. On 4 December 1708, in a terrible admission of royal weakness to the financial world, Desmaretz announced in a declaration that the crown was unable to reimburse all War bills or even some bills of exchange issued by the treasurers general. Instead it was going to try to make these instruments 'useful'. The conversion opportunities announced back in February would be continued for War bearer bills, while those that were renewed by the treasurers general would get 6 per cent annual interest on them from the date of their scheduled maturity until their final redemption. All bills of exchange drawn on Lyon by the treasurers general would, however, be *compulsorily* converted into Extraordinaire *billets*, also carrying 6 per cent interest. A few sentences later came the really bad news: those bearer bills that had matured in 1707 and 1708 would be converted into bills payable in 1710, and those due to mature in 1709 would be pushed back to 1711; interest on the bills from the 1706 and 1707 *exercices* would be paid in further bearer bills. Of course, the king was reassuring holders by detailing Dubuisson, one of his *intendants des finances*, to oversee all this.[42]

Though some repayments continued to be made in 1709, Desmaretz was still putting back the discharge of Extraordinaire debts (as he had more generally in February 1708), presumably because he felt the credibility of War bills was already shattered. He was also taking a last-ditch approach to interest payments: a contract was signed with Louis Waubert, a *traitant*, for him to pay the interest on behalf of the Extraordinaire, as directed by Desmaretz—for a price we do not know but

[40] AN G⁷1782, no. 122: note on 1707 *exercice*, 11 August 1708; no. 170: comte de l'Isle to [Desmaretz], 2 November 1708; no. 147: anonymous to Desmaretz, n.d. [1708–9]; CCG, III, 47: Le Guerchoys to Desmaretz, various letters between 25 August and 8 September 1708.

[41] AN G⁷1782, nos 148, 149: Montargis to Desmaretz, and attached note, 12 September 1708.

[42] BNF F-23619: *déclaration*, 4 December 1708; AN G⁷1783, no. 59: Moreau to Desmaretz, 12 March 1709; G⁷655: memorandum by Legendre, [1711].

which cannot have been cheap.[43] All this was a desperate attempt to free up funds for 1709 and 1710 that had previously been assigned for servicing and repaying Extraordinaire debts from 1706 and 1707. But (as Desmaretz realized by February 1709) this was counterproductive for the flow of credit: it did not make it at all easy for treasurer general Mongelas (the duty treasurer for 1706 who was again on duty in 1709) or his successors to raise short-term credit in any form. This was also because Desmaretz's drastic move involved a penalty for investors: some of the outstanding bearer bills (most?) had previously been carrying higher interest rates of 10 per cent or more. These moves only contributed to the crisis that was starting to stir in Lyon over bills of exchange and Mint bills. Although with these decisions in December 1708 Desmaretz might have freed up some *assignations* for current spending, he undoubtedly worsened the credit situation, which had indeed been why the treasurers general had opposed his policy.

As they had feared, the treasurers general now found their bearer bills plummeting in value. By February–March 1709, before the banking storm in Lyon blew up, War bills were being traded away for cash in a widespread fashion by army officers for 30–40 per cent discounts. In July an infantry lieutenant in the régiment de Tournaisis had to sell 1,200 *livres* of War bills for only 360 *livres*, to the fury of one of the captains, who described it as the worst usury he had encountered in twenty-five years of service. By the end of the year, 60–70 per cent discounting applied to the full variety of War bills, and this continued.[44] To give a sense of how far France's financial situation had deteriorated in fifteen years, during the great economic crisis of 1692–4 War bills were trading for a loss of only 10 per cent, a discount considered unacceptable at the time.[45] Just when the second great economic crisis of the reign was erupting in 1709, when they needed all their reserves to keep going and recover, merchants were also being hit very hard by the Extraordinaire defaulting on its debts. They could not even use the Extraordinaire bills they were holding to secure their own basic cash-flow needs and pay off their own creditors. In October the Paris merchant draper firm of Berault and Sougit reported that they were owed 2 million *livres* for uniforms and cloth supplied to the army, for which they had received 1.7 million *livres* of useless Extraordinaire and regimental bearer bills.[46] With such astronomical debts now no longer even being serviced, it was clear to all that the military treasury was in a state of meltdown which would be very hard to bring under control. Towards the end of the year Desmaretz offered creditors one-third of their back-interest, with the rest deferred to later dates, but the slide in War bills only got worse. A few people, however, were doing well out of this disastrous situation. By mid-1710 Desmaretz was convinced, with good

[43] AN G^{7}1782, no. 198: Waubert to Desmaretz, 26 November 1708.

[44] CCG, III, 105: Bernières to Desmaretz, 2 March 1709; AN G^{7}1784, no. 242: *mémoire* by Desmaretz, 27 February 1709; G^{7}1783, no. 257: Captain Gaye to Desmaretz, 3 July 1709; G^{7}1784, no. 156: Vignemont to Desmaretz, 29 November 1709; G^{7}1786, no. 336: Danoue to [Le Rebours?], 23 June 1710.

[45] SHD A^{1}1285, no. 208: de Sève to Barbezieux, 11 June 1694.

[46] AN G^{7}1784, no. 102: placet of Delabelle, [October 1709]; no. 160: placet from Sr Brochant, [October 1709]; G^{7}1786, no. 323: note on the *marchands-drapiers* of Paris, 8 October 1710.

reason, that 'the largest part of these bills is to be found in the hands of people who have made immense gains by the low prices at which they have bought them up'.[47]

While bearer bills continued to be emitted by the Extraordinaire, the government continued to try to withdraw some of the mass and convert the rest from 1710. The commitment the government made to restart systematically the withdrawal of Extraordinaire bearer bills at the start of that year began well enough, and Desmaretz was willing to give people further time to report their possession of all War bills. But in August 1711 the government renewed and pushed back onto 1712 all those bills not redeemed in 1711, continuing the ungenerous 6 per cent interest rate.[48] After 1709 some 1706 and 1707 bills were withdrawn, though they were worth only a few million, and the borrowings from 1709 onwards were redeemed through close ministerial direction of the treasurers general to discharge specific liabilities, presumably to get the goodwill of those whose credit the crown needed most. But other creditors, especially the small traders out in the provinces, were left hanging out to dry. Ministers also arbitrarily intervened to ensure that those who bought up War bills from others were given a lower priority for repayment, even if the bill was long overdue for redemption. This was a terrible situation to be in, despite the Caisse Legendre being able to break up War bills into smaller notes for partial discharges. The War bills remained thoroughly discredited, trading at best for 50 per cent of their face value for the rest of the war and beyond.[49]

Instead of repaying the capital it was therefore predominantly a question of *converting* as many of the remaining bills as possible without entirely destroying public confidence in the Extraordinaire des Guerres. The open-ended invitation to convert War bills into *rentes* on the Hôtel de ville did lead some holders to pursue this route, but the illiquid nature of these *rentes* continued to be a major stumbling block to efforts by army officers to pass them on to suppliers in payment of their invoices: one regiment had to hand over the *rentes* it had so acquired at a 50 per cent loss in order to get Mint bills which it could then pass on to get cash from merchants, but for a further loss of one-third of *their* face value! This was piling usury upon usury. Moreover, the voluntary conversion of War bills to *rentes* was clearly not working, so in October 1710 Desmaretz targeted those high up in the judiciary, in the bread supply companies, and in the revenue-gathering machinery (particularly *traitants* and tax farmers) for a series of forced loans: he demanded the payment of 1.25 million *livres* of *augmentations des gages* from those who held venal offices. Three-quarters of each payment could be made in War bills. He was, though, disappointed by the response, which was, in retrospect, unsurprisingly poor given the soaking magistrates and other venal officers had been given, the

[47] AN G[7]1784, no. 229: timetable for interest payments, [late 1709]; CCG, III, 698: Desmaretz to Le Bret *fils*, 27 October 1710 (quotation).

[48] AN G[7]1786, no. 77: memorandum on *billet* renewals, 22 February 1710; no. 129: *arrêt*, 29 March 1710; BNF F-23620: *déclaration*, 4 June 1712.

[49] AN G[7]1788, no. 102: [Mongelas] to Desmaretz, 6 May 1714; G[7]655: memorandum by Legendre, [1711]; G[7]1788, no. 11: Kerpen to Desmaretz, 18 June 1713.

drying up of *affaires extraordinaires*, and the inability of the bread suppliers and farmers to make advances to the state as part of their contracts.[50]

What worked better was the decision in August 1711 to push back withdrawal of all unredeemed and unconverted War bills by a further year. This seems to have induced some holders to use some of them to buy up new 5 per cent *rentes* on the Hôtel de ville and prompted others to pay for all sorts of venal-related forced loans with them. But this did not lead to the conversion or withdrawal of 'the largest part of them', as the crown mendaciously implied (in a declaration) had happened.[51] And some people demanded 'promesses'—promissory notes—as security from treasurer general Duplessis for converting their War bills into *rentes*.[52] In June 1712, Desmaretz gave people until the end of that year to swap their War bills for 6 per cent *rentes perpétuelles*, for 10 per cent life annuities (*rentes viagères*), for the *tontine* created back in May 1709, for *promesses* of the Caisse des emprunts, or for new venal offices. Alternatively, they could be used in deposits with the royal mints, but in all these cases a proportion in cash—which varied according to which transaction was involved—was demanded as well. From 1 January 1713 all War bills were to become null and void.[53]

This effort, too, failed to clear France of such poisonous instruments before the end of hostilities, in spite of several extensions to the cut-off date. As Desmaretz was already inflicting unpopular 'haircuts' on *rente*-holders—to the dismay of those who had converted their War bills into such instruments—it is not surprising that those who could afford to hold on to their War bills continued to do so.[54] So after peace had returned Desmaretz tried again, in a similar vein, bastardizing an already hybrid form of *rentes*: in June 1714 a lottery based upon a *tontine* issue was created, subscription to which was to be three-quarters in War bills and one-quarter in cash. This too failed to reduce the volume of unredeemed and unconverted War bills, despite a further declaration allowing them to be divided into smaller amounts to purchase lottery *rentes*. One reason may have been the fact that such *rentes* were to be backed by revenues hypothecated from the equally exhausted *fermes générales*.[55] The following year the efforts to withdraw War bills took on an air of deeper desperation. On 2 March 1715 a declaration reiterated that there were 10,000 lottery shares available, worth a total of 10 million *livres* of capital subscription, and War bills could be used to cover three-quarters of the cost of each purchase. But a second declaration later that very same day suddenly allowed the *entire* cost to be met in War bills if presented before 31 July—because army officers who still held these bills claimed they could not supply enough cash to cover even

[50] AN G[7]1787, no. 114: Mongelas to Desmaretz, 25 June 1711; G[7]652: memorandum to Desmaretz by officers of the régiment de Manière cavalerie, 9 January 1710; G[7]1031: placet of Thevenard, [May–June 1712]; McCollim, 307, 315, 319; CCG, III, 612: 'Mémoire', [early 1715].

[51] BNF F-23620: *déclaration*, 4 June 1712. This claim only works if the crown was muddling the total number that had been withdrawn since their original issue with the number withdrawn since August 1711.

[52] AN G[7]655: 'Memoire' to Desmaretz from several anonymous individuals, [1711].

[53] BNF F-23620: *déclaration*, 4 June 1712.

[54] AN G[7]1788, no. 48: Bonot to Desmaretz, 29 December 1713.

[55] Seligmann, 115; BNF F-23741: *déclaration*, 28 August 1714.

one-quarter of a share. According to a later edict this produced a massive rush to convert, flushing out 20 million *livres* of War bills, though the lottery only had provision to absorb half this amount.[56] In July 1715 Desmaretz therefore halted the entire conversion process, ordering instead, specifically for this purpose, the creation of *rentes héréditaires* worth 25 million *livres* of capital investment. Most unusually, a certain proportion of the capital would be reimbursed each year, based on a sinking fund fed by *capitation* revenues levied in the city of Paris. To accompany this there would be a 'visa' of all War bills, to establish who owned them: all those bills that were no longer held by their original recipients would be slashed in value by 50 per cent. Although this was officially announced in August, the death of Louis XIV prevented this extremely crude scheme from being carried through, and the new regency government, in which the duc de Noailles now held the financial whip hand, suspended the edict.[57]

FINAL LIQUIDATION, 1715–16

One cannot fault Desmaretz's desire to convert and withdraw the Extraordinaire des Guerres bearer bills, nor question his sincerity. At the start of May 1715 he made it clear to the king that for discharging liabilities his order of priorities was as follows: (1) the Caisse Legendre (which was now collapsing); (2) the *rentes* on the Hôtel de ville (the rock of credit on which the state ultimately stood); (3) the military treasurers; (4) the various food and equipment suppliers including, by name, Titon (the greatest of the gun suppliers); (5) the navy treasurers (revealingly, two places below the various army treasurers); (6) the bankers (who could sustain themselves more easily by rotating bills of exchange through various places); (7) discharging new *assignations*; (8) the various other royal treasurers; and (9) the payment of *gages* and the reimbursement of capital on suppressed venal offices.[58] The Extraordinaire des Guerres was clearly a very high priority, and the duc de Noailles—for the same reasons as those that influenced Desmaretz—held to this approach. Given the volume of prolonged short-term credit notes in circulation, he had little choice.

It is not possible to state with certainty the number of Extraordinaire des Guerres bearer bills outstanding on 1 September 1715—the day of Louis XIV's death—but by 31 January 1716 the unconverted War bills presented to the commission of ex-*intendants* conducting the *visa* of these instruments came to a total of 52,319,513 *livres*, as against 8,960,695 *livres* for the navy. Naturally this excluded all those which were not brought forward to the *visa* commission, and we know that people often held on to instruments despite 'last chance' decrees promulgated by the

[56] BNF F-23621: *déclaration*, 2 March 1715; F-27022: *édit*, August 1715.

[57] CCG, III, 634–5: 'Mémoire de M. Desmaretz', August 1715; BNF F-27022: *édit*, August 1715; Howard J. Shakespeare, *France: The Royal Loans—Les Emprunts Royaux, 1689–1789* (Shrewsbury, 1986), 86.

[58] CCG, III, 632: [*Mémoire* of Desmaretz], 1 May 1715.

crown.[59] At most, though, there were probably no more than 5–10 million *livres* of undeclared War bills still in circulation. All in all, then, for all the restraint exercised in issuing more bearer bills, the Extraordinaire had not made serious progress in reducing its enormous liabilities, worth around half its annual expenditure, since the spring of 1709. The repayment of some liabilities surely kept some credit flowing towards the Extraordinaire, and Desmaretz was determined to avoid re-escalating its debts. But it was as well that this was the case, for the continued failure to discharge perhaps 20 million *livres* of debts relating to the 1706 and 1707 *exercices* was an enormous millstone round the Extraordinaire's neck. Moreover, up to 10 million of the 52 million *livres* of debts the *visa* acknowledged were accounted for by interest bills on undischarged original capital. All of this made it harder in the final years of the War of the Spanish Succession to find short-term loans, never mind at reasonable rates—a problem that was compounded by the misguided attempts to convert War bills into illiquid *rentes*, and the determination to hold the official annual interest on Extraordinaire des Guerres instruments at ludicrously low rates of 6–7 per cent.[60] To be fair, any conversions would have been difficult when the government was living hand to mouth in 1709–10. But once the immediate crisis had passed it might well have been wiser, as Desmaretz instinctively seems to have realized, to return to the policy of repaying prolonged short-term debts in order to attract the capital back into the financial system as fresh loans, this time to the Caisse Legendre and other primary revenue receivers. However, it did not really happen.

On 7 April 1716 the regency government announced the conversion process for the *billets* of the various military treasurers. The aim was less to reimburse the bills than to convert them (and other debts) into a single class of new *billets d'état*, in which the state for the first time assumed royal liability for the quantity of short-term paper in circulation. It involved a further *visa*, in which some 56 million *livres* of War bills were reduced to the sum value of only 38.5 million *livres*, thus saving the crown somewhere in the region of 17.5 million *livres*. This was achieved by dividing the holders of these instruments into four categories, and in some respects the liquidation was far more brutal than the conversion mooted in July the previous year. In category one were the army officers and those who had supplied funds for the troops, even those who had not sold on their bills: they were subject to a forced reduction of one-fifth of the face value of their bills. In category two were those holders to whom the state felt less of an obligation or who had bought up the bills for a reduced price and still held them: they suffered a two-fifths reduction in value. In category three were those who had profited from these bills while supplying the armies, charging huge amounts to accept discounted War bills—they lost three-fifths of the value of their bills. And in category four were those bills that had

[59] CCG, III, 681: 'Compte rendu de M. Desmaretz au Régent', 1716; Dom H. Leclercq, *Histoire de la Régence pendant la minorité de Louis XV* (3 vols, Paris, 1921), I, 297; Natalia Platonova, 'Le visa des papiers royaux en France au début du XVIIIe siècle', in Marie-Laure Legay, ed., *Les modalités de paiement de l'État moderne: Adaptation et blocage d'un système comptable* (Paris, 2007), 183.

[60] Malet, *Comptes*, 136–7. One suspects the 6–7 per cent level was to take account of purchasing at a discount, but it merely depressed the trading value of such bills.

passed through many hands, and which were now reduced to only one-fifth of their original value. The Regent Orléans shed crocodile tears for those army and navy officers now being hit by reductions, who had, he intoned, 'sacrificed their ease and spilled their blood for the service of the State', and who should not be exposed to such treatment but who could nevertheless take it on the chin, stoically.[61] What they made of this betrayal is not known but one can only imagine. The Regent's decision was symptomatic of a gap that was beginning to widen between the super-elites and the rest of the nobility, and which only got larger over the following decades.

The excessive amount of debt issued by the Extraordinaire des Guerres was not, to do them justice, something that the treasurers general had wanted to see. And it was not something that finance ministers in the *ancien régime*, with the exception of Chamillart, wanted to encourage. However, it happened. In addition to problems with Mint bills and *assignations*, the quantity of Extraordinaire short-term debt that was prolonged, followed by clumsy and desperate attempts to convert it, drove up the cost of borrowing and threatened to bring lending to a complete halt in 1712–13. To sound again a refrain now familiar in this book, this was putting France in great peril of complete military defeat as the logistical structures surrounding the army began, finally, to collapse altogether under the weight of junk financial instruments and the withdrawal of credit. Had Chamillart not overexposed the treasurers general of the Extraordinaire, and instead directed the *receveurs généraux des finances* to cover most of that debt much earlier in the war, in the fashion of 1710–15, then this might have promoted better credit flow and reduced interest payments a little, not least as primary receivers' instruments would usually have been subject to smaller write-downs by purchasers. As early as 1704 one financier noted how actual *assignations* drawn on the Extraordinaire's coffers (a sign, in itself, of the bastardization of this treasury) 'were always the worst and the most distant' (regarding their maturity) compared with those drawn upon other revenue receivers.[62] Certainly, the alternative approach of relying more on primary revenue receivers would have preserved the credit of the Extraordinaire des Guerres for real short-term and local emergencies and for the covering of bills of exchange. At the very least, the financial system would have been better coordinated.

By and large, the *contrôleurs généraux* who held office from 1708 down to the collapse of the absolute monarchy in 1787 recognized the need to maintain some discipline over short-term paper lending and overall government expenditure, by restricting military and naval treasurers in the issuing of promissory notes and other devices. But it was not always possible to do this successfully. With the advent of leading courtiers and *grands* in ministerial office during the 1750s, and the sudden massive increases of expenditure in the Seven Years War, the secretaries of state for War and the Marine authorized or acquiesced in huge issues of departmental bearer bills and other instruments once again, this time in a somewhat cavalier

[61] Léon Bouchard, *Système financier de l'ancienne monarchie* (Paris, 1891), 213; Seligmann, 127, 131.

[62] AN G^{7}1776, no. 483: request by Charpentier of Les Invalides, [1704].

manner and (unlike Chamillart) without the excuse that they did not know it would produce chaos. Although *contrôleur général* Bertin came to office in 1759 determined to clamp down on this, nevertheless in 1765, two years after the end of this worldwide conflict, the debts of the Extraordinaire still stood at 58.9 million *livres*, and those of the artillery and engineers at a further 21.5 million *livres*.[63] This was a sign of things to come, for in the 1780s the Naval Ministry under the maréchal de Castries ran up enormous debts to pay for rearmament, the development of the port infrastructure, and the expansion of the navy, with the tacit blessing of Louis XVI. The enormous dangers of allowing departmental debt to go unchecked were finally brought home when, at the start of 1787, Claude Baudard de Saint-James, one of the treasurers general of the navy, went bankrupt, much as La Touanne and Sauvion of the Extraordinaire des Guerres had done back in 1701. This time, however, the Assembly of Notables, which was to mark the end of the absolute monarchy, was just about to convene, and this collapse of one of the most powerful financiers in the kingdom—followed six months later by the equally spectacular fall of Antoine-Jean-François Mégret de Sérilly, treasurer general of the Extraordinaire des Guerres—did enormous damage to public confidence in royal finances. These implosions did nothing to help royal efforts to get fiscal reform through the assembly, and were followed soon afterwards by declining fisco-financier confidence in the monarchy's ability to meet its credit obligations.[64] A smooth transition to a more consultative monarchy, but with the king still in real charge, became impossible. France had seen the collapse of armed forces treasurers before, but this time the public as a whole was no longer willing to tolerate such mismanagement of short-term debt.

[63] I am exceedingly grateful to Joël Félix for providing me with the data from 1765 garnered from AN F[4]1009. It is worth noting that the combined Extraordinaire, artillery, and engineering debt of 1765 was, in 1715 monetary terms, less than the amount subject to the 1716 conversion (47 million *livres* as against 56 million *livres*). The amount of silver in the country was also greater than in 1715, thus lowering this equivalence even further in terms of financial pain. Moreover, the various War Ministry bearer bills of the Seven Years War accounted for a smaller proportion of the state's stopgap borrowing through paper instruments than had been the case in 1702–14. See also Joël Félix, *Finances et politique au siècle des Lumières: Le ministère L'Averdy, 1763–1768* (Paris, 1999), 52, 160, 164, 394.

[64] Legohérel, 341–54; J. F. Bosher, *French Finances 1770–1795: From Business to Bureaucracy* (Cambridge, 1970), 185–8.

10

Rent-Seeking in the Military Paymaster World

The degeneration of royal finances provided a set of threats, challenges, and opportunities for all those involved in handling the 'deniers royaux'. At a minimum, those serving the king in financial matters wanted to be protected from excessive liabilities. However, the men who handled the military finances, through the Extraordinaire des Guerres and loosely in conjunction with it, also had ambitions to improve their social status and their financial positions. One of the least appreciated aspects of Chamillart's tenure of ministerial office is that he failed to keep the military financiers and other leading suppliers under sufficient control: he allowed, if not actively connived at, the penetration of the corridors of power by a group of deeply self-interested men on a scale not seen since the 1650s. This was harmful to orderly government and contributed to the financial incontinence of the time. The activities and demands of these men may not have been as damaging as those of their predecessors under Fouquet, but they added to royal expenses for the same reasons that exchange costs increased. France was running a financial and supply system that was being overstretched by geopolitical circumstances and strategic needs, and it functioned under poor ministerial oversight. There was, additionally, a willingness to take seriously and accept with insufficient caution some of the self-interested proposals for short-term financial palliatives that in fact set up longer-term dangers. It is therefore worth examining what sort of rent-seeking—lobbying for personal gain and protection—was going on in the Extraordinaire des Guerres and associated circles, and how successful it was.

Although there were narrowing opportunities for outright corruption from the 1660s, the rise of Mint bills and *billets de l'Extraordinaire des Guerres*, coinage manipulations, poor appropriations, and greater compensation and reimbursements all provided scope after 1700 for rent-seeking that was wider in scope than in the first forty years of Louis XIV's personal rule. Furthermore, the poor grasp of affairs on the part of Chamillart, the weak hand dealt to Desmaretz in 1708, and the intertwining of junior ministerial positions with the war financiers and big supply companies also made for a degree of complaisance and even outright favouritism towards the world of military finance, only some of which was really justified by necessity. At the very least, manipulations inside the Extraordinaire des Guerres and deficient oversight in the War Ministry and Finance Ministry ensured that while soldiers and small-scale suppliers suffered tremendous hardship, some people really did quite nicely out of the war. At worst, from what we can ascertain from the surviving evidence, the behaviour of these men in government and in the paymaster treasuries contributed to the further discrediting of financial instruments, higher war costs, and a general air of financial decay. Prices were inflated, and such inflated prices were often more or less accepted by the ministries. Furthermore, there were diversions of funds for legitimate purposes, but also some illegitimate or at least unauthorized diversions, especially of financial instruments. Additionally, anyone in a position to profit from financial instruments, especially Mint bills and those of the Extraordinaire des Guerres, seems to have been inclined to do so, which, given such difficult circumstances, is not surprising.

COMPENSATION AND INDEMNIFICATION IN THE EXTRAORDINAIRE DES GUERRES

To begin with authorized activity, we should look at the compensation and indemnification arrangements for financiers associated with the Extraordinaire. When the appropriations and payments mechanisms for this treasury failed to deliver, or when the Extraordinaire was forced into discounting instruments to make its payments, this cost it a lot of money, and in the 1700s such costs rocketed beyond anything seen since the 1650s. The demand for and need for compensation and indemnities in handling royal finances were far greater for the Extraordinaire des Guerres—and for other armed forces suppliers and financiers—than for primary revenue receivers such as the *receveurs généraux* and the farmers general, largely by virtue of the fact that they had to pass a lot of money to people outside the royal fisco-financier networks. The essential roles of the suppliers and remitters were also so tied up with the projection of royal power that they had to be protected from the worst consequences of revenue reductions and counterproductive financial and monetary policies. They could not be allowed to fail.

In the course of the decade 1691–1701 it became increasingly evident that the treasurers general of the Extraordinaire were being forced into shouldering a level of structural debt in their operations that the existing arrangements could not adequately service. From its 'taxations' (rake-offs) the Extraordinaire was expected to deal with the payment of interest on loans it contracted, as well as losses associated with coinage manipulations and exchange rate charges. In the early years of the Nine Years War it was up to the treasurer general to make whatever arrangements he felt necessary to get money to where it was needed, and the government took the rather stern line that the costs of doing this were his responsibility. However, as the scale of these costs and losses mounted, the treasurers general found themselves overwhelmed. By the mid-1690s ad hoc additional compensation payments were made by the Trésor royal to the Extraordinaire, sometimes for six-figure sums, but by 1695 the absence of any prior agreements or settled arrangements with the king was having a corrosive effect upon the army's financing.[1] The problem exploded in the summer of 1701 when one of the two treasurers general,

[1] AN G^{7}1778, no. 110: note on Turmenyes, 14 April 1706.

Charles Renouard de La Touanne, went bankrupt, most likely through negligent juggling of his own private finances with his official responsibilities. He had borrowed 9,000,987 *livres* to fund his official responsibilities and additionally owed army officers 400,000 *livres*. On the credit side he had only 6 million *livres* of resources from the king. Rapidly convinced that a formal legal bankruptcy would mean the destruction of the credit 'of those who handle our money or who are involved in our financial affairs', Louis issued a declaration in which the government stepped in to cover the outstanding liabilities, assigning reimbursement to the creditors on the already heavily committed *aides* and *gabelles* receipts from the *fermes générales*, with 5 per cent interest until final discharge. Later that year it was also understood by the public that the 3.6 million *livres* generated by the reorganization of the Extraordinaire's treasurers general would go to the king to help him repay some of La Touanne's creditors. Nevertheless, the fallout from La Touanne's collapse lasted over ten years: the interest payments on the whole affair cost the king 1 million *livres*, paid—like the capital reimbursements—out of the revenues of the *fermes générales*, while he lost over 6 million *livres* in total. The message was sent out that Louis XIV would support the debts of his greatest forces paymasters, as he was already doing secretly and with no fanfare for the *fermes générales*. This certainly upheld the credit of the Extraordinaire and calmed nerves quickly, but at the price of exacerbating a pre-existing principal-agent problem and generating moral hazard on a scale not seen in French finances for decades. To try to reduce the risks of corruption, the message of financial support for creditors was complemented, in the declaration of 3 June 1701, by a reiteration of the old ordinances, stretching back to 1532, against the holding-back or perversion of royal funds to the detriment of the state: in future the death penalty would be applied, and the sentence would not be commutable by judges. Unfortunately this draconian announcement probably cast a cloud over the king's willingness to help La Touanne's creditors, for it sent a worrying message to fisco-financiers who only prospered or even kept afloat because they had the opportunity to park dormant royal funds with other men and agencies to gain interest.[2]

Already, a month before La Touanne's collapse, the other treasurer general, Arnauld, had found himself overcommitted and was removed from office.[3] With both main treasurers general having foundered, and only Arnauld's junior colleague Mongelas holding the state up, additional steps were taken to maintain the credit of the Extraordinaire des Guerres. It was now clear that the ad hoc, arbitrary injection of extra funds was an unsuitable way to support the treasurers general when a large borrowing requirement year after year would clearly exist for the foreseeable future. Accordingly, Chamillart increased the number of treasurers general from two to three to spread the load. More importantly, he altered the risk-sharing arrangements between the king and the treasurers general for 1702 in order

[2] Saint-Simon, VIII, 302–5; Dangeau, VIII, 118, 252; Claeys, II, 850; BNF F-21054: *déclaration*, 3 June 1701; F-23741: *déclaration*, 12 December 1711; CCG, II, 310: Morant to Chamillart, 5 March 1706, Chamillart's marginalia.

[3] AN $G^7$1780, no. 181: *mémoire* on Extraordinaire, [1707]; $G^7$1775, no. 32: *mémoire* on Arnauld, [*c.*1701–2]; no. 233: Arnauld to Chamillart, April 1703.

to reflect monetary difficulties and the increased need for foreign exchange and credit: instead of the king expecting a treasurer general's *taxations* to cover losses and interest charges, the latter should bear no more than 300,000 *livres* of these costs. The king would ultimately cover anything above and beyond this through additional allocations to the treasurer general from the Trésor royal. Without such a royal guarantee nobody had been willing to take on the role of treasurer general for 1702. In other words, the new treasurer general Montargis—La Touanne's step-son, no less—had wrung this concession out of Louis. Thereafter it became the standard expectation for *exercices* that fell during wartime. The king also came to pick up the losses on Mint bill discounting.[4]

The size of the claims for indemnity could be huge, as we can see from Table 10.1, which shows the compensation sought by the treasurers general of the Extraordinaire.

Table 10.1 Extraordinaire des Guerres compensation claims

DUTY-YEAR	INTEREST ON BORROWING AND DISCOUNT LOSSES ON INSTRUMENTS TRADED—SUMS CLAIMED (in *livres*)
1704	4,728,010
1705	5,391,794
1706	10,609,343
1707	5,015,525
1708	564,989
1709	1,557,377

Source: Figures have been taken from: AN G^{7}1786, no. 218: memorandum, 19 June 1710. N.B. there were few bearer bill issues in 1708 (see Chapter 9).

This reflects the patterns of borrowing, Mint bill discounting, and international remittances covered by the Extraordinaire des Guerres, though it is not possible to separate out the relative strengths of these influences. There is no evidence these claims were not met, even if they were met with yet more degraded paper instruments that would in turn require further compensation for discount losses, and so on...

Chamillart was very keen that this compensation arrangement be kept secret, not least because the public would otherwise identify what nowadays would be thought of as very serious problems of moral hazard and principal-agent relations. As Chamillart put it, for the financiers involved in the Extraordinaire 'the profit is certain',[5] while all losses but a manageable 300,000 *livres* were covered. It was better that the public should think that the treasurers general and their associates were

4 SHD A^{1}1613, no. 185: Montargis to Chamillart, 18 April 1702; no. 199: Pleneuf to Chamillart, 14 November 1702; A^{1}1699, no. 199: Pleneuf to Chamillart, 14 November 1702; AN G^{7}1775, no. 33: *mémoire* by Arnauld, [1704]; no. 107: 'Ordonnances expediées... 1702', list, 3 August [1703]; no. 306: Chamillart to [Le Rebours?], 9 December 1703; G^{7}1782, no. 89: Chamillart to [Desmaretz?], 11 June 1708; G^{7}1011: memorandum: 'Fonds et surseances. demandez', 17 May 1708.

5 SHD A^{1}1699, no. 148: Jérôme de Pontchartrain to Chamillart, 31 January 1703 (quotation from Chamillart's marginalia).

kept under control by ministers and that they were liable for all costs, so that they would therefore act responsibly in the *apparent* absence of unlimited royal guarantees. Nevertheless, as time went on it gradually became more obvious to the public what had been agreed, to the point at which financiers and suppliers happily accepted paper instruments (mainly bearer bills and bills of exchange) from the Extraordinaire and then, having used them in their own payments, claimed compensation from the king for the losses they bore on these instruments.[6] Though it is not possible to put a global figure on the amount involved, indemnities became a larger and larger part of royal expenditure. Growing awareness of the opportunities this presented only discouraged paper-holders from squeezing their dues out of revenue-raising officials and farmers, and gave the latter, in turn, a chance to hold on to any revenues that came in above the rough estimate the public placed upon their yields.

The treasurers general and their associates—who had various non-liability agreements with the crown—were not entirely cosseted from the unfolding financial catastrophe of the 1700s, but after 1701 the crown did afford them protection on a scale not enjoyed by other fisco-financiers, never mind army and navy officers. This extended to blocking judicial proceedings against them for debts. In June 1707 Chamillart ordered the halting of all civil debt enforcement procedures against Montargis. At the start of 1708, when the Extraordinaire was threatening to implode under the weight of debt, Mongelas even had his office of treasurer general and its emoluments—the *taxations* and *gages*—sequestered by a court order, whereupon his creditors began trying to sell it! This was blocked, no doubt because it represented an unacceptable challenge to the king's right to install men of his choosing at the head of a para-royal treasury so closely tied to the great prerogative power of making war. The court orders continued, though.[7] Under pressure from creditors, in late summer 1708 Montargis asked the king to uphold the right of all financial transactions involving the Extraordinaire, and by extension those involved in issuing and discharging its instruments, to be judged solely before the military tribunal of the *Connétablie et Maréchaussée* sitting in the Paris palace of justice. But this would come at a cost. One government adviser feared that if such paper were only subject to the *Connétablie*,

> it is to be feared… this would diminish the credit of these sorts of instruments which are traded, and the same for all other *billets*, and bills of exchange which are made out or drawn by merchant traders, bankers, business men or others.

What made matters more complicated was the proclivity of treasurers general and agents inside the Extraordinaire to issue bills that were ostensibly official but were really to cover borrowing that had no direct relationship to the Extraordinaire's activities. Such was the problem of agency government in which the finances were

[6] Lüthy, I, 249; SHD Ya2: Chamillart to Vrevins, 12 January 1708.

[7] AN $G^7$1782, no. 61: Mongelas to [Desmaretz], 26 June 1708; no. 70: Mongelas to ?, 11 July 1708; no. 131: placet to Desmaretz by Ferlet, [August 1708]; $G^7$1011: Mongelas to Chamillart, 16 January 1708; memorandum entitled 'Extraord^{re}. des guerres', [January 1708].

handled in the manner of a franchise. In the end it appears the crown did opt to shield the Extraordinaire and its agents from the irritating activity of litigants and civil courts, but it came at the price of further diminishing the credibility of Extraordinaire debt instruments, which (for this and other reasons) went into free fall during 1709.[8] Formal associates of the Extraordinaire treasurers general were also in trouble by 1707, and in this case ministers had to protect them too in order to keep the entire non-liability arrangements for their participation in the Extraordinaire secret.[9] This only further dented the credibility of the paymaster system in general. There was, then, no easy way of supporting the credit rating of the Extraordinaire if sufficient effort were not made to reduce its volume of debt. This became abundantly obvious in the summer of 1709. *Contrôleur général* Desmaretz—under enormous pressure from the banking crisis and sharp revenue contractions—grew increasingly frustrated with treasurer general Mongelas. The essential problem was that the Finance Ministry was now building massive amounts of protection into contractual arrangements for the Extraordinaire, yet by this time a treasurer general was faced with such a gargantuan debt problem that even the Herculean Mongelas could not procure the necessary fresh loans.[10]

Absolving men from liability for Extraordinaire debts as either treasurers general or as associates, common sense suggests, led them into contracting or guaranteeing more borrowing than they would have been willing to authorize had they had some sort of longer-term liability. These flotations might have been useful in the short term, but over months and years they became a nightmare to handle, as we have seen. Although two associates bailed out in the face of mounting liabilities in early 1704, on the whole associates did not call a halt when the Extraordinaire's borrowing levels became extreme by 1706. It is worth noting in this regard that *commis* of the Extraordinaire, who issued bearer bills on the treasurers general to make payments out in the provinces or with the army, also in theory had no liability for the sums involved if the expenditure had been ordered and they had acted properly, at least as far as the crown was concerned. Moreover, they deliberately claimed royal legal protection for dealings that were in reality private ones too.[11] How responsibility and restraint might have been maintained, though, is a mystery. At best the king would have had to authorize other incentives for these men to take on the risks, and at a time of hand-to-mouth resourcing of para-royal agencies other methods of remuneration would also have been unreliable, if not worse. The only way to avoid the problem was to prevent the Extraordinaire becoming a gigantic credit machine in the first place. The Extraordinaire des Guerres was not meant to be a large-scale lending bank or 'corps intermédiaire' for royal borrowing, and to use it as such invited

[8] AN $G^7$1782, nos 148–9: Montargis to Desmaretz, 12 September 1708, and related note (quotation from latter).

[9] AN $G^7$1780, no. 181: *mémoire*, [1707]; $G^7$1782, no. 62: royal council order, 3 March 1707.

[10] AN $G^7$1785, no. 124: de La Garde to Desmaretz, 10 August 1709, latter's marginalia; $G^7$1784, no. 319: de La Garde to Desmaretz, 23 August 1709.

[11] SHD Ya2: Chamillart to d'Angervilliers, 12 October 1707; Bib. Maz. Ms. 2626, fos 58v, 59v: 'Memoire. Billets et decomptes de l'extraord. de la guerre', n.d.

enormous problems with maintaining the war effort at the sharp end, aggravated the principal-agent problem, and impaired royal sovereignty.

CORRUPTION AND RENT-SEEKING IN THE EXTRAORDINAIRE DES GUERRES

Given that the monarchy did use the Extraordinaire as a 'banque', the steps taken to protect and indemnify the military paymasters in the face of the mounting financial chaos were both necessary and morally justifiable, as long as the financiers involved were behaving honestly towards the king and their creditors. However, there is plenty of evidence that in the many ways military paymasters and other suppliers sought to protect and advance their interests—including in their claims for compensation—a degree of corruption, moral or legal, was present. It is not, though, a simple black-and-white matter.

At its loosest, political corruption involves the exploitation of office, power, or influence for personal/private gain, but this is essentially a modern definition, founded upon ideals of the separation of the state from private interest, and upon an idea of the state as an arbiter of all private interests. It is simply inadequate for understanding what was going on under Louis XIV or his immediate successors. France was a patrimonial absolute monarchy in which the king enjoyed a monopoly on the various marques of sovereign power, as defined by jurists. It was also a dynastic state in which the myriad private interests of the monarch's subjects were fused together, successfully or unsuccessfully, in an effort to maintain order and advance the interests of the country as represented first and foremost through the ruling dynasty, its prestige, and its influence abroad. Financial corruption in such a system of government is best defined as diverting revenues for personal gain (or personal protection) without the permission (tacit or explicit) of one's superior in the hierarchies of authority that met at the very top in the person of the king.[12] Alas, even from the 1670s this was not a clear-cut matter. To modern eyes, in the fisco-financier and entrepreneurial system of the French state there might appear to be no sharp distinction between opportunistic reimbursement of expenses and straightforward theft, and contemporaries were certainly uneasy about indemnity claims in a franchise system, especially when a farming contract was the basis for operations. On top of this, the growing complexity of royal finances continued to muddy the waters. In a period characterized by extreme cash shortages and financial instruments, the distribution of devalued instruments to creditors or those one was supposed to pay—and even discounting such instruments oneself—could be construed as corruption, especially if one claimed compensation from the king. But whether it deserved blanket condemnation is arguable. Be that as it may, if there was, as Richard Bonney has rightly argued, a reduced potential for serious

[12] See Rowlands, 16–17, for more discussion of the problem of conceptualizing corruption in this period.

illicit gain in state service under Louis XIV,[13] the diminished scope for graft rested in part upon ensuring that those in significant positions of power did not abuse the opportunity to talk ministers and ministry officials into favouring their interests unduly. Stealing was harder, but manipulating the system for still rather lucrative gain remained possible, especially when foreign exchange was involved.

Rent-seeking in the Extraordinaire des Guerres was more than just about getting protection from losses by securing indemnity agreements, structured payments, and legal injunctions. We should not underestimate the potential for legitimate and illegitimate gain, as well as for minimizing their own financial pain, that the treasurers general of the Extraordinaire des Guerres enjoyed, even in the tightened-up system after the early 1680s. Not least this came from proximity to the ministers. It is true that there was a risk of bankruptcy in their line of business, and Louis Jossier de La Jonchère did fall from grace spectacularly in 1683–84. Yet Gérard Michel de La Jonchère—no relation—was in no real difficulties at the end of the final wartime duty-year in December 1714.[14] Rather more of a risk than becoming completely insolvent under a mountain of unpayable net debt—especially after they received sizeable indemnities in the eighteenth century—was that a treasurer general would face a crisis of liquidity. Arnauld's claim in 1704 that all treasurers general had been ruined was self-serving and self-pitying hyperbole, especially from a man who was now a farmer general![15] The office of treasurer general of the Extraordinaire, if exercised with diligence, could lead on to the highest fisco-financier position in the realm, that of *Garde du Trésor royal*, or could provide a stepping stone to professional advancement or social ascension for immediate offspring and later descendants. It was really rather an attractive position in the king's service for an upwardly mobile family.

More immediately, the principal concern of a treasurer general was to protect or build up his wealth, and the position provided plenty of opportunities for this. The emoluments that came with the office had greater potential as a source of wealth-enhancement than is realized. Although associates and people with shares in the office would have to take a proportion of the remuneration from the *gages* and *taxations*, and these were also used to cover administrative costs and salaries for the scores of *commis* employed, the amount left over for treasurers general to devote to their own situation still put their incomes amongst the largest in France. The real gains came from staying in office over the long term and eventually getting out without debt liabilities. A document written by one official in the ministries in 1703 gives a strong hint that a treasurer general could personally expect to gain around 50,000 *livres* per annum, and thus over a forty-year period in which a family held the office (and some, such as the Dureys, did) a treasurer could cover the entire purchase price, and still have the right to sell it on and recoup his original costs. What appears to emerge, and it reflects the gambling nature of these men, is

[13] Richard Bonney, 'France, 1494–1815', in Richard Bonney, ed., *The Rise of the Fiscal State in Europe, c.1200–1815* (Oxford, 1999), 127.

[14] CCG, III, 567: Desmaretz to Le Rebours, 28 December 1714. La Jonchère was ruined in 1723, however.

[15] AN G^{7}1775, no. 33: memorandum by Arnauld, [1704].

that treasurers general did the job in wartime in extremely trying circumstances because they either hoped to gain advancement thereby, or they hoped for a long enjoyment of the post in peacetime: service for years would allow them to amass a lot of money through the vastly overvalued official *taxation* that gave them a rake-off of 4 *deniers* for every *livre* that passed through their agency. In particular, after 1702 the 300,000 *livres* per annum built into the *taxations* to cover interest payments on Extraordinaire debts would probably—if continued in peacetime—be freed up for the treasurer general to use as he pleased.[16] It should therefore not be surprising that the treasurers general were particularly keen to pocket their *taxations*, and this led them to throw their weight about or exercise influence to their own advantage. Treasurers general were supposed to take their *taxation* on a rolling basis, as each item of expenditure came up. Yet at least some of them, knowing the projected annual allocations for the bread supply companies, would take their entire rake-off in a single bite, perhaps as much as 200,000 *livres*, in the process disrupting the finances of the *munitionnaires*.[17] This depended, to an extent, on how closely a particular treasurer general was aligned to the *vivres* company in question. What this shows is how ruthless treasurers general could be with other financiers without actually straying over the line into theft.[18]

Just as much of a moral grey area (at the time, as now) is the issue of the use of political influence to gain advantages in a perfectly legal way, something which will crop up on several occasions in this chapter. Here, some further attention to what has been suggested in other chapters should yield insight. Until 1708–9 and the advent to ministerial power of Desmaretz and then Voysin, the treasurers general were able to persuade Chamillart and the king to follow their self-serving advice on a number of occasions, and even after the downfall of Chamillart they were still favoured beyond what their undoubtedly essential situation might naturally suggest. The proposals emanating from the treasurers general were self-serving in that they might benefit or protect themselves personally, or their suggestions might enhance the war effort in the short term and thus make themselves appear fully committed to it. But in either case their prescriptions could be very dangerous. There was precedent for this, when, towards the end of the Nine Years War, the treasurers general had successfully demanded the *receveurs généraux des finances* hand over some funds by means of bearer bills rather than cash or bills of exchange. They sought this arrangement partly so that they could, in turn, invoice the crown for interest payments stemming from the inevitable delays in getting this money using such promissory notes.[19] In the following decade they had greater success.

[16] AN G[7]1775, no. 32: memorandum on Arnauld, [*c.*1701–2]; no. 103: memorandum on discharging Montargis' debts, [1703]; G[7]1779, no. 8: 'Conditions sur lesquelles...', 11 December 1706.

[17] Iung, I, 68.

[18] They also billeted troops on their debtors, held on to *assignations* from the *receveurs généraux* on whom they were drawn if the man paid up from another source, and, when involved in *affaires extraordinaires*, mercilessly pursued venal office-holders for outstanding payments in the courts: e.g. AN G[7]1786, no. 244: Paparel to Desmaretz, 11 July 1710. All this was legal.

[19] AN G[7]1774, no. 12: *receveurs généraux* to Pontchartrain, 30 January 1697; André Navereau, *Le logement et les ustenciles de gens de guerre de 1439 à 1789* (Poitiers, 1924), 191–2.

Up to 1704 one still gets a feeling that the treasurers general were the agents of the ministers rather than important advisers. But as affairs turned worse, Chamillart became overwhelmed, more pronounced cronyism started to entrench itself in the Finance and War ministries in a more insidious way than previously, and the influence of some treasurers general grew and remained strong for a period of about five years. Some came to shape overall strategic financial questions, and thus the war effort, far more than in previous or subsequent decades.

The indices of this are multiple, and it was not just a question of jostling with ministers over funding priorities, or proffering advice on a range of matters connected with royal finance. From early 1706 the treasurers general of the Extraordinaire stepped up their pressure on the crown, using their influence to the detriment of other sorts of financiers and in such a way as to alter the nature and form of some financial instruments. Treasurer general Mongelas, who was in any case an impressive operator, seems to have had considerable influence over Chamillart, whom he pushed into carrying through an alarming extension of damaging policies with his short-term interests at heart. In February 1706 Chamillart greatly increased the number of Mint bills with a value of 500 *livres* to allow Mongelas and other treasurers to discharge their bills of exchange.[20] Three months later, also at the request of Mongelas, Chamillart allowed him to issue payment orders upon local *commis* of the *receveurs généraux* in the form of *rescriptions* with priority payment, even though it was normally the *receveurs généraux* themselves who issued such documents. For months to come Mongelas was locked in a struggle with a number of these men to get payments out of them. What Mongelas had done in these few months was persuade Chamillart to inflate the volume of Mint bills beyond all reasonable bounds, and to bypass the *assignation* system, instead of restoring confidence in cash and paper in Paris, with the effect that the appropriations system in the months and years ahead became even more raddled. Then in November Chamillart authorized Mongelas to strip a large number of leading fisco-financiers of their paper holdings the following March. This was, to be sure, tantamount to the seizure of massive advances in cash and paper for the following autumn months.[21] And it was a highly arbitrary move that did more harm than good, and as it turned out helped dry up finances by October 1707, to Chamillart's very painful despair. By the end of 1706 the treasurers general were in some respects taking over the initiative from Chamillart in assigning revenues: by negotiating bills of exchange for the 1707 *exercice* on future funds due to come from various *affaires extraordinaires*, Montargis forced Chamillart to order *intendants* to release this money, which he had not planned to do for this purpose.[22] As the Extraordinaire entered a crisis in the summer of 1707, thanks to the drawing of large quantities of bills of exchange, Chamillart was forced to react with funds in ways he had not anticipated doing, and he was by now bitterly resentful of 'the lack of help that

[20] AN G^{7}1778, no. 52: memorandum by Mongelas, 17 February 1706.

[21] AN G^{7}1778, nos 123–4: memorandum by Mongelas, 8 May 1706, and list of *receveurs généraux*; no. 146: note from Mongelas to Chamillart, 14 June 1706; no. 236: [Mongelas to Chamillart], [November 1706]; no. 239: [same], 13 November 1706.

[22] AN G^{7}1778, nos 266–70: Chamillart to various *intendants*, 19 December 1706.

I am receiving from the treasurer [Montargis]', who in turn responded angrily to Chamillart's chastisement.[23] To compound the growing chaos in appropriating funds within the Finance Ministry, the treasurers general were thus bouncing Chamillart into major, sometimes structural, funding decisions. It was only in 1709 that the ministers restored an adequate degree of control over these people, and that was in large part because the available revenues were now so paltry that a tight rationing of expenditure and closer Finance Ministry supervision had to be brought in.

Whether they were exercising undue influence or not, the big war financiers and suppliers were in any case highly favoured by the monarchy. Although ministers said one thing to some officials and another to others, the evidence is abundant that the big financial and supply contractors (as well as the rank-and-file troops) were the ministers' real priority most of the time in the difficult years after 1706, whatever the nuances of this. By October 1709 the most essential thing for supporting the armies was to meet payments to the grain suppliers and the directors of the *vivres*, that is, the big entrepreneurs, not just the ordinary bakers (or troop pay).[24] If pay arrears for the most important troops were kept at tolerable levels, those for other units, for the officers, and for local small-scale contractors built up in a crippling fashion. Meanwhile, those who had done the serious lending, either in Paris and Lyon or on the northern frontiers where intense warfare was ongoing, were getting a fair amount of the money. The pattern of ministerial direction on spending, of course, suited somewhat the treasurers general of the Extraordinaire des Guerres: although from early 1708 they had less autonomy than previously, there was still room for a lot of manoeuvring, and the Finance Ministry was now formally helping them to string out their payments and to maintain their stamina. Their correspondents and potential creditors among the most important suppliers were also kept solvent. All of this was, in effect, a further extension of the protection offered by the ministers to their favoured financiers and suppliers.

Opportunities for gain, or for minimizing their financial pain at the expense of others, thus came in a number of forms. Some were distasteful and at odds with the spirit of the king's interests, but those described so far (and other operations such as exchange arbitrage when moving money to other currency zones like Alsace) were not outrightly corrupt. All this was authorized, or at least not directly counter to ministerial directions. But in such a complex and large-scale system of remittances and payment mechanisms, the opportunities for the treasurers general of the Extraordinaire des Guerres to protect themselves or advance their own interests in an *ultra vires* manner were also there to be taken. Some activities involved stepping way over the line into outright abuse of either the king or those who depended upon them.

[23] CCG, II, 423: Chamillart to Le Gendre, 16 July 1707; AN G^{7}1780, no. 156: Montargis to Chamillart, 14 July 1707.

[24] CCG, III, 127: Desmaretz to d'Angervilliers, 23 May 1709; III, 222: Desmaretz to La Houssaye and other *intendants*, 6 October 1709; Ars. Ms. 4494 fo. 11r: 'Discours de M^r. Paris de la Montagne…', n.d.; AN G^{7}1784, nos 337 and 338: 'Etat' copy, [*c.* 23 October 1709].

To begin with, there appear to have been ways in which the treasurers general could make money out of dubious lending to the crown, not least because there was an opaqueness in their debt contracting arrangements that made it possible to shield the real lenders even from the prying eyes of War Ministry *commis* stationed in their Paris bureaux. Treasurers general could, in effect, issue bearer bills on themselves to straw men and associates, and thereby pocket the interest. Second, Forbonnais, who saw more of the papers than are left to us, argued that treasurers general of the armed forces in the Nine Years War and the War of the Spanish Succession exaggerated the amount of money that failed to come in from revenue sources on time and in the right form. They then failed to pass on such funds to troops and suppliers, instead forcing bearer bills on them, or they indulged in fictional borrowing to make these payments. This came to be seen 'indecently [...] as a right attached to their office', and they could make interest-payment indemnity claims for such supposed shortfalls. At times when it knew that *assignations* and funds *had* been transmitted regularly this left the government, unaware of the ruses involved, puzzled.[25]

This brings on the problem of how treasurers general disobeyed or distorted ministerial orders about making items of expenditure. It was not so much a matter of simple stealing as of diverting funds to prop up one's financial activities as one saw fit. Though his occupation of the two major offices of state was supposed to bring greater coordination to the war effort, Chamillart's poor oversight of financial allocations during most of his tenure of power allowed the treasurers general of the Extraordinaire to string out their payments selectively, with unexpectedly disruptive effects, and gave them far too much leeway in deciding what to prioritize. Taking a stance that would have been anathema to his predecessor Louvois, Chamillart even beseeched his fellow minister Jérôme de Pontchartrain not to ask him to intervene in too much of the detail of the treasurers' work. Accordingly, from as early as February 1703, those who were supposed to receive the king's money suffered more than they need have done—even favoured men like the arms entrepreneur Titon. By February 1706 Chamillart had to admit that he had no idea whether the Extraordinaire treasurer general for 1705 still owed the army of Italy any money.[26] This was no way to run a state by this period. After February 1708 Desmaretz, as the new *contrôleur général*, was not only determined to re-establish order in the appropriations of revenues for the War Ministry, he also saw a greater involvement of the Finance Ministry in the Extraordinaire des Guerres as an integral part of ensuring that the king's money was well used. But the quid pro quo was closer management of actual expenditure by the Finance Ministry, and Desmaretz' orders did not always accord with the wishes of the War Ministry, the treasurers general, or other military suppliers. However, by summer 1710 close Finance Ministry control was proving impractical 'because of continual changes' of

[25] Forbonnais, II, 60 (quotation); SHD A[1]1965, no. 61: Chamillart to d'Andrezel, 23 February 1706.

[26] SHD A[1]1699, no. 148: Jérôme de Pontchartrain to Chamillart, 31 January 1703, Chamillart's marginalia; no. 271: Titon to Chamillart, 17 February 1703; A[1]1965, no. 61: Chamillart to d'Andrezel, 23 February 1706.

circumstances, and because of the volume of work involved.[27] These efforts notwithstanding, ministers did not want, and could not afford, to pry too deeply into the registers of the Extraordinaire to confront the treasurers general with evidence of corruption. This would be to risk further breakdowns and hiatuses in the system. In order to keep credit flowing, a certain licence to partake in questionable manipulation of the king's revenues was in fact still allowed, even after the king decreed the death penalty in 1701 for those *comptables* who diverted royal funds without approval. As stated explicitly in one memorandum, in order to maintain their creditworthiness treasurers had to make secret payments, 'the knowledge of which has to be kept hidden from a *contrôleur*', and also from ministers, the tone of the document suggests.[28]

Most of the time the treasurers general, if they diverted funds earmarked for paying the troops, did so to prevent the breakdown of credit and therefore, by extension, troop pay in other places. This happened a fortiori at times when the treasurers general were being given insufficiently liquid *assignations* and their own borrowing opportunities were limited.[29] Yet even if some of the diversions by treasurers and their agents were understandable and even justifiable, it was risking a breakdown of the war effort not to keep a tight rein on the actual realization of spending decisions. When considering diversions of funds it would not be fair to say the treasurers general were fundamentally and callously indifferent about the ordinary soldiers (at least not until the onset of severe financial crisis in 1709), who may well have been their principal concern.[30] However, to a large extent this was enlightened self-interest: if the field armies suffered logistical collapse and the troops melted away through lack of support then the Extraordinaire would face the full wrath of the king and his ministers. These diversions were often allowed by the ministers, as long as those originally destined to receive the funds were given other monies very soon afterwards and bankers' payments were not disrupted (which they sometimes were).[31] Nevertheless, in the provinces of 'la France profonde'—far from the frontlines, from the anxieties of the treasurers general, and from the attention of the ministers—it became quite routine for underlings in the Extraordinaire to be completely starved of cash or viable instruments, building up arrears running into millions when taken altogether.[32] At times Voysin sought to spread money around as evenly as possible but, owing to frontier priorities, he found this hard. Diversions happened under both *contrôleurs généraux* during the War of the Spanish Succession, indicating the cynicism of the treasurers general and just how hard it was to maintain strict discipline over them, even when these men were

[27] SHD Ya2: Voysin to Bernières, 26 April 1710 (quotation); to Malet, 25 July 1710; A[1]2272, no. 236: Le Meuve to Voysin, 9 July 1710; AN G[7]1782, no. 92: Sauroy to Chamillart, 21 June 1708.

[28] Legohérel, 290, citing AN G[7]1828, 'Mémoire sur la situation des Trésoriers de la Marine', 8 January 1704.

[29] SHD Ya2: Chamillart to Desmaretz, 27 December 1708.

[30] AN G[7]1779, no. 185: note from Mercy to Montargis, [May 1706]; no. 81: Montargis to [Chamillart], 10 January 1707.

[31] AN G[7]1122: 'Estat des depenses faites par le S[r]. Hogguer le jeune pour le service de 1712…', [1712].

[32] For example, SHD Ya2: Chamillart to Bâville, 6 July 1708.

pursuing options they felt were the least damaging for the war effort. And sometimes they were not being so publicly minded about the fisco-strategic situation.

As suggested above, it seems to have been expected that any unauthorized manipulations were to be kept to a minimum, that diverted funds would be made up very quickly, and that there should be no damage to the king's interests. That was the acid test for all manipulations by royal treasurers, but it was very hard to enforce. At times, ministers certainly suspected treasurers general of going too far in preserving or enhancing their own positions over and above the needs of the state. This was not on the scale of the 1630s–1650s, but outright perversions—even if the funds concerned were merely being 'borrowed'—were made possible because the deficient accounting of the time made it well nigh impossible to keep track of the incomings and outgoings of the central *caisses* of the Extraordinaire des Guerres. In 1710 Voysin castigated Duplessis for the disorder of his chief cashier, whom he accused of deliberately confusing his registers and summary rolls and of 'preventing the *controlleur* [auditor of the Extraordinaire] from seeing things clearly'. Cashiers and clerks may have been carrying on like this without the approval of the treasurers general but this is open to debate, and Mongelas, in 1709, was suspected of diverting the better *assignations* and fresh loans the Finance Ministry procured for him in order to ease his own creditworthiness and maybe even indulge his own fancies, instead of channelling them solely—as was *explicitly* intended—to the army of Flanders. Furthermore, the treasurers general tended to support their central staff against the demands of ministerial auditors.[33] The treasurers general were also on occasions quite willing to defy royal payment orders so as to protect their own circles at the expense of everyone else. By August 1709 the Franche-Comté had advanced to the crown some 600,000 *livres* of taxes during 1708, and this was now supposed to be reimbursed to the local communities in Extraordinaire bearer bills. However, contrary to orders, treasurer general Durey de Sauroy kept some bills back for other purposes and handed others to the duty *receveur général* of the province—his own brother.[34] What the Durey family was doing was protecting their wider family business at the expense of the king's subjects and other treasurers.

Yet the people who probably suffered the most from the manipulations by the treasurers general were not ordinary civilians but the army officers. Technically they were being paid, but in reality they were being ripped off. They had Mint bills, bills of exchange, and various Extraordinaire bearer bills pressed on them as payment of their salaries and as allowances for maintaining their regiments. To keep things going the officers had to mortgage their own property, borrow at very low interest rates from their senior officers (if they were lucky), trade the depreciating financial instruments for cash, or pay their suppliers with them—and the merchants often took them only at discounts that generally grew heavier as the war

[33] SHD Ya2: Chamillart to Sauroy, 30 January 1709; Voysin to Duplessis, 25 February 1710 (quotation); A[1]2272, no. 46: Quesneau to Voysin, 12 June 1710; AN G[7]1785, no. 124: de La Garde to Desmaretz, 10 August 1709, Desmaretz's marginalia; G[7]1784, no. 304: Desmaretz to [?], 3 May 1709.

[34] AN G[7]1783, nos 295–6: Le Guerchois to Desmaretz, 2 and 29 August 1709.

ground on. It should be noted that army officers were forced to take such instruments not just because Extraordinaire *commis* on the ground insisted (which they did), but because the treasurers general also intended this to be the case. The ministers themselves stepped in to try to ensure some proportionality between cash and instruments, but ministers were under few illusions that the Extraordinaire followed such directions.[35] By these means, the burden of paying for the war was also shared by the king's forces, and the treasurers general—when thrusting discredited instruments on them without clear ministerial direction—were as good as perverting royal funds. Sometimes they may well have had no choice when the whole of the financial world was in turmoil, and Montargis made a powerful argument to Chamillart that this was the case.[36] Nevertheless, at our most generous we can say that they did it without leaving much trace of remorse, and apart, perhaps, from the state of their nerves, they were not the ones to suffer.

The treasurers general were also making up losses by turning the screw on their own *commis*, who were in turn misappropriating and perverting army funds.[37] With ruthless bosses to answer to, it was not surprising that military paymasters' *commis* and junior treasurers were bywords for corruption throughout the Grand Siècle. Foremost in the mind of most *commis* was a desire to remain solvent, and hopefully advance their position. If this could be done honestly then most were satisfied with remaining within the rules, and some were scrupulous indeed.[38] But the turbulent financial circumstances of the War of the Spanish Succession blurred the boundaries between regular and abusive behaviour, as they did for the treasurers general at the apex of the organization. Some *commis* paid the most urgent invoices with available cash, rather than using it in the exact way the treasurer general or minister might instruct. Many *commis* would receive funds and then use them to discharge borrowing they had undertaken in previous years, which—if a sound principle to ensure continued availability of credit—was not something the war ministers always appreciated. This was at least more honourable than indulging in fraud or abusing those who depended upon good treatment from the *commis*. For decades *commis* had invested temporarily idle money in local revenue-gatherers: although a string of bankruptcies in the mid-1690s made them more wary, those *commis* who were well integrated into their local areas persisted in this practice and had greater opportunities for fraud in general.[39] Only as the cash-flow situation deteriorated during the War of the Spanish Succession did the incidence of diverting money for other investment decline. Beyond this, however, much of the abuse was not so much about making money from the king as defrauding his troops. *Commis* of the Extraordinaire could and did manipulate foreign exchange and the coinage system in frontier provinces and occupied zones to gain some advantage

[35] SHD Ya2: Voysin to various *intendants*, 17 January 1710; Voysin to Bernières, 23 September 1710.

[36] AN G[7]1779, no. 43: Montargis to Chamillart, 15 April 1707.

[37] SHD Ya2: Voysin to all *intendants*, 13 July 1709.

[38] CCG, III, 443: Voysin to Desmaretz, 2 October 1712.

[39] SHD A[1]1526, no. 259: *mémoire* by Mairon, August 1701; CCG, II, 39: *nouveaux convertis* of Montauban to Chamillart, 6 June 1700.

when paying the troops beyond the old provinces of the kingdom. The opportunities for this were greater after 1701 than they had been in any of Louis XIV's previous wars, and when *commis* of the Extraordinaire were not humble petit bourgeois but, as in several cases, leading merchants and even bankers—or men working with the bankers—it was especially hard to police currency manipulations that contributed to the rising costs of the war. Similar devious practices were associated with those involved with the *vivres*. Joseph Bonnier, who became treasurer of the estates of Languedoc in 1709, and died in 1726 with a fortune reputedly one of the greatest in the *ancien régime*, had begun as a central *commis* of treasurer general Montargis. Then in 1707 and 1708 he was both the local *commis* of the Extraordinaire in Languedoc and responsible for supplying food to the army in the Dauphiné. He seemingly siphoned off small amounts of food on a regular basis and substituted different, unauthorized crops to get a profit. He was also one of the biggest participants in *affaires extraordinaires*. Such conflicts of interest were even stronger higher up the chain, as we shall see in the following section.[40]

More significant than food fraud or currency manipulation, the Extraordinaire des Guerres itself was responsible to a very large extent for the depreciated market values of its own bearer bills, and the inflated costs that came with this. One can understand the need for *commis* to issue IOUs of some sort to units and suppliers so that they in turn could either borrow using them as collateral or sell them on for cash. It was not, however, speculators outside the military system who were always the ones to exploit the neediness of Extraordinaire *billet*-holders, far from it. There is too much anecdotal evidence of gross manipulation by *commis* to think the usurious discounting of Extraordinaire instruments was anything other than integral to this agency's activities. There had been some fraud and trafficking in War bills during the Nine Years War, but as with many irregularities this was mostly visible during the troubled years of 1692–4.[41] In the following decade it became an epidemic. In northern Italy *commis* insisted on taking a cut from *billets d'ustencile* they were issuing for discharge in Lyon on the grounds that it would have cost the same amount in foreign exchange—20 per cent—to produce the equivalent cash in the duchy of Milan. This was suspect to say the least, but it did reflect the mysterious world of foreign exchange costs and Chamillart reluctantly seems to have let it pass.[42]

Other practices, however, aroused the fury of Versailles. *Commis* used devious sleights of hand to avoid paying the troops what they were owed beyond their basic pay, providing them with *billets* in which they promised to pay the remaining allowances—but the officers of the units provided discharges for the full amount, and some *commis* could therefore later claim they owed them nothing more! This did nothing for the credibility of War bills. Whether such devious practices were

[40] DAPS, 251–2, 544; Sven Stelling-Michaud, 'Deux aspects du rôle financier de Genève pendant la guerre de Succession d'Espagne', *Bulletin de la société d'histoire et d'archéologie de Genève* 6(ii) (1936), 151; Michaud, 684; Chaussinand, 53; CCG, II, 438: Bâville to Chamillart, 23 December 1707; II, 440: D'Angervilliers to Chamillart, 28 October 1707.

[41] Ars. Ms. 4575, fo. 96r: Guiscard to Barbezieux, 7 May [1694].

[42] SHD A[1]1594, nos 221, 233: Chamillart to Bouchu, 10 and 25 May 1702.

involved or not, in order to meet their needs the regiments had to borrow more money from elsewhere or persuade others, such as merchants, artisans, and armourers, to accept War bills at discounts. When officers became desperate, some *commis* ruthlessly seized their chance of making a profit: they offered to accept back the bearer bills they had themselves issued, for a discount. One senior officer, Henri Colbert, chevalier de Maulevrier, credibly alleged in 1710 that over half of all infantry officers had sold their *billets d'ustencile*—representing major allowances for regimental upkeep—back to Extraordinaire *commis* for a discount. To compound the sin, the *commis* were buying them back with cash earmarked for other more urgent purposes—weekly pay, for example. To describe minister Voysin's reaction to such news as annoyed would be an understatement.[43] However, despite the later investigations of 1716–17 few corrupt *commis* were prosecuted and heavily fined. It was usually the most brazen (and most greedily stupid) who got caught, especially if they were also involved in loan-sharking that took place beyond the view of notarial registration—something that was deeply resented and easily denounced. Even then, one egregious individual, who was duly convicted of financial abuse and sentenced to a fine of 100,000 *livres* and life in the galleys, was—like so many others caught up in the tribunals after Louis XIV's death—pardoned by the Regent, who even restored his money![44]

Proof of fraud in the paymaster world, run as a series of agencies at arm's length from the ministers, was hard to come by. Not all allegations may have been true, and treasurer general Duplessis defended one of his *commis*—accused of buying up War bills at 25–30 per cent discounts—by pointing out that the very nature of their dealings gave rise to grudges and malicious accusations.[45] True or not, when the trafficking was elevated to a fine art, proving anything was hard. It was widely held that most *commis* were careful to cover their tracks by enlisting the support of cronies, sometimes 'confidants', who would do their dirty work for them: they would 'hire' people as agents to buy up War bills at a heavy discount. One army captain alleged that this outrageous practice was carried on at the very top: the central cashiers of the treasurers general would supply limited funds to a frontman who bought up War bills at huge discounts; such bills were therefore either withdrawn for less than would otherwise have been the case, or they were palmed off again for their face value (or a more moderate discount) to other people.[46]

It is, at this distance in time, impossible to prove all sorts of allegations made against personnel of the Extraordinaire des Guerres but clearly contemporaries thought that a good deal of the manipulation and abuse of financial instruments

[43] AN G[7]1784, no. 242: *mémoire* by Desmaretz, 27 February 1709; SHD Ya2: Voysin to Bernières, 24 September 1710. See also, CCG, II, 440: D'Angervilliers to Chamillart, 28 October 1707 (on the head *commis* in the Dauphiné capital Grenoble).

[44] BNF F-21076: *arrest de la Chambre de Justice*, 19 August 1716; Erik Henry Goldner, 'Public Thieves: French Financiers, Corruption, and the Public in the Chamber of Justice of 1716–17' (unpublished PhD dissertation, Columbia University, 2008), 213–14. See also DAPS, 252, 754.

[45] SHD A[1]2272, no. 56: Duplessis to Voysin, 15 June 1710.

[46] Bib. Maz. Ms. 2626, fos 58r–61r: 'Memoire. Billets et decomptes de l'extraord. de la guerre', n.d.; SHD Ya2: Chamillart to all *intendants*, 26 December 1707; AN G[7]1783, no. 257: Gaye to Desmaretz, 3 July 1709.

was not just a matter of local officials pursuing their own interests. Those at the very top of this treasury may or may not have been ordering abuse, but they were certainly making unrefusable demands, influencing key policies, pulling strings, and acting in a complaisant manner towards those they favoured. This was not, however, as far as it went. When the king actually allowed people from the Extraordinaire des Guerres and the revenue-raising machinery into the heart of the ministries, even if they left their previous job behind, it was a recipe for favouritism and greatly exacerbated the risk and dangers of rent-seeking in government. When the inner corridors of power were penetrated by the military suppliers and paymasters, they had less need to siphon money illegitimately to their own operations. They were becoming part of the highest echelons of government that ordered the destination of funds, decided on the awarding of contracts, and made key policy decisions.

THE MILITARY-INDUSTRIAL COMPLEX IN THE MINISTRIES

It had been quite standard for men working for Jean-Baptiste Colbert both to provide finances for the navy and involve themselves as *receveurs généraux*, tax farmers, and other suppliers working for the Finance Ministry, either at the same time or sequentially. The most prominent was Samuel Daliès de La Tour. It was also not unknown for men who worked as officials in the Navy Ministry under Colbert and his successors to have interests in contracting for supplies or finance for the fleet, men such as François d'Usson de Bonrepaus, for example.[47] However, Colbert kept a tight rein on these people, and he knew very well what they were capable of. Also, the Navy Ministry was not like the War Ministry or the Finance Ministry, institutions, in the one case, of greater significance and, in the other, requiring considerable probity and a degree of detachment from the suppliers and fisco-financiers. The War of the Spanish Succession, by contrast with earlier decades, in fact saw the penetration of both the War and Finance ministries by men who had enjoyed a direct stake in the Extraordinaire des Guerres, and who continued to be involved directly or indirectly in military paymaster activity, the oversight of the Extraordinaire, or the supply of the armies. Furthermore, because loyalties and a sense of honour could be multidimensional, contractors who had made the move into the royal ministries were often trying to satisfy their 'amis' and relatives as well as the king's needs, regardless of whether they personally held any residual material interest in the supply of money, equipment, or food to Louis XIV's forces.

The remarkable thing is that they were all part of the same tightly knit circle, even within the rarefied world of the senior military fisco-financiers, and they were closely identified with bread supply for the armies. They enjoyed an astonishing degree of favour from Michel Chamillart, and we certainly need to banish any

[47] Daniel Dessert, *La Royale: Vaisseaux et marins du Roi-Soleil* (Paris, 1996), 74–9.

sense that Chamillart lacked a close group of clients in the fiscal-military system. It is a strange sort of clientage system, though, in which it is far from clear who was really the leader and who the follower, at least in matters of policy. Desmaretz had his clients too, although the closest were drawn from his relatives, from *colbertiste* families, and from the *robe* nobility—those upon whom ministers, since 1661, had habitually relied—with generally more positive results than had been the case prior to 1661 or during 1701–9. Those new men who came into his immediate orbit from the world of military finance and supply, such as the Paris brothers, more than delivered what was expected of them, and if Desmaretz retained some suppliers and suspect junior ministers he inherited from Chamillart, he also kept them at a greater distance. Moreover, he showed the suppliers in general far less favour than had Chamillart. Desmaretz simply ran a tighter ship, but he was still contending with the legacy of Chamillart's tenure of power. Voysin, as we shall see, took a similar line, if a slightly fiercer one with some of the suppliers.

At the heart of this group of Chamillart men was Jean-Etienne Berthelot de Pleneuf, who in 1702 became a treasurer general of the Extraordinaire and took on the duty for the 1703 *exercice*. In 1701 and 1702 he had organized the bread supply for French forces in northern Italy, bringing in wheat from Africa through Marseille at inflated prices, and he had simultaneously run the military hospitals for maximum profit and less than the minimum comfort of the patients. Indeed, such unacceptable profiteering would form the basis of his disgrace shortly after Louis XIV's death.[48] He was also *commissaire général des poudres et salpêtres* of France; in fact his family had been interested in the gunpowder monopoly from the late 1650s until just after the Nine Years War. From 1703 the powder business was more or less dominated once again by friends and relatives of the Berthelot family (such as their cousin Charles Lallemant, comte de Levignan—also a farmer general), or by the inner family itself.[49] After Pleneuf moved from the Extraordinaire to become director general of the artillery in 1704, Lallemant was then subject to his orders and under his protection. Indeed, in September 1706, when the gunpowder contract was up for renewal, Pleneuf brazenly admitted to the duc du Maine (Grand Master of the Artillery) that he had been trying to concentrate the powder contract in the hands of a small number of his friends and close relatives, but Chamillart had forced him to dilute their power by taking other people into the monopoly company that was formed. With chutzpah that almost defies belief, Pleneuf complained that these people so dear to him would now get less of a profit from the business! On top of this, although as artillery director general he was supposed to audit the accounts of the gunpowder suppliers, Pleneuf was also the man who drew up the accounts in 1710 for presentation to the Secretary of War, Voysin.[50] This sort of thing was highly questionable.

48 SHD A^{1}1519, no. 7: Berthelot de Duchy to Chamillart, 14 January 1701; Pierre Bonnassieux, *Les grandes compagnies de commerce: Etude pour servir à l'histoire de la colonisation* (Paris, 1892), 221.

49 SHD A^{1}1795: Pleneuf to Chamillart, 26 April 1704; DAPS, 314, 617; Claeys, II, 68.

50 SHD A^{1}1990, no. 1207: Pleneuf to Maine, 17 September 1706; A^{1}2409: Pleneuf to Camus des Touches, 8 June 1710; Pleneuf to Belloy, 3 August 1710.

By this time not only had Pleneuf's two brothers, Berthelot de Duchy and Berthelot de Saint-Laurent, taken on positions of *receveur général* and farmer general respectively, but when Duchy gave up his *recette générale* he moved fully into the management of the bread supply for the armies of Flanders and Germany, having previously—with Pleneuf himself—been the principal figure for supplying the army of Italy. As such he was very much under Pleneuf's orders, for in 1707 Pleneuf had become *premier commis* of the entire War Ministry, now working directly under Chamillart on so much of the ministry's business. It did not stop there. Pleneuf had been the one who lobbied for Duchy to be given this role with the northern armies' *vivres* company. Pleneuf certainly donated to, as well as profited from, the supply companies his family organized, but he was determined to keep up a public pretence of total impartiality regarding contractors of all kinds, as befitted his sub-ministerial dignity. He was, though, economical with the truth about his undertakings: to those outside the charmed circle he insisted that he had no personal interest in the transport contracts for the bread supply to Italy, though he admitted that Duchy was charged with the task and that he sometimes involved himself with facilitating operations. It is hard to imagine that Pleneuf did not provide insider information or advice to his cronies about costs, and how to present them in such a way that they could profit from the king's service more than would have been the case without such a well-placed friend in the ministry. Pleneuf as good as admitted he did this. He also advised his brothers to propose exploitative *affaires extraordinaires* to the ministers as a way of gaining greater financial backing for their supply operations. Pleneuf saw nothing wrong in helping his kith and kin, regardless of the benefit or loss to the king, though he would draw the line at overt lobbying for favours that departed from the rules or usual customs.[51]

Pleneuf also helped and protected his close friend Etienne II Landais, treasurer general of the artillery throughout this period, and was even 'indulgent towards him' when he could be, which was not surprising given how much Landais had supported him by sharing his office of treasurer general of the Extraordinaire des Guerres in 1702–4. By joining Pleneuf in this venture Landais did make it far more likely that his real focus of attention, the artillery, would get the funds it needed from the Extraordinaire des Guerres, through which most of its wartime income was then channelled. Pleneuf's protection of Landais was manifested in a number of ways: lobbying ministers on his behalf for financial relief; trying to keep his pay bill down by discriminating against artillery officers who had not bought their offices since they were venalized in 1703; and finally getting the artillery liberated from the financial stranglehold of the Extraordinaire treasurers general from 1705. Pleneuf also seems to have favoured the activities of the Compagnie de la Chine in bringing in raw materials from across the world for munitions manufacture: in 1701 this company had merged with the Compagnie de la Mer du Sud, in

[51] Claeys, I, 223; CCG, III, 55, 236: D'Angervilliers to Desmaretz, 16 September 1708, 20 October 1709; SHD A[1]1894: Pleneuf to *commissaire* Bernard, 31 August 1705; A[1]1990, no. 217: Pleneuf to Buttet, 25 May 1706; no. 475: Pleneuf to Chamillart, 26 January 1706; A[1]2409: Pleneuf to Saint-Laurent, 2 April 1708; Pleneuf to Belloy, 21 September 1710, 20 July 1712.

which Landais and Maximilien Titon, the arms manufacturer, were leading investors. In return, as part of his responsibilities, Landais appears to have made a priority of paying the invoices of all sorts of entrepreneurs if the Berthelot clan had a stake, even an indirect one, in their affairs.[52]

The only thing Pleneuf was kept away from was direct supervision of the Extraordinaire des Guerres, both before he became *premier commis* of the War Ministry in May 1707 and afterwards, and this continued for as long as he held this post until October 1715. Truthfully he told one artillery official in 1706 that 'I have no right whatsoever to involve myself' in the Extraordinaire, but he was a close friend of Chamillart's favourite treasurer general, Mongelas, who continued in this office until 1711 and who then held a part-share in his successor La Jonchère until 1715.[53] Otherwise little seems to have been off-limits to him, at least in the world of contracting, and he was quite willing to stretch the truth about this. On at least one occasion we can find Pleneuf telling a barefaced lie, when in 1706 he informed one correspondent that he had 'no dealings with the *traitants*' responsible for the 1703 contract to sell the hundreds of offices in the artillery corps.[54] The truth is, he was about as closely connected to these men as any government official could be. The man who had 'composed the edict for creating the offices of the artillery' was Jacques Poulletier, who continued to be the leading figure of the group of *traitants* who were contracted for this 5 million *livres* deal, and he was certainly its representative in government. In 1706 Pleneuf was even providing his own money to bail out this dreadful *affaire extraordinaire*. This was, to say the least, a very cosy set of arrangements.[55]

As a young man Jacques Poulletier had been the *premier commis* of his relative Louis Jossier de La Jonchère (the treasurer general who was disgraced in 1683–84), and in the early 1680s he had occupied the most important position among the Extraordinaire's junior treasurers (for an investment of 220,000 *livres*). From 1685 until 1704 he was *receveur général* of the Rouen *généralité*, was involved in two dozen financial contracts, and in 1701–3 also served as a farmer general. Chamillart had been *intendant* of Rouen briefly at the end of the 1680s, and this is almost certainly when the two men became close. Poulletier even came to live very close to Chamillart's beloved estate of L'Étang after 1701.[56] In the 1680s and 1690s Poulletier developed a good relationship with treasurer general Turmenyes, and his background and solidity made him a natural to support the Extraordinaire des Guerres at the start of the War of the Spanish Succession. This began in 1701 with Chamillart asking him to oversee the kingdom-wide payment of the *ustencile* pay

[52] SHD A[1]1795: Pleneuf to Grossolles, 21 February 1706; A[1]1894: Pleneuf to chevalier des Touches, 13 December [1704]; Pleneuf to Saint-Hilaire, 2 December 1705 (quotation); A[1]2409: Pleneuf to du Magny, 23 January 1708; Philippe Haudrère, *La Compagnie Française des Indes au XVIII*[e] *siècle (1719–1795)* (Paris, 1989), 29; Bonnassieux, *Les grandes compagnies*, 343.

[53] SHD A[1]1795: Pleneuf to Grossolles, 12 December 1706; A[1]1990, no. 1284: Pleneuf to chevalier des Touches, 11 December 1706; Pénicaut, 234.

[54] SHD A[1]1990, no. 841: Pleneuf to d'Albié, 23 March 1706.

[55] SHD A[1]1990, no. 421: Pleneuf to Manguin de Saint-Vallerin, 1 December 1706; no. 475: Pleneuf to Chamillart, 26 January 1706; A[1]1894: Pleneuf to Ferrand, 3 June 1705.

[56] Claeys, II, 765, 767; Pénicaut, 363.

supplement for the troops, and proceeded in 1702 when he was formally associated with Montargis for that year's Extraordinaire *exercice*, gaining a substantial 70,000 *livres* reward out of it. He was also given the job of deciding on the settling of monies owed to the *commis* of the late, bankrupt treasurer general La Touanne, which, given that La Touanne had been Montargis' stepfather, involved Poulletier in a glaring conflict of interest.[57] This was the first of a number of astonishing decisions by Chamillart that entrenched a small coterie of financiers with direct interests in the war effort at the heart of government, and even made them judges in their own cause.

Poulletier was clearly more than just any old *receveur général*, and this was confirmed in 1704 when he was elevated to the position of *Garde du Trésor royal*. By this point he was closer to the Berthelot family than to Montargis, as the former were the main military hospital contractors for the Milanese—Poulletier was a co-investor. They maintained good relations up to Poulletier's death in 1711. Meanwhile, Poulletier went from strength to strength. That he was allowed to work alongside Pleneuf on the rights and duties of the purchasers of artillery venal offices to whom he, as one of the *traitants*, had sold such positions is remarkable enough. To the horror of Chancellor Pontchartrain, though, he was plucked at the very end of Chamillart's time in the Finance Ministry to become one of the *intendants des finances*. For Pontchartrain, not normally squeamish about graft and corruption, this was to allow a barbarian into the citadel—those with such a record of financial contracting and administration should not be under-ministers and, in effect, formal judges of financial disputes. But Desmaretz upheld the appointment.[58] Within the Finance Ministry Poulletier was put in charge of nothing less than the oversight of all military funding, covering the Extraordinaire des Guerres, the suppliers, the network of route-march stops, and the artillery, of which Pleneuf remained director general even after he had become *premier commis* of the War Ministry. He was active in his tasks, and was, amongst other things, involved in negotiating loans as well as discounts on paper instruments for the Extraordinaire.[59] Pontchartrain might well have shuddered to think what turn such negotiations took. If there is no direct proof that Poulletier was outrageously corrupt in office, and the disappearance of most of the Extraordinaire des Guerres papers makes it hard to pull together a case for this, he was certainly complacent about other people's monopolies and what this might mean for good governance. He completely failed to see that the stranglehold over much foreign exchange business of the *agents de change* in Paris, with whom he regularly dealt for discounting instruments and sourcing funds abroad for the Extraordinaire, was detrimental to holding down the costs of the war effort.[60] If he did understand, then he did not flag this up or try to

[57] SHD A[1]1595, no. 162: Poulletier to Chamillart, 23 November 1701; A[1]1604, no. 28: 'Mémoire', [January 1702].

[58] Pénicaut, 99; AN G[7]1097: placet of *Gardes du Trésor royal*, Gruyn and Turmenyes, [*c*. February–December 1708]; Saint-Simon, XV, 386.

[59] SHD Ya2: Chamillart to Desmaretz, 14 November 1708; Voysin to Duplessis, 5 August 1710; CCG, III, 99: Bernage to Desmaretz, 9 April 1709; McCollim, 171, 178.

[60] CCG, III, 53: Desmaretz to Poulletier, 7 September 1708.

counteract it. Nor did he flinch from giving some of the choicest roles in emergency finance to his own cronies. From late 1708 Louis Waubert, a man who had been his own *commis* when Poulletier was a *receveur général* and then *Garde du Trésor royal*, was given a plum task: to act as a *traitant* and pay the interest on the outstanding Extraordinaire des Guerres bearer bills on behalf of the treasurers general.[61] This was, in other words, handing a contract worth several million *livres*, for a cut of probably seven figures over several years, to a man intimately connected with a fisco-financier turned *intendant des finances*. It is more than likely Waubert was a cover for Poulletier himself in this affair. Pontchartrain was right. Poulletier was not suitable for the role of impartial *juge de finance*.

The links between Chamillart, the Berthelots, and Poulletier were reinforced and completed by a small group of men associated with the Hôtel Royal des Invalides and the enormous business of food supply for the armies. One of Pleneuf's associates in the 1703 Extraordinaire duty-year had been Anne Alexis de Carqueville, the *receveur général* of Poitiers, who was the brother-in-law of Louis L'Héritier, seigneur de Merval. L'Héritier and his father had been *commis* of the Extraordinaire over several decades, and he had a share in Carqueville's office. In return Carqueville took a share in L'Héritier's 1701 purchase of one of the two offices of treasurer general of Les Invalides, the two men continuing in association until 1715. Furthermore, since at least 1693 the principal beef supplier for Les Invalides was one Jacques Charpentier, who appears to have had a share in one of the two offices of treasurer general of this Hôtel Royal. In the War of the Spanish Succession he can be found supplying beef to the army of Flanders, and became involved in the *vivres* company for Italy (with the Berthelots) and in its counterpart for the armies of Flanders and Germany.[62] Inside the War Ministry Pleneuf was even prepared to maintain funds to his friends the Les Invalides treasurers at the expense of the artillery officers he was supposed to be protecting.[63] The military-industrial complex was protecting its own.

Neither Charpentier nor L'Héritier was as powerful and influential as their colleague, the other treasurer general of Les Invalides, François Mauricet de La Cour, who also occupied the post from its re-creation in 1701. He was very close to Jacques Poulletier, Chamillart's *eminence grise* for war finance, but that was not all. Mauricet had invested 350,000 *livres* in the office of treasurer general of the Extraordinaire held by Arnauld and Mongelas between 1696 and 1701, and he remained close to Mongelas. Mauricet, too, became an *intime* of Chamillart to the extent that he was the minister's property developer and was treated by him as a friend. The great source of his power and wealth, however, was in his organization of the *vivres* companies that were formed each year to service the bread requirements of the armies of Flanders and Germany. Between 1701 and 1708 Chamillart worked on *vivres* matters himself and formed the *vivres* companies as he wished.

[61] AN G[7]1782, no. 198: Waubert to Desmaretz, 26 November 1708; Claeys, II, 1192; DAPS, 703.

[62] Claeys, I, 464; II, 268–9; Iung, I, vii.

[63] SHD A[1]1990, no. 207: Pleneuf to d'Allart, 18 May 1706.

For the companies supplying the armies of Flanders and Germany Mauricet became the dominant figure in these years, governing them, as one resentful *commis* put it, 'despotically'.[64] He even stumped up some of the investments for his colleagues on their behalf, making them his pawns, while he and Chamillart seem to have carved up much business tête-à-tête. Though Chamillart was willing to entertain other offers for the contracts, it is quite clear he had no intention of casting Mauricet aside. Desmaretz, in turn, maintained him at the head of the 1708 company and agreed to his leadership of the 1709 company.

The Flanders and Germany *vivres* contracts ran to several million *livres*, roughly 6.9 million *livres* in 1708 according to the Finance Ministry, and the total contract value for all *vivres* companies reached an average of 12 million *livres* per annum in 1704–6. This was up from 10 million *livres* in 1702. But as the deals for the Flanders and Germany *vivres* had been habitually struck at 5 million *livres*, there was clearly an increase in costs as the years went on, and as each year's operations got under way. This was partly because the *munitionnaires* put in inflated bids for their services, which were reduced by only a small amount by government officials deputed to assess them. The actual costs of the *vivres*, however, were greater than the headline figures of the contracts. The directors of the *vivres*, usually Mauricet, also claimed reimbursement for large losses they made during the course of a year: not only did they claim that prices had gone up since their original estimates, but they also claimed for losses in currency exchange for coin movement to Flanders. Moreover, they incurred further losses because the Trésor royal and the Extraordinaire des Guerres fed them substandard *assignations* and Mint bills, which they had to discount heavily for cash. They therefore either claimed retrospectively for such losses, or they anticipated them by building 'insurance premiums' into their cost estimates. They appear, in fact, to have pursued both options. At the end of 1705 the estimates for a new company put forward for 1706 by Mauricet were 16.7 per cent greater than those of the previous year, and this was agreed by Chamillart. The royal councillor Le Peletier de La Houssaye, asked to investigate the bread costs at that time, acknowledged that a large proportion of the *munitionnaires*' costs, perhaps one-third, was built into their estimates to cover problems they anticipated in realizing resources from the king's revenue collectors. Appropriations difficulties and monetary problems were, as Forbonnais charged, causing significant increases in the costs of war. The *munitionnaires*, who invested up to 3 million *livres* in their company in 1708 up front (a typical sum), were obviously not content with the generous 10 per cent interest the king was offering on their personal investments. In all, the historian of the *vivres*, Jean-Éric Iung, suggests the *munitionnaires* were legitimately getting 9–10 per cent of the total value of a contract each year—perhaps 700,000 *livres*—in interest, compensation, and permitted rake-offs.

The gains (or protection) the *munitionnaires* were seeking came on top of the manifold ways in which the king's money was being wasted or, in effect, stolen through mismanagement and outright fraud. If there was little noticeable decline in bread quality before 1709 (when it plummeted), there were all sorts of creative

[64] Quoted in Iung, II, 60. The comment was made in May 1710.

ways in which the suppliers could profit, especially through collusion with muster-masters and muster-auditors, allowing a lot of bread that was not needed to be billed to the government. With *commis* of the Extraordinaire doing the same to inflate the pay bill,[65] it is not altogether surprising if the government endorsed money for larger notional deliveries of bread than were needed or actually distributed in practice, leaving a nice profit. It would not be unreasonable to suggest that, owing to poor financial instruments, discounting, insurance-influenced pricing, and fraud, the king was losing 40 per cent or even 50 per cent of the value of his *vivres* contracts, a sum worth globally perhaps 5–7 million *livres* per annum, and he was having to pump more funds into each year's companies. Chamillart indeed seems to have disrupted the financial system on behalf of the *munitionnaires*. He was even suspected of diverting funds away from pressing military needs in order to extricate Mauricet from the ostensible financial overextension into which Chamillart was pushing him. Given Chamillart's repeated financial protection of other leading war financiers, this is only too plausible. As if this were not problematic enough, there were other issues concerning conflict of interest and good order in the war effort: Nicolas Dunoyer, a Mauricet client, was the principal Extraordinaire *commis* for the army of Flanders after 1702 *and* a director of all the *vivres* companies for this army between then and 1710. This remarkable conflict of interest (and similar arrangements existed with the Berthelots for the Italy company) gave all sorts of opportunities for manipulation of funds.

On top of their main role, the *munitionnaires* were also favoured with the awarding of contracts for exploitative *affaires extraordinaires* which, wearing their other hats as *traitants*, they often managed themselves or through their proxies. Here, Mauricet seems to have cornered the very best contracts for the most lucrative forced loans, including those concerned with the waterways and forests administration, at the expense even of his colleagues in the *vivres* company. Mauricet confused those contracts he took on for the *vivres* company with those he signed on his own account, making it hard to disentangle them. In 1701, moreover, he was even awarded the ultra-special contract to collect fines from fellow financiers arising from the royal investigation into them, just prior to the Spanish Succession conflict. Although Mauricet and his colleagues did not see every item on their wish lists of *affaires extraordinaires* nodded through, and some proposals were rejected, they were being directly favoured with probably the most lucrative form of lending to the government that then existed. Though it still needs investigation, the same may hold true for the *vivres* companies for Italy and the Spanish theatres. Just as the Extraordinaire des Guerres had become a major source of medium- and long-term credit for the monarch by 1707, so too had the *vivres* companies. But in this case the *munitionnaires* were being given the opportunity of far greater returns over the long term than the treasurers general of the Extraordinaire, whose interest reimbursements were far less than the 'remises de dedans' and the 'remises de dehors' rake-offs that came with most *affaires extraordinaires*.[66] This was not the

[65] SHD A[1]1526, nos 258–9: *mémoires* by Mairon, August 1701.

[66] See Chapter 4.

only opportunity for gain separate from their core business that they were offered: Mauricet and others took on contracts for forage supply and for supplying the route-march stopping points, the *étapes*, in Alsace. For this latter contract, Mauricet was joined by his Les Invalides colleague L'Héritier. The *munitionnaires* took on numerous other contracts.[67]

Chamillart also advanced Mauricet's social prestige as well as his fortune. In 1703 he was installed as *intendant* of the most prestigious chivalric order in France, the Ordre du Saint-Esprit, buying the post for 800,000 *livres*. Because of his success and favour at court, and his ruthless business practices, Mauricet was unpopular with fellow financiers and contractors. Because of his ostentation his name was odious with the wider public too. In this respect he was well matched with his associate and brother-in-law, Pierre Deschiens de Ressons, with whom he resided in Paris and who was the epitome of the social-climbing, amoral financier. Indeed, Deschiens was the principal character in *Pluton maltôtier*, a biting satire against greedy fisco-financiers published four years after his death in 1704. The Deschiens clan were protected throughout this period by the House of Orléans—the king's brother and his son, the future regent—and also by the royal bastard interest, notably the duc de Vendôme and the duc du Maine (who protected Mauricet's and Poulletier's man Waubert as well). This was an exceedingly powerful nexus which could support Mauricet's pursuit of his fiscal-military interests, and it was needed because as Chamillart's situation weakened and Mauricet ceased to deliver the goods, the latter's own position began to crumble.[68]

The management and oversight of the *vivres* companies by the government show how far conflict of interest went under both Chamillart and, to a lesser extent, Desmaretz, but it also reveals just how limited ministerial oversight over logistical contractors could be. As to the formal supervision inside the ministries, it can be outlined thus. One should doubt Chamillart's commitment to careful scrutiny of the *vivres*, not least because in practice the point man for this business inside the Finance Ministry was Poulletier, even from 1704 to 1708 when he was *Garde du Trésor royal* and thus not a ministry official. Once he became an *intendant des finances* the *vivres* were made part of his official remit, an arrangement which Desmaretz continued for eighteen months. Within the War Ministry Poulletier's counterpart was Pleneuf, who from mid-1707 had considerable influence over *vivres* matters. The conflicts of interest and the scope for collusion were thus enormous: for much of the period Chamillart was in office, it was his own inner circle of

[67] For the previous four paragraphs I have drawn upon Iung, I, 32–7, 68–76, 79, 82–4, 92, 98–100, 105. See also, AN G^{7}1787, no. 236: memorandum on the widow and heirs of Arnauld, [late 1711]; Jean-Claude Waquet, *Les Grands Maîtres des Eaux et Forêts de France de 1689 à la Révolution* (Paris, 1978), 14; Saint-Simon, XVII, 191, 193–4; Pénicaut, 362; Mathieu Stoll, 'Une commission extraordinaire du Conseil: le Bureau des vivres (1690–1787)', in Bernard Barbiche and Yves-Marie Bercé, eds, *Études sur l'ancienne France offertes en hommage à Michel Antoine* (Paris, 2003), 393; SHD A^{1}1613, no. 155: Mauricet de La Cour to Chamillart, 17 October 1702; A^{1}1699, nos 261, 274: same, 30 January, 26 February 1703.

[68] Alexandre Teulet, *Liste chronologique et alphabétique des chevaliers et des officiers de l'ordre du Saint-Esprit depuis sa création, en 1578, jusqu'à son extinction, en 1830* (Paris, 1864), 102; DAPS, 703.

trusted military financiers who were inflating the costs of war, and the excessive costs of the *vivres* of Italy in the early 1700s was the basis for Pleneuf's downfall in 1713–15. Pleneuf's reaction to the growing pressure on this matter, in particular his concealment of his assets and his subsequent flight to northern Italy (surely no coincidence either—he had financial interests there), suggests he had been involved in far more suspect activity than just that in 1701 and 1702. That this and many other problems could grow and spread stems in part from Chamillart's approach to governance and management. Most dangerously, the minister totally neglected the detail of the king's debts towards the *munitionnaires*. The Finance Ministry's estimates of the king's debt to the Flanders–Germany *vivres* company were more than 1 million *livres* adrift from those of the company itself by 1707.[69] This was a major failure of government.

While the chances of profit as a *munitionnaire* in the king's service were high, and the chances of becoming a net debtor were fairly low, the real problem these men faced was a crisis of liquidity, and in late 1708 this began to creep up on them. By this time the *vivres* company of Flanders and Germany claimed the king owed it over 8 million *livres*, a sum greater than an entire annual contract. When agricultural and climatic disaster struck in the first months of 1709, sending costs soaring while crown resources shrank and were also diverted to prop up the banker Samuel Bernard, it sealed the fate of this company. At the end of April 1709 Mauricet had to confess its inability to fulfil the contract for that year's campaign season, as he failed to realize *assignations* and was stymied by the collapse of Mint bills. By the following month others—notably Fargès, the Berthelots, and the Paris brothers, who became close to Desmaretz—were in the driving seat for the *vivres* of northern France, and remained so for the rest of the war.[70] In October Mauricet found himself pursued for debts, forced to renounce his role in military supplies, and having to give up his various prestigious and lucrative offices. He died in 1710 during the investigation into his accounts, which revealed that he in fact enjoyed enormous assets of 17.8 million *livres*, of which 5.6 million, the largest bloc of funds, were invested in the bread supply system for the armies. He had advanced money to courtiers and in addition had invested in numerous tax farms and revenue contracts, as well as in the finances of the artillery (like Poulletier) and the gunpowder farm, both dominated by the Berthelots. On the other side of the balance sheet, he owed 11–12 million *livres*. This still left his heirs with a net fortune of some 3–4 million *livres*, a huge sum, and he was also able to pass the intendancy of the Saint-Esprit on to his nephew, Charles Deschiens.[71]

Mauricet had taken on too much in an increasingly dangerous climate, but his fall was brought about not through net debt but because he suffered a serious crisis of liquidity as the king's agent shortly after Chamillart's fall, and he was left exposed to Voysin, who was set on his downfall by the end of June 1709. What counted for

[69] Iung, I, 24–6, 76, 227.

[70] Iung, I, 76–7, 235–6.

[71] Saint-Simon, XVII, 193 (note by Boislisle); AN G[7]1825, no. 25: 'Etat des effets…', [1711–12]; no. 69: note to Desmaretz, [1712–13]; M. Lemaire, *Relevé des documents intéressants le département de Seine-et-Marne …* (Fontainebleau, 1883), 211.

contractors, at a time of discredited paper (from which one could prosper), was getting the government to pay up what it owed. This was fundamentally a matter of having the ministers' confidence and support. When it vanished a financier could be left stranded, even if he was a net creditor.[72] Mauricet had also failed to protect himself sufficiently, despite Chamillart's warnings of the need to do so. This reveals that Chamillart—a naif in only some respects—was willing to help his principal support behind the scenes. At the time he left the War Ministry in June 1709 Chamillart had sought to shield his closest clients, recommending Mauricet draw up a complete inventory of everything he had gained since he started investing in the bread supply business, of everything he had gained from other activities, of everything he owned in his own name, and what the bread supply company owned separately. (This was because the law prevented the sequestration of assets held by a person before they entered a contract, when subsequent debts related to that contract.) Mauricet should then present this list to Desmaretz and have him read it to the king, along with an offer to donate some of his fortune back to Louis to assist in the war effort. But Mauricet had not followed this sage advice, and in his letter to Mauricet in January 1710, Chamillart even remarked: 'If you had taken this path, there would have been many people blocked.'[73] Chamillart therefore knew that *his* financiers were loathed, that others were out to bring them down, especially with himself out of government, and he was more partisan than we have previously thought. He therefore did have a tight group of financiers upon whom he relied for active involvement in the war effort and for advice, almost certainly far too much in both cases. He presided over levels of profiteering that were not negligible, and he pushed these clients into overextending their activities, causing the government, in turn, to support their borrowing on a huge scale. These men were military financiers whose revenue sources were unstable, but most of them and their families—barring Mauricet—came through the War of the Spanish Succession more or less unscathed, and even got through the subsequent squall of the regency's Chambre de Justice without a major reduction in their circumstances.

In the War of the Spanish Succession royal finances were not just dominated by fisco-financiers as in Louis XIV's previous wars and Louis XV's subsequent ones. During this particular, formative period of the French monarchy royal finances were influenced preponderantly by *military* financiers and those directly associated with them, much more so than in any other conflict of the *ancien régime*. They also had unparalleled opportunities for enrichment without even having to steal much directly. All that was required was a steady nerve and skill at manipulating both financial instruments and the king's ministers. This situation arose particularly as a result of Chamillart's occupation of both the War and Finance ministries together

[72] Iung, I, 269–70, 291; II, 169. Iung regards Mauricet as having been ruined, but he does not make the vital distinction between being a net debtor and being simply illiquid. As long as a man retained the ministers' support he would not necessarily be descending year after year further into the abyss through involvement in the *vivres*.

[73] AN G^{7}1825, no. 1: Chamillart to Mauricet de La Cour, 2 January 1710.

for seven crucial years, his limited skills as the king's aide, and the backgrounds of the men whom he placed in a number of crucial positions. However, it was also a product of the reckless emphasis that was placed upon the pursuit of the war, on an unprecedented geographical scale, at almost any financial cost during the period 1701–9. The military financiers understandably kept up pressure to maintain the flow of funds for the operations the king ordered them to undertake, and they were willing to accept and promote all sorts of payment devices at times. The ministers on occasions made serious missteps in their efforts to keep the war effort going. Their imposition of colossal debts on the Extraordinaire des Guerres itself, which might have been resisted by the treasurers general, was accepted in return for unlimited indemnification, which only encouraged further debt issues and manipulations by this ubiquitous agency. And Chamillart lost much of his grip on the *vivres*, hospital, and powder contractors. By allowing themselves to be pushed down unsound roads, Chamillart, along with Desmaretz, Voysin, and the king, achieved the unhappy distinction of further inflating the costs of the war and pumping up the debts.

Conclusion

At the height of the French government's financial troubles in the War of the Spanish Succession Nicolas Desmaretz lamented 'the complete disturbance of business that the excess of expenditure has caused'.[1] He might have added that these high levels of spending, which continued for another six years, would destabilize the financial affairs of the state for decades to come. The Nine Years War and the War of the Spanish Succession caused an immense increase in state spending and built up an astronomical sovereign debt, but this obvious generalization about nearly a quarter of a century of military and naval campaigning fails to explain why the costs of war rose so much in the course of the 1700s—and why the War of the Spanish Succession was so disastrous for France. It was not that the excessive spending of the years after 1701 had been on more troops or more equipment than in the Nine Years War, although defeats after 1704 had meant shelling out money to cover heavy losses of both. In fact during the second great conflict of Louis XIV's 'third reign' the army had fewer men and the navy fewer ships. Nor can inflationary pressures account for more than a minor proportion of the additional financial burdens. The explanations for the escalation in costs must be sought elsewhere.

First, after November 1700 the Bourbon dynasty found itself in a far more demanding geostrategic and geopolitical situation, defending the Spanish *monarquía* across much of southern and western Europe, as well as holding the frontiers of the French hexagon and seeing off the Camisard rebels in the Cévennes. Foreign exchange costs for the armies would therefore have increased anyway as more French troops were stationed abroad in regions that, frankly, could meet only a fairly small proportion of their expenses. Second, the French government mismanaged its finances. This is not to issue a blanket condemnation of the king and his ministers for so doing, although by the standards of the time they understood some fiscal and monetary issues poorly compared with other players in the game at home and abroad (such as Orry in Spain, never mind Godolphin in Britain). To be fair, no minister—or financier, however expert they were—could know at this time just how far to push various financial instruments or revenue-raising devices, or what their mutation might entail. And it was all too understandable for ministers to interpret valid, reasoned objections as the defence of vested interests (some of which, of course, ministers were more than willing to accommodate). Nevertheless, by

[1] AN G[7]1120: Bernard to Desmaretz, 13 April 1708, Desmaretz's note.

1707, if not earlier, even the ministers themselves recognized that they had gone way too far with Mint bills, bearer bills on the Extraordinaire des Guerres, and other methods of funding the war effort, with counterproductive results.

The French state had been carrying a large debt from the Nine Years War, burdening future revenues, especially the *fermes générales*, and it entered the War of the Spanish Succession handicapped by the after-effects of the 1692–94 economic and demographic crisis, by the currency manipulations since 1689, and by declining revenue yields which only got worse. The king was also showing marked reluctance to tax the clergy at levels their wealth could sustain. With a *contrôleur général* well versed in the financial arcana, better organization of the fisco-financiers, and a government more willing to increase land and income-related taxes on the wealthy and privileged very early in the war far more than it did (and it finally did bite this bullet with the *dixième* in 1710), France might not have got into such a financial mess, even though the debt would still have grown considerably. Instead, Louis XIV appointed Michel Chamillart—a decent man and a competent second fiddle (in the more straightforward parts of government)—not only to the contrôle général but also to the position of Secretary of State for War. On his watch after January 1701 the affairs of both departments were not so much harmonized as utterly confused, even by the standards of the old regime when the investment interests and responsibilities of fisco-financiers overlapped. He understood little about the psychology of lending, and, though Colbert too had expected financiers to make sacrifices for the good of the state, Chamillart was under far more illusions than the cold and cynical 'le Nord' about the likelihood of them doing so. When financiers and the markets failed to respond to his expressed wishes or to his avowed good intentions in the way he expected, Chamillart was both baffled and exasperated, and only compounded his misjudgements by his subsequent reactions to apparent defiance and greed.

Moreover, between 1701 and 1708 Chamillart took a number of dubious and dangerous decisions, especially on monetary issues, on the issuing of bearer bills, and on short-term borrowing. It would probably have been far better to organize the *receveurs généraux* into a solid corporate body to manage revenue sources and discounting—had this happened in 1702 rather than 1710 they could have performed many of the roles of the Bank of England, and many of the worst expedients could have been avoided or used on a smaller scale. Chamillart was also unable to restrain the compensation demands and contract inflation of his financial and material suppliers. Some of these demands had to be allowed, given the circumstances, but Chamillart kept few tabs on their accounts compared with Louvois before him, and he was naïve in permitting his most favoured contractors, in effect, to dictate terms to him. In 1707 he even contractually allowed the banker Samuel Bernard open-ended compensation for foreign exchange costs to an extent not seen in the years before or after.[2] Some of Chamillart's most important, and most damaging, decisions were taken under the influence of one or other member of a

[2] Esnault, II, 215: 'Articles de demandes du Sieur Bernard [...]', [27 April 1709].

small group of very important men with special war-related financial interests—particularly Pleneuf, Mauricet de La Cour, Mongelas, Montargis, and Bernard, a veritable military-industrial complex. They were not entirely dispassionate in their policy prescriptions or recommendations for financial allocations, far from it. The upshot in most of these cases was to add to the financial disorder which further increased the costs of funding the war effort. On top of this, Chamillart was unable to maintain order in the appropriations system, something that would have been difficult anyway as revenue sources failed or came up short, but he allowed Le Rebours to preside over chaos in the earmarking of revenues to expenditure. This contributed to the deterioration in credibility and value of the tradable financial instruments of the appropriations system—notably the *assignations*—and thereby provoked further issues of these documents (which often failed, too), fraudulent diversion of revenues under cover of failure claims, fraudulent interest demands, and higher costs to keep the war machine going.

Desmaretz, implicated in some but by no means all of the problems of the Chamillart era, had to try to disentangle the fiscal-administrative Gordian knot when he inherited the contrôle général in 1708, but he was no financial demigod, perhaps a semi-demigod at best. Desmaretz put his understanding of financial psychology to great use on behalf of the king, but he overreached himself with the 1709 currency manipulations (despite the good that resulted from the recoining) and his efforts to withdraw expensive forms of debt. He also came to anticipate revenues on a massive scale, though this was the best way to proceed if debt was to remain orderly (relatively so). Desmaretz was faced with an underlying difficulty in withdrawing or converting dangerous, unstable, and excessively prolonged short-term debt instruments, in that the main long-term, funded form of royal debt—bonds in the form of *rentes* on the Paris Hôtel de ville, serviced mainly by hypothecated revenues from the *fermes générales*—were rather illiquid and clumsy devices, tradable in a most sluggish manner, and not much good for passing on at face value when people such as regimental suppliers wanted something they could use quickly to pay off their own liabilities. This made the bulk of the French debt far less attractive than the more liquid British national debt. While Desmaretz was far more cautious, conservative, and skilled than Chamillart in his handling of government borrowing and the credit markets, his financial policies from mid-1709 onwards were placing Louis XIV in a race between utter bankruptcy and a tolerable diplomatic solution to the conflict. He was, of course, doing the king's bidding in keeping the essentials of the war effort going as best he could, while financial outlays were slashed almost in half and the army suffered from huge shortfalls in equipment. Up to 1711 (Marlborough's final campaign) French financiers and suppliers as well as international bankers had been willing to accept a lot of discredited and suspect paper instruments, with some coin. However, from then on it became harder to persuade people to do this now the king was postponing or cancelling a big chunk of the payments (in any form) to meet his spending orders, and particularly once it became clear he was inflicting big 'haircuts' on holders of bonds and on short-term lenders, in the form of reduced interest rates and selective defaulting. This may well have been desirable as a means to rein back profiteering and demonstrate that it would not pay massive dividends. Nevertheless, it was a recipe for drying up a significant portion of available lending when the armies were already fighting on their knees. It is true that the king's word was still seen to count for something at this time,[3] despite the manipulations, and this can only be put down to the sheer longevity of his firm personal rule, which had brought unprecedented internal political stability to the realm. The prospect of the regime, in its social and constitutional characteristics, collapsing internally was most likely not considered realistic by the financiers of the time. But if this was a correct assessment, the country by 1712 was nonetheless teetering on the brink of international disaster, something that only those with access to the full picture of logistical overstretch and munitions shortages, that is, the king and a handful of others, could have appreciated. Only the exit of Great Britain from the war in the early summer of 1712, and major diplomatic developments arising from this, allowed France to avoid logistical collapse and financial shutdown—and escape that rare thing for this period, a shattering military defeat that would have ensued. In 1712 France was in the same situation as Frederick the Great's Prussia fifty years later on the eve of the death of Elisabeth, Empress of Russia. The country was heading over a cliff.

The arguments advanced in this book have been drawn overwhelmingly from examining both the fisco-financier system, especially as it related to the war effort, and the monetary policies established by the government. This has allowed a richly complex picture to be painted of the financial degeneration of France at this time. The book has explained the interrelationship of revenue-raising and military spending, and laid out the *prima mobiles* of French financial decline, which compelled or tempted bankers, suppliers, and financiers alike to escalate the costs of the French war effort in the War of the Spanish Succession. The bankers, especially Samuel Bernard, have therefore appeared where relevant to the discussion, but this book would be incomplete—and the claims about the huge increase in costs between the Nine Years War and the Spanish Succession war would not add up—without some brief explanation of the sheer scale of their operations and how much they added to the state's costs. While Herbert Lüthy's masterful study of the bankers in this period should be consulted by anyone wishing to understand how developments unrolled in detail, there is still room to relate banking activities to the overall costs of the French war effort in a sharply focused way.

As I have argued, the international and geostrategic scenario of the Spanish Succession war meant that exchange costs would have been higher anyway than in the Dutch War or Nine Years War, reflecting not only the larger French forces stationed and operating way beyond the homeland year after year, but also the localized exchange prices, and the supply and demand in one place for exchange on another—a factor that could produce heavy costs if a link (such as Lyon to Genoa, or to Milan, or to Cadiz and Madrid) was used extensively.[4] For all that there was

[3] Saint-Germain, *Bernard*, 203.

[4] AN G7 1123: Antoine Hogguer to [Daniel] Hogguer, 3 May 1706; 'Memoire pour les freres Hogguer touchant le traité qu'ils ont fait pour l'Italie', [November 1706]; G7 1097: Mongelas to Chamillart, 22 August 1706; and G7 1093: Méliand to Desmaretz, 28 April 1708.

now a multilateral system of 'touring' bills of exchange around major European centres to prolong their final redemption,[5] the delivery of money for military purposes—necessarily in bulk—tended to involve only a score or so of cities and towns on the French frontiers and abroad, as well as Paris and Lyon. Too much demand in one place put up the exchange rate there.

On top of this, exchange costs were further inflated by concerns in the international banking and mercantile community about the means that the French government and its agents would use to settle up exchange contracts at their final payment stage. Exchange contracts between the French government and a banker to remit funds for the state took account of three principal cost items: the actual exchange rate (the 'change'); the commission for the banker and his contacts; and the loss incurred by correspondents discounting the face value of French currency or financial instruments with which they anticipated they might find themselves repaid, the so-called 'perte'. These *pertes* were substantial, reflecting not just particular moments of currency manipulation but a general air of uncertainty about French monetary values. The deterioration of Mint bills, as well as their introduction into Lyon and the mere threat of this, not only pushed *perte* costs up but *change* costs as well.[6] On top of this, bankers were also charging the government interest for prolonging their bills of exchange, much of which was to cover their own costs of proroguing final settlement (based on as yet undelivered royal funds) with their correspondents. This became the essence of Samuel Bernard's system in 1704–9.[7] Bankers were therefore discounting instruments or claiming interest and compensation for much the same reasons as fisco-financiers, suppliers, and other lenders in this period.

It was difficult enough for governments to control those involved in foreign exchange, owing to the transnational nature of these people and their operations. It was made doubly hard by the great secrecy surrounding exchange dealings, something the French government reluctantly conceded was vital, though they deplored the way currency dealers, the *agents de change*, took advantage of this. Foreign exchange was seen by Louis XIV's ministers as something mysterious, even alchemical. The prices of exchange were largely a matter of subjective judgement (even more so than in subsequent centuries), often based on very limited knowledge, and the bases on which rates of *change* and commission were calculated were thoroughly opaque, predominantly reflecting very rough notions of current balances of payments between different places. This, however, left the door wide open to the other cause of inflated exchange costs, outright profiteering through the charging of excessive prices for remitting money. In a fit of disgust Desmaretz even exclaimed of *agents de change*, 'I mistrust them to such a degree, and I have such a

[5] J. Sperling, 'The International Payments Mechanism in the Seventeenth and Eighteenth Centuries', *Economic History Review* 14 (1962), esp. 464.

[6] CCG, II, 77: Le Bret to Chamillart, 20 June 1701; AN G^{7}1777, no. 91: 'Memoire' by Macaire, 21 November 1705; G^{7}1123: memorandum: 'Italie. Les Sieurs Hogguer', 15 December 1707.

[7] AN G^{7}1120: 'Conditions sous lesquelles M. Bernard offre a Monseigneur de fournir les fonds necessaires pour la subsistance [...] December 1704', September 1704; and see footnote 2.

horror for their manoeuvres, that I cannot bring myself to speak with them.'[8] As to the bankers, Desmaretz condemned them as 'men who have no other object than the profit from their trade, often very illegitimate, and who are in the habit of sacrificing everything to their own interest'. This is best seen in the way they charged commission not just on the sums to be remitted but on the amount of money that was eventually given to them to indemnify them for all other costs too![9] One Lyonnais merchant, deputed to investigate the accounts of the Hogguer brothers and Bernard in 1712–13, revealingly told Desmaretz, 'Here one is in the pernicious habit of believing everything is permitted to oneself, in matters regarding the interests of the King, so I am no longer surprised by the immense expenditure that has been made.'[10] Whether the government channelled its exchange operations through a single dominant banker such as Samuel Bernard or through a consortium, as in 1701–2—and it never allowed one man or syndicate to dominate remises for *all* war theatres combined—what is certain is that the nature of the War of the Spanish Succession made the largest bankers too useful and too big to be allowed to fail. Not only did Finance Ministry officials acknowledge this, so too did Bernard himself.[11] The main bankers were also too big to control, it turned out. This all injected a colossal degree of principal-agent imbalance, rent-seeking, and moral hazard into foreign remitting for the armies, while bankers such as Lullin of Geneva could further profit with impunity from additional opportunities for buying up royal and para-royal instruments at heavy discounts, and would short-sell them to boot.[12]

In addition, the most important set of bankers working with the king—the Hogguer brothers—and the most important individual banker of them all—Samuel Bernard—bastardized the most dangerous of all royal financial instruments, the Mint bills, ultimately precipitating the great Lyon credit crunch of April 1709.[13] They not only got more and more of them issued, as hybrid credit devices, and parcelled out these volatile instruments as guarantees for borrowing and exchange deals, knowing full well this would provoke further discounting of these devices. From late 1706 they also allowed creditors to withhold a portion of their exchange loans in the form of Mint bills. Creditors would only hand these Mint bills over when the Hogguers and, later, Bernard made final settlement of what they owed them from their bills of exchange. But the disconnecting of the bills of exchange from Bernard's Mint bills by some of his correspondents, which may not

[8] *Manuel des agens de change et des courtiers de commerce*... (Paris, 1823), 33–4 (council *arrêt* of 24 March 1711); AN G[7]1784, no. 252: note on a letter from La Garde, 4 March 1709 (quotation).

[9] CCG, II, 425: Desmaretz to Bernage, 12 August 1707 (quotation); AN G[7]1123: 'Bordereau du compte dressé par les S[rs]. Hogguer pour la fourniture qu'ils ont faite en Italie pendant 1706', [November? 1706].

[10] AN G[7]1124–6: Clapeyron, 1 February 1713.

[11] AN G[7]1098: Le Rebours and Bercy to Desmaretz, 16 April 1712; G[7]1120: Bernard to Chamillart, 15 March 1707.

[12] André-E. Sayous, 'La crise financière de 1709 à Lyon et à Genève', *Revue d'histoire économique et sociale* 24 (1938), 74; CCG, II, 411: Trudaine to Chamillart, 10 May 1707.

[13] A good narrative of the crisis can be found in W. Gregory Monahan, *Year of Sorrows: The Great Famine of 1709 in Lyon* (Columbus, OH, 1993).

have been appreciated by Bernard himself (as he used agents), brought the system crashing down in 1709. Short-selling seems to have been the immediate cause of the crisis, but given the government's appalling record in maintaining monetary discipline, the bankers had every reason to go down this road.[14] Had Bernard been given more reliable funds, and not asked to overstretch himself, as Desmaretz reproached Chamillart for doing, the crash might have been avoided, or at least happened on a smaller scale.[15] But the king's main bankers brought on trouble through avarice, too. They were guilty of artificially underbidding for the army remittance contracts in order to advance their positions, and by 1708 Bernard found himself operating what could now be termed a pyramid scheme: taking on more royal contracting to keep his increasingly unviable operations going, while prolonging many of his settlements further and further into the future.[16] Had he felt less certain of the king's confidence in him and willingness to reward him, and less sure of the crown's open-ended commitment to paying him huge indemnities for his operations, Bernard might have been more restrained. But he was a gambler, in both his professional and his private life, and such people often cannot help rolling the dice again and again.

The French government was fortunate in one way: the spring 1709 meltdown came at a time when the state's need for foreign exchange was much diminished compared with three years earlier. But it was still large, and remained so until 1712. Moreover, Louis paid a heavy price in the inflated exchange costs that Mint bills had caused, and in the additional 16–18 million *livres* that the government appears to have employed in 1709 to bail out Bernard and his creditors—a far higher sum than was needed to bail out the creditors of treasurer general La Touanne of the Extraordinaire des Guerres.[17] These additional funds thrown at the 1709 crisis diverted essential sums from front-line military expenditure and the covering of other debts, thereby causing greater chaos in the fisco-financier system and higher debt premiums.

How much, then, was being transferred abroad through bankers and other mercantile contacts, and how much did this all cost the French state? It is not possible to provide an accurate global figure for the whole of the War of the Spanish Succession, or even for any particular theatre or year of the conflict. But a good impression of the size and costs of the remittances can be given. In the years 1703–6, during the height of the Bourbon empire in Europe, the French state through exchange deals was sending abroad at least 41 million and in 1706 as much as 60 million *livres*. This was somewhere between half and two-thirds of its military expenditure, a truly staggering proportion whose sheer magnitude (when combined with far too few exports or re-exports of goods) pushed up the underlying rates of foreign exchange to France's disfavour. The amount expatriated dropped to

[14] AN G[7]1120: Bernard to [Le Rebours?], 3 January 1706; to Chamillart, 24 June 1706; G[7]363: Trudaine to Desmaretz, 16 May 1709, cited in full in Sayous, 'La crise financière', 170; Lüthy, I, 177, 198–202, 209–11.

[15] SHD A[1]2182, no. 96: Desmaretz to Chamillart, 6 March 1709.

[16] AN G[7]1120: Bernard to Chamillart, 8 October 1707.

[17] Monahan, *Year of Sorrows*, 110; Lüthy, I, 213–19.

about one-third of total spending in 1707–9, before settling at around one-quarter in 1709 onwards (although some of the later foreign exchange transactions were technically the raising of credit abroad for *importation into France* to support the armies). Most of the time, at best, this was costing the French state—in the form of *change*, *perte*, and commission—in the region of an additional 20–30 per cent of the value of the contracts. Often it went over 30 per cent. Well over half of this was usually compensation for 'pertes sur les espèces'. To put this into a longer perspective, the great authority on French trade, Jacques Savary, thirty years earlier, reckoned that a *change* rate alone approaching 15 per cent for a transaction was high, not mentioning the costs of *pertes*. Sending money to Casale in Italy at the start of the Nine Years War there in 1690 cost only 1–2 per cent, whereas remitting money to Milan in January 1703 cost 8.5 per cent *change* and a further 14.5 per cent in *perte*.[18] At times, the total costs approached the usurious 'Fuggerei' levels of 50–55 per cent of big contracts. Even this was small beer compared with the costs of using the Hogguer brothers for most Italian remitting in 1706: for 17.16 million *livres* delivered the final costs were 34.48 million *livres*, a record 101 per cent remittance charge! These costs were largely because of Mint bill losses or, from 1712, because state finances had collapsed to a level commensurate with that of a second- or third-rank power. All of this adds up to the French state sometimes paying another 15–20 million *livres* per annum for its war effort through foreign remittances or borrowing abroad.[19] No wonder the military budget, however variously estimated, soared in the years after 1701.

When to this are added the additional inflation of the *vivres* contracts by some 6–7 million *livres* per annum in many years; compensation to the Extraordinaire des Guerres itself for various causes to the tune of between 4 and 10 million *livres* in 1704–7; and considerable discounting of *assignations* and Mint bills passing through the military paymasters' hands, then, on top of geographical overstretch more generally, it becomes far clearer why in 1705 and 1707 French military

[18] Jacques Savary, *Le Parfait Negociant*... (2nd edn, Paris, 1679), 217; SHD A^{1}1007, no. 32: Louvois to Crenan, 9 August 1690; A^{1}1699, no. 304: list of 'Lettres de change' for January 1703, 31 December 1702.

[19] Various documents provide indications that lead me to these overall estimations in this paragraph. See, *inter alia*: AN G^{7}1097: memorandum: 'Fonds pour la Flandre et l'Espagne pendant 1706', [1705]; G^{7}1120: 'Estat detaillé des fonds', 15 September 1704; *bordereaux*: 'Mr Bernard a fourny a l'extraord^{re}. des guerres 1704 [ ]', 16 December 1704, and 'Remises Faites en 1705', [late December 1705]; 'Etat des sommes fournies par M. Bernard pour l'exercice 1705', 20 February 1706; 'Estat des fournitures faites par M. Bernard, pour Flandres, Italie et Espagne pendant les 8 premiers mois de l'exercice de M^{r}. de Montargis 1707', [September? 1707]; contract entitled 'M. Bernard 1708', 20 December 1707; G^{7}1121: 'Compte des fournitures faits par M. Bernard a M de Sauroy pendant l'année 1711' [for Flanders], [1712]; G^{7}1122: accounts: 'Ex^{re}. des Guerres exercice de Mr de Vieuxcourt 1704', [1706 or 1713?]; 'Estat des depenses faites par le S^{r}. Hogguer le jeune pour le service de 1711', [1712]; *bordereau*: 'Compte de Mr Bernard pour 1713', 24 March 1714; G^{7}1123: 'Bordereau du compte dressé par les S^{rs}. Hogguer pour la fourniture qu'ils ont faite en Italie pendant 1706', [November? 1706]; accounts: 'Italie. Compte des Remises faites par les S^{rs}. Hogguer', 15 December 1707; G^{7}1124–6: memorandum: 'Strasbourg et Metz', 1 October 1708; G^{7}1776, no. 294: documents on *remises* sent by the Extraordinaire des Guerres, Bernard, and the Hogguer brothers, 12 December 1704; G^{7}1779, no. 228: memorandum: 'Fonds a fournir', 31 March 1707; SHD Ya2: Voysin to Nointel, 24 December 1709; Lüthy, I, 174–9; Saint-Germain, *Bernard*, 149.

expenditure was nudging close to 150 million *livres*. After 1708 expenditure remained high, not least because economic crisis drove up the *vivres* costs by perhaps 30 million *livres* for a couple of years. This was nothing less than disastrous for the future of the country, as it forced the state into huge debt.

The debt bequeathed by Louis XIV, arising largely from the War of the Spanish Succession, was far too big for the system created in his reign to cope with. Colbert had reduced the royal debt from around 450 million *livres* in 1661 and developed a financial apparatus capable of comfortably sustaining a debt of some 200–300 million (and at least roughly the same again in venal office capital). But his distaste for borrowing and failure to evolve methods for handling potentially much higher levels of long-term debt condemned his successors to adopting costly hand-to-mouth expedients in the thirty years after his death. The result was a royal debt of somewhere in the region of 1.8 to 2.3 billion *livres*, some thirty-five to forty-five times the net disposable revenue! In itself this is an astonishing achievement, and reflects the greater stability of both the monarchy and the fisco-financier system, developments in short-term debt instruments, and larger flows of international capital compared with the time of the Frondes, when the monarchy had been brought to the edge of an abyss by a far smaller debt burden (and far higher interest rates). Nevertheless, this volume of debt could never be paid off, and neither the central government nor even provincial authorities in the *pays d'états* were even willing to try to tax the country to redeem a majority of the total. In fact, taxes were cut in the early years of the Regency at both local and 'national' levels. For the rest of the *ancien régime* it is striking that there was a huge mismatch between the tax levels people were prepared to pay under an absolute monarchy and the amount of money it took to fund a sustainable fiscal-military state. And the government ran shy of pushing the propertied elites too far for fear of a backlash. Governments from 1689 to 1789 hesitated for too long at the start of every war before trying to tax the surplus wealth of the country more effectively, as Desmaretz himself suggested. The monarchy also repeatedly baulked at 'selling' higher taxes to the public, for meeting the whole costs of war, which would carry over into subsequent peacetime eras too. Instead, ministers argued that taxes were necessary during wartime and would be scaled back or withdrawn when the emergency passed. This was not a recipe for a sustainable fiscal-military state. The fiscal base in the 1750s was really no larger than in the early 1710s, after adjusting for price and coin changes. It grew thereafter but the government ended up in the worst of all situations: war expenditure and ensuing levels of debt increased so much that the fiscal base was still far from strong enough to sustain them without periodic crises, yet the amount and methods by which the tax burden climbed generated growing political resentment in the context of an expanding public sphere. The final two wars of Louis XIV, and the management of taxation between 1689 and 1717, had set the pattern for the rest of the *ancien régime*.[20]

[20] Rafe Blaufarb, 'The Survival of the *pays d'états*: The Example of Provence', *Past and Present* 209 (2010), 103, 107–9; James C. Riley, *The Seven Years War and the Old Regime in France: The Economic and Financial Toll* (Princeton, 1986), 58, 70–1.

In direct relation to this, the fisco-financier system that had been refined on Colbert's watch became entrenched under his four successors, and in the end was neither dislodged by John Law nor brought under control by Jacques Necker. Their structural reforms were largely reversed after their dismissals from office. In the shape of the farmers general—many of whom had been involved closely in military finance in 1701–14—the fisco-financiers arguably gained the upper hand over the state under Louis XV, backed by some of the leading nobles and enjoying increasingly independent sources of wealth through overseas ventures and 'industrial' investment. Up to a point, a continuation of the fisco-financier system was probably essential. The determination of the broad spectrum of French propertied society to maintain secrecy over their finances, and the government's weary recognition that this was the necessary price to pay for the maintenance of a monopoly of sovereign powers in the king's hands, favoured continued contractual arrangements for so much of the royal fiscal machinery. Moreover, the sheer size, diversity, and lack of integration of the country, and the weak communications infrastructure before the final third of the eighteenth century, meant the monarchy could not create a state-run financial apparatus on the English model. John Law's efforts to supplant the fisco-financiers in 1718–20 were, moreover, selective: the War of the Spanish Succession had entrenched the departmental-based military and naval paymaster system, and the Regency did little more than reform its internal structures. As the Finance Ministry failed to achieve dominance in government until late 1787, this left the door open to renewed flotation of departmental debt in subsequent wars. Mismanagement of this portion of the state debt by the ministers and treasurers intensified the financial and political crisis of that fateful year. Furthermore, for all the closer supervision of the bread supply companies for the armies, ministers still felt they were being ripped off by entrepreneurs in the 1770s, if not later.[21]

In the decades after 1715 there were certainly some improvements to the way the government handled the funding of the state and, by extension, its war efforts, but these were cautious and incremental, probably too much so. This was understandable after the calamitous experiment with John Law's 'System' during the Regency, which had only been possible and thinkable because of the accumulation of debt and the development of poorly understood financial instruments in the period 1701–15. The ministers of Louis XV and Louis XVI largely renounced the resumption of venal-related *affaires extraordinaires* to raise loans during wartime, and similarly avoided the use of anything like Mint bills. The establishment of the Paris Bourse in 1724 produced a more regular and predictable system of discounting instruments and acquiring foreign exchange, however volatile it remained. From the tenure of Philibert Orry as *contrôleur général* the government was using *rescriptions* on revenue collectors as the principal means of allocating revenues to expenditure, creating greater flexibility in the appropriations system and diminishing the amount of 'parked' money people like the *receveurs généraux* had at their disposal. From 1726 until 1785 the French coinage was stable in relation to the

[21] *Mémoires de M. le Comte de S^t. Germain* (Amsterdam, 1779), 24.

livre, being set (unintentionally) at a level that turned out to be broadly suitable for preserving a balance between retaining monetary stock and acquiring foreign exchange at a reasonable price. It helped that the need for foreign exchange was proportionally much smaller in the wars after 1715 than it had been in the War of the Spanish Succession, and the volume of all international payments (which facilitated international war remittances) was much greater by the 1750s. Moreover, the government tried to manage instrument discounting in a more subtle way, in particular through the use of 'Court bankers' (and later the *Gardes du Trésor royal*) who, on the crown's behalf in mid-century, traded *rescriptions* for loans and advances at smaller discounts than under Louis XIV. The advances were managed and came largely through the more solid revenue collectors, with *receveurs généraux* often acting collectively, much like the Caisse Legendre in 1710–15.[22] All this made it possible for Extraordinaire des Guerres bills and other instruments to account for a smaller proportion of short-term debt in the Seven Years War and American War of Independence than in the Spanish Succession conflict.

However, as to the main royal debt instrument, the *rentes*, after 1715 the ministers did very little to make them more liquid. Arguably, the shift to life annuities—the *rentes viagères*—and the imposition of a tax on transfers in 1764 made them more illiquid, just as the British long-term debt was becoming very attractive and cheap by contrast. All this acted as a brake on any development of the notarial system for loan brokering as a substitute for large, developed secondary markets. The only thing that could be said for the relatively low levels of *rente* trading is that this was one means by which the markets could not signal a general and possibly disastrous verdict on the French state's overall credit rating in the form of trading prices for these pale imitations of government bonds. The French government did nothing to enhance its credibility during the Regency in the way it converted short-term debt into new *billets d'état* and bearer bills on the *receveurs généraux*, followed this by transforming most of the state's liabilities into Law's Indies Company shares, and then inflicted brutal 'haircuts' on *rente*-holders during the unravelling and liquidation of the Law System. The likelihood of similar future write-downs was going to be priced into any further borrowing the French monarchy undertook.

The state debt was technically around the same level by the end of the Regency that it had been in 1715, but the colossal reduction in interest rates by royal *fiat* in effect brought it down to somewhere in the region of 1 billion *livres* and there were further forced capital reductions in 1726. Although *contrôleur général* Orry got something of a grip on the finances in the 1730s, his successes were possible because of the modest demands of the War of the Polish Succession, and by 1741, when France began mobilizing for the War of the Austrian Succession, the debt was still another 400–500 million *livres* higher than in 1726, in spite of the general avoidance of war in the previous quarter-century. The 1740s, early 1750s, and Seven

[22] Riley, *Seven Years War*, 152; Joël Félix, *Finances et politique au siècle des Lumières: Le ministère L'Averdy, 1763–1768* (Paris, 1999), 394; J. F. Bosher, *French Finances 1770–1795: From Business to Bureaucracy* (Cambridge, 1970), 94–7; *Dictionnaire des Surintendants*, 136.

Years War saw a further increase in the debt because of big hikes in war spending, but matters were made worse after 1750 by excessive debt-servicing costs, which were partly self-inflicted through miscalculations about the interest rates the market would tolerate on *rentes viagères*. By the end of the Seven Years War the total of royal and para-royal debt capital had soared above the level of 1715 in absolute terms, and might have hit 3.3 billion *livres* by 1788, after the American War and ministers' recklessness in 1783–6. Even so, taking into account coinage revaluations and economic growth over the previous seventy-three years, this amounted to 1.9–2 billion *livres* in 1715 terms. The monarchy was back to square one.

The War of the Spanish Succession had created very large debts combined with a weak tax base and high de facto yields on the debt, and this was storing up a great deal of trouble if the debt were not brought down dramatically before another punishing spate of warfare. But by the 1740s the problems of the fiscal-military structure, of the credibility of the monarchy's commitment to honouring its obligations, and of the size of the debt had not been sufficiently addressed. The final fifteen years of Louis XIV's reign had established a huge and unstable debt base, shown the weakness of absolute monarchy in the face of fresh developments in the money markets and financial instruments, and embedded a political-fiscal set-up on which the French state stood for the rest of the *ancien régime* and from which—for as long as it continued to act as a great power—the monarchy could not escape. Louis XVI proclaimed in an edict at the start of his reign, in 1774, that '[The facility] to render our peoples happy depends principally on a wise administration of the finances.'[23] By that measure his great-great-great-grandfather had not only caused misery for his subjects at the time, but he had also ensured that future French generations would suffer too. Louis XIV did not cause the French Revolution, but the War of the Spanish Succession made the eventual political implosion of France much more likely.

[23] Clamageran, 211–12, 244, 279, 283, 358–60; Riley, *Seven Years War*, 230; Félix, *Finances et politique*, 143; BNF F-21188: *édit*, May 1774 (quotation).

Select Bibliography

The sources cited here are only those which appear in the footnotes to this book.

ARCHIVAL SOURCES (FRANCE)

Archives Nationales de France, Paris (AN)
series: G^7
Bibliothèque de l'Arsenal, Paris (Ars. Ms.)
Bibliothèque Mazarine, Paris (Maz. Ms.)
Bibliothèque Nationale de France, Paris (BNF)
series: Manuscrits Français (Ms. Fr.)
Service Historique de la Défense, Vincennes (SHD)
series: A^1; Ordonnances militaires (OM); Ya

PRINTED PRIMARY SOURCES

André, Louis, ed., *Deux mémoires historiques* (Paris, 1906)

Bibliothèque Nationale de France, series F—numerous *ordonnances, édits*, etc.

Boislisle, A. M. de, ed., *Correspondance des contrôleurs généraux des finances* (3 vols, Paris, 1874–97)

Challe, Robert, *Mémoires: Correspondance complète*, ed. Frédéric Deloffre and Jacques Popin (Geneva, 1996)

Chamillard [*sic*], Michel, *Correspondance et papiers inédits recueillis et publiés par l'abbé G. Esnault* (2 vols, Le Mans, 1884)

Dangeau, Philippe de Courcillon, marquis de, *Journal du marquis de Dangeau*..., ed. E. Soulié, L. Dussieux, and P. de Chennevières (19 vols, Paris, 1854–60)

Depping, G. B., ed., *Correspondance administrative sous le règne de Louis XIV* (4 vols, Paris, 1850–55)

Forbonnais, François Véron de, *Recherches et considérations sur les finances de France, depuis l'année 1595 jusqu'à l'année 1721* (2 vols, Basel, 1758)

La Chesnaye des Bois, François de, et Badier, *Dictionnaire de la noblesse* (19 vols, Paris, 1863–76)

Lemaire, M. *Relevé des documents intéressants le département de Seine-et-Marne*... (Fontainebleau, 1883)

Louis XIV, *Correspondance de Louis XIV avec Michel Amelot, son ambassadeur à Madrid*, ed. baron de Girardot (Paris, 1864)

Malet, Jean-Roland, *Comptes rendus de l'administration des finances du royaume de France* (Paris, 1789)

Manuel des agens de change et des courtiers de commerce... (Paris, 1823)

Pluton maltôtier, nouvelle galante (Cologne[?], 1708)

Quincy, Charles Sevin, marquis de, *Histoire militaire du règne de Louis le Grand* (8 vols, Paris, 1726)

Quincy, Joseph Sevin, comte de, *Mémoires du chevalier de Quincy*, ed. Léon Lecestre (3 vols, Paris, 1898–1901)

Saint-Germain, Claude, comte de, *Mémoires de M. le Comte de S^{t}. Germain* (Amsterdam, 1779)
Saint-Simon, Louis de Rouvroy, duc de, *Mémoires de Saint-Simon*, ed. A. M. de Boislisle (43 vols, Paris, 1879–1928)
Savary, Jacques, *Le Parfait Négociant*... (2nd edn, Paris, 1679)

SECONDARY SOURCES

André, Louis, *Michel Le Tellier et l'organisation de l'armée monarchique* (Paris, 1906)
Antoine, Michel, *Le coeur de l'État: Surintendance, contrôle général et intendances des finances 1552–1791* (Paris, 2003)
Antonetti, Guy, 'Colbert et le crédit public', in Roland Mousnier, ed., *Un nouveau Colbert: Actes du Colloque pour le tricentenaire de la mort de Colbert* (Paris, 1985)
Bayard, Françoise and Daniel Dessert, 'Les financiers dans l'état monarchique en guerre au XVIIe siècle', in Emmanuel Le Roy Ladurie, ed., *Les monarchies* (Paris, 1986)
Bayard, Françoise, Joël Félix, and Philippe Hamon, eds, *Dictionnaire des surintendants et des contrôleurs généraux des finances* (Paris, 2000)
Beaulieu, Eugène-Pierre, *Les gabelles sous Louis XIV* (Paris, 1903)
Blaufarb, Rafe, 'The Survival of the *pays d'états*: The Example of Provence', *Past and Present* 209 (2010), 83–116
Bonnassieux, Pierre, *Les grandes compagnies de commerce. Etude pour servir à l'histoire de la colonisation* (Paris, 1892)
Bonney, Margaret and Richard Bonney, *Jean-Roland Malet, premier historien des finances de la monarchie française* (Paris, 1993)
Bonney, Richard, *The King's Debts: Finance and Politics in France, 1589–1661* (Oxford, 1981)
——, 'France, 1494–1815', in Richard Bonney, ed., *The Rise of the Fiscal State in Europe, c.1200–1815* (Oxford, 1999)
——, '"Le secret de leurs familles": The Fiscal and Social Limits of Louis XIV's *Dixième*', *French History* 7 (1993), 383–416
——, 'France and the First European Paper Money Experiment', *French History* 15 (2001), 254–72
Bosher, J. F., *French Finances 1770–1795: From Business to Bureaucracy* (Cambridge, 1970)
Bouchard, Léon, *Système financier de l'ancienne monarchie* (Paris, 1891)
Brewer, John, *The Sinews of Power: War, Money and the English State, 1688–1783* (London, 1988)
Cans, Albert, *La contribution du clergé de France à l'impôt pendant la seconde moitié du règne de Louis XIV (1689–1715)* (Paris, 1910)
——, 'L'Organisation financière du clergé de France à l'époque de Louis XIV', *Revue d'histoire moderne et contemporaine* 16 (1911), 334–45
Chapman, Sara, *Private Ambition and Political Alliances: The Phélypeaux de Pontchartrain Family and Louis XIV's Government, 1650–1715* (Rochester, NY, 2004)
Chaunu, Pierre and Richard Gascon, *Histoire économique et sociale de la France. Tome 1: De 1450 à 1660. Premier volume: l'État et la Ville* (Paris, 1977)
Chaussinand-Nogaret, Guy, *Les Financiers de Languedoc au XVIIIe siècle* (Paris, 1970)
Claeys, Thierry, *Dictionnaire biographique des financiers en France au XVIIIe siècle* (2nd edn, 2 vols, Paris, 2009)
Clamageran, Jean-Jules, *Histoire de l'impôt en France* (3 vols, Paris, 1867–76)

Clément, Pierre, *Le Gouvernement de Louis XIV ou la Cour, l'Administration, les Finances et le Commerce de 1683 à 1689* (Paris, 1848)

——, *Histoire de Colbert et de son administration* (2nd edn, 2 vols, Paris, 1874)

Collins, James B., *Classes, Estates and Order in Early Modern Brittany* (Cambridge, 1994)

Dahlgren, E. W., *Les rélations commerciales et maritimes entre la France et les côtes de l'océan Pacifique (commencement du XVIIIe siècle). Tôme Premier: le commerce de la Mer du Sud jusqu'à la paix d'Utrecht* (Paris, 1909)

Dee, Darryl, *Expansion and Crisis in Louis XIV's France: Franche-Comté and Absolute Monarchy, 1674–1715* (Rochester, NY and Woodbridge, 2009)

Dent, Julian, *Crisis in Finance: Crown, Financiers and Society in Seventeenth-Century France* (Newton Abbot, 1973)

Dermigny, Louis, 'Circuits de l'argent et milieux d'affaires au XVIIIe siècle', *Revue historique* 212 (1954), 239–78

Dessert, Daniel, *Argent, pouvoir et société au Grand Siècle* (Paris, 1984)

——, *La Royale. Vaisseaux et marins du Roi-Soleil* (Paris, 1996)

——, *Le royaume de Monsieur Colbert 1661–1683* (Paris, 2007)

—— and J.-L. Journet, 'Le lobby Colbert: Un royaume ou une affaire de famille?' *Annales ESC* 30 (1975), 1303–36

Dickson, P. G. M., *The Financial Revolution in England: A Study in the Development of Public Credit 1688–1756* (London, 1967)

Doyle, William, *Venality: The Sale of Offices in Eighteenth-Century France* (Oxford, 1996)

Dubet, Anne, *Jean Orry et la réforme du gouvernement de l'Espagne (1701–1706)* (Clermont-Ferrand, 2009)

Dumas, René, *La politique financière de Nicolas Desmaretz, Contrôleur Général des Finances (1708–1715)* (Paris, 1927)

Fantacci, Luca, 'The Dual Currency System of Renaissance Europe', *Financial History Review* 15 (2008), 55–72

Félix, Joël, *Finances et politique au siècle des Lumières. Le ministère L'Averdy, 1763–1768* (Paris, 1999)

Felloni, Giuseppe, *Gli investimenti finanziari genovesi in Europa tra il Seicento e la Restaurazione* (Milan, 1971)

Fontaine, Laurence, 'Antonio and Shylock: Credit and Trust in France, *c.* 1680–*c.* 1780', *Economic History Review* 54 (2001), 39–57

Frémont, P. J. M. R., *Les payeurs d'armées: Historique du service de la trésorerie et des postes aux armées (1293–1870)* (Paris, 1906)

Frostin, Charles, *Les Pontchartrain, ministres de Louis XIV: Alliances et réseau d'influence sous l'Ancien Régime* (Rennes, 2006)

Germain-Martin, Henry, 'Le financement des guerres de Louis XIV et les trésoriers de l'extraordinaire des guerres', *Revue des travaux de l'Académie des sciences morales et politiques* 126 (1973), 15–25

Giraud, Marcel, 'Crise de conscience et crise d'autorité à la fin du règne de Louis XIV', *Annales. Histoire, Sciences sociales* 7 (1952), (2) 172–90 and (3) 293–302

Goldner, Erik Henry, 'Public Thieves: French Financiers, Corruption, and the Public in the Chamber of Justice of 1716–17' (unpublished PhD dissertation, Columbia University, 2008)

Gouberville, Michel de, 'Armes et argent: les Berthelot, munitionnaires du Roi Soleil', *Annales de généalogie et d'héraldique* (2 parts:) 52 and 53 (1994), (52) 5–23 and (53) 3–29

Guéry, Alain, 'Les finances de la monarchie française sous l'ancien régime', *Annales ESC* 33 (1978), 216–39

Harsin, Paul, *Les doctrines monétaires et financières en France du XVIe au XVIIIe siècle* (Paris, 1928)

——, *Crédit public et Banque d'État en France du XVIe au XVIIIe siècle* (Paris, 1933)

——, 'La finance et l'état jusqu'au système de Law', in Ernest Labrousse, Pierre Léon et al., *Histoire économique et sociale de la France. Tome 1: Des derniers temps de l'âge seigneurial aux préludes de l'âge industriel (1660–1789)* (Paris, 1970)

Haudrère, Philippe, *La Compagnie Française des Indes au XVIIIe siècle (1719–1795)* (Paris, 1989)

Herlaut, Colonel, 'Projet de création d'une banque royale en France à la fin du règne de Louis XIV (1702–1712)', *Revue d'histoire moderne* 8(NS2) (1933), 143–60

Hoffman, Philip T., Gilles Postel-Vinay, and Jean-Laurent Rosenthal, *Priceless Markets: The Political Economy of Credit in Paris, 1660–1870* (London, 2000)

Hurt, John J., *Louis XIV and the Parlements: The Assertion of Royal Authority* (Manchester, 2002)

Iung, Jean-Éric, 'Service des vivres et munitionnaires de l'Ancien Régime: la fourniture du pain de munition aux troupes de Flandre et d'Allemagne de 1701 à 1710' (dissertation for the *diplôme d'archiviste-paléographe*, École Nationale des Chartes, Paris, 1983)

Jacquart, Jean, 'Colbert et la réformation de la domaine', in Roland Mousnier, ed., *Un nouveau Colbert: Actes du Colloque pour le tricentenaire de la mort de Colbert* (Paris, 1985)

Johnson, Noel D., 'Banking on the King: The Evolution of the Royal Revenue Farms in Old Regime France', *Journal of Economic History* 66 (2006), 963–91

Jones, D. W., *War and Economy in the Age of William III and Marlborough* (Oxford, 1988)

Kamen, Henry, *The War of Succession in Spain 1700–15* (London, 1969)

Kwass, Michael, *Privilege and the Politics of Taxation in Eighteenth-Century France. Liberté, égalité, fiscalité* (Cambridge, 2000)

Labrousse, Ernest, Pierre Léon et al., *Histoire économique et sociale de la France. Tome 1: Des derniers temps de l'âge seigneurial aux préludes de l'âge industriel (1660–1789)* (Paris, 1970)

Lachiver, Marcel, *Les années de misère: La famine au temps du Grand Roi* (Paris, 1991)

Leclercq, Dom H., *Histoire de la Régence pendant la minorité de Louis XV* (3 vols, Paris, 1921)

Legohérel, Henri, *Les Trésoriers généraux de la Marine (1517–1788)* (Paris, 1963)

Lemarchand, Yannick, 'Introducing Double-Entry Bookkeeping in Public Finance: A French Experiment at the Beginning of the Eighteenth Century', *Accounting, Business and Financial History: An International Comparative Review* 9 (1999), 225–54

Levasseur, E., *Histoire du commerce de France: Première partie: avant 1789* (Paris, 1911)

Lévy, Claude-Frédéric, *Capitalistes et pouvoir au siècle des Lumières* (3 vols, Paris, 1969–80)

Lüthy, Herbert, *La Banque Protestante en France de la Révocation de l'Édit de Nantes à la Révolution* (2 vols, Paris, 1959–61)

Martin, Germain and Marcel Bezançon, *L'Histoire du crédit en France sous le règne de Louis XIV* (Paris, 1913)

Matthews, George T., *The Royal General Farms in Eighteenth-Century France* (New York, 1958)

McCollim, Gary Bruce, 'The Formation of Fiscal Policy in the Reign of Louis XIV: The Example of Nicolas Desmaretz, Controller General of Finances (1708–1715)' (unpublished PhD dissertation, Ohio State University, 1979)

Meyer, Jean, *Colbert* (Paris, 1981)

Michaud, Claude, *L'Eglise et l'argent sous l'Ancien Régime: Les receveurs-généraux du clergé de France aux XVIe–XVIIIe siècles* (Paris, 1991)

Monahan, W. Gregory, *Year of Sorrows: The Great Famine of 1709 in Lyon* (Columbus, OH, 1993)

Morineau, Michel, 'Budgets de l'état et gestion des finances royales en France au dix-huitième siècle', *Revue historique* 536 (1980), 289–336

——, *Incroyables gazettes et fabuleux métaux: Les retours des trésors américains d'après les gazettes hollandaises (XVIe–XVIIIe siècles)* (Cambridge/Paris, 1985)

Moulin, Mathilde, 'Les rentes sur l'Hôtel de Ville de Paris sous Louis XIV', *Histoire, économie et société* 17 (1998), 623–648

Mousnier, Roland, ed., *Un nouveau Colbert: Actes du Colloque pour le tricentenaire de la mort de Colbert* (Paris, 1985)

Navereau, André, *Le logement et les ustenciles de gens de guerre de 1439 à 1789* (Poitiers, 1924)

Parrott, David, *Richelieu's Army: War, Government and Society in France, 1624–1642* (Cambridge, 2001)

Pénicaut, Emmanuel, *Faveur et pouvoir au tournant du Grand Siècle: Michel Chamillart, Ministre et secrétaire d'État de la guerre de Louis XIV* (Paris, 2004)

Platonova, Natalia, 'Le visa des papiers royaux en France au début du XVIIIe siècle', in Marie-Laure Legay, ed., *Les modalités de paiement de l'État moderne: Adaptation et blocage d'un système comptable* (Paris, 2007)

Potter, Mark, *Corps and Clienteles: Public Finance and Political Change in France, 1688–1715* (Aldershot, 2003)

Riley, James C., *The Seven Years War and the Old Regime in France: The Economic and Financial Toll* (Princeton, 1986)

Roosen, William, 'The Origins of the War of the Spanish Succession', in Jeremy Black, ed., *The Origins of War in Early Modern Europe* (Edinburgh, 1987)

Roux, Pierre, *Les fermes d'impôts sous l'ancien régime* (Paris, 1916)

Rowlands, Guy, *The Dynastic State and the Army under Louis XIV: Royal Service and Private Interest, 1661–1701* (Cambridge, 2002)

Rule, John C., 'The Partition Treaties, 1698–1700: A European View', in Esther Mijers and David Onnekink, eds, *Redefining William III: The Impact of the King-Stadholder in International Context* (Aldershot, 2007)

Rupprecht, Benoît, 'Michel Chamillart, contrôleur général des finances' (*Mémoire de maîtrise*, Université Paris-Sorbonne (Paris IV), 1997)

Sagnac, Philippe, 'Le crédit de l'État et les banquiers à la fin du XVIIe et au commencement du XVIIIe siècle', *Revue d'histoire moderne et contemporaine* 10 (1908), 257–72

Saint-Germain, Jacques, *Les financiers sous Louis XIV: Paul Poisson de Bourvalais* (Paris, 1950)

——, *Samuel Bernard, le banquier des rois* (Paris, 1960)

Sarmant, Thierry, ed., *Les ministres de la guerre 1570–1792: Histoire et dictionnaire biographique* (Paris, 2007)

——, Hervé Lemoine, and Marc Boulanger, *Guerre, pouvoir et finance dans l'Alsace du Roi-Soleil: La famille Dietrich de 1681 à 1715* (Vincennes, 2000)

——, and Mathieu Stoll, *Régner et gouverner: Louis XIV et ses ministres* (Paris, 2010)

Sayous, André-E., 'La crise financière de 1709 à Lyon et à Genève', *Revue d'histoire économique et sociale* 24 (1938), 57–86 and 163–77

Seligmann, Armand, *La première tentative d'émission fiduciaire en France: Etude sur les billets de monnaie du Trésor Royal à la fin du règne de Louis XIV (1701–1718)* (Paris, 1925)

Shakespeare, Howard J., *France: The Royal Loans—Les Emprunts Royaux, 1689–1789* (Shrewsbury, 1986)

Sperling, J., 'The International Payments Mechanism in the Seventeenth and Eighteenth Centuries', *Economic History Review* 14 (1962), 446–68

Spooner, Frank C., *The International Economy and Monetary Movements in France, 1493–1725* (Cambridge, MA, 1972)

Stelling-Michaud, Sven, 'Deux aspects du rôle financier de Genève pendant la guerre de Succession d'Espagne', *Bulletin de la société d'histoire et d'archéologie de Genève* 6(ii) (1936), 147–68

Stoll, Mathieu, 'Une commission extraordinaire du Conseil: le Bureau des vivres (1690–1787)', in Bernard Barbiche and Yves-Marie Bercé, eds, *Études sur l'ancienne France offertes en hommage à Michel Antoine* (Paris, 2003)

Storrs, Christopher, ed., *The Fiscal-Military State in Eighteenth-Century Europe: Essays in Honour of P. G. M. Dickson* (Farnham, 2009)

Swann, Julian, *Provincial Power and Absolute Monarchy: The Estates-General of Burgundy, 1661–1790* (Cambridge, 2003)

Swarte, Victor de, *Un banquier du Trésor Royal au XVIIIe siècle: Samuel Bernard. Sa vie—sa correspondance (1651–1739)* (Paris/Nancy, 1893)

Teulet, Alexandre, *Liste chronologique et alphabétique des chevaliers et des officiers de l'ordre du Saint-Esprit depuis sa création, en 1578, jusqu'à son extinction, en 1830* (Paris, 1864)

Velde, François R., 'French Public Finance between 1683 and 1726', in Fausto Piola Caselli, ed., *Government Debts and Financial Markets in Europe* (London, 2008)

Vuitry, Adolphe, *Le désordre des finances et les excès de la spéculation à la fin du règne de Louis XIV et au commencement du règne de Louis XV* (Paris, 1885)

Walker, Geoffrey J., *Spanish Politics and Imperial Trade, 1700–1789* (London, 1979)

Waquet, Jean-Claude, *Les Grands Maîtres des Eaux et Forêts de France de 1689 à la Révolution* (Paris, 1978)

Weir, David R., 'Tontines, Public Finance, and Revolution in France and England, 1688–1789', *Journal of Economic History* 49 (1989), 95–124

White, Eugene N., 'From Privatized to Government-Administered Tax Collection: Tax Farming in Eighteenth-Century France', *Economic History Review* 57 (2004), 636–63

Index

Lightning Source UK Ltd.
Milton Keynes UK
UKHW031158180119
335659UK00010B/275/P

9 780199 585076